Trigonometry
Second Edition

Photo by Dennis di Cicco/*Sky & Telescope*.

Trigonometry is useful because of its help in studying periodic phenomena —things that repeat at regular intervals. The photograph above shows the *analemma:* a curve recording the sun's position in the sky at the same time throughout a year. To produce the photograph, a camera was set to take an exposure at 8:30 A.M. on forty-five different days over a year's time. Complicated calculations using a programmable calculator along with advanced formulas from trigonometry were needed to find the dates for the exposures. The three streaks represent time exposures from sunrise to 8:25 A.M. on days near the winter and summer solstice, and at the crossover point. These streaks show the shorter days of winter and the longer days of summer. The long axis of the analemma makes a 42° angle with the horizontal; this angle gives the latitude at which the photograph was taken—about 42° north of the equator. The building and trees were added in a separate, single exposure. For further information, see *Exposing the Analemma,* by Dennis di Cicco, *Sky and Telescope*, June 1979, p. 536.

Margaret L. Lial / Charles D. Miller

American River College   Sacramento, California

Trigonometry

Second Edition

Scott, Foresman and Company   Glenview, Illinois

Dallas, Tex.   Oakland, N.J.   Palo Alto, Cal.   Tucker, Ga.   London

Credits

Cover photo by James Tallon/OUTDOOR EXPOSURES

Photos by Charles D. Miller *77, 201*

Photo courtesy of P. Dugan, M.D., and B. Gorham, R.N. *93*

Photos courtesy of James A. Tomlinson *117*

Howard Eves. *A Survey of Geometry*, Volume One. Boston: Allyn and
Bacon, Inc., 1963, p. 39, problem #1.5-12.

Thomas, Finney, *Calculus and Analytic Geometry*, © 1979, 5/e,
Addison-Wesley Publishing Company, Inc., Pages 462–3 of text and figure 10-7
"Communication of Bees." Reprinted with permission.

Foerster, *Trigonometry: Functions and Applications*, © 1977, Addison-Wesley
Publishing Company, Inc. Reprinted with permission: 64, 65 (27–32); 118
(Example 2); 121 (13); 122 (14); 182 (41, 42); 220 (47); 226 (22, 23).

Ralph H. Hannon, *Basic Technical Mathematics with Calculus*.
Philadelphia: W. B. Saunders Co., 1978, p. 300.

Barbara M. Lando and Clifton A. Lando. "Is the Graph of Temperature
Variation a Sine Curve?" *The Mathematics Teacher*, 70, (September, 1977) 535.

Library of Congress Cataloging in Publication Data

Lial, Margaret L
 Trigonometry.

 Includes index.
 1. Trigonometry. I. Miller, Charles David, 1942–
joint author. II. Title.
QA531.L5   1981   516.2′4   80-26117
ISBN 0-673-14910-2

12345678910–RRC–9291908988878685848 3

Preface

The Second Edition of *Trigonometry* is designed for a one-semester or one- or two-quarter course covering the ideas needed for success in later classes. In particular, we have been careful to make sure that thorough preparation is offered both to those students going into calculus as well as to students planning further work in electronics and other technical fields. Suitable applications for both groups of students occur throughout the book.

We assume a background equivalent to a second course in algebra. A course in geometry is a desirable prerequisite, but many students take trigonometry with little or no geometry background. For this reason, all necessary ideas from geometry are explained in the text as needed. In addition, a geometry review unit is given in the *Instructor's Guide*. This unit can be reproduced and made available to students as desired.

The Second Edition of *Trigonometry* offers the following features:

- The basic ideas of trigonometry are presented very early. Angles are discussed in Section 1.2 and trigonometric functions are defined in Section 1.3.
- Triangles are presented early. In Chapter 2 we show how triangles are used to obtain the trigonometric functions for acute angles, and then show some applications of trigonometry. This quickly gives students a feel for the usefulness of trigonometry.
- Chapter 4 has been extensively rewritten to provide a step-by-step method of graphing the basic functions.
- A new section on polar graphs has been added at the end of Chapter 8.
- The chapter on logarithms has been changed to give a calculator emphasis; this chapter now comes last in the book.
- The number of examples and exercises has been increased.
- Calculator exercises, identified by the symbol ⬛, occur throughout the text. Almost all exercise sets feature calculators. A scientific calculator is not needed—few problems in the text can't be worked with other than a four-function calculator and the tables we supply.

- The number and variety of applications has been greatly increased. As in the first edition, these applications are spread throughout the book rather than being concentrated in one chapter.
- Each chapter concludes with a sample Chapter Test.
- Tables of decimal degrees, as well as degrees and minutes, the Greek Alphabet, a table of values of trigonometric functions for special angles, and a list of trigonometric identities is supplied in the appendix.
- All text and answer art has been redrawn, both to enhance accuracy and to make the graphs more attractive.
- All answers were checked by Carolyn Funk from Thornton Community College.

The *Instructor's Guide* features answers to even-numbered exercises, a unit reviewing geometry, three alternate forms of each chapter test, two sample final examinations, and a solutions guide giving complete solutions to about two thirds of the even-numbered exercises.

This revision is based on suggestions from many people. In particular, we would like to thank Kenneth Bradshaw, San Jose State University; Douglas Crawford, College of San Mateo; Arthur P. Dull, Diablo Valley College; Carolyn Funk, Thornton Community College; Stanley J. Guberud and Dorothy Johnson, Milwaukee School of Engineering; Gary Krause, Southwest Texas State University; Charlene Pappin, Wright City College; David Sanders, Miami-Dade Community College; Dorothy Schwellenback, Hartnell College; W. W. Watson, Louisiana Tech University.

The staff at Scott, Foresman did an excellent job helping us with this revision.

Margaret L. Lial
Charles D. Miller

Contents

6 Inverse Trigonometric Functions and Trigonometric Equations 163

7 Triangles and Vectors 189

8 Complex Numbers 229

Throughout this book you will find exercises designed for use with a calculator. These exercises are identified by the symbol ⬛. Some instructors will assign these exercises; others may not. Even if these exercises are not assigned, you should still work on them. We are now in the calculator age, and ability to use calculators will be assumed when you get to more advanced classes or when you get a job.

You don't really need a scientific calculator for the great bulk of our calculator exercises—for the most part, a calculator with a square-root key will be sufficient. However, if you do plan to do much further work in mathematics you may want to consider the purchase of a scientific calculator. The price of the basic models of these calculators is not much more than the price of this textbook. Scientific calculators offer the advantage of doing away with most tables; it is not necessary to look up logarithms or antilogarithms, for example. This can save a lot of time, especially in the trigonometry portion of the course. However, a basic calculator together with the tables in this book is really all you need for most of the exercises in this book.

How sophisticated a calculator do you want to buy? It is a waste of money to buy one with more features than you will ever need. On the other hand, you should try to get those features that you expect to use in the future. Here are some features to consider when looking at calculators.

Memory. A memory is an electronic scratch pad. You can store intermediate calculations in the memory and then recall them later. This feature is very helpful and usually adds on a few dollars to the cost of a calculator.

Automatic Constant. The formula for the circumference of a circle is $C = 2\pi r$. To find the circumference of a circle, you would have to enter r and then multiply by 2 times π. If you had to do this for a great many circles, you could save time by finding 2 times π and then activating the automatic constant key. In this way, for every circle you need to do calculations for, you need enter only r and then push the multiplication key in order to get $2\pi r$ displayed. For each value of r you enter, the answer would be displayed automatically.

Scientific Notation.   Machines with this feature usually have a key labeled EE. Using this key, numbers can be entered into the machine in scientific notation, so that numbers from 1×10^{-99} to $9.999999999 \times 10^{99}$ may be used. Very large and very small numbers such as these occur often in science.

Logarithms.   Logarithms, both common logarithms and natural logarithms (which we study in detail in Chapter 5), occur again and again in mathematics. You will very likely use this key enough to make its purchase worthwhile.

Trigonometric Functions.   Again, these keys will come in very handy in this course as well as in further work in mathematics, physics, or engineering.

Powers and Roots.   These functions are used often in mathematical work.

Statistical Functions.   Some machines do factorials, mean, standard deviation, and linear regression. Will you need these?

There are two types of logic in common use on calculators today. Both algebraic and Reverse Polish Notation (RPN) have advantages and disadvantages. Algebraic logic is the easiest to learn. For example, the problem $8 + 17$ is entered into an algebraic machine by pressing

$$8 + 17 = .$$

On a machine with Reverse Polish Notation, this same problem would be entered as

$$8 \text{ ENTER } 17 + .$$

Some people claim that Reverse Polish machines work advanced problems more easily than algebraic machines. Others claim that algebraic machines are easier to use for the great bulk of ordinary, common problems. It's up to you to decide which to buy. Our recommendation: one of us has a Reverse Polish machine and the other has an algebraic machine.

Calculator Errors. A calculator can store only so many digits in its memory. Because of this, numbers which have more digits than can be stored must be rounded. For example, $\frac{1}{3}$ is not stored as the exact fraction $\frac{1}{3}$, but rather as a decimal, perhaps .3333333333333. Since this rounded form of $\frac{1}{3}$ is used, errors can occur in calculations. To see how this happens, use a calculator to divide 1 by 3, and then multiply the result by 3. You should get 1 (exactly), but many machines produce

$$(1 \div 3) \times 3 = \left(\frac{1}{3}\right) \times 3 = .9999999999.$$

Some machines round this result to 1; however, the machine does not treat the number internally as 1. To see this, subtract 1 from the result above; you should get 0 but probably won't. Another calculator error results when numbers of greatly different size are used in addition. For example,

$$10^9 + 10^{-5} - 10^9 = 10^{-5}.$$

However, most calculators would give

$$10^9 + 10^{-5} - 10^9 = 0.$$

These calculator errors seldom occur in realistic problems, but if they do occur you should know what is happening.

EXERCISES   *The following numbers represent approximate measurements. State the range represented by each of the measures.*

1. 5 pounds   **2.** 8 feet   **3.** 9.6 tons

4. 7.8 quarts   **5.** 8.95 meters   **6.** 2.37 kilometers

7. 19.7 liters   **8.** 32 centimeters   **9.** 253.741 meters

10. 47.358 ounces

11. When the area around Mt. Everest was first surveyed, the surveyors obtained a height of 29,000 feet to the nearest foot. State the range represented by this number. (The surveyors felt that no one would believe a measurement of 29,000 feet, so they reported it as 29,002.)

12. At Denny's, a chain of restaurants, the Low-Cal Special is said to have "approximately 472 calories." What is the range of calories represented by this number? By claiming "approximately 472 calories," they are probably claiming more accuracy than is possible. In your opinion, what might be a better claim?

Give the number of significant digits in each of the following.

13. 21.8   **14.** 37   **15.** 42.08   **16.** 600.9

17. 31.00   **18.** 20,000   **19.** 3.9×10^7 **20.** 5.43×10^3

21. 2.7100×10^4 **22.** 3.7000×10^3

Round each of the following numbers to three significant digits. Then refer to the original numbers and round each to two significant digits.

23. 768.7   **24.** 921.3   **25.** 12.53   **26.** 28.17

27. 9.003   **28.** 1.700   **29.** 7.125   **30.** 9.375

31. 11.55   **32.** 9.155

Use a calculator to work the following problems to the correct number of significant digits.

33. $(8.742)^2$ **34.** $(.98352)^2$

35. $\dfrac{.746}{.092}$ **36.** $\dfrac{.375}{.005792}$

37. $(.425)(89.3)(746,000)$ **38.** $\dfrac{1.0000}{897.62}$

39. $\dfrac{3.0000}{521.84}$ **40.** $\dfrac{2.000}{(74.83)(.0251)}$

41. $\dfrac{1.000}{(.0900)^2 + (3.21)^2}$ **42.** $\dfrac{(6.93)^2 + (21.74)^2}{(38.76)^2 - 29.4}$

43. $\dfrac{8.92}{[(3.14)^2 + 2.79]^2}$ **44.** $\dfrac{4.63 - (2.158)^2}{[(5.728)^2 - 33.9142]}$

45. $\sqrt{74.689}$ **46.** $\sqrt{215.89}$

47. $\sqrt{89,000,000}$ **48.** $\sqrt{253,000}$

49. $\dfrac{1.00}{\sqrt{28.6} + \sqrt{49.3}}$ **50.** $\dfrac{4.00}{\sqrt{59.7} - \sqrt{74.6}}$

51. $\dfrac{-5.000(2.143)}{\sqrt{.009826}}$ **52.** $\dfrac{78.9(258.6)}{\sqrt{.05382}}$

53. $6.0(7.4896) + 58\sqrt{79.42} - 38(489.7)$

54. $128.9(3.02) + 97.6(.0589) - \sqrt{700.9}$

55. $\left[\dfrac{89^2(25.8) + (314.2)(5.098) - \sqrt{910.593}}{258(.0972) - \sqrt{104.38} + (65.923)^2}\right]^2$

56. $\left[\dfrac{(.00900)(74)}{1.0 - (.0382)\sqrt{741.6} + \sqrt{98.32}}\right]^2$

1

The Trigonometric Functions

Trigonometry is over three thousand years old. The ancient Egyptians, Babylonians, and Greeks developed trigonometry to find the lengths of the sides of triangles and the measures of their angles. In Egypt trigonometry was used to reestablish land boundaries after the annual flood of the Nile River. In Babylonia it was used in astronomy. The very word *trigonometry* comes from Greek words for triangle *(trigon)* and measurement *(metry)*. Today trigonometry is used in electronics, surveying, and other engineering areas, and is necessary for further courses in mathematics, such as calculus.

Perhaps the most exciting thing to happen to trigonometry in the last few years is the widespread availability of inexpensive calculators. With these calculators, arithmetic calculations that formerly required many hours, or were not done at all, can now be done in a few moments. In this book, while a calculator is not required, it would be a big help. Exercises where a calculator would be especially helpful are identified by the symbol

1.1 Basic Terms

Number lines are basic to all of mathematics. To make a **number line**, draw a horizontal line. Choose any point on the line and label it 0. Now choose a point to the right of 0 and label it 1. The distance from 0 to 1 gives a unit measure which can be used to find points representing other numbers, labeled 2, 3, 4, 5, . . . , going to the right, and −1, −2, −3, −4, . . . , to the left. A number line and points representing several different numbers are shown in Figure 1.1.

Figure 1.1

The set of all numbers which represent points on a number line is called the set of **real numbers**. The numbers shown in Figure 1.1 are examples of real numbers.

The distance between a point on the number line and 0 is called the **absolute value** of the number represented by the point. The distance from 0 to −6 is 6, so the absolute value of −6 is 6. Absolute value is written using vertical bars, so that

$$|-6| = 6 \quad \text{and} \quad |5| = 5.$$

EXAMPLE 1 (a) $|-\pi| = \pi$*

(b) $|-6 + 8| = |2| = 2$

(c) $-|2 - (-9)| - |-4| = -|11| - |-4|$ Work first inside absolute value
$$= -11 - 4 \qquad \text{bars.}$$
$$= -15$$

(d) $|0| = 0$ ●

The symbol $|x|$ represents the distance from 0 to the number x. In a similar way,

$$|x - a|$$

represents the distance from x to a. For example, the distance from −8 to −3 is

$$|-8 - (-3)| = 5.$$

We can give a more formal definition of absolute value as follows.

$$|x| = \begin{cases} x & \text{if } x \geq 0 \\ -x & \text{if } x < 0 \end{cases}$$

(Recall: $\geq$ means "greater than or equal to" and $<$ means "less than.")

A pair of numbers inside parentheses, such as $(-2, 4)$, is called an **ordered pair**. In the ordered pair $(-2, 4)$, the number −2 is called the *first component*, or *first element*, and 4 is called the *second component*, or *second element* of the ordered pair.

A real number such as −4 can be represented by a point on a number line. An ordered pair of numbers such as $(-2, 4)$ can be represented by a point in a coordinate system. To make a **coordinate system**, use two number lines, called **axes**, which are placed at right angles. (See Figure 1.2.) To locate the point $(-2, 4)$, start at the point O, called the **origin**. Because the first component, −2, is a negative number, go 2 units to the left along the horizontal number line, or **x-axis**. Because the second component, +4, is a positive number, turn and go up 4 units parallel to the vertical number line, or **y-axis**. The point $(-2, 4)$ and other sample points are shown in Figure 1.2.

The axes divide the coordinate system into four regions called **quadrants**. The quadrants are numbered in a counterclockwise direction, as shown in Figure 1.3. The points on the coordinate axes themselves belong to none of the quadrants. Figure 1.3 also shows that in quadrant I both the x-coordinate and the y-coordinate are positive; in quadrant II x is negative and y is positive; and so on.

*π, the ratio of the circumference of a circle to its diameter, is approximately 3.14159.

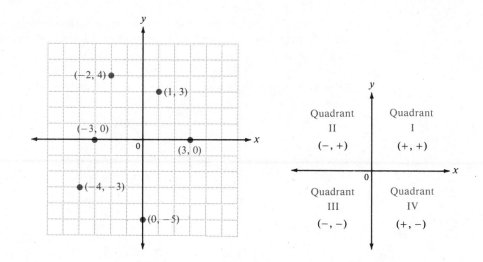

Figure 1.2

Figure 1.3

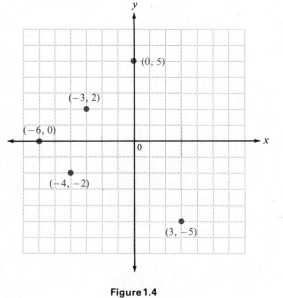

Figure 1.4

EXAMPLE 2 Identify the quadrants for the points in Figure 1.4.

Point	Quadrant
$(-3, 2)$	II
$(-4, -2)$	III
$(3, -5)$	IV
$(-6, 0)$	none
$(0, 5)$	none

Given two points in the coordinate system, we often need to find the distance between them. This distance can be found with the **Pythagorean theorem** of geometry.

If the two shorter sides of a right triangle have lengths a and b and the length of the longest side, the hypotenuse, is c, then

$$a^2 + b^2 = c^2.$$

Figure 1.5 shows a right triangle with sides a, b, and c (the hypotenuse).

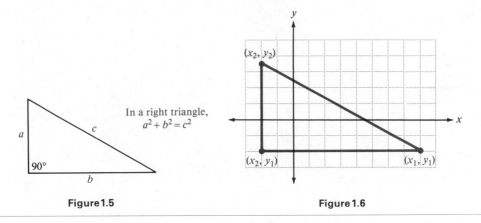

In a right triangle,
$a^2 + b^2 = c^2$

Figure 1.5

Figure 1.6

The coordinate system in Figure 1.6 shows the points (x_1, y_1) and (x_2, y_2) joined by a line segment. Complete a right triangle by drawing a line through (x_1, y_1) parallel to the x-axis and through (x_2, y_2) parallel to the y-axis. The ordered pair at the right angle of this triangle is (x_2, y_1).

The horizontal side of the right triangle in Figure 1.6 has length $|x_2 - x_1|$, while the vertical side has length $|y_2 - y_1|$. We can find the length of the hypotenuse by using the Pythagorean theorem. (This will give the distance between the two original points.)

$$d^2 = |x_2 - x_1|^2 + |y_2 - y_1|^2$$

Since $|x_2 - x_1|^2 = (x_2 - x_1)^2$ and $|y_2 - y_1|^2 = (y_2 - y_1)^2$,

$$d^2 = (x_2 - x_1)^2 + (y_2 - y_1)^2$$

or

$$d = \sqrt{(x_2 - x_1)^2 + (y_2 - y_1)^2} \quad \bullet$$

This result is called the **distance formula**.

EXAMPLE 3   Use the distance formula to find the distance, d, between each of the following pairs of points.

(a) (2, 6) and (5, 10)

We can use either point as (x_1, y_1). If we choose $(2, 6)$ as (x_1, y_1), then $x_1 = 2$, $y_1 = 6$, $x_2 = 5$, and $y_2 = 10$.

$$d = \sqrt{(5 - 2)^2 + (10 - 6)^2}$$
$$= \sqrt{3^2 + 4^2}$$
$$= \sqrt{9 + 16}$$
$$= \sqrt{25}$$
$$= 5$$

(b) $(-7, 2)$ and $(3, -8)$

$$d = \sqrt{[3 - (-7)]^2 + (-8 - 2)^2}$$
$$= \sqrt{10^2 + (-10)^2}$$
$$= \sqrt{100 + 100}$$
$$= \sqrt{200}$$
$$= 10\sqrt{2} \qquad \text{Notice that } \sqrt{200} = \sqrt{100 \cdot 2}$$
$$= \sqrt{100} \cdot \sqrt{2} = 10\sqrt{2}. \quad \bullet$$

A **relation** is a set of ordered pairs. Almost all relations have a rule or formula showing the connection between the two components of the ordered pairs. For example, the formula

$$y = -5x + 6$$

shows that a value of y can be found from a given value of x by multiplying the value of x by -5 and then adding 6. For example, if $x = 2$, then $y = -5 \cdot 2 + 6 = -4$, so that $(2, -4)$ belongs to the relation defined by this formula. In the relation $y = -5x + 6$, the value of y depends on the value of x, so that y is the **dependent variable** and x is the **independent variable**.

Most of the relations in trigonometry are also *functions*.

A **function** is a relation where for each value of the independent variable there is exactly one value of the dependent variable.

For example, $y = -5x + 6$ is a function. If we choose one value of x, then $y = -5x + 6$ gives exactly one value of y. On the other hand, $y^2 = x$ is a relation that is not a function. If we choose $x = 16$, then $y^2 = x$ becomes $y^2 = 16$, from which $y = 4$ or $y = -4$. The one x-value, $x = 16$, leads to *two* y-values, 4 and -4. Thus, $y^2 = x$ is not a function.

Functions are often named with letters such as f, g, or h. For example, the function $y = -5x + 6$ can be written as

$$f(x) = -5x + 6,$$

where $f(x)$ is read "f of x." The $f(x)$ notation is used to show that x is the independent variable. For the function $f(x) = -5x + 6$, if $x = 3$ then $f(x) = -5 \cdot 3 + 6 = -15 + 6 = -9$. This can be written as

$$f(3) = -9.$$

Also, $\qquad\qquad\qquad f(-6) = -5 \cdot (-6) + 6 = 36.$

EXAMPLE 4   Let $f(x) = -x^2 + |x + 5|$. Find each of the following.

(a) $f(0)$

Use $f(x)$ and replace x with 0.

$$f(0) = -0^2 + |0 + 5|$$
$$f(0) = 5$$

(b) $f(-4) = -(-4)^2 + |-4 + 5|$
$$= -16 + |1|$$
$$f(-4) = -15$$

(c) $f(a) = -a^2 + |a + 5|$ Replace x with a.

(d) Is f a function?

For each value of x, there is exactly one value of $f(x)$. Thus f is a function.   ●

The set of all possible real number values that can be used as a replacement for the independent variable is called the **domain** of the relation. The set of all possible real number values for the dependent variable is the **range** of the relation.

EXAMPLE 5   Find the domain and range for each of the following relations. Identify any functions.

(a) $y = x^2$

Here x can take on any value, so the domain is the set of all real numbers. Since y equals the square of x, and a square is never negative, the range is the set of all nonnegative numbers, $y \geq 0$. Each value of x leads to exactly one value of y, so $y = x^2$ is a function.

(b) $3x + 2y = 6$

In this relation x and y can take on any value at all. Thus, both the domain and the range are the set of all real numbers. For any value of x that we might choose, we find exactly one value of y. Thus, $3x + 2y = 6$ is a function.

(c) $x = y^2 + 2$

Since $y^2 \geq 0$ for all values of y, we have $x = y^2 + 2 \geq 0 + 2 = 2$. Thus the domain of the relation is $x \geq 2$. Any real number can be squared, so the range is the set of all real numbers. If we choose the single real number 6 for x, we get

$$6 = y^2 + 2$$
$$4 = y^2$$
$$y = 2 \quad \text{or} \quad y = -2.$$

Since one x-value, 6, leads to two y-values, 2 and -2, the relation $x = y^2 + 2$ is not a function.   ●

EXAMPLE 6   Find the domain for the following.

(a) $y = \dfrac{1}{x - 2}$

Since division by 0 is undefined, we cannot have $x = 2$. (This value of x would make the denominator become $2 - 2$, or 0.) Any other value of x is acceptable, so that the domain is all values of x other than 2, written $x \neq 2$.

(b) $y = \dfrac{8 + x}{(2x - 3)(4x - 1)}$

This denominator is 0 if either

$$2x - 3 = 0 \quad \text{or} \quad 4x - 1 = 0.$$

Solve each of these equations.

$$
\begin{array}{ll}
2x - 3 = 0 & 4x - 1 = 0 \\
2x = 3 & 4x = 1 \\
x = \dfrac{3}{2} & x = \dfrac{1}{4}
\end{array}
$$

The domain here is made up of all real numbers x such that $x \neq 3/2$ and $x \neq 1/4$. ●

In order for a relation to be a function, for each value of x in the domain of the function, we must be able to find exactly one value of y. Figure 1.7 shows the graph of a relation. A point x_1 has been chosen on the x-axis. A vertical line drawn through x_1 cuts the graph in more than one point. Thus, for the x-value x_1, we have more than one y-value, so that this graph is not the graph of a function. This suggests the **vertical line test for a function**:

If any vertical line cuts the graph of a relation in more than one point, then the graph is not the graph of a function.

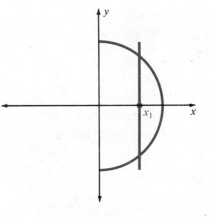

Figure 1.7

1.1 EXERCISES   *Find each of the following. See Example* 1.

1. $|-6| + 2$

2. $-|-2| + 4$

3. $-|8| + |-3|$

4. $-|12| + |-9|$

5. $-|-8| - |7|$

6. $-|-3| - |-2|$

7. $-|-8 - 9| + 4$

8. $-|16 - (-2)| - 3$

9. $|-14 - (-3)| - |-2 + 1|$

10. $|-8 - (-9)| - |-4 - (-2)|$

11. $-9.4765 + |8.32179 - 12.4025|$

12. $-|-14.4720 - 3.8976| + |-4.1214|$

Find the quadrant in which each of the following points lie. See Example 2.

13. $(-4, 2)$ **14.** $(-3, -5)$ **15.** $(-9, -11)$ **16.** $(8, -5)$

17. $(9, 0)$ **18.** $(-2, 0)$ **19.** $(0, -2)$ **20.** $(0, 6)$

21. $(-5, \pi)$ **22.** $(\pi, -3)$ **23.** $(\sqrt{3}, -1)$ **24.** $(-2\sqrt{2}, 2\sqrt{2})$

Suppose that the point (x, y) is, in turn, in each of the following quadrants. Decide if x is positive or negative and if y is positive or negative.

25. I   **26.** II   **27.** III   **28.** IV

Suppose r is a positive number and the point (x, y) is in the indicated quadrant. Decide if the given ratio is positive or negative.

EXAMPLE   Quadrant II, ratio y/x

In quadrant II, x is negative and y is positive. Thus, the quotient y/x is negative.   ●

29. II, y/r **30.** II, x/r **31.** III, y/r **32.** III, x/r

33. III, y/x **34.** III, x/y **35.** IV, x/r **36.** IV, y/r

37. IV, y/x **38.** IV, x/y

Find the distance between each of the following pairs of points. See Example 3.

39. $(-2, 7)$ and $(1, 4)$

40. $(8, -2)$ and $(4, -5)$

41. $(2, 1)$ and $(-3, -4)$

42. $(-5, 2)$ and $(3, -7)$

43. $(-1, 0)$ and $(-4, -5)$

44. $(-2, -3)$ and $(-6, 4)$

45. $(3, -7)$ and $(-2, -5)$

46. $(-5, 8)$ and $(-3, -7)$

47. $(-3, 6)$ and $(-3, 2)$

48. $(5, -2)$ and $(5, -4)$

49. $(7, -2)$ and $(3, -2)$

50. $(-4, -1)$ and $(2, -1)$

51. $(3.7492, 8.1125)$ and $(-2.9082, 3.4147)$

52. $(-1.2004, .8619)$ and $(.2438, -.2199)$

Let $f(x) = -2x^2 + 4x + 6$. Find each of the following. See Example 4.

53. $f(0)$ **54.** $f(-2)$

55. $f(-1)$ **56.** $f(3)$

57. $f(.9461)$ **58.** $f(-.2247)$

59. $f(a)$ **60.** $f(-m)$

61. $f(1 + a)$ **62.** $f(2 - p)$

For each of the following, replace x, in turn, by $-2, -1, 0, 1, 2,$ and 3. Then plot the resulting six points on a coordinate system.

63. $y = -3x + 5$ **64.** $y = 2x - 4$

65. $y = -x^2 + 2x$ **66.** $y = x^2 - 4x + 1$

Find the domain and range of each of the following. Identify any which are functions. See Example 5.

67. $y = 4x - 3$

68. $2x + 5y = 10$

69. $y = x^2 + 4$

70. $y = 2x^2 - 5$

71. $y = -2(x - 3)^2 + 4$

72. $y = 3(x + 1)^2 - 5$

73. $x = y^2$

74. $-x = y^2$

75. $y = \sqrt{4 + x}$

76. $y = \sqrt{x - 2}$

77. $y = \sqrt{x^2 + 1}$

78. $y = \sqrt{1 - x^2}$

Find the domain for each of the following. See Example 6.

79. $y = \dfrac{1}{x}$

80. $y = \dfrac{-2}{x + 1}$

81. $y = \dfrac{3 + x}{(3x - 7)(2x + 1)}$

82. $y = \dfrac{4 + x^2}{(5x + 1)(3x + 8)}$

1.2 Angles

One basic idea in trigonometry is the angle, which we define in this section. Figure 1.8 shows a line through the two points A and B. This line is named **line AB**.

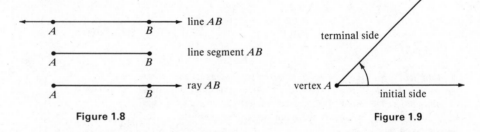

Figure 1.8   Figure 1.9

The portion of the line between A and B, including points A and B themselves, is called **line segment AB**. The portion of line AB that starts at A and continues through B, and on past B, is called **ray AB**. Point A is the endpoint of the ray. See Figure 1.8.

An **angle** is formed by rotating a ray around its endpoint. The initial position of the ray is called the **initial side** of the angle, while the location of the ray at the end of its rotation is called the **terminal side** of the angle. The endpoint of the ray is called the **vertex** of the angle. Figure 1.9 shows the initial and terminal sides of an angle with vertex A.

If the rotation of an angle is counterclockwise, the angle is **positive**. If the rotation is clockwise, the angle is **negative**. Figure 1.10 shows two angles, one positive and one negative.

An angle can be named by using the name of its vertex. For example, the angle on the right in Figure 1.10 can be called angle *C*. Alternatively, an angle can be named using three letters. For example, the angle on the right could also be named angle *ACB* or angle *BCA*. (Put the vertex in the middle of the three letters.)

There are two systems in common use for measuring the size of angles. The most common unit of measure is the **degree**. (The other unit of measure is called the *radian*, which is discussed in Chapter 3.) Degree measure has remained unchanged since the Babylonians developed it four thousand years ago. To use degree measure, assign 360 degrees to a complete rotation of a ray. In Figure 1.11, notice that the terminal side of the ray corresponds with its initial side when it makes a complete rotation.

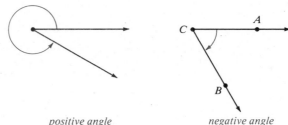

positive angle   *negative angle*

Figure 1.10

   A complete rotation of a ray gives an angle whose measure is 360°.

Figure 1.11

A plant will grow the fastest if none of its leaves shade other leaves on the plant from sunlight. It turns out that to ensure the maximum amount of sunlight to its leaves, a plant should have its leaves in a spiral, with the angle between successive leaves given by

$$360°\left(\frac{3 - \sqrt{5}}{2}\right)$$

For further information on this, see The Curves of Life, *by T. A. Cook, a Dover Reprint, 1979.*

Cinder Cone, in Lassen Volcanic National Park, is one of the most symmetric such cones in the world. The slides slope at an angle of 35°, the angle of repose. The sides can't be any steeper; if they were, the cinders would roll down. This cone is on an old emigrant trail. It was not on the trail in 1850; when the emigrants of 1851 came through the area, they found it.

One degree, written 1°, represents 1/360 of a rotation. For example, 90° represents 90/360 = 1/4 of a rotation, and 180° represents 180/360 = 1/2 of a rotation. Angles of measure 1°, 90°, and 180° are shown in Figure 1.12.

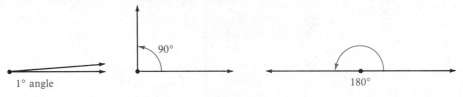

Figure 1.12

Angles are named according to the chart of Figure 1.13.

Name	Angle measure	Example
acute angle	between 0° and 90°	
right angle	exactly 90°	
obtuse angle	between 90° and 180°	
straight angle	exactly 180°	

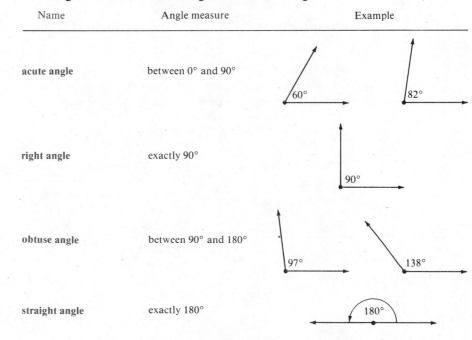

Figure 1.13

Angles are measured with a tool called a **protractor**. Figure 1.14 shows a protractor measuring an angle of 35°.

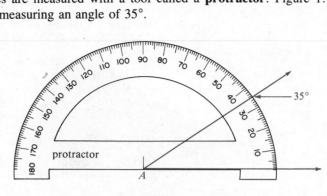

Figure 1.14

Do not confuse an angle with its measure. Angle A of Figure 1.14 is a rotation; the measure of the rotation is 35°. This is often expressed by saying that $m(\text{angle } A) = 35°$, where $m(\text{angle } A)$ is read "the measure of angle A." However, it will save a lot of work for us if we agree to abbreviate $m(\text{angle } A) = 35°$ as simply angle $A = 35°$.

Traditionally, portions of a degree have been measured with minutes and seconds. One **minute**, written $1'$, is $1/60$ of a degree:

$$1' = \frac{1}{60}^{\circ} \quad \text{or} \quad 60' = 1°,$$

while one **second**, $1''$, is $1/60$ of a minute:

$$1'' = \frac{1}{60}' = \frac{1}{3600}^{\circ} \quad \text{or} \quad 60'' = 1'.$$

The measure $12° 42' 38''$ represents 12 degrees, 42 minutes, 38 seconds.

With the increasing use of calculators, it is now common to measure angles in **decimal degrees**. For example, $12.4238°$ represents

$$12.4238° = 12 \frac{4238}{10,000}^{\circ}.$$

The next example shows how to change between decimal degrees and degrees, minutes, seconds.

EXAMPLE 1   (a) Convert $74° 28' 15''$ to decimal degrees. Round to the nearest thousandth.

Since $1' = \frac{1}{60}^{\circ}$ and $1'' = \frac{1}{3600}^{\circ}$,

$$74° 28' 15'' = 74° + \frac{28}{60}^{\circ} + \frac{15}{3600}^{\circ}$$
$$= 74° + .4667° + .0042°$$
$$= 74.471° \quad \text{(rounded)}.$$

(b) Convert 34.817° to degrees, minutes, seconds.

$$34.817° = 34° + .817°$$
$$= 34° + (.817)(60')$$
$$= 34° + 49.02'$$
$$= 34° + 49' + .02'$$
$$= 34° + 49' + (.02)(60'')$$
$$= 34° + 49' + 1'' \quad \text{(rounded)}$$
$$= 34° \, 49' \, 1''$$

An angle is in **standard position** if its vertex is at the origin of a coordinate system and its initial side is along the positive x-axis. The two angles of Figure 1.15 are in standard position. An angle in standard position is said to lie in the quadrant

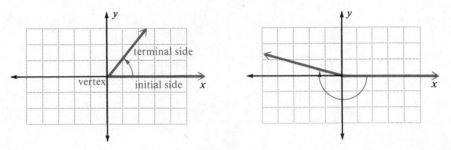

Figure 1.15

where its terminal side lies. For example, an acute angle is in quadrant I and an obtuse angle is in quadrant II.   ●

EXAMPLE 2   Find the quadrants for each of the following angles.

(a) 225°

As shown in Figure 1.16(a), the angle is in quadrant III.

(b) −47°

This angle is in quadrant IV. See Figure 1.16(b).

(c) 90°

An angle of 90° is not in any quadrant, since its terminal side lies along the y-axis.   ●

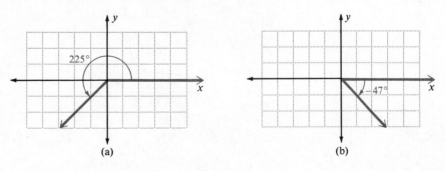

Figure 1.16

Angles in standard position having their terminal side along the *x*-axis or *y*-axis are called **quadrantal angles**. By Example 1(c), a 90° angle is a quadrantal angle. Can you name others?

A complete rotation of a ray results in an angle of measure 360°. But there is no reason why the rotation need stop at 360°. By continuing the rotation, we get angles of measure larger than 360°. The angles in Figure 1.17(a) have measures 60° and 420°. These two angles have the same initial side and the same terminal side, but different amounts of rotation. Angles which have the same initial sides and the same terminal sides are called **coterminal angles**. As shown in Figure 1.17(b), the angles with measures 110° and 830° are coterminal.

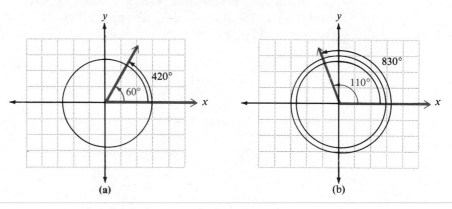

Figure 1.17

EXAMPLE 3 Find the angles of smallest possible positive measure coterminal with the following angles.

(a) 908°

Add or subtract 360° as many times as needed to get an angle with measure at least 0° but less than 360°. Here, 908° − 2 · 360° = 908° − 720° = 188°. Thus, an angle of 188° is coterminal with an angle of 908°. See Figure 1.18.

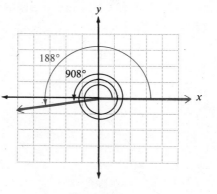

Figure 1.18

(b) $-75°$

Here we need a rotation of $360° + (-75°) = 285°$. See Figure 1.19.   ●

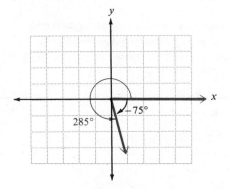

Figure 1.19

EXAMPLE 4   A phonograph record revolves 45 times per minute. Through how many degrees will a point on the edge of the record move in 2 seconds?

The record revolves 45 times per minute or

$$\frac{45}{60} = \frac{3}{4}$$

times per second (since there are 60 seconds in a minute). In 2 seconds, the record will revolve

$$2 \cdot \frac{3}{4} = \frac{3}{2}$$

times. Each revolution is $360°$. Thus, a point on the edge will revolve

$$\frac{3}{2} \cdot 360° = 540°$$

in 2 seconds.   ●

1.2 EXERCISES   *Find the angles of smallest possible positive measure coterminal with the following angles. See Example* 3.

1. $-40°$	**2.** $-98°$	**3.** $-125°$	**4.** $-203°$
5. $450°$	**6.** $489°$	**7.** $539°$	**8.** $699°$
9. $850°$	**10.** $1000°$	**11.** $-985.4063°$	**12.** $-1762.3974°$

Place the following angles in standard position. Draw an arrow representing the correct amount of rotation. Find the measure of two other angles, one positive and one negative that are coterminal with the given angle. Give the quadrant of each angle. See Example 2.

13. $75°$	**14.** $89°$	**15.** $122°$	**16.** $174°$

17. 234°   **18.** 250°   **19.** 300°   **20.** 324°

21. 438°   **22.** 593°   **23.** 512°   **24.** 624°

25. −52°   **26.** −61°   **27.** −159°   **28.** −214°

Locate the following points in a coordinate system. Draw a ray through the given point, starting at the origin. Use the ray you draw, along with the positive x-axis, to determine an angle. Use a protractor to measure the angle to the nearest degree. (Hint: $\sqrt{3}$ is approximately 1.7.)

29. (1, 1)   **30.** (−4, 4)

31. (−3, −3)   **32.** (5, −5)

33. (3, 4)   **34.** (−4, 2)

35. (−5, 2)   **36.** (−3, −5)

37. (−6, 1)   **38.** (−5, −3)

39. ($\sqrt{3}$, 1)   **40.** (−2, 2$\sqrt{3}$)

41. (4$\sqrt{3}$, −4)   **42.** (−5, −5$\sqrt{3}$)

Solve each of the following. See Example 4.

43. A tire is rotating 600 times per minute. Through how many degrees does a point on the edge of the tire move in 1/2 second?

44. An airplane propeller rotates 1000 times per minute. Find the number of degrees that a point on the edge of the propeller will rotate in 1 second.

Convert as indicated. In Exercises 48–50, round to the nearest thousandth of a degree. See Example 1.

45. 31.4296° to degrees–minutes–seconds

46. 102.3771° to degrees–minutes–seconds

47. 89.9004° to degrees–minutes–seconds

48. 20° 51′ 35″ to decimal degrees

49. 374° 18′ 59″ to decimal degrees

50. 164° 51′ 09″ to decimal degrees

1.3   Definition of the Trigonometric Functions

The study of trigonometry covers six trigonometric functions that are defined in this section. Most of the sections of this book involve at least one of these functions. To define these six basic functions, start with an angle θ (the Greek letter *theta**) in standard position. Choose any point P, having coordinates (x, y) on the terminal side of angle θ. (The point P must not be the vertex of θ.) See Figure 1.20.

*Greek letters are often used to name angles. A list of Greek letters appears in the appendix.

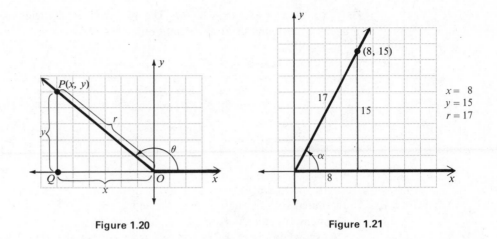

Figure 1.20   Figure 1.21

A perpendicular from P to the x-axis at point Q determines a triangle having vertices at O, P, and Q. The distance from P to O is r. Since distance is never negative, $r > 0$. The six **trigonometric functions** of angle θ are defined as follows.

$$\text{sine } \theta = \sin \theta = \frac{y}{r} \qquad\qquad \text{cotangent } \theta = \cot \theta = \frac{x}{y}$$

$$\text{cosine } \theta = \cos \theta = \frac{x}{r} \qquad\qquad \text{secant } \theta = \sec \theta = \frac{r}{x}$$

$$\text{tangent } \theta = \tan \theta = \frac{y}{x} \qquad\qquad \text{cosecant } \theta = \csc \theta = \frac{r}{y}$$

EXAMPLE 1 The terminal side of an angle α goes through the point $(8, 15)$. Find the values of the six trigonometric functions of angle α.

Figure 1.21 shows angle α and the triangle formed by dropping a perpendicular from the point $(8, 15)$. The point $(8, 15)$ is 8 units to the right of the y-axis and 15 units above the x-axis, so that $x = 8$ and $y = 15$. To find r, use the Pythagorean theorem.

$$r^2 = x^2 + y^2$$
$$r = \sqrt{x^2 + y^2}$$

(Recall: $\sqrt{a}$ represents the nonnegative square root of a.) Substitute the known values, $x = 8$ and $y = 15$.

$$r = \sqrt{8^2 + 15^2}$$
$$= \sqrt{64 + 225}$$
$$= \sqrt{289}$$

From a calculator or Table I in the Appendix,

$$r = 17.$$

Thus, $x = 8$, $y = 15$, and $r = 17$. The values of the six trigonometric functions of angle α are found using the definitions given above.

$$\sin \alpha = \frac{y}{r} = \frac{15}{17} \qquad \cot \alpha = \frac{x}{y} = \frac{8}{15}$$

$$\cos \alpha = \frac{x}{r} = \frac{8}{17} \qquad \sec \alpha = \frac{r}{x} = \frac{17}{8}$$

$$\tan \alpha = \frac{y}{x} = \frac{15}{8} \qquad \csc \alpha = \frac{r}{y} = \frac{17}{15} \qquad \bullet$$

EXAMPLE 2   The terminal side of angle β goes through $(-3, -4)$. Find the values of the six trigonometric functions of β.

As shown in Figure 1.22, $x = -3$ and $y = -4$. Use the Pythagorean theorem to find that $r = 5$. (Remember: $r > 0$.) Then, by the definitions given above,

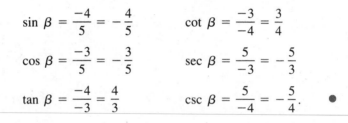

$$\sin \beta = \frac{-4}{5} = -\frac{4}{5} \qquad \cot \beta = \frac{-3}{-4} = \frac{3}{4}$$

$$\cos \beta = \frac{-3}{5} = -\frac{3}{5} \qquad \sec \beta = \frac{5}{-3} = -\frac{5}{3}$$

$$\tan \beta = \frac{-4}{-3} = \frac{4}{3} \qquad \csc \beta = \frac{5}{-4} = -\frac{5}{4}. \qquad \bullet$$

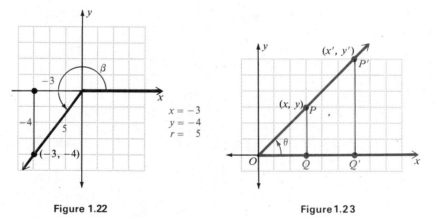

$x = -3$
$y = -4$
$r = 5$

Figure 1.22   **Figure 1.23**

To find the six trigonometric functions, we can choose *any* point on the terminal side of the angle except the origin itself. To see why any point may be used, refer to Figure 1.23, which shows an angle θ and two points on its terminal side. Point P has coordinates (x, y) and point P' (read "P-prime") has coordinates (x', y'). Let r be the length of the hypotenuse of triangle OPQ and let r' be the length of the hypotenuse of triangle $OP'Q'$. By the theory of similar triangles from geometry,

$$\sin \theta = \frac{y}{r} = \frac{y'}{r'},$$

so that sin θ is the same no matter which point is used to find it. A similar result holds for the other five functions.

EXAMPLE 3   Find the values of the six trigonometric functions for an angle of 90°.

First, select any point on the terminal side of a 90° angle. Let us select the point (0, 1), as shown in Figure 1.24. Here $x = 0$ and $y = 1$. Verify that $r = 1$.

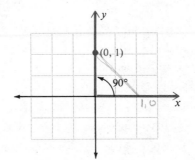

Figure 1.24

Then

$$\sin 90° = \frac{1}{1} = 1 \qquad\qquad \cot 90° = \frac{0}{1} = 0$$

$$\cos 90° = \frac{0}{1} = 0 \qquad\qquad \sec 90° = \frac{1}{0} \text{ (undefined)}$$

$$\tan 90° = \frac{1}{0} \text{ (undefined)} \qquad \csc 90° = \frac{1}{1} = 1.$$

(Recall: division by zero is not defined.)   ●

In the same way, we could find the values of the six trigonometric functions for the quadrantal angles 0°, 180°, 270°, and 360°. These results are summarized in the following table. This table is for reference only; you should either memorize it or be able to reproduce it quickly.

θ	$\sin \theta$	$\cos \theta$	$\tan \theta$	$\cot \theta$	$\sec \theta$	$\csc \theta$
0°	0	1	0	undefined	1	undefined
90°	1	0	undefined	0	undefined	1
180°	0	−1	0	undefined	−1	undefined
270°	−1	0	undefined	0	undefined	−1
360°	0	1	0	undefined	1	undefined

1.3 EXERCISES

Use a protractor to draw angles of the following measures in standard position. On the terminal side of each angle lay off a length r = 100 mm*. Use a millimeter ruler to measure x and y as accurately as possible. Then find the sine, cosine, and tangent for each angle.

1. 15°	**2.** 20°	**3.** 25°	**4.** 30°
5. 35°	**6.** 40°	**7.** 45°	**8.** 50°
9. 55°	**10.** 60°	**11.** 70°	**12.** 80°

Evaluate each of the following. An expression such as $\cot^2 90°$ means $(\cot 90°)^2$.

13. $\cos 90° + 3 \sin 270°$

14. $\tan 0° - 6 \sin 90°$

15. $3 \sec 180° - 5 \tan 360°$

16. $4 \csc 270° + 3 \cos 180°$

17. $\tan 360° + 4 \sin 180° + 5 \cos^2 180°$

18. $2 \sec 0° + 4 \cot^2 90° + \cos 360°$

19. $\sin^2 180° + \cos^2 180°$

20. $\sin^2 360° + \cos^2 360°$

21. $\sec^2 180° - 3 \sin^2 360° + 2 \cos 180°$

22. $5 \sin^2 90° + 2 \cos^2 270° - 7 \tan^2 360°$

23. $2 \sec^2 360° - 4 \sin^2 90° + |5 \cos 180°|$

24. $3 \csc^2 270° + 2 \sin^2 270° - |3 \sin 270°|$

25. $-4|\sin 90°| + 3|\cos 180°| + 2|\csc 270°|$

26. $-|\cos 270°| - 2|\sin 90°| + 5|\cos 180°|$

Find the values of the six trigonometric functions for the angles in standard position having the following points on their terminal sides. See Examples 1 and 2.

27. $(-3, 4)$	**28.** $(-4, -3)$
29. $(5, -12)$	**30.** $(-12, -5)$
31. $(6, 8)$	**32.** $(-9, -12)$
33. $(-7, 24)$	**34.** $(24, 7)$
35. $(0, 2)$	**36.** $(-4, 0)$
37. $(8, 0)$	**38.** $(0, -9)$
39. $(1, \sqrt{3})$	**40.** $(-2\sqrt{3}, -2)$
41. $(5\sqrt{3}, -5)$	**42.** $(8, -8\sqrt{3})$
43. $(2\sqrt{2}, -2\sqrt{2})$	**44.** $(-2\sqrt{2}, 2\sqrt{2})$

---

*mm is an abbreviation for *millimeter*, a unit of measure in the metric system (1 inch = 25.4 mm). Here is a millimeter ruler.

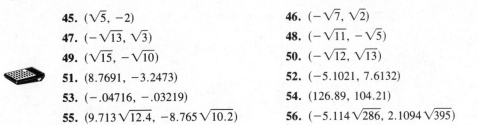

45. $(\sqrt{5}, -2)$

47. $(-\sqrt{13}, \sqrt{3})$

49. $(\sqrt{15}, -\sqrt{10})$

51. $(8.7691, -3.2473)$

53. $(-.04716, -.03219)$

55. $(9.713\sqrt{12.4}, -8.765\sqrt{10.2})$

46. $(-\sqrt{7}, \sqrt{2})$

48. $(-\sqrt{11}, -\sqrt{5})$

50. $(-\sqrt{12}, \sqrt{13})$

52. $(-5.1021, 7.6132)$

54. $(126.89, 104.21)$

56. $(-5.114\sqrt{286}, 2.1094\sqrt{395})$

1.4 Using the Definitions of the Trigonometric Functions

Recall the definitions of the six trigonometric functions: if an angle θ is in standard position, with (x, y) a point on the terminal side of the angle and with r the distance from the origin to (x, y), then

$$\sin \theta = \frac{y}{r} \qquad\qquad \cot \theta = \frac{x}{y}$$

$$\cos \theta = \frac{x}{r} \qquad\qquad \sec \theta = \frac{r}{x}$$

$$\tan \theta = \frac{y}{x} \qquad\qquad \csc \theta = \frac{r}{y}.$$

In this section we derive several useful results from these definitions. First recall the definition of a reciprocal: if x is a nonzero real number, the reciprocal of x is $1/x$. (There is no reciprocal for 0.) Many calculators have a $1/x$ key which is used to find reciprocals.

EXAMPLE 1   The table below shows several real numbers and the reciprocal of each number.

Number	Reciprocal
6	1/6
1/4	4
3/8	$\dfrac{1}{3/8} = 8/3$
−9/7	−7/9
0	none ●

Looking back at the definitions of the trigonometric functions, we see that y/r and r/y are reciprocals of each other. Thus, $\sin \theta$ and $\csc \theta$ are reciprocals.

$$\sin \theta = \frac{1}{\csc \theta} \qquad\qquad \csc \theta = \frac{1}{\sin \theta}$$

Also, $\cos \theta$ and $\sec \theta$ are reciprocals, as are $\tan \theta$ and $\cot \theta$.

$$\cos \theta = \frac{1}{\sec \theta} \qquad \sec \theta = \frac{1}{\cos \theta}$$

$$\tan \theta = \frac{1}{\cot \theta} \qquad \cot \theta = \frac{1}{\tan \theta}$$

These formulas, called the **reciprocal identities**, hold for any angle θ that does not lead to a 0 denominator. (*Identities* are equations that are true for all values of the variable that are meaningful. We study identities in more detail in Chapter 5.)

EXAMPLE 2   Find $\sin \theta$ for each of the following.

(a) $\csc \theta = 4/3$
    Since $\sin \theta = 1/\csc \theta$,

$$\sin \theta = \frac{1}{4/3} = 3/4.$$

(b) $\csc \theta = -\sqrt{12}/2$

$$\sin \theta = \frac{1}{-\sqrt{12}/2} = \frac{-2}{\sqrt{12}}$$

We can remove $\sqrt{12}$ from the denominator (called *rationalizing the denominator*) as follows.

$$\sin \theta = \frac{-2}{\sqrt{12}} = \frac{-2\sqrt{12}}{\sqrt{12} \cdot \sqrt{12}} = \frac{-2\sqrt{12}}{12} = \frac{-\sqrt{12}}{6}$$

By simplifying $\sqrt{12}$ as $\sqrt{4 \cdot 3} = 2\sqrt{3}$,

$$\sin \theta = \frac{-\sqrt{12}}{6} = \frac{-2\sqrt{3}}{6} = \frac{-\sqrt{3}}{3} \qquad \bullet$$

In the definition of the trigonometric functions, r is the distance from the origin to the point (x, y). Distance is never negative, so we always have $r > 0$.

If we choose a point (x, y) in quadrant I, then both x and y will be positive. Since $r > 0$, all six of the fractions used in the definitions of the trigonometric functions will be positive, so that the values of all six functions will be positive in quadrant I.

A point (x, y) in quadrant II has $x < 0$ and $y > 0$. Thus, sine and cosecant are positive for quadrant II angles, while the other four functions take on negative values. Similar results can be obtained for the other quadrants, as summarized in the following tables. Again, you should memorize these results.

θ in quadrant	$\sin \theta$	$\cos \theta$	$\tan \theta$	$\cot \theta$	$\sec \theta$	$\csc \theta$
I	+	+	+	+	+	+
II	+	−	−	−	−	+
III	−	−	+	+	−	−
IV	−	+	−	−	+	−

II sine and cosecant positive	I all functions positive
III tangent and cotangent positive	IV cosine and secant positive

Figure 1.25 shows an angle θ as it increases in size from near 0° toward 90°. In each case, r is the same. As the size of the angle increases, y increases but never exceeds r, so that $y \le r$. Thus, dividing by r,

$$\frac{y}{r} \le 1.$$

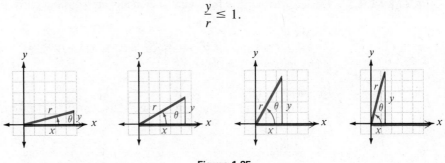

Figure 1.25

In a similar way, angles in the fourth quadrant suggest that

$$-1 \le \frac{y}{r},$$

so
$$-1 \le \frac{y}{r} \le 1.$$

Since $y/r = \sin \theta$,

$$-1 \le \sin \theta \le 1$$

for any angle θ. In the same way,

$$-1 \le \cos \theta \le 1.$$

The tangent of an angle is defined as y/x. It is possible that $x < y$, that $x = y$, or that $x > y$. Thus, y/x can take on any value at all, so that tan θ can be any real number, as can cot θ.

Sec θ and csc θ are reciprocals of cos θ and sin θ, respectively. Thus,

$$\sec \theta \leq -1 \quad \text{or} \quad \sec \theta \geq 1,$$
$$\csc \theta \leq -1 \quad \text{or} \quad \csc \theta \geq 1.$$

For any angle θ:

1. $-1 \leq \sin \theta \leq 1$ and $-1 \leq \cos \theta \leq 1$.

2. tan θ and cot θ may be equal to any real number.

3. $\sec \theta \leq -1$ or $\sec \theta \geq 1$.

4. $\csc \theta \leq -1$ or $\csc \theta \geq 1$.

(sec θ and csc θ are *never* between -1 and 1.)

EXAMPLE 3   Decide whether the following statements are possible or impossible.

(a) $\sin \theta = \sqrt{8}$

For any value of θ, $-1 \leq \sin \theta \leq 1$. Since $\sqrt{8} > 1$, there is no value of θ such that $\sin \theta = \sqrt{8}$.

(b) $\tan \theta = 110.47$

Tangent can take on any value. Thus, $\tan \theta = 110.47$ is possible.

(c) $\sec \theta = .6$

We know that $\sec \theta \leq -1$ or $\sec \theta \geq 1$. Thus, $\sec \theta = .6$ is impossible. ●

The six trigonometric functions are defined in terms of x, y, and r, where $r^2 = x^2 + y^2$, and $r > 0$. With these relationships, it is possible to find the values of all six trigonometric functions, knowing the value of only one function and the quadrant in which the angle lies. This is shown in the next example.

EXAMPLE 4   Suppose α is in quadrant II and $\sin \alpha = 2/3$. Find the values of the other five functions.

We can choose any point on the terminal side of angle α. For simplicity, let us choose the point with $r = 3$. Since $\sin \alpha = y/r$,

$$\frac{y}{r} = \frac{2}{3}.$$

If $r = 3$, then y will be 2. To find x, we use the fact that $x^2 + y^2 = r^2$.

$$x^2 + y^2 = r^2$$
$$x^2 + 2^2 = 3^2$$
$$x^2 + 4 = 9$$
$$x^2 = 5$$
$$x = \sqrt{5} \quad \text{or} \quad x = -\sqrt{5}$$

Since α is in quadrant II, x must be negative. See Figure 1.26. Thus, $x = -\sqrt{5}$ and the point $(-\sqrt{5}, 2)$ is on the terminal side of α.

Now that we know the value of x, y, and r, we can find the values of the trigonometric functions.

$$\cos \alpha = \frac{x}{r} = \frac{-\sqrt{5}}{3}$$

$$\tan \alpha = \frac{y}{x} = \frac{2}{-\sqrt{5}} = \frac{2\sqrt{5}}{-\sqrt{5}\cdot\sqrt{5}} = \frac{-2\sqrt{5}}{5}$$

$$\cot \alpha = \frac{x}{y} = \frac{-\sqrt{5}}{2}$$

$$\sec \alpha = \frac{r}{x} = \frac{3}{-\sqrt{5}} = \frac{-3\sqrt{5}}{5}$$

$$\csc \alpha = \frac{r}{y} = \frac{3}{2} \quad \bullet$$

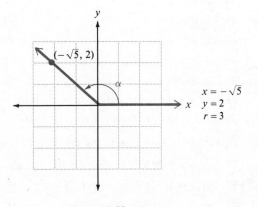

Figure 1.26

1.4 EXERCISES   *Find the sine of each of the following angles. See Example 2.*

1. $\csc \theta = 3$ **2.** $\csc \alpha = -4$

3. $\csc \beta = \sqrt{5}$ **4.** $\csc \gamma = \sqrt{12}$

 5. $\csc \theta = 1.42716$ **6.** $\csc \gamma = -9.102795$

Find the tangent of each of the following angles.

7. $\cot \gamma = 2$

8. $\cot \phi = -3$

9. $\cot \omega = \sqrt{3}/3$

10. $\cot \theta = \sqrt{6}/12$

11. $\cot \alpha = -.01$

12. $\cot \beta = .4$

Identify the quadrant or quadrants for the angles satisfying the following conditions.

13. $\sin \alpha > 0$, $\cos \alpha < 0$

14. $\cos \beta > 0$, $\tan \beta > 0$

15. $\sec \theta < 0$, $\csc \theta < 0$

16. $\tan \gamma > 0$, $\cot \gamma > 0$

17. $\sin \beta < 0$, $\cos \beta > 0$

18. $\cos \beta > 0$, $\sin \beta > 0$

19. $\tan \omega < 0$, $\cot \omega < 0$

20. $\csc \theta < 0$, $\cos \theta < 0$

21. $\sin \alpha > 0$

22. $\cos \beta < 0$

23. $\tan \theta > 0$

24. $\csc \alpha < 0$

Give the signs of the six trigonometric functions for each of the following angles.

25. $74°$ **26.** $129°$ **27.** $183°$ **28.** $298°$

29. $302°$ **30.** $372°$ **31.** $406°$ **32.** $412°$

33. $-82°$ **34.** $-14°$ **35.** $-121°$ **36.** $-208°$

Decide whether each of the following statements is possible *or* impossible. *See Example 3.*

37. $\sin \theta = 2$

38. $\cos \alpha = -1.001$

39. $\tan \beta = 0.92$

40. $\cot \omega = -12.1$

41. $\csc \alpha = 1/2$

42. $\sec \gamma = 1$

43. $\tan \theta = 1$

44. $\sin \alpha = -0.82$

45. $\sin \beta + 1 = .6$

46. $\sec \omega + 1 = 1.3$

47. $\csc \theta - 1 = -.2$

48. $\tan \alpha - 4 = 7.3$

49. $\sin \alpha = 1/2$ and $\csc \alpha = 2$

50. $\cos \theta = 3/4$ and $\sec \theta = 4/3$

51. $\tan \beta = 2$ and $\cot \beta = -2$

52. $\sec \gamma = .4$ and $\cos \gamma = 2.5$

53. $\sin \alpha = 3.251924$ and $\csc \alpha = .3075103$

54. $\tan \alpha = 4.67129$ and $\cot \alpha = .214074$

Find all the other trigonometric functions for each of the following angles. See Example 4.

55. $\cos \alpha = -3/5$, α in quadrant III

56. $\tan \alpha = -15/8$, α in quadrant II

57. $\sin \beta = 7/25$, β in quadrant II

58. $\cot \gamma = 6/8$, γ in quadrant III

59. $\csc \theta = 2$, θ in quadrant II

60. $\tan \beta = \sqrt{3}$, β in quadrant III

61. $\cot \gamma = -2$, γ in quadrant IV

62. $\tan \theta = 3$, θ in quadrant III

63. $\sin \theta = -5/6$, $\cos \theta > 0$

64. $\sec \theta = -8/5$, $\cot \theta < 0$

65. $\cot \alpha = 3/8$, $\sin \alpha > 0$

66. $\sin \alpha = 5/7$, $\tan \alpha > 0$

67. $\tan \theta = 3/2$, $\csc \theta = \sqrt{13}/3$

68. $\sec \alpha = -2$, $\cot \alpha = \sqrt{3}/3$

69. $\sin \alpha = .164215$, α in quadrant II

70. $\cot \theta = -1.49586$, θ in quadrant IV

71. $\tan \gamma = .642193$, γ in quadrant III

72. $\cos \beta = -.425847$, β in quadrant III

73. $\sin \gamma = a$, γ in quadrant I

74. $\tan \omega = m$, ω in quadrant III

Chapter 1   Test

[1.1]   *Find each of the following.*

    1. $|-4|$ **2.** $|-3| + |-2| - |-4 + 6|$

    Find the distance between each of the following pairs of points.

    3. $(4, -2)$ and $(1, -6)$ **4.** $(-6, 3)$ and $(-2, -5)$

    Let $f(x) = -x^2 + 3x + 2$. Find each of the following.

    5. $f(0)$ **6.** $f(-2)$ **7.** $f(a)$

[1.2]   *Find the angles of smallest possible positive measure coterminal with the following angles.*

    8. $-51°$ **9.** $-174°$ **10.** $792°$

[1.3]   *Find the sine, cosine, and tangent of each of the following angles.*

11.   **12.**

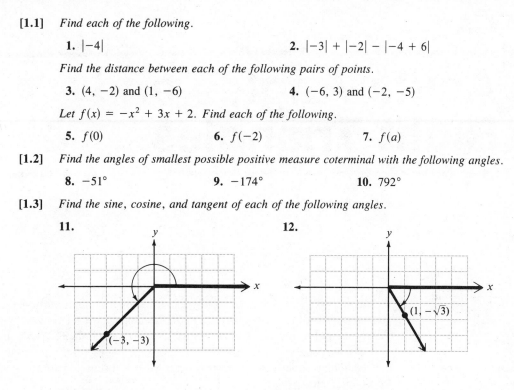

13. $180°$ **14.** $360°$

15. The angle in standard position having $(-8, 15)$ on its terminal side

Decide whether each of the following statements are possible *or* impossible.

[1.4]   **16.** $\sin \theta = 3/4$ and $\csc \theta = 4/3$ **17.** $\sec \theta = -2/3$

    18. $\tan \theta = 1.4$

    Find the values of the other trigonometric functions, given the following.

    19. $\sin \theta = \sqrt{3}/5$ and $\cos \theta < 0$ **20.** $\cos \gamma = -5/8$, γ in quadrant III

2

Acute Angles and Right Triangles

So far we have been able to use the definition of trigonometric functions only for angles such as 0°, 90°, 180°, or 270°. In this chapter we see how to find the values of trigonometric functions of other useful angles, such as 30°, 45°, and 60°. We also discuss the use of tables and calculators for angles whose function values cannot be found directly. The chapter ends with a discussion of some applications of trigonometry.

2.1 Trigonometric Functions of Acute Angles

Figure 2.1 shows an acute angle A in standard position. In order to find the trigonometric functions of A, we need to know x, y, and r. As drawn in Figure 2.1, x and y are the lengths of the two shorter sides of right triangle ABC, while r is the length of the hypotenuse.

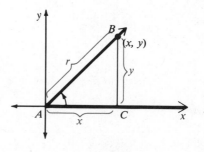

Figure 2.1

The side of length y is called the **side opposite** angle A, while the side of length x is called the **side adjacent** to angle A. We can use the length of these sides to replace x and y in the definitions of the trigonometric functions. For any acute angle A,

$$\sin A = \frac{y}{r} = \frac{\text{side opposite}}{\text{hypotenuse}} \qquad \cot A = \frac{x}{y} = \frac{\text{side adjacent}}{\text{side opposite}}$$

$$\cos A = \frac{x}{r} = \frac{\text{side adjacent}}{\text{hypotenuse}} \qquad \sec A = \frac{r}{x} = \frac{\text{hypotenuse}}{\text{side adjacent}}$$

$$\tan A = \frac{y}{x} = \frac{\text{side opposite}}{\text{side adjacent}} \qquad \csc A = \frac{r}{y} = \frac{\text{hypotenuse}}{\text{side opposite}}.$$

EXAMPLE 1   Find the values of the trigonometric functions for angles A and B in the right triangle of Figure 2.2.

The length of the side opposite angle A is 7. The length of the side adjacent to angle A is 24, and the length of the hypotenuse is 25. Thus,

$$\sin A = \frac{\text{side opposite}}{\text{hypotenuse}} = \frac{7}{25} \qquad \cot A = \frac{\text{side adjacent}}{\text{side opposite}} = \frac{24}{7}$$

$$\cos A = \frac{\text{side adjacent}}{\text{hypotenuse}} = \frac{24}{25} \qquad \sec A = \frac{\text{hypotenuse}}{\text{side adjacent}} = \frac{25}{24}$$

$$\tan A = \frac{\text{side opposite}}{\text{side adjacent}} = \frac{7}{24} \qquad \csc A = \frac{\text{hypotenuse}}{\text{side opposite}} = \frac{25}{7}.$$

The length of the side opposite angle B is 24, while the length of the side adjacent to B is 7. Thus,

$$\sin B = \frac{24}{25} \qquad \tan B = \frac{24}{7} \qquad \sec B = \frac{25}{7}$$

$$\cos B = \frac{7}{25} \qquad \cot B = \frac{7}{24} \qquad \csc B = \frac{25}{24}. \qquad \bullet$$

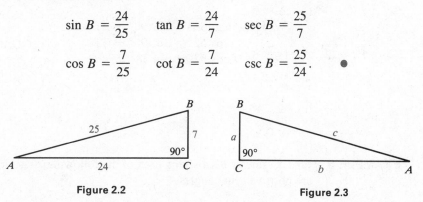

Figure 2.2   Figure 2.3

In Example 1, you may have noticed that $\sin A = \cos B$, $\cos A = \sin B$, and so on. We can show that relationships such as these are always true for the two acute angles of a right triangle. Figure 2.3 shows a right triangle with acute angles A and B and a right angle at C. (Whenever we use A, B, and C to name the angles in a right triangle, C will be the right angle.) The length of the side opposite angle A is a, and the length of the side opposite angle B is b. The length of the hypotenuse is c.

By the definitions given above, $\sin A = a/c$. However, it is also true that $\cos B = a/c$. Thus,

$$\sin A = a/c = \cos B.$$

In the same way,

$$\tan A = a/b = \cot B \quad \text{and} \quad \sec A = c/b = \csc B.$$

The sum of the three angles in any triangle is 180°. Angle C is 90°. Thus, angles A and B must have a sum of 90°. Angles having a sum of 90° are called **complementary angles**. Since angles A and B are complementary and since $\sin A = \cos B$, the functions sine and cosine are called **cofunctions**. Also, tangent and cotangent are cofunctions, as are secant and cosecant.

Since $A + B = 90°$,

$$B = 90° - A,$$

and $\sin A = \cos B = \cos(90° - A)$. Similar results are true for the other functions, leading to the following **cofunction identities**, for an acute angle A. (It would be wise to memorize all the identities presented in this book.)

$$\sin A = \cos(90° - A) \qquad \cot A = \tan(90° - A)$$
$$\cos A = \sin(90° - A) \qquad \sec A = \csc(90° - A)$$
$$\tan A = \cot(90° - A) \qquad \csc A = \sec(90° - A)$$

EXAMPLE 2   Write each of the following in terms of the cofunctions.

(a) $\cos 52°$
  We know that $\cos A = \sin(90° - A)$. Thus,
$$\cos 52° = \sin(90° - 52°)$$
$$\cos 52° = \sin 38°.$$

(b) $\tan 71° = \cot 19°$

(c) $\sec 24° = \csc 66°$ ●

EXAMPLE 3   Find a value of θ satisfying each of the following. Assume that all angles involved are positive acute angles.

(a) $\cos(\theta + 4°) = \sin(3\theta + 2°)$
  Since sine and cosine are cofunctions, this equation is true if the sum of the angles is 90°. Thus,

$$(\theta + 4°) + (3\theta + 2°) = 90°$$
$$4\theta + 6° = 90°$$
$$4\theta = 84°$$
$$\theta = 21°.$$

(b) $\tan(2\theta - 18°) = \cot(\theta + 18°)$
Here we have

$$(2\theta - 18°) + (\theta + 18°) = 90°$$
$$3\theta = 90°$$
$$\theta = 30°. \qquad \bullet$$

Figure 2.4 shows three right triangles. From left to right, the length of each hypotenuse is held fixed, but angle A increases in size. As angle A increases in size from 0° to 90°, the length of the side opposite angle A also increases.

To find $\sin A$, we use the formula

$$\sin A = \frac{\text{side opposite}}{\text{hypotenuse}}.$$

As angle A increases, the numerator of the fraction in the formula also increases, while the denominator is fixed. Because of this, $\sin A$ *increases* as A increases from 0° to 90°.

In the same way, $\tan A$ and $\sec A$ also *increase* as A increases from 0° to 90°. On the other hand, $\cos A$, $\cot A$, and $\csc A$ all *decrease* as A increases from 0° to 90°.

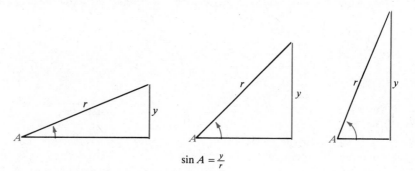

$$\sin A = \frac{y}{r}$$

As A increases, y increases. Since r is fixed, $\sin A$ increases

Figure 2.4

EXAMPLE 4   Answer true or false for each of the following.

(a) $\sin 21° > \sin 18°$
In the interval from 0° to 90°, as the angle increases, so does the sine of the angle. Thus, $\sin 21° > \sin 18°$ is a true statement.

(b) $\cos 49° \leq \cos 56°$
As the angle increases, the cosine decreases. The statement $\cos 49° \leq \cos 56°$ is false. $\bullet$

2.1 EXERCISES   *Find the values of the six trigonometric functions for each of the following indicated angles. Leave answers as fractions. See Example 1.*

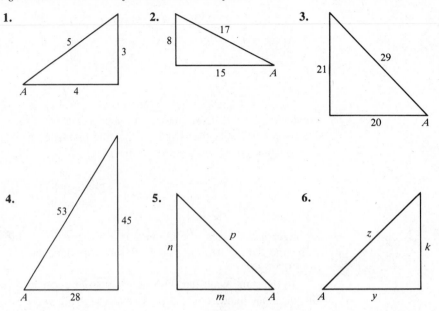

1.

2.

3.

4.

5.

6.

 Use a calculator to find the values of the six trigonometric functions for each angle A. See Example 1.

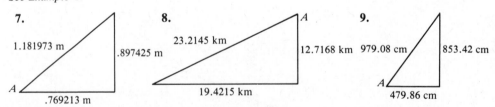

7.

8.

9.

Write each of the following in terms of the cofunction. Assume that all angles are positive acute angles. See Example 2.

10. cot 73°   **11.** tan 50°   **12.** sec 39°

13. csc 47°   **14.** cos 43°   **15.** cos 52° 49′

16. sin 38° 29′   **17.** tan 25° 43′   **18.** sec 75° 58′

19. sin γ **20.** cot α **21.** sec 2A

22. tan 3B   **23.** cos (α + 20°)   **24.** cot (β − 10°)

Solve each of the following equations. Assume that all angles are positive acute angles. See Example 3.

25. cos θ = sin 2θ **26.** tan α = cot(α + 10°)

27. sec(β + 10°) = csc(2β + 20°)   **28.** sin(2γ + 10°) = cos(3γ − 20°)

29. cot(5θ + 2°) = tan(2θ + 4°)   **30.** csc(β + 6°) = sec(2β + 21°)

31. sin(6A + 2°) = cos(4A + 8°)   **32.** tan(3B + 4°) = cot(5B − 10°)

33. $\sec\left(\dfrac{\beta}{2} + 5°\right) = \csc\left(\dfrac{\beta}{2} + 15°\right)$ **34.** $\sin\left(\dfrac{3A}{2} - 5°\right) = \cos\left(\dfrac{2}{3}A + 30°\right)$

Answer true *or* false *for each of the following. See Example* 4.

35. $\tan 28° \le \tan 40°$ **36.** $\sin 50° > \sin 40°$

37. $\sec 80° < \sec 82°$ **38.** $\cot 52° > \cot 58°$

39. $\sin 46° < \cos 46°$ **40.** $\cos 28° < \sin 28°$
(*Hint:* $\cos 46° = \sin 44°$)

41. $\tan 41° < \cot 41°$ **42.** $\cot 30° < \tan 40°$

43. $\sin 60° \le \cos 30°$ **44.** $\sec 80° \ge \csc 10°$

2.2 Trigonometric Functions of Special Angles

Certain special angles, particularly 30°, 45°, and 60°, occur so often in trigonometry that they deserve careful study. The trigonometric functions of 30° and
60° are found by using a 30°–60° right triangle. Figure 2.5(a) shows an **equilateral
triangle**, a triangle with all sides equal. Each angle of such a triangle has a measure
of 60°.

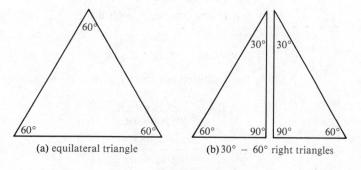

(a) equilateral triangle   (b) 30° − 60° right triangles

Figure 2.5

If we bisect one angle of an equilateral triangle, we obtain two right triangles,
each of which has angles of 30°, 60°, and 90° as shown in Figure 2.5(b). If the
hypotenuse of one of these right triangles has a length of 2, then the shortest side
will have a length of 1. (Why?) If we use x to represent the length of the medium
side, then we can use the Pythagorean theorem.

$$2^2 = 1^2 + x^2$$
$$4 = 1 + x^2$$
$$3 = x^2$$
$$\sqrt{3} = x.$$

The length of the medium side is thus $\sqrt{3}$. In summary,

in a 30°–60° right triangle, the hypotenuse is always twice as long as the shortest side, and the medium side has a length which is $\sqrt{3}$ times as long as that of the shortest side. Also, the shortest side is opposite the 30° angle, and the medium side is opposite the 60° angle.

EXAMPLE 1 The hypotenuse of a 30°–60° right triangle has a length of 7. Find the lengths of the other two sides.

In a 30°–60° right triangle, the hypotenuse is twice as long as the shortest side. If we use y to represent the length of the shortest side, then

$$2y = \text{length of hypotenuse}$$
$$2y = 7$$
$$y = \frac{7}{2}.$$

The medium side has a length $\sqrt{3}$ times that of the shortest side. Thus,

$$\text{length of medium side} = \frac{7}{2}\sqrt{3}. \quad \bullet$$

EXAMPLE 2 Find the trigonometric function values for 30°.

Figure 2.6 shows a 30°–60° right triangle having a hypotenuse of length 2. As shown above, the side opposite the 30° angle has length 1. That is, for the 30° angle,

$$\text{hypotenuse} = 2, \quad \text{side opposite} = 1, \quad \text{side adjacent} = \sqrt{3}.$$

Using the definitions of the trigonometric functions,

$$\sin 30° = \frac{\text{side opposite}}{\text{hypotenuse}} = \frac{1}{2} \qquad \csc 30° = \frac{2}{1} = 2$$

$$\cos 30° = \frac{\text{side adjacent}}{\text{hypotenuse}} = \frac{\sqrt{3}}{2} \qquad \sec 30° = \frac{2}{\sqrt{3}} = \frac{2\sqrt{3}}{3}$$

$$\tan 30° = \frac{\text{side opposite}}{\text{side adjacent}} = \frac{1}{\sqrt{3}} = \frac{\sqrt{3}}{3} \qquad \cot 30° = \frac{\sqrt{3}}{1} = \sqrt{3}$$

The denominator was rationalized for tan 30° and sec 30°. $\quad \bullet$

If you have a calculator which finds trigonometric function values at the touch of a key, you may wonder why we spend so much time in finding values for special angles. We do this because a calculator gives only *approximate* values in most cases, while we need *exact* values. For example, a calculator might give the tangent of 30° as

$$\tan 30° \approx 0.5773502692$$

($\approx$ means "is approximately equal to"); we found the *exact* value:

$$\tan 30° = \frac{\sqrt{3}}{3}$$

Since an exact value is frequently more useful than an approximation, you should be able to give exact values of all the trigonometric functions for the special angles.

EXAMPLE 3   Find the values of the trigonometric functions for 60°.

To find those values, use the 30°–60° right triangle of Figure 2.6. The side of length $\sqrt{3}$ is the side opposite the 60° angle, while the side of length 1 is adjacent. Thus,

$$\sin 60° = \frac{\sqrt{3}}{2} \qquad \tan 60° = \sqrt{3} \qquad \sec 60° = 2$$

$$\cos 60° = \frac{1}{2} \qquad \cot 60° = \frac{\sqrt{3}}{3} \qquad \csc 60° = \frac{2\sqrt{3}}{3}. \qquad \bullet$$

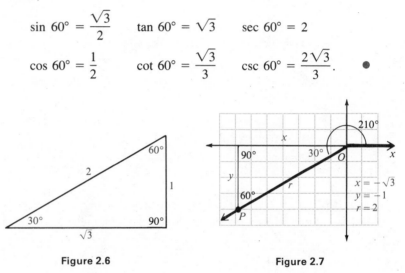

Figure 2.6   Figure 2.7

EXAMPLE 4   Find the values of the trigonometric functions for 210°.

A 210° angle is not an angle of a right triangle. The easiest way to find the value of the trigonometric functions of 210° is to draw an angle of 210° in standard position, as shown in Figure 2.7. Choose point P on the terminal side of the angle so that the distance from the origin O to P is 2. By our knowledge of 30°–60° right triangles, the coordinates of point P become $(-\sqrt{3}, -1)$, with $x = -\sqrt{3}$, $y = -1$, and $r = 2$. This gives us the following trigonometric values.

$$\sin 210° = -\frac{1}{2} \qquad \tan 210° = \frac{\sqrt{3}}{3} \qquad \sec 210° = -\frac{2\sqrt{3}}{3}$$

$$\cos 210° = -\frac{\sqrt{3}}{2} \qquad \cot 210° = \sqrt{3} \qquad \csc 210° = -2 \qquad \bullet$$

To find the values of the trigonometric functions for 45°, start with a 45°–45° right triangle, as shown in Figure 2.8. This triangle is *isosceles* and thus has two sides of equal length.

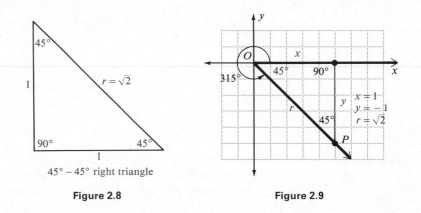

Figure 2.8

Figure 2.9

If we let the sides of shorter length each have length 1 and if r represents the length of the hypotenuse, then

$$1^2 + 1^2 = r^2$$
$$2 = r^2$$
$$\sqrt{2} = r.$$

In a 45°–45° right triangle, the hypotenuse has a length which is $\sqrt{2}$ times as long as the length of either of the shorter sides.

EXAMPLE 5   Find the values of the trigonometric functions for 45°.

Using the measures indicated on the 45°–45° right triangle of Figure 2.8,

$$\sin 45° = \frac{1}{\sqrt{2}} = \frac{\sqrt{2}}{2} \qquad \tan 45° = \frac{1}{1} = 1 \qquad \sec 45° = \frac{\sqrt{2}}{1} = \sqrt{2}$$

$$\cos 45° = \frac{1}{\sqrt{2}} = \frac{\sqrt{2}}{2} \qquad \cot 45° = \frac{1}{1} = 1 \qquad \csc 45° = \frac{\sqrt{2}}{1} = \sqrt{2}. \qquad ●$$

EXAMPLE 6   Find the values of the trigonometric functions for an angle of 315°.

Figure 2.9 shows an angle of measure 315°. Choose point P on the terminal side of the angle so that the distance from O to P is $r = \sqrt{2}$. By drawing the 45°–45° right triangle shown in Figure 2.9, we find that $x = 1$ and $y = -1$. Thus,

$$\sin 315° = -\frac{\sqrt{2}}{2} \qquad \tan 315° = -1 \qquad \sec 315° = \sqrt{2}$$

$$\cos 315° = \frac{\sqrt{2}}{2} \qquad \cot 315° = -1 \qquad \csc 315° = -\sqrt{2}. \qquad ●$$

EXAMPLE 7   Evaluate $\cos 60° + 2 \sin^2 60° - \tan^2 30°$.

We know that $\cos 60° = 1/2$, $\sin 60° = \sqrt{3}/2$, and $\tan 30° = \sqrt{3}/3$.

$$\cos 60° + 2 \sin^2 60° - \tan^2 30° = \frac{1}{2} + 2\left(\frac{\sqrt{3}}{2}\right)^2 - \left(\frac{\sqrt{3}}{3}\right)^2$$

$$= \frac{1}{2} + 2\left(\frac{3}{4}\right) - \frac{3}{9}$$

$$= \frac{5}{3}. \quad \bullet$$

It is important to be able to find the exact trigonometric function values of angles of 30°, 45°, and 60°. To find these values, you should be able to quickly reproduce the triangles of Figure 2.10 and be able to use them with the definitions of the trigonometric functions given earlier.

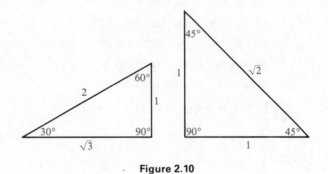

Figure 2.10

2.2 EXERCISES

Find the values of the six trigonometric functions for each of the following angles. Do not use tables or a calculator. See Examples 2–6.

1. 120°	**2.** 135°	**3.** 150°
4. 225°	**5.** 240°	**6.** 300°
7. 330°	**8.** 390°	**9.** 420°
10. 495°	**11.** 510°	**12.** 570°

Complete the following table. Do not use tables or a calculator. See Examples 2–6.

	θ	$\sin \theta$	$\cos \theta$	$\tan \theta$	$\cot \theta$	$\sec \theta$	$\csc \theta$
13.	30°	$1/2$	$\sqrt{3}/2$	___	___	$2\sqrt{3}/3$	2
14.	45°	___	___	1	1	___	___
15.	60°	___	$1/2$	$\sqrt{3}$	___	2	___
16.	120°	$\sqrt{3}/2$	___	$-\sqrt{3}$	___	___	$2\sqrt{3}/3$
17.	135°	$\sqrt{2}/2$	$-\sqrt{2}/2$	___	___	$-\sqrt{2}$	$\sqrt{2}$
18.	150°	___	$-\sqrt{3}/2$	$-\sqrt{3}/3$	___	___	2
19.	210°	$-1/2$	___	$\sqrt{3}/3$	$\sqrt{3}$	___	-2
20.	240°	$-\sqrt{3}/2$	$-1/2$	___	___	-2	$-2\sqrt{3}/3$

Evaluate each of the following. See Example 7.

21. $\sin^2 120° + \cos^2 120°$ **22.** $\sin^2 225° + \cos^2 225°$

23. $2\tan^2 120° + 3\sin^2 150° - \cos^2 180°$ **24.** $\cot^2 135° - \sin 30° + 4\tan 45°$

25. $\sin^2 225° - \cos^2 270° + \tan 60°$ **26.** $\cot^2 90° - \sec^2 180° + \csc^2 135°$

27. $\cos^2 60 + \sec^2 150° - \csc^2 210°$ **28.** $\cot^2 135° + \tan^4 60° - \sin^4 180°$

29. $\sec 30° - \sin 60° + \cos 210°$ **30.** $\cot 30° + \tan 60° - \sin 240°$

Answer true *or* false *for each of the following.*

31. $\sin 30° + \sin 60° = \sin(30° + 60°)$

32. $\sin(30° + 60°) = \sin 30° \cdot \cos 60° + \sin 60° \cdot \cos 30°$

33. $\cos 60° = 2\cos^2 30° - 1$ **34.** $\cos 60° = 2\cos 30°$

35. $\sin 120° = \sin 150° - \sin 30°$ **36.** $\sin 210° = \sin 180° + \sin 30°$

37. $\sin 120° = \sin 180° \cdot \cos 60° - \sin 60° \cdot \cos 180°$

38. $\cos 300° = \cos 240° \cdot \cos 60° - \sin 240° \cdot \sin 60°$

39. $\cos 150° = \cos 120° \cdot \cos 30° - \sin 120° \cdot \sin 30°$

40. $\sin 120° = 2\sin 60° \cdot \cos 60°$

Find all values of the angle θ, when $0° \leq \theta < 360°$, for which the following are true.

41. $\sin \theta = \dfrac{1}{2}$ **42.** $\cos \theta = \dfrac{\sqrt{3}}{2}$

43. $\tan \theta = \sqrt{3}$ **44.** $\sec \theta = \sqrt{2}$

45. $\cos \theta = -\dfrac{1}{2}$ **46.** $\cot \theta = -\dfrac{\sqrt{3}}{3}$

47. $\sin \theta = -\dfrac{\sqrt{3}}{2}$ **48.** $\cos \theta = -\dfrac{\sqrt{2}}{2}$

49. $\tan \theta = -1$ **50.** $\cot \theta = -\sqrt{3}$

51. $\cos \theta = 0$ **52.** $\sin \theta = 1$

53. $\cot \theta$ is undefined   **54.** $\csc \theta$ is undefined

Use a calculator with sine and tangent keys and find each of the following. (Be sure to set the machine for degree measure.) Then explain why these answers are not really "correct" if the exact value has been requested.

55. $\sin 45°$ **56.** $\tan 60°$

2.3 Related Angles and Trigonometric Tables

So far we have seen how to find the values of the trigonometric functions for angles such as 0°, 30°, 45°, 60°, 90°, and so on. The values for angles other than these (and their multiples) must be found from tables or by using calculators.

Angle measure has traditionally been given in degrees, minutes, and seconds.

Recall that

$$1 \text{ minute} = 1' = 60 \text{ seconds} = \frac{1}{60}^{\circ}$$

$$1 \text{ second} = 1'' = \frac{1}{60}' = \frac{1}{3600}^{\circ}.$$

For example, an angle of 12° 25′ 56″ is

$$12 + \frac{25}{60} + \frac{56}{3600} \text{ degrees.}$$

Most calculators work in **decimal degrees**. For example, 56.832° is

$$56\frac{832}{1000} \text{ of a degree.}$$

When using a calculator to find the values for an angle given in degrees, minutes, and seconds, it is often necessary to convert to decimal degrees, as reviewed in Example 1.

EXAMPLE 1   Convert to decimal degrees.

(a) $58° \ 30' = 58\frac{30^{\circ}}{60} = 58\frac{1}{2}^{\circ} = 58.5°$

(b) $29° \ 51' = 29\frac{51^{\circ}}{60} = 29.85°$

(c) $171° \ 08' = 171\frac{8}{60}^{\circ} \approx 171.13333°$

(d) $39° \ 15' \ 37'' = \left(39 + \frac{15}{60} + \frac{37}{3600}\right)^{\circ} \approx 39.260278°$ ●

EXAMPLE 2   Use a calculator with sine, cosine, and tangent keys to find each of the following. Round to five decimal places. Make sure the calculator is set for degree measure.

(a) sin 49° 12′

Convert 49° 12′ to decimal degrees.

$$49° \ 12' = 49\frac{12^{\circ}}{60} = 49.2°$$

Then push the sine button.

$$\sin 49.2° = 0.75700$$

(b) $\tan 132° \ 41' = \tan 132\frac{41^{\circ}}{60}$

$$= \tan 132.68333°$$
$$= -1.08432$$

(c) $\sec 97° \, 58' \, 37'' = \sec \left(97 + \dfrac{58}{60} + \dfrac{37}{3600}\right)^{\circ}$

$$= \sec 97.97694°$$

Calculators do not have secant keys. However,

$$\sec \theta = \frac{1}{\cos \theta}$$

for all angles θ when $\cos \theta$ is not 0. Thus, $\sec 97.97694°$ is found by pushing the cosine key, and then taking the reciprocal. (Push the $1/x$ key.)

$$\sec 97.97694° = \frac{1}{\cos 97.97694°} = -7.20593$$

(d) $\cot 51.4283°$

This angle is already in decimal degrees. Use the identity $\cot \theta = 1/\tan \theta$.

$$\cot 51.4283° = \frac{1}{\tan 51.4283°} = 0.79748 \quad \bullet$$

If your calculator does not have sine, cosine, and tangent keys, you can find the values of the trigonometric functions by using the tables in the back of this book. Table II is used to find four digit approximations of angles measured to the nearest ten minutes. Table III is used for angles measured to the nearest tenth of a degree. Portions of Table II and Table III are shown here. (Note: the column in Table II headed "radians" will be used in Chapter 3.)

Table II (Portion)

Angle θ									
Degrees	**Radians**	**sin θ**	**csc θ**	**tan θ**	**cot θ**	**sec θ**	**cos θ**		
36° 00′	.6283	.5878	1.701	.7265	1.376	1.236	.8090	.9425	**54° 00′**
10	312	901	695	310	368	239	073	396	50
20	341	925	688	355	360	241	056	367	40
30	.6370	.5948	1.681	.7400	1.351	1.244	.8039	.9338	30
40	400	972	675	445	343	247	021	308	20
50	429	995	668	490	335	249	004	279	10
37° 00′	.6458	.6018	1.662	.7536	1.327	1.252	.7986	.9250	**53° 00′**
		cos θ	**sec θ**	**cot θ**	**tan θ**	**csc θ**	**sin θ**	**Radians**	**Degrees**

Remember: Table II is used for angles measured to the nearest ten minutes, such as 41° 20′, or 76° 50′. Table III is used for angles measured to the nearest tenth of a degree, such as 11.4° or 56.5°.

Table III (Portion)

θ deg	deg min		sin θ	csc θ	tan θ	cot θ	sec θ	cos θ			
36.0	36	0	0.5878	1.7013	0.7265	1.3764	1.2361	0.8090	54	0	54.0
36.1	36	6	0.5892	1.6972	0.7292	1.3713	1.2376	0.8080	53	54	53.9
36.2	36	12	0.5906	1.6932	0.7319	1.3663	1.2392	0.8070	53	48	53.8
36.3	36	18	0.5920	1.6892	0.7346	1.3613	1.2408	0.8059	53	42	53.7
36.4	36	24	0.5934	1.6852	0.7373	1.3564	1.2424	0.8049	53	36	53.6
36.5	36	30	0.5948	1.6812	0.7400	1.3514	1.2440	0.8039	53	30	53.5
36.6	36	36	0.5962	1.6772	0.7427	1.3465	1.2456	0.8028	53	24	53.4
36.7	36	42	0.5976	1.6733	0.7454	1.3416	1.2472	0.8018	53	18	53.3
36.8	36	48	0.5990	1.6694	0.7481	1.3367	1.2489	0.8007	53	12	53.2
36.9	36	54	0.6004	1.6655	0.7508	1.3319	1.2505	0.7997	53	6	53.1
37.0	37	0	0.6018	1.6616	0.7536	1.3270	1.2521	0.7986	53	0	53.0
			cos θ	sec θ	cot θ	tan θ	csc θ	sin θ	deg min		θ deg

EXAMPLE 3   Use the portions of Tables II and III above, when appropriate, to find the following.

(a) sin 36° 40′

Since the angle is measured to the nearest ten minutes, we need Table II. For angles between 0° and 45°, read down the *left* of the table and use the function names at the *top* of the table. Doing this here gives

$$\sin 36° 40′ = .5972.$$

The value .5972 is only an approximation of sin 36° 40′, so we really should write sin 36° 40′ ≈ .5972. However, just about all values of trigonometric functions can only be approximated as decimals anyway, so = is used for convenience.

(b) csc 53° 40′

Use the right "degree" column of the table for angles between 45° and 90°. Use the function names at the bottom. Notice that 53° 40′ is above the entry for 53°. We have

$$\csc 53° 40′ = 1.241.$$

(c) tan 36.7°

Use Table III, because of the decimal degrees.

$$\tan 36.7° = .7454$$

(d) cot 53.9° = .7292   Table III

(e) tan 37° = .7536   From either table.   ●

It is not practical to give tables that can be used for all of the infinite number of angle measures that exist. For this reason, most tables give values only for angles between 0° and 90°. Function values for an angle having a larger or smaller measure must be calculated using an angle in this range. Let us start with angles larger than 360° or smaller than 0°.

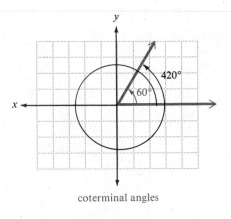

coterminal angles

Figure 2.11

Figure 2.11 shows an angle of 60°. Coterminal with this angle, we can draw angles of 360° + 60° = 420°, or 720° + 60° = 780°, or −360° + 60° = −300°, and so on. Because the trigonometric functions are defined by a point on the terminal side of the angle (and not by the amount of rotation),

$$\sin 60° = \sin 420° = \sin 780° = \sin(-300°),$$

and so on. Similar statements are true for the other five functions. Rotating the terminal side of an angle 360° results in a new angle having its terminal side coterminal with that of the original angle. The values of the trigonometric functions of both angles are the same, leading to the following **identities for coterminal angles**, for any angle θ.

$$\sin \theta = \sin(360° + \theta) \qquad \cot \theta = \cot(360° + \theta)$$
$$\cos \theta = \cos(360° + \theta) \qquad \sec \theta = \sec(360° + \theta)$$
$$\tan \theta = \tan(360° + \theta) \qquad \csc \theta = \csc(360° + \theta)$$

EXAMPLE 4   Evaluate each of the following by first expressing the function in terms of an angle between 0° and 360°.

(a) cos 780°

Add or subtract 360° as many times as necessary so that the final angle is between 0° and 360°. Here we subtract 720°, which is 2 · 360°, to get

$$\cos 780° = \cos(780° - 720°)$$
$$= \cos 60°$$
$$\cos 780° = 1/2.$$

(b) tan (−210°)

Adding 360° gives us an angle between 0° and 360°.

$$\tan(-210°) = \tan(-210° + 360°)$$
$$= \tan 150°$$
$$\tan(-210°) = -\sqrt{3}/3$$

(c) sec (−318.8°)

Add 360° to get

$$\sec(-318.8°) = \sec(-318.8° + 360°)$$
$$= \sec 41.2°$$
$$= 1.3291 \quad \bullet$$

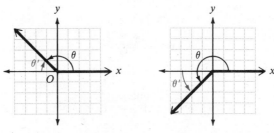

θ in quadrant II θ in quadrant III

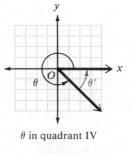

θ in quadrant IV

Figure 2.12

By adding or subtracting multiples of 360°, the values of any trigonometric function can be found by considering only angles between 0° and 360°. Angles from 0° to 90° can be read directly from Table II or Table III. For angles from 90° to 360°, we need to find the related angle θ' for any angle θ. A **related angle**, or **reference angle** for an angle θ, written θ', is the positive acute angle made by the terminal side of angle θ and the x-axis. Figure 2.12 shows angles θ in quadrants II, III and IV respectively, with the related angle θ' also shown. (In quadrant I, θ and θ' are the same.)

A very common error is to find the related angle with reference to the y-axis.

The related angle is always found with reference to the x-axis.

EXAMPLE 5 Find the related angles for the following.

(a) 218°

As shown in Figure 2.13, the positive acute angle made by the terminal side of this angle and the x-axis is $218° - 180° = 38°$. Thus, for $\theta = 218°$, we have $\theta' = 38°$.

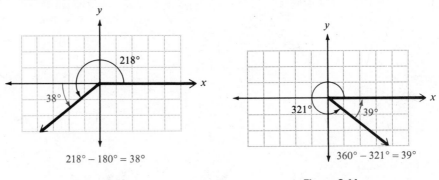

Figure 2.13   Figure 2.14

(b) 321°

The positive acute angle made by the terminal side of this angle and the x-axis is $\theta' = 360° - 321° = 39°$. See Figure 2.14.

(c) 1387°

Divide 1387° by 360° to get a quotient of about 3.9. Begin by subtracting 360° three times (because of "3" in 3.9):

$$1387° - 3 \cdot 360° = 307°$$

The related angle for 307° is $360° - 307° = 53°$.   ●

In general, based on the examples above, we can use the following table to find the related angle θ' for any angle θ between 0° and 360°.

θ in quadrant	θ' is
I	θ
II	$180° - \theta$
III	$\theta - 180°$
IV	$360° - \theta$

Figure 2.15 shows an angle θ and related angle θ', drawn so that θ' is in standard position. Point P, with coordinates (x_1, y_1), has been located on the terminal side of angle θ. Let r be the distance from O to P.

Choose point P' on the terminal side of angle θ', so that the distance from

O to P' is also r. Let P' have coordinates (x_2, y_2). By congruent triangles, verify that

$$x_1 = -x_2 \quad \text{and} \quad y_1 = y_2.$$

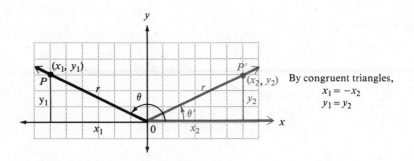

By congruent triangles,
$$x_1 = -x_2$$
$$y_1 = y_2$$

Figure 2.15

Thus,

$$\sin \theta = \frac{y_1}{r} = \frac{y_2}{r} = \sin \theta'$$

$$\cos \theta = \frac{x_1}{r} = \frac{-x_2}{r} = -\cos \theta'$$

$$\tan \theta = \frac{y_1}{x_1} = \frac{y_2}{-x_2} = -\tan \theta',$$

and so on. Notice that the values of the trigonometric functions of the related angle θ' are the same as those of angle θ, except perhaps for signs. We have shown the truth of this statement for an angle θ in quadrant II; similar results can be proven for angles in the other quadrants.

Based on this work, the values of the trigonometric functions for any angle θ can be found by finding the function value for an angle between $0°$ and $90°$. To do this, go through the following steps.

1. If $\theta \geq 360°$, or if $\theta < 0°$, add or subtract $360°$ as many times as needed to get an angle at least $0°$ but less than $360°$.

2. Find the related angle θ'. (Use the table given above.)

3. Find the necessary values of the trigonometric functions for the related angle θ'.

4. Find the correct signs for the values found in Step 3. This gives you the trigonometric values for angle θ.

EXAMPLE 6   Find each of the following values.

(a) tan 315°

To begin, find the related angle of 315°. See Figure 2.16. Since 315° is in quadrant IV, we subtract 315° from 360°.

$$360° - 315° = 45°$$

We know that tan 45° = 1 and that the tangent for quadrant IV angles is negative. Thus,

$$\tan 315° = -\tan 45° = -1.$$

(b) cos(−570°)

To begin, find the smallest possible positive angle coterminal to −570°. See Figure 2.17. Add 2 · 360°, or 720°, to −570°.

$$-570° + 720° = 150°$$

Since 150° is in quadrant II, we find its related angle by subtracting 150° from 180°.

$$180° - 150° = 30°$$

We know that cos 30° = $\sqrt{3}/2$. The cosine for quadrant II angles is negative. Thus,

$$\cos(-570°) = -\cos 30° = -\sqrt{3}/2.$$

(c) cot 600°

$$600° - 360° = 240° \qquad \text{Subtract } 360°.$$

Verify that $\theta' = 240° - 180° = 60°$, and that

$$\cot 600° = \cot 60° = \sqrt{3}/3. \qquad \bullet$$

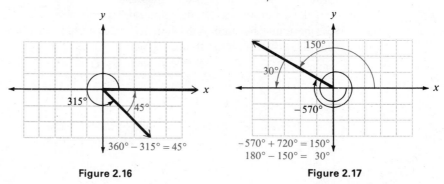

Figure 2.16   Figure 2.17

EXAMPLE 7   Use Table II or III in the back of the book to find each of the following.

(a) sin 190° 10′

Figure 2.18 shows the related angle 10° 10′. An angle of 190° 10′ is in quadrant III, where sine is negative. Thus,

$$\sin 190° \, 10′ = -\sin 10° \, 10′ = -.1765.$$

Here we used Table II.

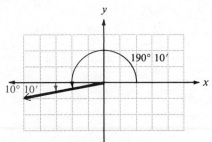

Figure 2.18

(b) tan 305° 20′

The related angle is 54° 40′. (To subtract 305° 20′ from 360°, first change 360° to 359° 60′.) Since 305° 20′ is in quadrant IV, tangent is negative and

$$\tan 305° \, 20′ = -\tan 54° \, 40′ = -1.411.$$

(c) cos 1045.6°

$$\cos 1045.6° = \cos(1045.6 - 720)°$$ Subtract 720 to get an angle
$$= \cos 325.6°$$ between 0° and 360°.

Since 325.6° is in quadrant IV, its reference angle is

$$360° - 325.6° = 34.4°$$

Finally, cos 1045.6° = cos 34.4° = .8251
(Why is the answer positive?)

(d) cot 100.8° = −cot 79.2° = −.1908   ●

EXAMPLE 8   Use Table II and find a value of θ in the interval $0° \le \theta \le 90°$ satisfying each of the following.

(a) sin θ = .5807

Use Table II and read columns having sine at either the top or the bottom. Here we find .5807 in a column having sine at the top. Thus, we use angles at the left.

$$\theta = 35° \, 30′$$

(b) tan θ = 2.699

Since 2.699 is in a column having tangent at the bottom, use angles at the right.

$$\theta = 69° \, 40′ \quad ●$$

2.3 EXERCISES   *Find an angle θ, where $0° \le \theta < 360°$, that is coterminal with each of the following. See Example* 4.

1. 425°	**2.** 589°	**3.** 615°	**4.** 708°
5. 483°	**6.** 592°	**7.** 458° 20′	**8.** 506° 40′

9. 738° 30'   **10.** 815° 40'   **11.** 948° 50'   **12.** 1000° 10'

13. 428.9°   **14.** 765.4°   **15.** −250°   **16.** −321°

17. −198° 10'   **18.** −243° 30'   **19.** −582.1°   **20.** −325.8°

Find a related angle for each of the following. See Example 5.

21. 98°   **22.** 143°   **23.** 212°   **24.** 239°

25. 285°   **26.** 314°   **27.** 389°   **28.** 427°

29. 538°   **30.** 619°   **31.** 114° 40'   **32.** 138° 50'

33. 215.7°   **34.** 312.9°   **35.** −110° 10'   **36.** −183° 20'

37. −214° 30'   **38.** −429° 10'   **39.** −579.1°   **40.** −682.5°

Use Table II or Table III to find the value of each of the following. See Examples 3 and 4.

41. sin 38° 40'   **42.** tan 29° 30'

43. cot 41° 20'   **44.** cos 27° 10'

45. sin 58° 30'   **46.** cos 46° 10'

47. tan 17.2°   **48.** sin 39.8°

49. cot 128° 30'   **50.** tan 153° 20'

51. sin 179.4°   **52.** cos 124.7°

53. sin 204° 20'   **54.** sec 218° 50'

55. cos 251° 10'   **56.** cot 298° 30'

57. sin 274.8°   **58.** cos 304.3°

59. csc 421° 10'   **60.** cot 512° 20'

61. sec(−108° 20')   **62.** csc(−29° 30')

63. tan(−197.8°)   **64.** cos(−378.4°)

Use Table II to find a value of θ for each of the following. See Example 8.

65. sin θ = .8480   **66.** tan θ = 1.473

67. cos θ = .8616   **68.** cot θ = 1.257

69. sin θ = .7214   **70.** sec θ = 2.749

71. tan θ = 6.435   **72.** sin θ = .2784

Convert to decimal degrees. Round to five decimal places if necessary. See Example 1.

73. 49° 15'   **74.** 71° 48'

75. 114° 13'   **76.** 201° 58'

77. 32° 41' 15"   **78.** 59° 52' 30"

79. 128° 42' 28"   **80.** 249° 57' 47"

Find each of the following to five decimal places.

81. sin 59.642°   **82.** cos 38.1219°

83. tan(−80.612°)   **84.** sec(−19.702°)

85. cos 74° 11′   **86.** tan 58° 46′

87. cot 125° 52′ 10″   **88.** csc 211° 40′ 38″

When a light ray travels from one medium, such as air, to another medium, such as water or glass, the speed of the light changes, and the direction that the ray is traveling changes. (This is why a fish under water is in a different position than it appears to us.) These changes are given by Snell's Law, from physics:

$$\frac{c_1}{c_2} = \frac{\sin \theta_1}{\sin \theta_2},$$

where c_1 is the speed in the first medium, c_2 is the speed in the second medium, and θ_1 and θ_2 are the angles shown in the figure.

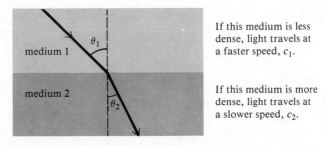

In the following exercises assume that $c_1 = 3 \times 10^8$ meters per second. Find the speed of light in the second medium.

89. $\theta_1 = 46°, \theta_2 = 31°$ **90.** $\theta_1 = 39°, \theta_2 = 28°$

2.4   Interpolation and Significant Digits (Optional)

Suppose we glance quickly at a room and guess that it is 15 feet by 18 feet. To calculate the length of a diagonal of the room, use the Pythagorean theorem.

$$d^2 = 15^2 + 18^2$$
$$d^2 = 549$$
$$d = \sqrt{549}.$$

On a calculator,

$$\sqrt{549} = 23.43074903.$$

Should we give this answer as the length of the diagonal of the room? Of course not. The number 23.43074903 contains 8 decimal places, while our original data of 15 feet and 18 feet are certainly not more accurate than to the nearest foot. In general, the results of a problem can be no more accurate than the least accurate number in any calculation. Thus, we really should say that the diagonal of our 15-by-18-foot room is 23 feet.

If we measure a wall to the nearest foot and say that it is 18 feet long, then we are saying that the wall has a length between 17.5 feet and 18.5 feet. If we measure the wall more accurately and say that it is 18.3 feet long, then we know that it is really between 18.25 feet and 18.35 feet long. A measurement of 18.00 feet would indicate that the wall is between 17.995 feet and 18.005 feet long. The measurement 18 feet is said to have 2 **significant digits** of accuracy; 18.3 has 3 significant digits and 18.00 has 4.

To find the number of significant digits in a measurement, count from left to right, starting at the first nonzero digit and counting to the right to the last digit.

EXAMPLE 1 The following chart shows some numbers, the number of significant digits in each number, and the range represented by each number.

Number	Number of significant digits	Range represented by number
29.6	3	29.55 to 29.65
1.39	3	1.385 to 1.395
.000096	2	.0000955 to .0000965
.03	1	.025 to .035
100.2	4	100.15 to 100.25 ●

There is one possible place for trouble when finding significant digits. We know that the measurement 19.00 meters is a measurement to the nearest hundredth meter. What about the measurement 93,000 meters? Does it represent a measurement to the nearest meter? the nearest ten meters? hundred meters? thousand meters? We can't tell by the way the number is written. To get around this problem, write the number in **scientific notation**, the product of a number between 1 and 10 and a power of 10. Depending on what we know about the accuracy of the measurement, we could write 93,000 using scientific notation as follows.

Measurement to nearest	Scientific notation	Number of significant digits
Meter	9.3000×10^4	5
Ten meters	9.300×10^4	4
Hundred meters	9.30×10^4	3
Thousand meters	9.3×10^4	2

In a formula such as the one for the perimeter of a rectangle, $P = 2L + 2W$, the number 2 is called an **exact number**; it is assumed to have as many significant digits as needed.

Virtually all values of trigonometric functions are approximations, and virtually all measurements are approximations. When performing calculations on such approximate numbers, use the following rules.

1. When *adding and subtracting,* add or subtract normally, and then round the answer so that the last digit you keep is in the right-most column in which all the numbers have significant digits.

2. When *multiplying or dividing*, round your answers to the *least* number of significant digits found in any of the given numbers.

3. For *powers and roots*, round the answer so that it has the same number of significant digits as the number whose power or root you are finding.

EXAMPLE 2 (a) A backyard field is 2.8 meters by 11.4 meters. Find its perimeter.

$$\text{perimeter} = 2(2.8 \text{ m} \times 11.4 \text{ m}) = 28.4 \text{ m}$$

Since 2.8 and 11.4 both have significant digits in the tenth's place, the answer is 28.4 m.

(b) Find the area of a field 125.0 meters by 38.50 meters.

$$\text{area} = 125.0 \text{ m} \times 38.50 \text{ m} = 4812.5 \text{ m}^2.$$

We must round the answer to four significant digits. There are two ways to round a number ending in 5: we can round *up* and get 4813, or we can round off so that the final digit is *even*, and get 4812. We use the second method in this book, so that area = 4812 m² (m² represents "square meters"). •

One place where rounding is needed is in **linear interpolation**, a process used to find values of trigonometric functions for angles not in the table. This process is illustrated in the next few examples.

EXAMPLE 3 Find sin 42° 37′.

First, locate sin 42° 30′ and sin 42° 40′. Recall that in the first quadrant values of sine increase as the angle measures increase, so

$$\sin 42° 30' < \sin 42° 37' < \sin 42° 40'.$$

Using the values from Table II, we obtain the inequality

$$.6756 < \sin 42° 37' < .6777.$$

The difference between the two sine values, .6777 and .6756, is

$$.6777 - .6756 = .0021.$$

Notice that the angle 42° 37′ is 7/10 of the way between 42° 30′ and 42° 40′, with sin 42° 37′

$$(.0021)\frac{7}{10} = .00147$$

$$\approx .0015 \quad \text{(rounded to four places)}$$

greater than sin 42° 30′.

$$\sin 42° 37' = \sin 42° 30' + .0015$$
$$= .6756 + .0015$$
$$\sin 42° 37' = .6771.$$

Using a more accurate table or a pocket calculator, we could find that to five decimal places, sin 42° 37′ = .67709.   ●

The work in Example 3 can be arranged in the following compact form.

$$10' \begin{bmatrix} 7' \begin{bmatrix} \sin 42° \, 30' = .6756 \\ \sin 42° \, 37' = \quad ? \end{bmatrix} d \\ \sin 42° \, 40' = .6777 \end{bmatrix} .0021$$

$$\frac{d}{.0021} = \frac{7}{10}$$

$$d = \frac{7(.0021)}{10}$$

$$d \approx .0015$$

$$\sin 42° \, 37' = .6756 + .0015$$
$$= .6771$$

EXAMPLE 4   Find cos 58° 54′.

In the first quadrant values of cosine *decrease* as the angle measures *increase*, so

$$\cos 58° \, 50' > \cos 58° \, 54' > \cos 59° \, 00'.$$

Because of this, we must modify the procedure used above, and *subtract* at the last step. Work as shown in the following compact form.

$$10' \begin{bmatrix} 4' \begin{bmatrix} \cos 58° \, 50' = .5175 \\ \cos 58° \, 54' = \quad ? \end{bmatrix} d \\ \cos 59° \, 00' = .5150 \end{bmatrix} .0025$$

$$\frac{d}{.0025} = \frac{4}{10}$$

$$d = \frac{4(.0025)}{10} = .0010$$

$$\cos 58° \, 54' = .5175 - .0010$$
$$= .5165$$

Therefore cos 58° 54′ = .5165.   ●

EXAMPLE 5   Find a value of θ where $0° \leq \theta \leq 90°$ so that tan θ = .6720.

To begin, find the two numbers closest to .6720 in Table II. Here

$$.6703 < .6720 < .6745$$
$$\tan 33° \, 50' < \tan \theta < \tan 34° \, 00'.$$

Then proceed as follows.

$$10' \begin{bmatrix} d \begin{bmatrix} \tan 33° \, 50' = .6703 \\ \tan \quad ? \quad = .6720 \end{bmatrix} .0017 \\ \tan 34° \, 00' = .6745 \end{bmatrix} .0042$$

$$\frac{d}{10} = \frac{.0017}{.0042}$$

$$d = \frac{10(.0017)}{.0042} \approx 4$$

$$33° \, 50' + 4' = 33° \, 54'$$

Therefore θ = 33° 54′.   ●

2.4 EXERCISES *The following numbers represent approximate measurements. State the range represented by each of the measures. See Example 1.*

1. 5 lb   **2.** 8 ft

3. 9.6 ton   **4.** 7.8 qt

5. 8.95 m   **6.** 2.37 km

7. 19.7 L   **8.** 32 cm

9. 253.741 m   **10.** 74.358 oz

11. When Mt. Everest was first surveyed, the surveyors obtained a height of 29,000 feet to the nearest foot. State the range represented by this number. (The surveyors felt that no one would believe a measurement of 29,000 feet, so they reported it as 29,002.)

12. At Denny's, a chain of restaurants, the Low-Cal Special is said to have "approximately 472 calories." What is the range of calories represented by this number? By claiming "approximately 472 calories," they are probably claiming more accuracy than is possible. In your opinion, what might be a better claim?

Give the number of significant digits in each of the following. See Example 1.

13. 21.8   **14.** 37   **15.** 42.08   **16.** 600.9

17. 31.00   **18.** 20,000   **19.** 3.0×10^7 **20.** 5.43×10^3

21. 2.7100×10^4 **22.** 3.7000×10^3

Round each of the following numbers to three significant digits. Then refer to the original numbers and round each to two significant digits.

23. 768.7   **24.** 921.3   **25.** 12.53   **26.** 28.17

27. 9.003   **28.** 1.700   **29.** 7.125   **30.** 9.375

31. 11.55   **32.** 9.155

Use interpolation to find each of the following values. Use related angles in Exercises 49–52. See Examples 3 and 4.

33. tan 29° 42′   **34.** sin 56° 38′

35. tan 49° 17′   **36.** sin 78° 32′

37. sec 62° 34′   **38.** sin 74° 08′

39. tan 42° 09′   **40.** sec 12° 14′

41. cos 14° 24′   **42.** cos 29° 37′

43. cot 71° 12′   **44.** cot 38° 29′

45. cos 78° 45′   **46.** cos 82° 24′

47. csc 42° 36′   **48.** csc 71° 08′

49. cot 212° 38′   **50.** cot 257° 44′

51. cos 324° 18′   **52.** cos 342° 38′

Find θ in each of the following. See Example 5.

53. sin θ = .5840   **54.** tan θ = 1.420

55. tan θ = .4850   **56.** sin θ = .5160

57. $\cos \theta = .9285$

58. $\cos \theta = .4670$

59. $\cot \theta = 2.340$

60. $\cot \theta = .7050$

61. $\sec \theta = 3.510$

62. $\csc \theta = 2.708$

Replace each of the following trigonometric functions with its value from Table II, interpolating if necessary. Then decide if the given statement is true *or* false. *Use a calculator for the arithmetic. It may be that a true statement will lead to results that differ in the last decimal place, due to rounding error.*

63. $\sin 10° + \sin 10° = \sin 20°$

64. $\cos 40° = 2 \cos 20°$

65. $\sin 50° = 2 \sin 25° \cdot \cos 25°$

66. $\cos 70° = 2 \cos^2 35° - 1$

67. $\cos 40° = 1 - 2 \sin^2 80°$

68. $\cos^2 28° 42' + \sin^2 28° 42' = 1$

69. $2 \cos 38° 22' = \cos 76° 44'$

70. $\tan 29° 32' = \dfrac{\sin 29° 32'}{\cos 29° 32'}$

71. $\sin 39° 48' + \cos 39° 48' = 1$

72. $\cot 76° 43' = \dfrac{1}{\tan 76° 43'}$

2.5 Solving Right Triangles

One of the main applications of trigonometry is solving triangles. **To solve a triangle** means to find the measures of all the angles and sides of the triangle. We will study the solution of general triangles in Chapter 7. In this section, however, we look at methods of solving right triangles.

When solving triangles, use the following table for deciding on significant digits in angle measure.

Number of significant digits	Angle measure to nearest
2	degree
3	Ten minutes, or nearest tenth of a degree
4	Minute, or nearest hundredth of a degree

EXAMPLE 1 For example, if an angle measures 52° 30' we say its measurement has 3 significant digits.

Solve right triangle ABC if $A = 61°$ and $b = 32$ meters.

Recall that in a right triangle, C is reserved for the right angle, a is the length of the side opposite angle A, b is the length of the side opposite angle B, and c is the length of the hypotenuse. To begin, draw a sketch of right triangle ABC with the measures given above. See Figure 2.19.

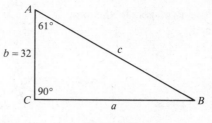

Figure 2.19

Angles A and B are complementary, so that the sum of their measures is $90°$. Thus,

$$A + B = 90°$$
$$61° + B = 90°$$
$$B = 29°.$$

We are given that $A = 61°$ and $b = 32$ meters. Side b is adjacent to angle A. To find the length of side a, we need a trigonometric function that involves angle A, the side opposite, and the side adjacent. We can use either tangent or cotangent. If we use tangent, we have

$$\tan A = \frac{\text{side opposite}}{\text{side adjacent}}.$$

Substituting $61°$ for A, 32 for the side adjacent, and a for the side opposite gives

$$\tan 61° = \frac{a}{32}.$$

$32 \tan 61° = a$	Multiply both sides by 32.
$32(1.8040) = a$	Use a calculator or look up
$a = 58$ m	$\tan 61°$ in Table II and substitute.

We rounded a to two significant digits to match the other numbers in the problem.

All that remains is to find c. Since $a^2 + b^2 = c^2$, we could use the Pythagorean theorem to find c. However, it is a good idea to *not* use a calculated value to find another calculated value. If an error was made in the first value, it would lead to an error in the second value also. We know that $A = 61°$ and $b = 32$. We want to find c. The cosine function relates A, the side adjacent, and the hypotenuse.

$$\cos A = \frac{\text{side adjacent}}{\text{hypotenuse}}.$$

$\cos 61° = \dfrac{32}{c}.$	Substitute the known values.
$c \cos 61° = 32$	Multiply both sides of this equation by c.
$c = \dfrac{32}{\cos 61°}$	Divide both sides by $\cos 61°$.
$c = \dfrac{32}{0.4848}$	From Table II, or a calculator, $\cos 61° = 0.4848$.
$c = 66$ m	

The Pythagorean theorem could be used as a check on the values found for a and c. ●

EXAMPLE 2 Solve right triangle ABC if $a = 29$ centimeters and $c = 53$ centimeters. Draw a sketch showing the given information, as in Figure 2.20.

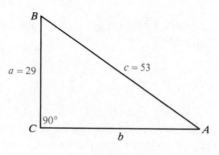

Figure 2.20

We can find angle A by using sine.

$$\sin A = \frac{\text{side opposite}}{\text{hypotenuse}}$$

$$\sin A = \frac{29}{53} = 0.5472$$

From Table II, or a calculator, $A = 33°$, to the nearest degree.
Since $A + B = 90°$,

$$B = 90° - A$$
$$= 90° - 33°$$
$$B = 57°.$$

To find b, use the Pythagorean theorem.

$$a^2 + b^2 = c^2$$
$$b^2 = c^2 - a^2$$

Since $a = 29$ and $c = 53$,

$$b^2 = 53^2 - 29^2$$
$$b^2 = 2809 - 841$$
$$b^2 = 1968$$

Finally, $b = 44$ cm ●

2.5 EXERCISES   *Solve each right triangle. See Examples 1 and 2.*

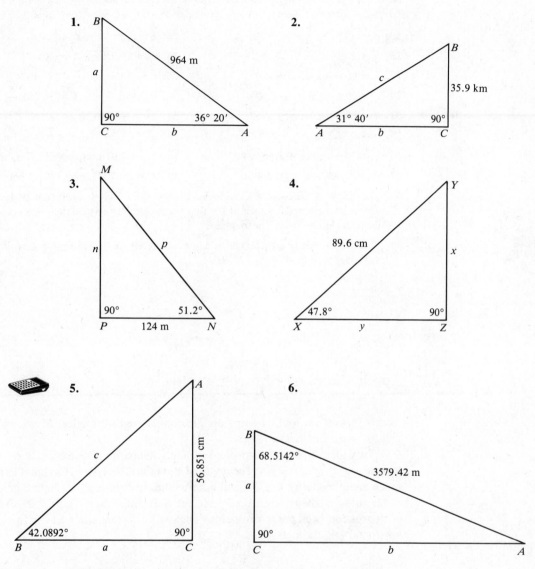

1. B, 964 m, a, 90°, 36° 20′, C, b, A

2. B, c, 35.9 km, 31° 40′, 90°, A, b, C

3. M, n, p, 90°, 51.2°, P, 124 m, N

4. Y, 89.6 cm, x, 47.8°, 90°, X, y, Z

5. A, c, 56.851 cm, 42.0892°, 90°, B, a, C

6. B, 68.5142°, 3579.42 m, a, 90°, C, b, A

Solve each right triangle. See Examples 1 and 2.

7. $b = 19$ ft, $B = 40°$ **8.** $a = 12$ yd, $A = 20°$

9. $a = 38$ m, $B = 32°$ **10.** $b = 59$ cm, $A = 54°$

11. $c = 36$ in, $A = 29°$ **12.** $c = 63$ mm, $A = 43°$

13. $c = 98$ m, $B = 32°$ **14.** $c = 74$ m, $B = 59°$

15. $a = 2.3$ m, $B = 63°$ **16.** $b = 7.9$ yd, $A = 12°$

17. $a = 80$ ft, $b = 74$ ft   **18.** $a = 60$ ft, $b = 38$ ft

19. $a = 73$ m, $b = 29$ m   **20.** $a = 86$ yd, $b = 92$ yd

21. $a = 3.8$ in, $b = 1.4$ in   **22.** $a = 7.6$ cm, $b = 9.4$ cm

Solve each of the following right triangles to the proper number of significant digits. Use a calculator or interpolation in Exercises 31–36. See Examples 1 and 2.

23. $a = 842$ cm, $A = 29° 30'$ **24.** $b = 325$ m, $B = 46° 10'$

25. $b = 62.9$ m, $A = 32° 50'$ **26.** $a = 79.1$ mm, $A = 40° 40'$

27. $c = 96.3$ m, $A = 36° 20'$ **28.** $c = 74.8$ cm, $B = 53° 10'$

29. $c = .298$ m, $B = 18° 40'$ **30.** $c = .0136$ mi, $A = 34° 50'$

 31. $a = 69.73$ m, $A = 32° 53'$ **32.** $b = 293.7$ ft, $B = 58° 12'$

33. $b = 7.982$ cm, $A = 29° 43'$ **34.** $a = 1.739$ km, $A = 59° 36'$

35. $c = 7.813$ m, $b = 2.467$ m   **36.** $c = 44.91$ mm, $a = 32.71$ mm

37. $B = 42.432°$, $a = 157.49$ m   **38.** $A = 36.704°$, $c = 1461.3$ cm

39. The length of the base of an isosceles triangle is 37 inches. Each base angle is 49°. Find the length of each of the two equal sides of the triangle. (Hint: break the triangle into two right triangles.)

40. Find the altitude of an isosceles triangle having a base of 125 centimeters, if the angle opposite the base is 72° 40'.

2.6 Applications of Right Triangles

In this section we look at some applications of right triangles. More applications are discussed in Chapter 7.

Two ideas that come up often in applications involve the angle of elevation and the angle of depression. The **angle of elevation** from point X to point Y (above X) is the angle made by line XY and a horizontal line through X. Note that the angle of elevation is always measured from the horizontal. See Figure 2.21. The **angle of depression** from point X to point Y (below X) is the angle made by line XY and a horizontal line through X.

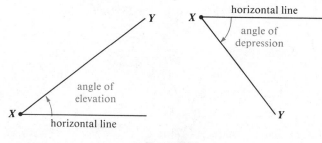

Figure 2.21

EXAMPLE 1   The angle of elevation from a point 49 meters from the base of a flagpole to the top is 27°. Find the height of the flagpole.

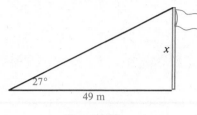

Figure 2.22

Draw a sketch showing the given information, as in Figure 2.22. We need to find x. The tangent function relates x, 49, and 27°.

$$\tan 27° = \frac{x}{49}$$

$$49 \tan 27° = x$$

$$49(.5095) = x \qquad \text{Use Table II or a calculator.}$$

$$x = 25 \text{ m.}$$

The height of the flagpole is 25 m.   ●

Other applications of trigonometry involve **bearing**, an important idea in navigation. There are two common ways to express bearing. *When a single angle is given, such as* 164°, *it is understood that the bearing is measured in a clockwise direction from due north.* Several sample bearings using this system are shown in Figure 2.23.

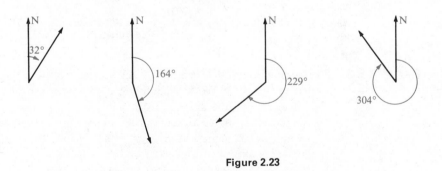

Figure 2.23

EXAMPLE 2   Radar stations A and B are on an east-west line, 3.7 kilometers apart. Station A detects a plane at C, on a bearing of 61°. Station B detects the same plane, on a bearing of 331°. Find the distance from A to C.

Draw a sketch showing the given information, as in Figure 2.24. Angle C is a right angle, since angles CAB and CBA are complementary. (If C were not a right angle, we would need the methods of Chapter 7.) We can find the desired distance, b, by using the cosine function.

$$\cos 29° = \frac{b}{3.7}$$
$$3.7 \cos 29° = b$$
$$3.7(.8746) = b$$
$$b = 3.2 \text{ km}$$

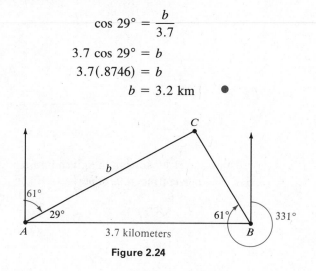

Figure 2.24

The other common system for expressing bearing starts with a north-south line and uses an acute angle to show the direction, either east or west, from this line. Figure 2.25 shows several sample bearings using this system. Either N or S always comes first, followed by an acute angle, and then E or W.

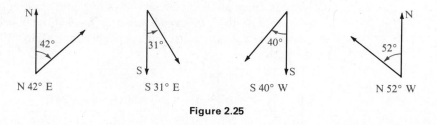

Figure 2.25

EXAMPLE 3 The bearing from A to C is S 52° E. The bearing from A to B is N 84° E. The bearing from B to C is S 38° W. A plane flying at 250 miles per hour takes 2.4 hours to go from A to B. Find the distance from A to C.

Figure 2.26 shows a sketch of the given information. Since the bearing from A to B is N 84° E, angle ABD is 180° − 84° = 96°. Thus, angle ABC is 46°. Also, angle BAC is 180° − (84° + 52°) = 44°. Angle C is 180° − (44° + 46°) = 90°. We know that a plane flying at 250 miles per hour takes 2.4 hours to go from A to B. The distance from A to B is the product of rate and time, or

$$c = \text{rate} \times \text{time}$$
$$= 2.4(250)$$
$$c = 600 \text{ miles.}$$

To find b, the distance from A to C, we use sine. (We could also use cosine.)

$$\sin 46° = \frac{b}{c}$$

$$\sin 46° = \frac{b}{600}$$

$$600 \sin 46° = b$$

$$600(.7193) = b$$

$$b = 430 \text{ miles} \quad \bullet$$

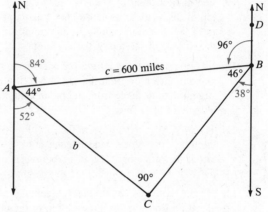

Figure 2.26

2.6 EXERCISES

Solve each of the following problems. Give angles to the nearest degree and lengths to two significant digits. See Examples 1–3.

1. A 22-foot ladder leans against a house. The top of the ladder is 12 feet above the ground. Find the angle the ladder makes with the ground.

2. A 15-foot ladder makes a 52° angle with the ground. How far will the top of the ladder be above the ground?

3. A guy wire on a telephone pole makes an angle of 64° with the ground. One end of the wire is 12 meters above the ground. How long is the wire?

4. When Scott Hardy stands 127 feet from the base of a bell tower, the angle of elevation to the top is 21°. Find the height of the tower.

5. The angle of elevation from a point 64 meters from the base of a building to the top of the building is 35°. Find the height of the building.

6. The angle of depression from the top of a building to a fountain is 38°. The fountain is 47 feet from the base of the building. Find the height of the building.

7. The angle of elevation from a point 140,000 feet horizontally from a point directly below the top of Mt. Everest to the top of the mountain is 8°. The point from which the observation is made is at an altitude of 9000 feet. Find the elevation of the top of the mountain.

8. The angle of depression from the top of Pike's Peak, at an altitude of 14,000 feet, to the city of Colorado Springs is 8°. The horizontal distance from the city to the peak is 58,000 feet. Find the altitude of Colorado Springs.

9. The highest point in Texas is Guadelupe Peak. The angle of depression from the top of this peak to a small miner's cabin at elevation 2000 feet is 26°. The cabin is 14,000 feet horizontally from a point directly under the top of the mountain. Find the altitude of the top of the mountain.

10. Mt. Rogers, with an altitude of 5700 feet, is the highest point in Virginia. The angle of elevation from the top of Mt. Rogers to a plane flying overhead is 33°. The straight line distance from the mountaintop to the plane is 4600 feet. Find the altitude of the plane.

11. The angle of elevation from the top of an office building in New York City to the top of the World Trade Center is 68°, while the angle of depression from the top of the office building to the bottom is 63°. The office building is 290 feet from the World Trade Center. Find the height of the World Trade Center.

12. A plane is flying 12,000 feet horizontally from a tall, vertical cliff. The angle of elevation from the plane to the top of the cliff is 45°, while the angle of depression from the plane to a point on the cliff at elevation 8000 feet is 14°. Find the height of the cliff.

13. The bearing from Winston-Salem, North Carolina, to Danville, Virginia, is N 42° E. The bearing from Danville to Goldsboro, North Carolina, is S 48° E. A small plane piloted by Calvin Taylor, traveling at 60 miles per hour, takes 1 hour to go from Winston-Salem to Danville and 1.8 hours to go from Danville to Goldsboro. Find the distance from Winston-Salem to Goldsboro.

14. The bearing from Atlanta to Macon is S 27° E, while the bearing from Macon to Augusta is N 63° E. A plane traveling at 60 miles per hour needs $1\frac{1}{4}$ hours to go from Atlanta to Macon and $1\frac{3}{4}$ hours to go from Macon to Augusta. Find the distance from Atlanta to Augusta.

15. The airline distance from Philadelphia to Syracuse is 260 miles, on a bearing of 335°. The distance from Philadelphia to Cincinnati is 510 miles, on a bearing of 245°. Find the bearing from Cincinnati to Syracuse.

16. A ship travels 70 kilometers on a bearing of 27°, and then turns on a bearing of 117° for 180 kilometers. Find the distance of the end of the trip from the starting point.

17. A plane is found by radar to be flying 18,000 m above the ground. The angle of elevation from the radar to the plane is 80°. Nine minutes later, the plane is directly over the station. See the Figure. Find the speed of the plane, assuming that it is flying level.

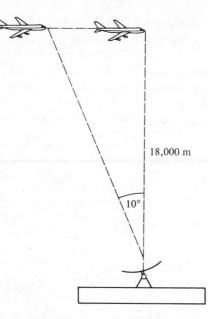

18,000 m

10°

18. A chisel is to be made from a steel rod with a diameter of 4.6 cm. If the angle at the tip is 64°, how long will the tip be? See the Figure.

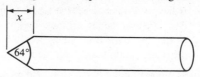

x

64°

Use a calculator or interpolation to work the following problems to the correct number of significant digits.

19. To measure the height of a flagpole, José finds that the angle of elevation from a point 24.73 feet from the base to the top is 38° 12'. Find the height of the flagpole.

20. A rectangular piece of land is 629.3 feet by 872.6 feet. Find an acute angle made by the diagonal of the rectangle.

21. To find the distance *RS* across a lake, a surveyor lays off *RT* = 72.6 meters, angle *T* = 32° 10', and angle *S* = 57° 50'. Find length *RS*.

22. A surveyor must find the distance *QM* across a depressed freeway. She lays off *QN* = 769 feet along one side of the freeway, with angle *N* = 21° 50', and angle *M* = 68° 10'. Find *QM*.

23. Forest fire lookouts are located at points *A* and *B*, which are 12.4 miles apart on an east-west line. From *A*, the bearing of a fire is 127° 10'. From *B*, the bearing of the same fire is 217° 10'. Find the distance from *B* to the fire.

24. Two lighthouses are located on a north-south line. From lighthouse *A* the bearing of a ship 3742 meters away is 129° 43'. From lighthouse *B* the bearing of the ship is 39° 43'. Find the distance between the lighthouses.

25. At a point 753 meters from the base of the Space Needle in Seattle the angle of elevation to the top is 13° 40'. Find the height of the needle.

26. The Tower of the Americas in San Antonio is 622 feet tall. Find the angle of depression from the top of the tower to Joske's Department Store, 972 feet from the base of the tower. Round to the nearest degree.

27. A beam of gamma rays is to be used to treat a tumor known to be 5.7 centimeters beneath the patient's skin. To avoid damaging a vital organ, the radiologist moves the source over 8.3 centimeters. See the Figure.
    a. At what angle to the patient's skin must the radiologist aim the gamma ray source to hit the tumor?
    b. How far will the beam have to travel through the patient's body before reaching the tumor?

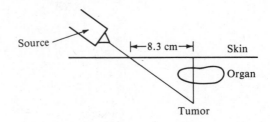

28. Commercial airliners fly at an altitude of about 10 kilometers. They start descending toward the airport when they are still far away so that they will not have to dive at a steep angle.
    a. If the pilot wants the plane's path to make an angle of 3° with the ground, how far from the airport must the pilot start descending?
    b. If the pilot starts descending 300 kilometers from the airport, what angle will the plane's path make with the horizontal?

29. From a point on the North Rim of the Grand Canyon, a surveyor measures an angle of depression of 1° 18′ to a point on the South Rim. See the Figure. From an aerial photograph, he determines that the horizontal distance between the two points is 10 miles. How many feet below the North Rim is the South Rim? (A mile is 5280 feet.)

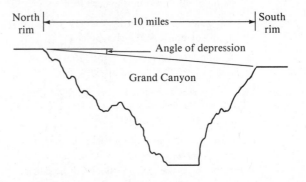

30. A submarine at the surface of the ocean makes an emergency dive, its path making an angle of 21° with the surface.
    a. If it goes for 300 meters along its downward path, how deep will it be? What horizontal distance is it from its starting point?
    b. How many meters must it go along its downward path to reach a depth of 1000 meters?

31. Scientists estimate the heights of features on the moon by measuring the lengths of the shadows they cast on the moon's surface. From a photograph, you find that the shadow cast on the inside of a crater by its rim is 325 meters long. See the Figure. At the time the photograph was taken, the sun's angle of elevation from this place on the moon's surface was 23° 37′. How high does the rim rise above the inside of the crater?

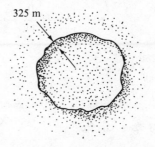

325 m

32. Suppose that you are on a salvage ship in the Gulf of Mexico. Your sonar system has located a sunken Spanish galleon at a slant distance of 683 meters from your ship, with an angle of depression of 27° 52′.

a. How deep is the water at the galleon's location?

b. How far must you sail to be directly above the galleon?

c. You sail directly toward the spot over the galleon. When you have gone 520 meters, what should the angle of depression be?

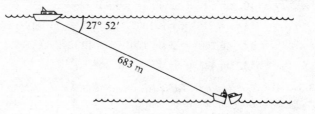

27° 52′

683 m

Chapter 2   Test

[2.1–2.2]   *Find the values of the trigonometric functions for each of the following angles. Do not use tables or a calculator. Give the exact values.*

1.

2. 120°

3. 225°

4. 300°

Solve each of the following. Assume that all angles are positive acute angles.

5. $\sin 4\beta = \cos 5\beta$ **6.** $\sec(2\gamma + 10°) = \csc(4\gamma + 20°)$

Evaluate each of the following. Do not use tables or a calculator. Give the exact values.

7. $\cos 60° + 2 \sin^2 30°$

8. $\tan^2 120° - 2 \cot 240°$

9. $\cot^2 300° + \cos^2 120° - 3 \sin^2 240°$

[2.2–2.3]   *Answer* true *or* false *for each of the following. Use a calculator or a table as necessary.*

10. $\sin 50° + \sin 40° = \sin 90°$

11. $\cos 210° = \cos 180° \cdot \cos 30° - \sin 180° \cdot \sin 30°$

12. $\sin 240° = 2 \sin 120° \cdot \cos 120°$

13. $\sin 42° + \sin 42° = \sin 84°$

[2.3–2.4]   *Use Table II, Table III, or a calculator to find the value of each of the following. Interpolate as necessary.*

14. $\sin 72° 30'$ **15.** $\sec 222° 30'$

16. $\cot 305.6°$ **17.** $\sin 47° 24'$

18. $\cot 32° 42'$ **19.** $\csc 78° 21'$

Find the related angle θ' for each of the following.

20. 142° 20'   **21.** 251.9°   **22.** 680° 30'

Use Table II to find a value of θ where $0° \leq \theta \leq 90°$, for each of the following.

23. $\sin \theta = .8258$ **24.** $\cot \theta = 1.124$ **25.** $\cos \theta = .9754$

Find the number of significant digits in each of the following.

26. 28.000   **27.** 9.70×10^{-7}

Round each of the following to three significant digits.

28. 975.5   **29.** .000143259

[2.5]   *Solve each of the following right triangles. The right angle is at C.*

30. $A = 43°$, $a = 76$ m   **31.** $B = 79° 20'$, $c = 896$ cm

[2.6]   *Work the following problems to the correct number of significant digits.*

32. The angle of elevation from a point 89.6 feet from the base of a tower to the top of the tower is $42° 40'$. Find the height of the tower.

33. The bearing of B from C is $254°$. The bearing of A from C is $344°$. The bearing of A from B is $32°$. The distance from A to C is 780 meters. Find the distance from A to B.

3

Radian Measure and Circular Functions

In most work in applied trigonometry, angles are measured in degrees, minutes, and seconds, or in decimal degrees. For thousands of years, the number 360 has been used to represent the number of degrees around a point. Originally, it may have been chosen because it is close to the number of days in a year.

In more advanced work in mathematics, especially in calculus, the use of degree measure for angles makes many formulas very complicated. These advanced formulas can be simplified if we measure angles with *radian measure* instead of degrees.

3.1 Radian Measure

Figure 3.1 shows an angle θ in standard position along with a circle of radius r. The vertex of θ is at the center of the circle. Angle θ cuts an arc on the circle. The length of this arc is equal to the radius of the circle. Because of this, angle θ is said to have a measure of one radian:

One radian is the measure of an angle whose vertex is at the center of a circle and which cuts an arc on the circle equal in length to the radius of the circle.

It follows that an angle of measure two radians cuts an arc equal in length to twice the radius of the circle, while an angle of measure one-half radian cuts an arc equal in length to half the radius of the circle, and so on.

The circumference of a circle is the distance around the circle. It is given by the formula $C = 2\pi r$, where r is the radius of the circle. The formula $C = 2\pi r$ shows that the radius can be laid off 2π times around a circle. Therefore, an angle of $360°$, which corresponds to a complete circle, cuts an arc equal in length to 2π times the radius of the circle. Because of this, an angle of 360° has a measure of 2π radians:

$$360° = 2\pi \text{ radians}$$

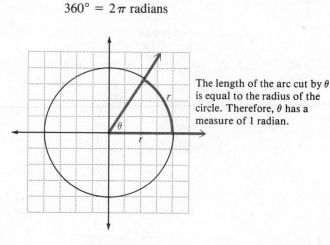

The length of the arc cut by θ is equal to the radius of the circle. Therefore, θ has a measure of 1 radian.

Figure 3.1

The radian measure of an angle is the ratio of the arc length cut by the angle to the radius of the circle. In this ratio, the units of measure "cancel," leaving only a number. For this reason, radian measure is just a real number—there are no units associated with a radian measure. Because of this, we can write 360° = 2π radians as just

$$360° = 2\pi.$$

An angle of 180° is half the size of an angle of 360°. Therefore, an angle of 180° would have half the radian measure of an angle of 360°.

$$180° = \frac{1}{2}(2\pi) \text{ radians}$$

$$180° = \pi \text{ radians}$$

Since π radians = 180°, we can divide both sides by π to find that

$$1 \text{ radian} = \frac{180°}{\pi}$$

or

$$1 \text{ radian} \approx \frac{180°}{3.14159}$$

$$\approx 57.296°$$

$$1 \text{ radian} \approx 57° \ 17' \ 45''.$$

Since 180° = π radians, we also have

$$1° = \frac{\pi}{180} \text{ radians,}$$

or

$$1° \approx \frac{3.14159}{180} \text{ radians}$$

$$1° \approx .0174533 \text{ radians.}$$

Angle measures can be converted back and forth between degrees and radians by either of two methods.

1. Proportion:

$$\frac{\text{radian measure}}{\pi} = \frac{\text{degree measure}}{180}$$

2. Formulas:

From	To	Multiply by
radians	degrees	$\dfrac{180°}{\pi}$
degrees	radians	$\dfrac{\pi}{180°}$

EXAMPLE 1 Convert each degree measure to radians.

(a) 45°

By the proportion method:

$$\frac{\text{radian measure}}{\pi} = \frac{45}{180}$$

Multiply both sides by π.

$$\text{radian measure} = \frac{45\pi}{180} = \frac{\pi}{4}$$

To use the formula method, multiply by $\pi/180°$ since we are converting from degrees to radians.

$$45° = 45°\left(\frac{\pi}{180°}\right) = \frac{45\pi}{180} = \frac{\pi}{4} \text{ radians}$$

(b) $240° = 240°\left(\dfrac{\pi}{180°}\right) = \dfrac{4\pi}{3} \text{ radians}$ ●

EXAMPLE 2 Convert to radians.

(a) 29° 40′

We know that 40′ = 40/60 = 2/3 of a degree. Thus,

$$29° \, 40′ = 29\frac{2}{3}°$$

$$= \frac{89°}{3}$$

$$= \frac{89}{3}\left(\frac{\pi}{180}\right) \text{ radians}$$

$$29° \, 40′ = \frac{89\pi}{540} \text{ radians.}$$

This answer is exact. If we now replace π with the approximation 3.14159, we get

$$29° \; 40' \approx \frac{89(3.14159)}{540}$$

$$29° \; 40' \approx .518 \text{ radians.}$$

(b) 74.9162°

$$74.9162° = 74.9162\left(\frac{\pi}{180}\right) \qquad \text{Multiply by } \pi/180°.$$

$$\approx 74.9162\left(\frac{3.14159}{180}\right)$$

$$\approx 1.30753 \text{ radians} \qquad \bullet$$

EXAMPLE 3 Convert each of the following radian measures to degrees.

(a) $\dfrac{9\pi}{4}$

Use a proportion, or multiply by 180°/π. Using this second method,

$$\frac{9\pi}{4} \text{ radians} = \frac{9\pi}{4}\left(\frac{180°}{\pi}\right)$$

$$\frac{9\pi}{4} \text{ radians} = 405°.$$

(b) $\dfrac{11\pi}{3}$ radians $= \dfrac{11\pi}{3}\left(\dfrac{180°}{\pi}\right) = 660°$ $\qquad \bullet$

EXAMPLE 4 Convert 4.2 radians to degrees. Write the result to the nearest minute.
By the formula,

$$4.2 \text{ radians} = 4.2\left(\frac{180°}{\pi}\right)$$

$$\approx \frac{4.2(180°)}{3.14159}$$

$$4.2 \text{ radians} \approx 240.64°$$

$$= 240° + .64°$$

$$= 240° + .64(60')$$

$$\approx 240° + 38'$$

$$= 240° \; 38'. \qquad \bullet$$

Many calculators will convert back and forth from radian measure to degree measure. A common difficulty is that the calculator works with decimal degrees, rather than degrees, minutes, and seconds. The next example shows how to handle this.

EXAMPLE 5 (a) Convert 146° 18′ 34″ to radians.
Since 1′ = 1/60° and 1″ = 1/60′,

$$146° \ 18′ \ 34″ = 146° + \frac{18}{60}° + \frac{34}{3600}°$$

$$= 146° + .3° + .00944°$$

$$= 146.30944°.$$

Now, activate the calculator keys that convert from degrees to radians to get

$$146° \ 18′ \ 34″ \approx 2.55358 \text{ radians.}$$

(b) Convert .97682 radians to degrees.
Enter .97682 in your calculator and use the keys that convert from radians to degrees to get

$$.97682 \text{ radians} = 55.967663°.$$

This result may be converted to degree–minute–second measure if desired.

$$55.967663° = 55° + (.967663)(60′)$$

$$= 55° + 58.05978′$$

$$= 55° + 58′ + (.05978)(60″)$$

$$= 55° + 58′ + 4″$$

$$= 55° \ 58′ \ 4″ \quad \bullet$$

EXAMPLE 6 Find $\tan \dfrac{2\pi}{3}$.

We first convert $2\pi/3$ radians to degrees.

$$\tan \frac{2\pi}{3} = \tan \frac{2\pi}{3} \cdot \frac{180}{\pi}$$

$$= \tan 120°$$

$$\tan \frac{2\pi}{3} = -\sqrt{3} \quad \bullet$$

A table giving the values of the trigonometric functions for common radian and degree measures is inside the front cover of this book.

3.1 EXERCISES *Convert each of the following degree measures to radians. Leave answers as multiples of π. See Example 1.*

1. 60°	**2.** 30°	**3.** 90°	**4.** 120°
5. 150°	**6.** 135°	**7.** 210°	**8.** 270°

9. 300°	**10.** 315°	**11.** 450°	**12.** 480°
13. 20°	**14.** 80°	**15.** 140°	**16.** 320°

Convert each of the following degree measures to radians. Write the results with three significant digits. See Example 2.

17. 39°	**18.** 74°	**19.** 42° 30′	**20.** 53° 40′
21. 139° 10′	**22.** 174° 50′	**23.** 64.29°	**24.** 85.04°

Convert each of the following radian measures to degrees. See Example 3.

25. $\dfrac{\pi}{3}$	**26.** $\dfrac{8\pi}{3}$	**27.** $\dfrac{7\pi}{4}$	**28.** $\dfrac{2\pi}{3}$
29. $\dfrac{11\pi}{6}$	**30.** $\dfrac{15\pi}{4}$	**31.** $-\dfrac{\pi}{6}$	**32.** $-\dfrac{\pi}{4}$
33. $\dfrac{8\pi}{5}$	**34.** $\dfrac{7\pi}{10}$	**35.** $\dfrac{11\pi}{15}$	**36.** $\dfrac{4\pi}{15}$
37. $\dfrac{7\pi}{20}$	**38.** $\dfrac{17\pi}{20}$	**39.** $\dfrac{11\pi}{30}$	**40.** $\dfrac{15\pi}{32}$

Convert radians to degrees and degrees to radians. Write radian measure with four significant digits and degree measure to four decimal places and also to the nearest minute. See Example 5.

41. 2 radians	**42.** 5 radians
43. 1.74 radians	**44.** 3.06 radians
45. .0912 radians	**46.** .3417 radians
47. 56° 25′	**48.** 122° 37′
49. 47.6925°	**50.** 83.0143°
51. −29° 42′ 36″	**52.** −157° 11′ 9″

Find each of the following without using a calculator or a table. See Example 6.

53. $\sin \dfrac{\pi}{3}$	**54.** $\cos \dfrac{\pi}{6}$	**55.** $\tan \dfrac{\pi}{4}$	**56.** $\cot \dfrac{\pi}{3}$
57. $\sec \dfrac{\pi}{6}$	**58.** $\csc \dfrac{\pi}{4}$	**59.** $\sin \dfrac{\pi}{2}$	**60.** $\csc \dfrac{\pi}{2}$
61. $\tan \dfrac{2\pi}{3}$	**62.** $\cot \dfrac{2\pi}{3}$	**63.** $\sin \dfrac{5\pi}{6}$	**64.** $\tan \dfrac{5\pi}{6}$
65. $\cos 3\pi$	**66.** $\sec \pi$	**67.** $\sin \dfrac{4\pi}{3}$	**68.** $\cot \dfrac{4\pi}{3}$
69. $\tan \dfrac{5\pi}{4}$	**70.** $\csc \dfrac{5\pi}{4}$	**71.** $\sin 3\pi$	**72.** $\cos 5\pi$
73. $\tan -\dfrac{\pi}{3}$	**74.** $\cot -\dfrac{2\pi}{3}$	**75.** $\sin -\dfrac{7\pi}{6}$	**76.** $\cos -\dfrac{\pi}{6}$

77. The figure shows the same angles measured in both degrees and radians. Complete the missing measures.

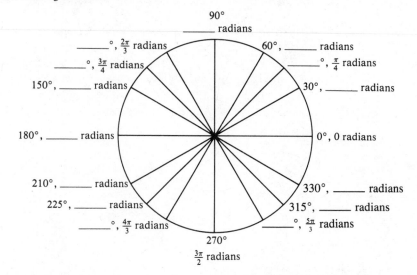

78. A spaceship is rotating along its axis. Through how many radians would it turn in 6 rotations?

79. A dart board is broken into sectors of various colors, with each sector of equal area. Find the total number of radians represented by

(a) red

(b) blue.

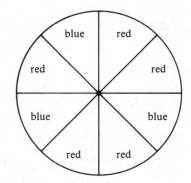

80. How many radians are in 12.4 revolutions?

Find the radian measure (as a multiple of π) of the smallest angle between the hands of a clock at each of the following times. Assume that the hour hand is exactly on the given hour.

81. 12:15   **82.** 12:30   **83.** 2:40

84. 3:35   **85.** 9:25   **86.** 10:40

3.2 Length of Arc and Area of a Sector

Using radian measure, we can obtain two useful formulas. The first formula is used to find the length of an arc on a circle. It depends on the fact from plane geometry that the length of an arc is proportional to the measure of its central angle.

In Figure 3.2, angle QOP has a measure of 1 radian and cuts an arc of length r on the circle. Angle ROT has a measure of θ radians and cuts an arc of length s on the circle. Since the lengths of the arcs are proportional to the measure of their central angles,

$$\frac{s}{r} = \frac{\theta}{1},$$

or

$$s = r\theta.$$

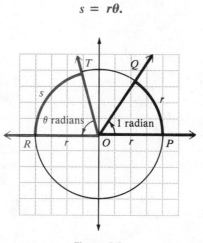

Figure 3.2

In words,

The **length s of the arc** cut on a circle of radius r by a central angle of measure θ radians is given by the product of the radius and the radian measure of the angle.

This formula is a good example of the usefulness of radian measure. To see why, try to write the equivalent formula for an angle measured in degrees.

EXAMPLE 1 A circle has a radius of 18.2 centimeters. Find the length of the arc cut by a central angle having the following measures.

(a) $\dfrac{3\pi}{8}$ radians

Here $r = 18.2$ cm and $\theta = 3\pi/8$. Since $s = r\theta$,

$$s = 18.2\left(\frac{3\pi}{8}\right)\ \text{cm}$$

$$s = \frac{54.6\pi}{8}\ \text{cm} \qquad \text{The exact answer}$$

or

$$s \approx 21.4\ \text{cm}$$

(b) 144°

The formula $s = r\theta$ requires that θ be measured in radians. First, convert θ to radians by the methods of the previous section.

$$144° = 144\left(\frac{\pi}{180}\right) \text{ radians}$$

$$144° = \frac{4\pi}{5} \text{ radians}$$

Now,

$$s = 18.2\left(\frac{4\pi}{5}\right) \text{ cm}$$

$$s = \frac{72.8\pi}{5} \text{ cm}$$

or

$$s \approx 45.7 \text{ cm} \qquad \bullet$$

EXAMPLE 2   Reno, Nevada, is approximately due north of Los Angeles. The latitude of Reno is 40°N, while that of Los Angeles is 34°N. (The N in 34°N means that the location is *north* of the equator.) If the radius of the earth is 6400 km, find the north–south distance between the two cities.

Latitude gives the measure of a central angle whose initial side goes through the earth's equator and whose terminal side goes through the location in question. As shown in Figure 3.3, the central angle between Reno and Los Angeles is 6°. The distance between the two cities can thus be found by the formula $s = r\theta$, after 6° is first converted to radians.

$$6° = 6\left(\frac{\pi}{180}\right) = \frac{\pi}{30} \text{ radians}$$

The distance between the two cities is thus

$$s = r\theta$$

$$= 6400\left(\frac{\pi}{30}\right) \text{ km}$$

$$s = 670 \text{ km} \qquad \bullet$$

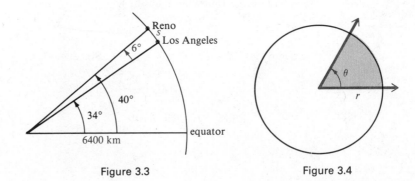

Figure 3.3   Figure 3.4

The other useful formula that we obtain in this section is used to find the area of a "piece of pie," or sector. A **sector of a circle** is the portion of the interior of a circle cut by a central angle. See Figure 3.4. To find the area of a sector, assume that the radius of the circle is r. A complete circle has a measure of 2π radians. If a central angle for the sector has measure θ radians, then the sector makes up a fraction $\theta/(2\pi)$ of a complete circle. The area of a complete circle is $A = \pi r^2$. Therefore, the area of the sector is given by the product of the fraction $\theta/(2\pi)$ and the total area, πr^2, or

$$\text{Area of sector} = \frac{\theta}{2\pi} \cdot \pi r^2$$

$$\textbf{Area of sector} = \frac{1}{2}\,\theta r^2.$$

This unusual corral is broken into 26 areas, many of which approximate sectors of a circle. Assume that the corral has a diameter of 50 m. Find the area that each horse has if we assume that the areas are sectors, with the fences meeting at the center. What would be the central angle for each area?

This field is a sector of a circle; see Example 3 on the next page.

EXAMPLE 3 The preceding photograph shows a field in the shape of a sector of a circle. The central angle is 15° and the radius of the circle is 321 m. Find the area of the field.

First, convert 15° to radians.

$$15° = 15\left(\frac{\pi}{180}\right) = \frac{\pi}{12} \text{ radians}$$

Now, use the formula

$$\text{Area of sector} = \frac{1}{2}\theta r^2$$

to get

$$= \frac{1}{2}\left(\frac{\pi}{12}\right)(321)^2$$

$$\approx \frac{1}{2}\left(\frac{3.14159}{12}\right)(103,041)$$

$$\text{Area of sector} \approx 13,500 \text{ m}^2 \quad \bullet$$

3.2 EXERCISES *Find the arc length cut by each of the following angles. See Example 1.*

1. $r = 8.00$ in, $\theta = \pi$ radians

2. $r = 72.0$ ft, $\theta = \pi/8$ radians

3. $r = 12.3$ cm, $\theta = 2\pi/3$ radians

4. $r = .892$ cm, $\theta = 11\pi/10$ radians

5. $r = 253$ m, $\theta = 2\pi/5$ radians

6. $r = 120$ mm, $\theta = \pi/9$ radians

7. $r = 4.82$ m, $\theta = 60°$

8. $r = 71.9$ cm, $\theta = 135°$

9. $r = 58.402$ m, $\theta = 52.417°$

10. $r = 39.4$ cm, $\theta = 68.059°$

Find the distance in miles between each of the following pairs of cities whose latitudes are given. Assume that the cities are on a north–south line and that the radius of the earth is 6400 km. See Example 2.

11. Grand Portage, Minnesota, 44°N, and New Orleans, Louisiana, 30°N

12. St. Petersburg, Florida, 28°N, and Detroit, Michigan, 42°N

13. Madison, South Dakota, 44°N, and Dallas, Texas, 33°N

14. Charleston, South Carolina, 33°N, and Toronto, Ontario, 43°N

15. Panama City, Panama, 9°N, and Pittsburgh, Pennsylvania, 40°N

16. Farmersville, California, 36°N, and Penticton, British Columbia, 49°N

17. New York City, New York, 41°N, and Lima, Peru, 12°S

18. Halifax, Nova Scotia, 45°N, and Buenos Aires, Argentina, 34°S

Find the distance between the following pairs of cities located along the equator.

19. Nairobi, Kenya, longitude 40°E, and Singapore, Republic of Singapore, 105°E

20. Quito, Ecuador, longitude 80°W, and Libreville, Gabon, 10°E

If a central angle is very small, there is little difference in length between an arc and the inscribed chord. See the figure. Approximate each of the following lengths by finding the necessary arc length.

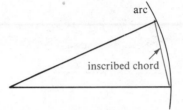

arc

inscribed chord

21. A tree 600 m away intercepts an angle of 2°. Find the height of the tree.

22. A building 500 m away intercepts an angle of 3°. Find the height of the building.

23. A railroad track in the desert is 3.5 km away. A train on the track intercepts (horizontally) an angle of 3° 20′. Find the length of the train.

24. An oil tanker 2.3 km at sea intercepts a 1° 30′ angle horizontally. Find the length of the ship.

25. The full moon intercepts an angle of 1/2°. The moon is 240,000 miles away. Find the diameter of the moon.

26. A building with a height of 58 m intercepts an angle of 1° 20′. How far away is the building?

27. The mast of Gale Stockdale's boat is 32 feet high. If it intercepts an angle of 2° 10′, how far away is it?

28. A television tower 530 m high intercepts an angle of 2° 40′. How far away is the tower?

Find the areas of each of the following sectors of a circle. See Example 3.

29. $r = 9.0$ m, $\theta = \pi/3$ radians

30. $r = 15$ ft, $\theta = \pi/5$ radians

31. $r = 29.2$ m, $\theta = 5\pi/6$ radians

32. $r = 59.8$ km, $\theta = 2\pi/3$ radians

33. $r = 52$ cm, $\theta = 3\pi/10$ radians

34. $r = 25$ mm, $\theta = \pi/15$ radians

35. $r = 12.7$ cm, $\theta = 81°$

36. $r = 18.3$ m, $\theta = 125°$

37. $r = 32.6$ m, $\theta = 38° 40′$

38. $r = 59.8$ ft, $\theta = 74° 30′$

39. $r = 86.243$ m, $\theta = 11.7142°$

40. $r = 111.976$ cm, $\theta = 29.8477°$

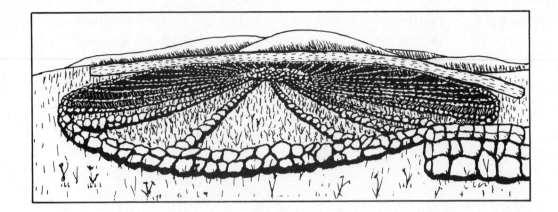

The sketch shows Medicine Wheel, an Indian structure in northern Wyoming. The circular structure is perhaps 200 years old. There are 32 spokes in the wheel, all equally spaced.

41. Find the measure of each central angle in degrees and radians.

42. If the radius of the wheel is 76 feet, find the circumference.

43. Find the length of each arc intercepted by consecutive pairs of spokes.

44. Find the area of each sector formed by consecutive spokes.

45. The area of a sector is given approximately by

$$A \approx 0.008727\,\theta r^2,$$

where r is the radius of the circle and θ is measured in *degrees*. Show how this formula was obtained.

Use the formula of Exercise 45 to find the areas of the following sectors.

46. $\theta = 27.472°$, $r = 11.946$ m

47. $\theta = 51.0382°$, $r = 25.1837$ cm

48. $\theta = 38° \, 42' \, 15''$, $r = 42.89734$ cm

49. $\theta = 246° \, 15' \, 37''$, $r = 8.76122$ mm

50. Eratosthenes (*ca.* 230 B.C.)* made a famous measurement of the earth. He observed at Syene, (the modern Aswan) at noon and at the summer solstice, that a vertical stick had no shadow, while at Alexandria (on the same meridian as Syene) the sun's rays were inclined 1/50 of a complete circle to the vertical. See the figure. He then calculated the circumference of the earth from the known distance of 5000 stades between Alexandria and Syene. Obtain Eratosthenes' result of 250,000 stades for the circumference of the earth. There is reason to suppose that a stade is about equal to

---

*Exercise reproduced with permission from *A Survey of Geometry*, v. 1, by Howard Eves, Boston: Allyn and Bacon, 1963.

516.7 feet. Assuming this, use Eratosthenes' result to calculate the polar diameter of the earth in miles. (The actual polar diameter of the earth, to the nearest mile, is 7900 miles.)

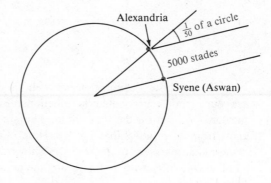

3.3 Circular Functions of Real Numbers

So far we have defined the six trigonometric functions for *angles*. The angles can be measured either by degrees or radians. While the domain of the trigonometric functions is a set of angles, the range is a set of real numbers. In advanced work, such as calculus, it is necessary to modify the trigonometric functions so that the domain contains not angles, but real numbers. Trigonometric functions having a domain of real numbers are called circular trigonometric functions, or just **circular functions**.

To find the values of the circular functions for any real number *s*, use a unit circle, as shown in Figure 3.5. (A **unit circle** has a radius of 1 unit.) Start at the

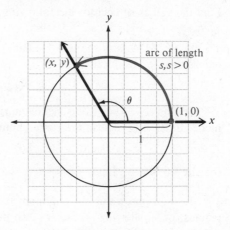

Figure 3.5

point (1, 0) and lay off an arc of length s along the circle. Go counterclockwise if s is positive, and clockwise if s is negative. Let the endpoint of the arc be at the point (x, y). The six **circular functions** are then defined as follows.

$$\sin s = y \qquad \tan s = \frac{y}{x} \qquad \sec s = \frac{1}{x}$$

$$\cos s = x \qquad \cot s = \frac{x}{y} \qquad \csc s = \frac{1}{y}$$

We can show a connection between the definitions of these circular functions and our familiar trigonometric functions. Figure 3.5 shows angle θ placed in standard position on the unit circle. The arc length cut off by angle θ is s. We know from Section 3.2 that $s = r\theta$. Here $r = 1$, so that $s = 1(\theta) = \theta$. Hence, s is the radian measure of angle θ. As shown in the figure, (x, y) is a point on the terminal side of θ, with $r = 1$. Using the definitions of the trigonometric functions from Chapter 1,

$$\sin \theta = \frac{y}{r} = \frac{y}{1} = y = \sin s$$

$$\cos \theta = \frac{x}{r} = \frac{x}{1} = x = \cos s.$$

Similar results hold for the other four functions.

Thus, the trigonometric functions and the circular functions lead to the same function values. Because of this, we can find a value such as $\sin \pi/2$ without worrying about whether $\pi/2$ is a real number or the radian measure of an angle. In either case, $\sin \pi/2 = 1$.

All the formulas we develop in this book are valid for either angles or real numbers. For example, the formula $\sin \theta = 1/\csc \theta$ is equally valid for θ as the measure of an angle in degrees or radians or for θ as a real number.

Function values of real numbers can be found by using the "radian" column of Table II, or by a calculator, as shown in the next examples.

EXAMPLE 1   Find the values of each of the following.

(a) cos .5149

Since .5149 is in the left "radian" column of Table II, find the word cosine across the top. Doing this,

$$\cos .5149 = .8704.$$

To find cos .5149 using a calculator, make sure the machine is set in "radian" mode. Enter .5149, push the cosine button, getting

$$\cos .5149 = .870342 \qquad \text{(to six decimal places)}.$$

(b) cot 1.3206 = .2555   ●

To find the value of trigonometric functions for angles larger than $\pi/2$ radians, or smaller than 0 radians, we use related angles. To find function values of real numbers larger than $\pi/2$ or smaller than 0, we use **related numbers**, as shown in the next example.

EXAMPLE 2   Find the value of each of the following. Use the number 3.1416 as an approximation for π.

(a) sin 6.6759

The circumference of the unit circle is $C = 2\pi r = 2\pi(1) \approx 2(3.1416) = 6.2832$. As Figure 3.6 shows, the related number for 6.6759 is $6.6759 - 6.2832 = .3927$. From Table II,

$$\sin 6.6759 = \sin .3927 = .3827.$$

The value of sin 6.6759 can also be found directly with a calculator.

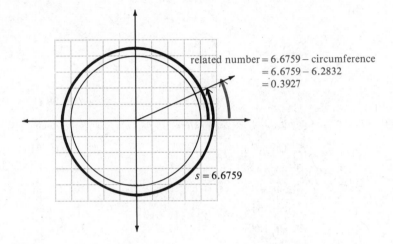

Figure 3.6

(b) tan 2.1031

As shown in Figure 3.7, the related number here is

$$3.1416 - 2.1031 = 1.0385.$$

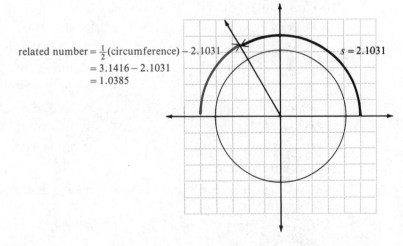

Figure 3.7

The number 2.1031 leads to an arc in quadrant II, where tangent is negative. Thus,

$$\tan 2.1031 = -\tan 1.0385 = -1.698. \quad \bullet$$

EXAMPLE 3   Find a value of s that makes $\cos s = 0.0581$.

Look in the body of Table II (in a column having cosine at top or bottom). The number 0.0581 is found in a column with cosine at the bottom. Thus, s is read from the right "radian" column.

$$s = 1.5126. \quad \bullet$$

3.3 EXERCISES   *Use Table II or a calculator to find each of the following. See Example* 1.

1. tan .4538
2. sin .6109
3. cot 1.0821
4. cos 1.1519
5. sin .8203
6. cot .6632
7. cos .6429
8. tan .9047
9. sin 1.5097
10. cot .0465
11. csc 1.3875
12. tan 1.3032

 Use related numbers or a calculator to find the value of each of the following. Use 3.1416 as an approximation of π. *See Example* 2.

13. sin 7.5835
14. tan 6.4752
15. cot 7.4526
16. cos 6.6701
17. tan 4.0230
18. cot 3.8426
19. cos 4.2528
20. sin 3.4645
21. sin(−2.2864)
22. cot(−2.4850)
23. cos(−3.0602)
24. tan(−1.7861)
25. cot 6.0301
26. cos 5.2825
27. sin 5.9690
28. tan 5.4513
29. cos 13.8143
30. sin 13.6572
31. cot 12.9795
32. tan 11.0392
33. csc 9.4946

Find a value of s, where $0 \le s \le 1.5708$, *that makes each of the following true. See Example* 3.

34. tan s = .2126
35. cos s = .7826
36. sin s = .9918
37. cot s = .2994

38. cot s = .6208

40. cos s = .5783

42. cot s = .0963

39. tan s = 2.605

41. sin s = .9877

 Use Table II and interpolation, or a calculator, to find each of the following.

EXAMPLE Find sin 0.9000 using interpolation.
Proceed as follows.

$$.0030 \begin{bmatrix} .0012 \begin{bmatrix} \sin .8988 = .7826 \\ \sin .9000 = \quad ? \end{bmatrix} d \\ \sin .9018 = .7844 \end{bmatrix} .0018$$

$$\frac{d}{.0018} = \frac{.0012}{.0030}$$

$$d = \frac{.0012(.0018)}{.0030}$$

$$d \approx .0007$$

$$.7826 + .0007 = .7833$$

Thus, sin 0.9000 = .7833.

43. cos 1.0000

46. cot 0.5

49. cos 1.3

44. sin 1.0000

47. sin 1.2

50. tan 1.4

45. tan 0.3

48. cot 1.1

51. sin 2.

The values of the circular functions repeat every 2π. For this reason, circular functions are used to describe things that repeat periodically. For example, the maximum afternoon temperature in a given city might be approximated by

$$t = 60 - 30 \cos \frac{x}{2},$$

where t represents the maximum afternoon temperature in month x, with x = 0 representing January, x = 1 representing February, and so on. Find the maximum afternoon temperature for each of the following months.

52. January

54. May

56. August

53. April

55. June

57. October

 Show that the following points lie (approximately) on a unit circle.

58. (.39852144, .91715902)

59. (−.81745602, −.57599102)

 Identify the quadrant in which arcs on a unit circle having the following lengths would terminate.

60. s = 10

62. s = −89.19

61. s = 18

63. s = −104.27

The temperature in Fairbanks is approximated by

$$T(x) = 37 \sin\left[\frac{2\pi}{365}(x - 101)\right] + 25*,$$

where $T(x)$ is the temperature in degrees Celsius on day x, with $x = 1$ corresponding to January 1 and $x = 365$ corresponding to December 31. Use a calculator to estimate the temperature on the following days.

64. March 1 (day 60) **65.** April 1 (day 91)

66. day 101 **67.** day 150

68. June 15 **69.** September 1

70. October 31

3.4 Linear and Angular Velocity

Suppose point P moves at a constant speed along a circle of radius r and center O. See Figure 3.8. The measure of how fast the position of P is changing is called **linear velocity**. We can express linear velocity v as

$$v = \frac{s}{t}$$

where s is the length of the arc cut by point P at time t.

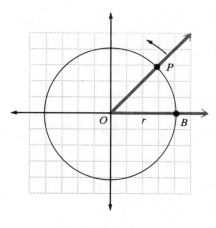

Figure 3.8

Look at Figure 3.8 again. As point P moves along the circle, ray OP rotates around the origin. Since the ray OP is the terminal side of angle POB, the measure

---

Barbara Lando and Clifton Lando, "Is the Graph of Temperature Variation a Sine Curve?" The Mathematics Teacher, 70 (September, 1977) 534–37.

of the angle changes as P moves along the circle. The measure of how fast angle POB is changing is called **angular velocity**. Angular velocity, written ω, can be given as

$$\omega = \frac{\theta}{t}$$

where θ is the measure of angle POB at time t.

Recall that in Section 3.2 we defined the length s of the arc cut on a circle of radius r by a central angle of measure θ radians as

$$s = r\theta.$$

Using this formula, the formula for linear velocity, $v = s/t$, becomes

$$v = \frac{r\theta}{t}$$

or $$v = r\omega.$$

This last formula relates linear and angular velocity.

EXAMPLE 1   Suppose point P is on a circle with a radius of 10 cm, and ray OP is rotating with angular velocity of $\pi/18$ radians per second.

(a) Find the angle generated by P in 6 seconds.

The velocity of ray OP is $\pi/18$ radians per second. Since $\omega = \theta/t$, then in 6 seconds

$$\frac{\pi}{18} = \frac{\theta}{6}$$

or $\theta = 6(\pi/18) = \pi/3$ radians.

(b) Find the distance traveled by P along the circle in 6 seconds.

In 6 seconds P generates an angle of $\pi/3$ radians. Since $s = r\theta$,

$$s = 10\left(\frac{\pi}{3}\right) = \frac{10\pi}{3} \text{ cm.}$$

(c) Find the linear velocity of P.

Since $v = s/t$, then in 6 seconds

$$v = \frac{10\pi/3}{6} = \frac{5\pi}{9} \text{ cm per second.} \qquad \bullet$$

EXAMPLE 2   A belt runs a pulley of radius 6 cm at 80 revolutions per minute.

(a) Find the angular velocity of the pulley in radians per second.

In one minute, the pulley makes 80 revolutions. Each revolution is 2π radians, for a total of

$$80(2\pi) = 160\pi \text{ radians per minute.}$$

Since there are 60 seconds in a minute, ω, the angular velocity in radians per second, is given by

$$\omega = \frac{160\pi}{60} = \frac{8\pi}{3} \text{ radians per second.}$$

(b) Find the linear velocity of the belt in centimeters per second.

The linear velocity of the belt will be the same as that of a point on the circumference of the pulley. Thus,

$$v = r\omega$$
$$v = 6\left(\frac{8\pi}{3}\right)$$
$$v = 16\pi \text{ cm per second}$$
$$v \approx 50.3 \text{ cm per second.} \quad \bullet$$

3.4 EXERCISES

Use the formula $\omega = \theta/t$ to find the value of the missing variable in each of the following.

1. $\omega = \pi/4$ radians per minute, $t = 5$ minutes
2. $\omega = 2\pi/3$ radians per second, $t = 3$ seconds
3. $\theta = 2\pi/5$ radians, $t = 10$ seconds
4. $\theta = 3\pi/4$ radians, $t = 8$ seconds
5. $\theta = 3\pi/8$ radians, $\omega = \pi/24$ radians per minute
6. $\theta = 2\pi/9$ radians, $\omega = 5\pi/27$ radians per minute
7. $\omega = .90674$ radians per minute, $t = 11.876$ minutes
8. $\theta = 3.871142$ radians, $t = 21.4693$ seconds

 Use the formula $v = r\omega$ to find the value of the missing variable in each of the following.

9. $r = 8$ cm, $\omega = 9\pi/5$ radians per second
10. $r = 12$ m, $\omega = 2\pi/3$ radians per second
11. $v = 18$ feet per second, $r = 3$ feet
12. $v = 9$ m per second, $r = 5$ m
13. $r = 24.93215$ cm, $\omega = .372914$ radians per second
14. $v = 107.692$ m per second, $r = 58.7413$ m

 Since $\omega = \theta/t$, we can write $\theta = \omega t$. Using ωt for θ, we can rewrite $s = r\theta$ as $s = r\omega t$. Use this formula to find the values of the missing variables in each of the following.

15. $r = 6$ cm, $\omega = \pi/3$ radians per second, $t = 9$ seconds
16. $r = 9$ yd, $\omega = 2\pi/5$ radians per second, $t = 12$ seconds

17. $s = 6\pi$ cm, $r = 2$ cm, $\omega = \pi/4$ radians per second

18. $s = 12\pi/5$ m, $r = 3/2$ m, $\omega = 2\pi/5$ radians per second

19. $s = 3\pi/4$ km, $r = 2$ km, $t = 4$ seconds

20. $s = 8\pi/9$ m, $r = 4/3$ m, $t = 12$ seconds

21. $r = 37.6584$ cm, $\omega = .714213$ radians per second, $t = .924473$ seconds

22. $s = 5.70201$ m, $r = 8.92399$ m, $\omega = .614277$ radians per second

Find ω for each of the following.

23. The hour hand of a clock.

24. The minute hand of a clock.

25. The second hand of a clock.

26. A line from the center to the edge of a phonograph record revolving $33\frac{1}{3}$ times per minute.

Find v for each of the following.

27. The tip of the minute hand of a clock, if the hand is 7 cm long.

28. The tip of the second hand of a clock, if the hand is 28 mm long.

29. A point on the edge of a flywheel of radius 2 m rotating 42 times per minute.

30. A point on the tread of a tire of radius 18 cm, rotating 35 times per minute.

31. The tip of an airplane propeller 3 m long, rotating 500 times per minute.

32. A point on the edge of a gyroscope of radius 83 cm, rotating 680 times per minute.

Solve the following, which review the ideas of this chapter.

33. A railroad track is laid along the arc of a circle of radius 1800 ft. The circular part of the track intercepts a central angle of 40°. How long (in seconds) will it take a point on the front of a train traveling 30 miles per hour to go around this portion of the track?

34. Two pulleys of diameter 4 m and 2 m respectively, are connected by a belt. The larger pulley rotates 80 times per minute. Find the speed of the belt in meters per second and the angular velocity of the smaller pulley.

35. The earth revolves on its axis once every 24 hours. Assuming the earth's radius is 6400 km, find the

(a) angular velocity of the earth in radians per day and radians per hour.

(b) linear velocity at the North Pole or South Pole.

(c) linear velocity at Quito, Equador, a city on the equator.

(d) linear velocity at Salem, Oregon (halfway from the equator to the North Pole).

36. Assume the radius of the earth is 6400 km, with a satellite orbiting the earth 320 km above the surface of the earth. See the Figure. Suppose the satellite orbits the earth once in 1.84 hours.

   (a) Find ω for the satellite. (Hint: the satellite takes how long to go through 2π radians?)

   (b) Find the linear velocity of the satellite.

 37. A teeter-totter rotates through an angle of 47.64°. The end of the teeter-totter goes through 1.783 m. How long is the teeter-totter?

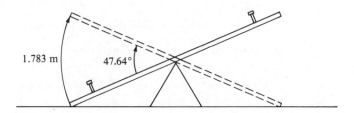

 38. The wheels of a bicycle are 60.96 cm in diameter. When the bike is ridden so that the wheels make 9.804 revolutions in one minute, how far will the bike travel in a half hour?

Chapter 3 Test

[3.1] *Convert each of the following degree measures to radians. Leave answers as multiples of π.*

   1. 45°   **2.** 120°   **3.** 80°

   4. 175°   **5.** 800°

Convert each of the following radian measures to degrees.

   6. $5\pi/4$ **7.** $9\pi/10$ **8.** $14\pi/15$

   9. $-6\pi/5$ **10.** $-11\pi/18$

Evaluate each of the following without using a table or a calculator.

   11. $\tan \dfrac{\pi}{3}$ **12.** $\cos \dfrac{2\pi}{3}$ **13.** $\sin -\dfrac{5\pi}{6}$

   14. $\cot \dfrac{11\pi}{6}$ **15.** $\tan -\dfrac{7\pi}{3}$

[3.2] *Solve each of the following problems.*

   16. The radius of a circle is 15.2 cm. Find the length of an arc of the circle cut by a central angle of $3\pi/4$ radians.

   17. Find the area of a sector of a circle cut by a central angle of 21° 40′ in a circle of radius 38 m.

   18. A tree 2000 yards away intercepts an angle of 1° 10′. Find the height of the tree to two significant digits.

[3.3] *Use Table II or a calculator to find each of the following. Use 3.1416 as an approximation for π.*

   19. sin 1.0472   **20.** tan 1.2275

   21. cos (−.2443)   **22.** cot 3.0543

   23. tan 7.3159   **24.** sin 4.8386

   25. cos 2.1   **26.** Find s if cos s = 0.9250.

[3.4] *Solve each of the following problems.*

   27. Use the formula $\omega = \theta/t$ to find t if $\theta = 5\pi/12$ radians and $\omega = 8\pi/9$ radians per second.

   28. Find ω if $t = 12$ seconds and $\theta = 2\pi/5$ radians.

   29. Use the formula $s = r\omega t$ to find ω if $s = 12\pi/25$ feet, $r = 3/5$ feet, and $t = 15$ seconds.

   30. Use the formula $v = r\omega$ to find the linear velocity of a point on the edge of a flywheel of radius 7 m if the flywheel is rotating 90 times per second.

4

Graphs of Trigonometric Functions

By studying the graph of a function, we can often identify properties of the function that are not easy to see from the equation of the function. For this reason, we study the graphs of the trigonometric functions in this chapter.

One important property which can be recognized from the graphs of the trigonometric functions is their repeating or cyclic nature. Functions which repeat are called *periodic*. Periodic functions are useful in many practical applications, especially in electrical engineering, physics, and economics. We show several of these applications in the last section of this chapter.

4.1   Graphs of Sine and Cosine

By the identities for coterminal angles,

$$\sin 0 = \sin 2\pi$$
$$\sin \pi/2 = \sin (\pi/2 + 2\pi)$$
$$\sin \pi = \sin (\pi + 2\pi),$$

and, in general, $\sin x = \sin (x + 2\pi)$, for any real number x. The value of the sine function is the same for x and $x + 2\pi$. Therefore, we say that $y = \sin x$ is a periodic function with period 2π. (We show the graph of $y = \sin x$ in Figure 4.1. Notice the repeating nature of the graph.)

In general, a **periodic function** has the property

$$f(x) = f(x + a),$$

for any real number x and for some positive real number a. The smallest number a for which the statement is true is called the **period**.

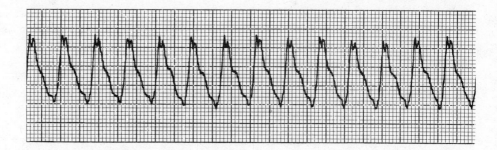

Periodic phenomena are very common in nature. One of the most common is the human heartbeat, as shown in this electrocardiogram (EKG). The EKG shows electrical impulses from the heart. Each small square represents .04 seconds, so that each large square represents .2 seconds. What is the period of this (abnormal) heartbeat?

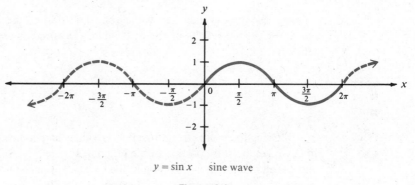

$y = \sin x$ sine wave

Figure 4.1

As we have seen, the sine function $y = \sin x$ has the set of real numbers for its domain, with range $-1 \le y \le 1$ or $-1 \le \sin x \le 1$. Since the sine function has period 2π, we can concentrate only on the values of x in the interval $0 \le x \le 2\pi$.

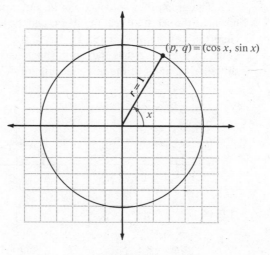

Figure 4.2

Figure 4.2 shows a unit circle with a point (p, q) on it. As we saw in Section 3.3, for any angle x measured in radians, $p = \cos x$ and $q = \sin x$. As x increases from 0 to $\pi/2$ (or $90°$), we see that q (or $\sin x$) increases from 0 to 1, while p (or $\cos x$) decreases from 1 to 0.

As x increases from $\pi/2$ to π (or $180°$), q decreases from 1 to 0, while p decreases from 0 to -1. Similar results can be found for the other quadrants, as shown in the following table.

As x increases from	$\sin x$	$\cos x$
0 to $\pi/2$	increases from 0 to 1	decreases from 1 to 0
$\pi/2$ to π	decreases from 1 to 0	decreases from 0 to -1
π to $3\pi/2$	decreases from 0 to -1	increases from -1 to 0
$3\pi/2$ to 2π	increases from -1 to 0	increases from 0 to 1

By selecting certain key values of x and finding the corresponding values of $\sin x$, we get the results of the next table. (Decimals were rounded to the nearest tenth.)

x	0	$\pi/4$	$\pi/2$	$3\pi/4$	π	$5\pi/4$	$3\pi/2$	$7\pi/4$	2π
$\sin x$	0	.7	1	.7	0	$-.7$	-1	$-.7$	0

Plotting the points from the table of values and connecting them with a smooth line, we get the solid portion of the graph of Figure 4.1. Since $y = \sin x$ is periodic and has all real numbers as domain, the graph continues in both directions infinitely, as indicated by the arrows. Note that the same scale is used on both axes so as not to distort the shape of the graph. This graph is sometimes called a **sine wave** or **sinusoid**. You should memorize the shape of this key graph and be able to sketch it quickly. The main points of the graph are $(0, 0)$, $(\pi/2, 1)$, $(\pi, 0)$, $(3\pi/2, -1)$, and $(2\pi, 0)$. By plotting these five points, then connecting them with the characteristic sine wave, you can quickly sketch the graph.

The graph of $y = \cos x$ can be found in much the same way. The domain of cosine is the set of all real numbers, and the range of $y = \cos x$ is $-1 \leq \cos x \leq 1$. Here the key points are $(0, 1)$, $(\pi/2, 0)$, $(\pi, -1)$, $(3\pi/2, 0)$, and $(2\pi, 1)$. The graph of $y = \cos x$ has the same shape as $y = \sin x$. In fact, it is the sine wave, shifted $\pi/2$ units to the left. See Figure 4.3.

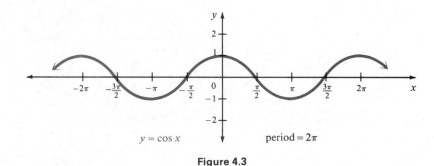

$y = \cos x$ period $= 2\pi$

Figure 4.3

The graphs of sine and cosine can be obtained directly from a unit circle, as shown in Figure 4.4. (Explain how the definition of the trigonometric functions in terms of a unit circle is used here.)

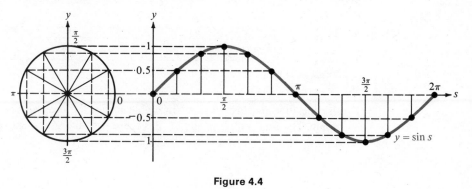

Figure 4.4

EXAMPLE 1   Graph $y = 3 \sin x$.

In this graph each y-value is 3 times the corresponding y-value for the basic sine function $y = \sin x$. This has the effect of stretching the graph in both directions away from the x-axis as shown in Figure 4.5. The five main points are given below, with a few other selected points.

x	0	$\pi/4$	$\pi/2$	π	$3\pi/2$	$7\pi/4$	2π
$3 \sin x$	0	2.1	3	0	-3	-2.1	0

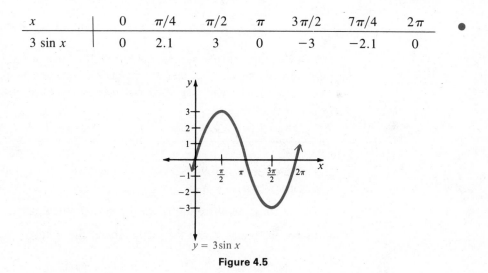

$y = 3 \sin x$

Figure 4.5

In the graphs of these sine and cosine functions, the maximum distance of the curve from the x-axis is called the **amplitude** of the curve. In Example 1 above, the amplitude is 3.

The amplitude of $y = a \sin x$ or $y = a \cos x$ is $|a|$.

EXAMPLE 2   Graph $y = \cos \dfrac{1}{4} x$.

For each x-value first find $(1/4)x$. Then find $\cos (1/4)x$. The following table gives enough ordered pairs so that we can graph one complete period.

x	0	π	2π	3π	4π	5π	6π	8π
$(1/4)x$	0	$\pi/4$	$\pi/2$	$3\pi/4$	π	$5\pi/4$	$3\pi/2$	2π
$\cos (1/4)x$	1	.7	0	$-.7$	-1	$-.7$	0	1

Use the first and last rows of the table to get the ordered pairs necessary for the graph. The final graph is shown in Figure 4.6; the graph shows that the period is 8π.   ●

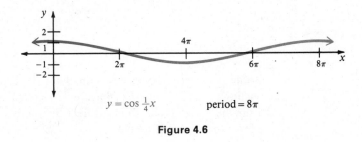

Figure 4.6

If $b > 0$, the graph of $y = \cos bx$ or $y = \sin bx$ has a period of $2\pi/b$.

Throughout this chapter we assume $b > 0$. If a function has $b < 0$, we can use the identities of the next chapter to change the function to one where $b > 0$.

Let us now list some steps that can be used to graph $y = a \sin bx$ or $y = a \cos bx$, where $b > 0$.

1. Find the period, $2\pi/b$. Start at 0 on the x-axis and lay off a distance $2\pi/b$.

2. Divide the interval from 0 to $2\pi/b$ into four equal parts.

3. Locate the points where the graph crosses the x-axis.

Function	Graph crosses x-axis at	
$y = a \sin bx$	$0, \dfrac{\pi}{b}, \dfrac{2\pi}{b}$	(beginning, middle, and end of interval)
$y = a \cos bx$	$\dfrac{\pi}{2b}, \dfrac{3\pi}{2b}$	(one-fourth and three-fourths points of interval)

4. Locate the points where the graph reaches its maximum and minimum values.

Function	Graph has a maximum when x is		
$y = a \sin bx$	$\dfrac{\pi}{2b}$ (for $a > 0$)	or	$\dfrac{3\pi}{2b}$ (for $a < 0$)
$y = a \cos bx$	0 and $\dfrac{2\pi}{b}$ (for $a > 0$)	or	$\dfrac{\pi}{b}$ (for $a < 0$)

5. Use the tables or a calculator to find as many additional points as needed. Then sketch the graph.

6. Draw additional periods of the graph, to the right and to the left, as needed.

EXAMPLE 3   Graph $y = -2 \sin 3x$.

   The period is $2\pi/3$. The amplitude is $|-2| = 2$. Sketch the graph using the steps shown in Figure 4.7.   ●

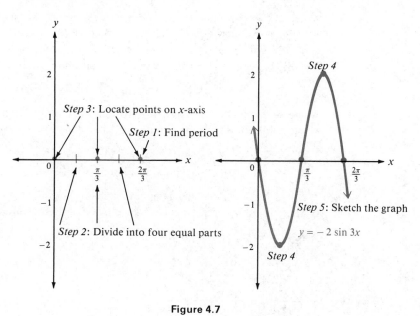

Figure 4.7

EXAMPLE 4   Graph $y = 3 \cos \dfrac{1}{2} x$.

   The period is $2\pi/(1/2) = 4\pi$. Follow the steps shown in Figure 4.8. The amplitude is 3.   ●

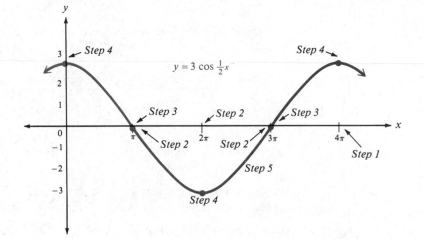

Figure 4.8

Radio stations send out a carrier signal in the form of a sine wave having equation

$$y = A_0 \sin (2\pi\omega_0 t),$$

where A_0 is the amplitude of the carrier signal, ω_0 is the number of periods the signal oscillates through in one second (its **frequency**), and t is time. A carrier signal received by a radio would be a pure tone. To transmit music and voices, the station might change or **modulate** A_0 according to the function

$$A_0(t) = A_0 + mA_0 \sin (2\pi\omega t),$$

where ω is the frequency of a pure tone and m is a constant called the **degree of modulation**. The transmitted signal has equation

$$y = A_0 \sin (2\pi\omega_0 t) + A_0 m \sin (2\pi\omega t) \sin (2\pi\omega_0 t)$$
$$= A_0[1 + m \sin (2\pi\omega t)] \sin (2\pi\omega_0 t)$$

A typical carrier signal and a typical graph of y are shown in Figure 4.9. This process of sending out a radio signal is called **amplitude modulation**, or AM, radio.

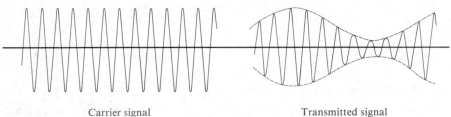

Carrier signal   Transmitted signal

Figure 4.9

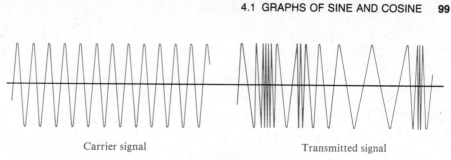

Carrier signal   Transmitted signal

Figure 4.10

Frequency modulation, or FM, radio involves altering the frequency of the carrier signal, rather than its amplitude. A typical graph is shown in Figure 4.10.

4.1 EXERCISES   *Graph the following functions over the interval* $-2\pi \leq x \leq 2\pi$. *Identify the amplitude. See Example* 1.

1. $y = 2 \cos x$

2. $y = 3 \sin x$

3. $y = \dfrac{2}{3} \sin x$

4. $y = \dfrac{3}{4} \cos x$

5. $y = -\cos x$

6. $y = -\sin x$

7. $y = -2 \sin x$

8. $y = -3 \cos x$

Graph each of the following functions over a two-period interval. Give the period and the amplitude. See Examples 2–4.

9. $y = \sin \dfrac{1}{2} x$

10. $y = \sin \dfrac{2}{3} x$

11. $y = \cos \dfrac{1}{3} x$

12. $y = \cos \dfrac{3}{4} x$

13. $y = \sin 3x$

14. $y = \sin 2x$

15. $y = \cos 2x$

16. $y = \cos 3x$

17. $y = -\sin 4x$

18. $y = -\cos 6x$

19. $y = 2 \sin \dfrac{1}{4} x$

20. $y = 3 \sin 2x$

21. $y = -2 \cos 3x$

22. $y = -5 \cos 2x$

23. $y = \dfrac{1}{2} \sin 3x$

24. $y = \dfrac{2}{3} \cos \dfrac{1}{2} x$

25. $y = -\dfrac{2}{3} \sin \dfrac{3}{4} x$

26. $y = -2 \cos 5x$

Graph each of the following functions over one period.

27. $y = (\sin x)^2$ (Hint: $(\sin x)^2 = \sin x \cdot \sin x$)

28. $y = (\cos x)^2$

29. $y = (\sin 2x)^2$

30. $y = (\cos 2x)^2$

The graph shown here gives the variation in blood pressure for a typical person. Systolic and diastolic pressures are the upper and lower limits of the periodic changes in pressure which produce the pulse. The length of time between peaks is called the period of the pulse.

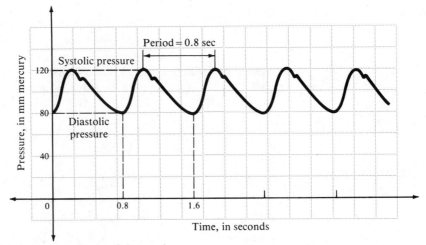

31. Find the amplitude of the graph.

32. Find the pulse rate for this person—the number of pulse beats in one minute.

33. The voltage E in an electrical circuit is given by

$$E = 5 \cos 120\pi t$$

where t is time measured in seconds.

(a) Find the amplitude and period.

(b) How many cycles are completed in one second? (The number of cycles completed in one second is the *frequency* of the function.)

(c) Find E when $t = 0$; .03; .06; .09; .12

(d) Graph E, for $0 \le t \le 1/30$.

34. For another electrical circuit, the voltage E is given by

$$E = 3.8 \cos 40\pi t$$

where t is time measured in seconds.

(a) Find the amplitude and the period.

(b) Find the frequency. See Exercise 33(b)

(c) Find E when $t = .02, .04, .08, .12, .14$.

(d) Graph one period of E.

4.2 Graphs of the Other Trigonometric Functions

We can graph the remaining four trigonometric functions, $y = \tan x$, $y = \cot x$, $y = \sec x$, and $y = \csc x$, as we graphed the sine and cosine functions. Although these are also periodic functions like sine and cosine, their graphs are not sine waves.

The period of $y = \tan x$ is π, so we need to investigate the tangent function only within an interval of π units. A convenient interval for this purpose is $-\pi/2 < x < \pi/2$. Although the endpoints are not in the domain (why?), $\tan x$ exists for all other values in this interval.

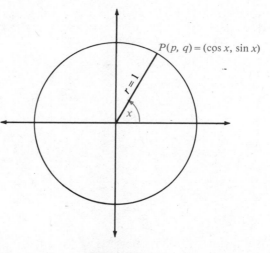

Figure 4.11

Just as we used a unit circle to help graph sine and cosine, we can use the unit circle to graph tangent and cotangent. Figure 4.11 shows a unit circle with point P located on it. If P has coordinates (p, q), then we have seen that $p = \cos x$ and $q = \sin x$. Since $\tan x = \sin x/\cos x$,

$$\tan x = \frac{q}{p} \quad \text{and} \quad \cot x = \frac{p}{q}.$$

As x increases from 0 to $\pi/2$, p will decrease from 1 to 0, while q will increase from 0 to 1. The quotient q/p will increase from 0, without bound. In a similar way, the quotient p/q will decrease to 0. Similar results hold for values of x in quadrant IV. In summary:

As x increases from	$\tan x$	$\cot x$
0 to $\pi/2$	increases from 0, without bound	decreases to 0
$-\pi/2$ to 0	increases to 0	decreases from 0

As x approaches $\pi/2$ (through values of x less than $\pi/2$), $\tan x$ gets larger and larger; as x approaches $-\pi/2$ (through values of x greater than $-\pi/2$), $\tan x$ gets more and more negative, again without bound. For this reason, there is no point on the graph of $y = \tan x$ corresponding to $x = \pi/2$ or $x = -\pi/2$.

Based on these results, the graph will approach the vertical line $x = \pi/2$ but never touch it. The line $x = \pi/2$ is called a **vertical asymptote**. The lines $x = \pi/2 + k\pi$, where k is any integer, are all vertical asymptotes. We indicate these asymptotes on the graph with a light dashed line. See Figure 4.12. In the interval $-\pi/2 < x < 0$, which corresponds to quadrant IV, $\tan x$ is negative, and as x goes from 0 to $-\pi/2$, $\tan x$ gets smaller and smaller. A table of values for $\tan x$, where $-\pi/2 < x < \pi/2$, is given below.

x	$-\pi/3$	$-\pi/4$	$-\pi/6$	0	$\pi/6$	$\pi/4$	$\pi/3$
$\tan x$	-1.7	-1	$-.6$	0	$.6$	1	1.7

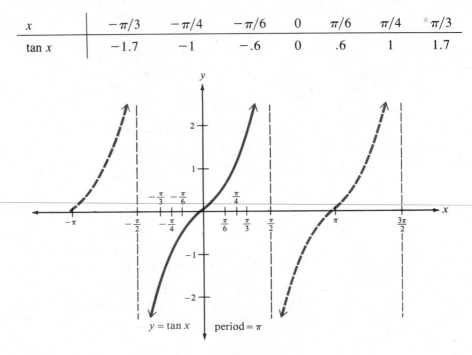

Figure 4.12

Plotting the points from the table and letting the graph approach the asymptotes at $x = \pi/2$ and $x = -\pi/2$, gives the portion of the graph shown with a solid line in Figure 4.12. We can sketch more of the graph by repeating the same curve, as shown in Figure 4.12. This graph, like the graphs for sine and cosine, should be memorized. Convenient main points are $(-\pi/4, -1)$, $(0, 0)$, $(\pi/4, 1)$. The vertical asymptotes are at $-\pi/2$ and $\pi/2$.

EXAMPLE 1   Graph $y = \tan 2x$.

Multiplying x by 2 changes the period to $\pi/2$. The effect on the graph is shown in Figure 4.13.

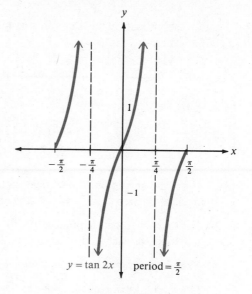

Figure 4.13

If $b > 0$, the graph of $y = \tan bx$ has period π/b.

We can use the fact that $\cot x = 1/(\tan x)$ to find the graph of $y = \cot x$. The period of cotangent, like tangent, is π. The domain of $y = \cot x$ excludes $0 + k\pi$, where k is any integer (why?). Thus, the vertical lines $x = k\pi$ are asymptotes. Values of x that lead to asymptotes for $\tan x$ will make $\cot x = 0$, so that $\cot (-\pi/2) = 0$, $\cot \pi/2 = 0$, $\cot 3\pi/2 = 0$, and so on. Tan x increases as x goes from $-\pi/2$ to $\pi/2$. Since $\cot x = 1/(\tan x)$, $\cot x$ will decrease as x goes from $-\pi/2$ to $\pi/2$. Using these facts and plotting points as necessary give the graph of $y = \cot x$ as shown in Figure 4.14.

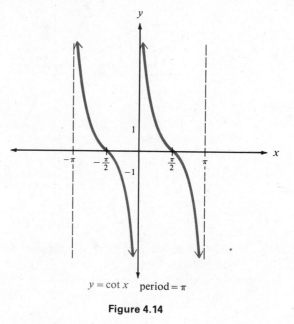

Figure 4.14

Let us summarize the steps in graphing one period of $y = a \tan bx$ or $y = a \cot bx$, where $b > 0$.

---

1. Find the period, π/b.

2. Start at 0 on the x-axis and lay off two intervals, each with length half the period. One interval goes to the left and the other goes to the right of 0.

3. Draw the asymptotes as vertical dotted lines: at the endpoints of the interval of Step 2 for tangent, and along the y-axis for cotangent.

4. For tangent, locate a point at $(0, 0)$. For cotangent, locate points on the x-axis at each end of the interval of Step 2.

5. Sketch the graph, finding additional points as needed.

6. Draw additional periods, both to the right and to the left, as needed.

EXAMPLE 2   Graph $y = -3 \tan \frac{1}{2}x$.

The period is $\pi/(1/2) = 2\pi$. Proceed as shown in Figure 4.15 ●

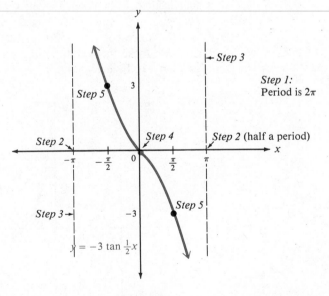

Figure 4.15

· The graph of $y = \csc x$ is restricted to values of $x \neq k\pi$, where k is any integer (why?). Hence, the lines $x = k\pi$ are asymptotes. Since $\csc x = 1/\sin x$, the period is 2π, the same as for $\sin x$. When $\sin x = 1$, we have $\csc x = 1$, and when $0 < \sin x < 1$, then $\csc x > 1$. Thus, the graph takes the shape of the solid line shown in Figure 4.16. To show how the two curves are related, the graph of $y = \sin x$ is also shown, as a dashed curve.

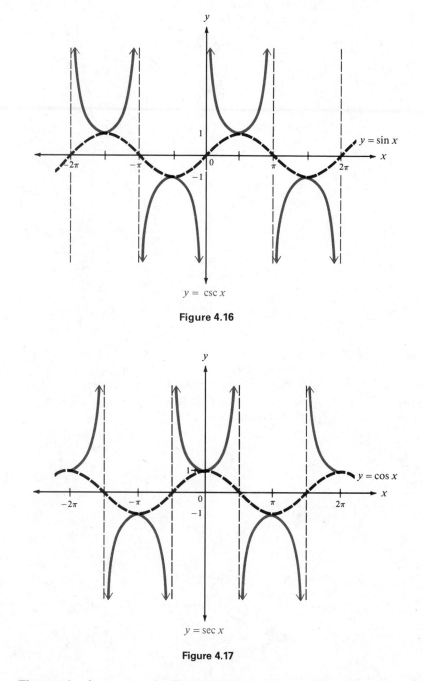

$y = \csc x$

Figure 4.16

$y = \sec x$

Figure 4.17

The graph of $y = \sec x$ in Figure 4.17 is related to the cosine graph in the same way that the graph of $y = \csc x$ is related to the sine graph.

EXAMPLE 3   Graph $y = \frac{1}{2}\sec x$.

The amplitude of the corresponding cosine graph is $1/2$ and the period is 2π. The graph of $y = (1/2)\sec x$ is shown in Figure 4.18.   ●

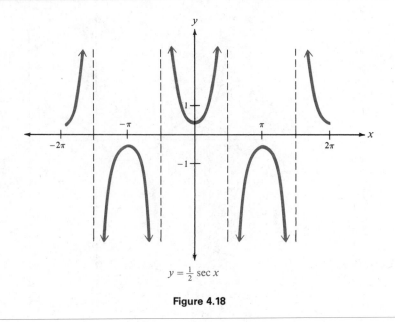

$$y = \frac{1}{2}\sec x$$

Figure 4.18

EXAMPLE 4   Graph $y = 2 + \tan x$.

Every y-value for this function will be 2 units more than the corresponding value of y in $y = \tan x$. Thus, the graph of $y = 2 + \tan x$ will be shifted up 2 units as compared to $y = \tan x$. See Figure 4.19. Such a shift is called a **vertical translation.**   ●

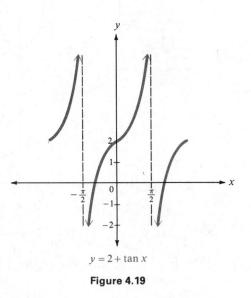

$$y = 2 + \tan x$$

Figure 4.19

4.2 EXERCISES   *Graph the following functions over the interval* $-2\pi \leq x \leq 2\pi$. *See Examples* 1–4.

1. $y = 2 \tan x$

2. $y = -\tan x$

3. $y = -\cot x$

4. $y = \frac{1}{2} \cot x$

5. $y = 1 + \tan x$

6. $y = -2 + \tan x$

7. $y = -1 + 2 \tan x$

8. $y = 3 + \frac{1}{2} \tan x$

9. $y = 1 - \cot x$

10. $y = -2 - \cot x$

11. $y = -2 \csc x$

12. $y = -\frac{1}{2} \csc x$

13. $y = -\sec x$

14. $y = -3 \sec x$

15. $y = -2 - \csc x$

16. $y = 1 - \sec x$

Graph the following functions over a two-period interval. Identify the period. See Examples 1–4.

17. $y = \tan 2x$

18. $y = 2 \tan \frac{1}{4} x$

19. $y = \cot 3x$

20. $y = -\cot \frac{1}{2} x$

21. $y = \csc 4x$

22. $y = \csc \frac{1}{4} x$

23. $y = \sec \frac{1}{2} x$

24. $y = -\sec 4x$

25. $y = 2 \csc \frac{1}{2} x$

26. $y = -2 \sec \frac{1}{4} x$

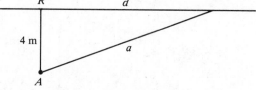

A rotating beacon is located at point A next to a long wall. The beacon is 4 m from the wall. The distance d is given by

$$d = 4 \tan 2\pi t,$$

where t is time measured in seconds since the beacon started rotating. (When t = 0, the beacon is aimed at point R.) Find d if

27. $t = 0$ **28.** $t = .4$ **29.** $t = .8$ **30.** $t = 1.2$

31. Why is .25 seconds a meaningless value for t?

32. What is a meaningful domain for t?

In the previous figure, a is given by

$$a = |4 \sec 2\pi t|.$$

Find a if

33. $t = 0$ **34.** $t = .86$ **35.** $t = 1.24$

36. Why are the absolute value bars needed here, but not in the function giving *d*?

4.3   Translations: Phase Shift

In the previous sections, we saw the role played by the real numbers a, b, and c in the graph of a trigonometric function such as $y = c + a \sin bx$. We saw that a, in the case of sine and cosine, determines the maximum distance of the graph from the line $y = c$. (Recall: the amplitude of the graph is $|a|$.) The number b affects the period, so that if the usual period is p, the new period becomes p/b. (Recall: we assume $b > 0$.) We also saw that in $y = c + a \sin bx$, the graph is translated c units up from the x-axis if $c > 0$ and translated $|c|$ units down if $c < 0$. Now we want to consider how the graph of a function like $y = \sin (x - d)$ compares with that of $y = \sin x$. In the function $y = \sin (x - d)$, the expression $x - d$ is called the **argument**.

EXAMPLE 1   Graph $y = \sin (x - \pi/2)$.

By plotting the points given in the table of values below, we get the graph of Figure 4.20.

x	0	$\pi/2$	π	$3\pi/2$	2π
$x - \pi/2$	$-\pi/2$	0	$\pi/2$	π	$3\pi/2$
$\sin (x - \pi/2)$	-1	0	1	0	-1

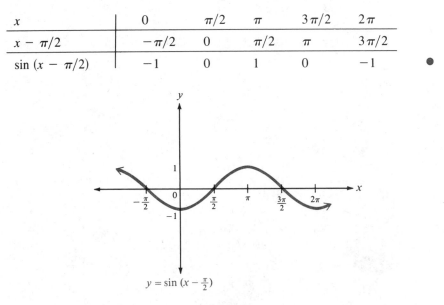

$$y = \sin \left(x - \tfrac{\pi}{2}\right)$$

Figure 4.20

The final result is a sine wave translated $\pi/2$ units to the *right*. This graph is said to have a *horizontal translation*, or **phase shift**, of $\pi/2$ to the right.

The phase shift could have been found by setting the argument equal to 0:

$$x - \frac{\pi}{2} = 0$$

$$x = \frac{\pi}{2}$$

Since $\pi/2 > 0$, the phase shift is to the right.

$y = \sin(x - d)$ has the shape of a basic sine graph, $y = \sin x$, translated $|d|$ units.

If $d > 0$, the graph has a **phase shift** of d to the right, while if $d < 0$, the graph has a phase shift of $|d|$ to the left. A similar definition also applies to the other five trigonometric functions.

EXAMPLE 2   Graph $y = 3 \cos\left(x + \frac{\pi}{4}\right)$.

The amplitude is 3 and the period is 2π. To find the phase shift, set the argument equal to 0 and solve for x.

$$x + \frac{\pi}{4} = 0$$

$$x = -\frac{\pi}{4}$$

Since $-\pi/4$ is negative, the phase shift is $|-\pi/4| = \pi/4$ to the left. The graph is shown in Figure 4.21.   ●

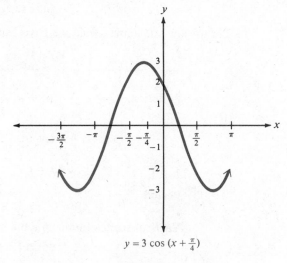

$$y = 3 \cos\left(x + \frac{\pi}{4}\right)$$

Figure 4.21

EXAMPLE 3   Graph $y = -2 \cos(3x + \pi)$.

The amplitude is $|-2| = 2$, and the period is $2\pi/3$. To find the phase shift, set the argument equal to 0.

$$3x + \pi = 0$$
$$3x = -\pi,$$
$$x = -\frac{\pi}{3}$$

The phase shift is $|-\pi/3| = \pi/3$ to the left. (Go to the left since $-\pi/3 < 0$.) See Figure 4.22.   ●

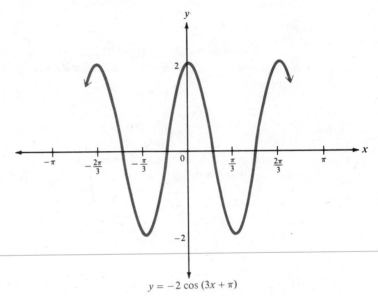

$$y = -2 \cos (3x + \pi)$$

Figure 4.22

Let us now summarize what we have learned about sine and cosine graphs. (Assume $b > 0$.)

Function $y = c + a \sin b(x - d)$

or

$y = c + a \cos b(x - d)$

Amplitude $|a|$

Period $\dfrac{2\pi}{b}$

Vertical translation   up c units if $c > 0$

down $|c|$ units if $c < 0$

Phase shift d units to the right if $d > 0$
(horizontal
translation) $|d|$ units to the left if $d < 0$

(To find d, set the argument equal to 0.)

EXAMPLE 4   Graph $y = \tan\left(2x + \dfrac{\pi}{2}\right)$.

Find the phase shift just as with sine and cosine: set the argument equal to 0.

$$2x + \frac{\pi}{2} = 0$$

$$2x = -\frac{\pi}{2}$$

$$x = -\frac{\pi}{4}$$

Since $-\pi/4 < 0$, the phase shift is $|-\pi/4| = \pi/4$ to the left. The period is $\pi/2$, so one complete cycle of the graph is compressed between points $\pi/2$ units apart. The usual origin point is translated to $-\pi/4$, with other x-intercepts every $\pi/2$ units. As shown in Figure 4.23, the asymptotes are at $x = 0 + \pi k/2$, where k is any integer.   ●

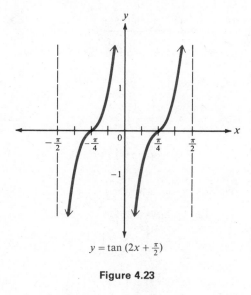

$$y = \tan\left(2x + \tfrac{\pi}{2}\right)$$

Figure 4.23

EXAMPLE 5   One example of a phase shift comes up in electrical work. A simple alternating current circuit is shown in Figure 4.24. The relationship between voltage V and current I in the circuit is also shown in the figure.

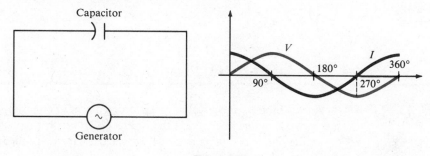

Figure 4.24

As this graph shows, current and voltage are *out of phase* by 90°. In this example, current *leads* the voltage by 90°, or voltage *lags* by 90°.   ●

4.3 EXERCISES   *For each of the following, find the amplitude (if applicable), the period, any vertical translation, and any phase shift. See Examples 1–4.*

1. $y = 2 \sin x$ **2.** $y = \dfrac{2}{3} \sin 5x$ **3.** $y = 4 \cos \dfrac{x}{2}$

4. $y = -\cos \dfrac{2}{3} x$ **5.** $y = \tan (2x - \pi)$ **6.** $y = \tan \left(\dfrac{x}{2} + \pi \right)$

7. $y = \cot \left(3x + \dfrac{\pi}{4} \right)$ **8.** $y = \cot \left(2x - \dfrac{3\pi}{2} \right)$

9. $y = 2 - \sin \left(3x - \dfrac{\pi}{5} \right)$ **10.** $y = -1 + \dfrac{1}{2} \cos (2x - 3\pi)$

11. $y = -2 + 3 \tan (4x + \pi)$ **12.** $y = \dfrac{3}{2} - 2 \cot \left(\dfrac{1}{2} x - \pi \right)$

Graph each of the following functions over a one period interval. See Examples 1–4.

13. $y = \cos \left(x - \dfrac{\pi}{2} \right)$ **14.** $y = \sin \left(x + \dfrac{\pi}{4} \right)$

15. $y = \sin \left(x - \dfrac{\pi}{4} \right)$ **16.** $y = \cos \left(x + \dfrac{\pi}{3} \right)$

17. $y = 2 \cos \left(x - \dfrac{\pi}{3} \right)$ **18.** $y = 3 \sin \left(x + \dfrac{3\pi}{2} \right)$

19. $y = \dfrac{3}{2} \sin 2 \left(x - \dfrac{\pi}{4} \right)$ **20.** $y = -\dfrac{1}{2} \cos 4 \left(x + \dfrac{\pi}{2} \right)$

21. $y = -4 \sin (2x - \pi)$ **22.** $y = 3 \cos (4x + \pi)$

23. $y = \dfrac{1}{2} \cos \left(\dfrac{1}{2} x - \dfrac{\pi}{4} \right)$ **24.** $y = -\dfrac{1}{4} \sin \left(\dfrac{3}{4} x + \dfrac{\pi}{8} \right)$

25. $y = -3 + 2 \sin \left(x - \dfrac{\pi}{2} \right)$ **26.** $y = 4 - 3 \cos (x + \pi)$

27. $y = \dfrac{1}{2} + \sin 2 \left(x + \dfrac{\pi}{4} \right)$ **28.** $y = -\dfrac{5}{2} + \cos 3 \left(x - \dfrac{\pi}{6} \right)$

29. $y = \tan \left(x - \dfrac{\pi}{4} \right)$ **30.** $y = \cot \left(x + \dfrac{3\pi}{4} \right)$

31. $y = \sec \left(x + \dfrac{\pi}{4} \right)$ **32.** $y = \csc \left(x + \dfrac{\pi}{3} \right)$

4.4   Graphing by Addition of Ordinates

An **ordinate** is the y-value of an ordered pair. For example, in the ordered pair $(\pi, -1)$, the number -1 is the ordinate. To graph trigonometric functions which are the sum of two or more terms, we can use a method called **addition of ordinates**.

EXAMPLE 1   Graph $y = x + \sin x$.

Begin by graphing the functions $y = x$ and $y = \sin x$ separately on the same coordinate axes. Figure 4.25 shows the two graphs. (We dashed $y = \sin x$ to make it easier to see.) Then select some x-values, and for these values add the two corresponding ordinates to get the ordinate of the sum, $x + \sin x$. For example, when $x = 0$, both ordinates are 0, so that $P_1 = (0, 0)$ is a point on the graph of $y = x + \sin x$. When $x = \pi/2$, the ordinates are $\pi/2$ and 1, their sum is $\pi/2 + 1$, and $P_2 = (\pi/2, \pi/2 + 1)$ is on the graph. At $x = 3\pi/2$, the sum is $3\pi/2 + (-1)$, or $3\pi/2 - 1$. The point with ordinate $3\pi/2 - 1$ is indicated by P_3 on the graph. As many points as necessary can be located in this way. The graph is then completed by drawing a smooth curve through the points. The graph of $y = x + \sin x$ is shown in color in Figure 4.25.   ●

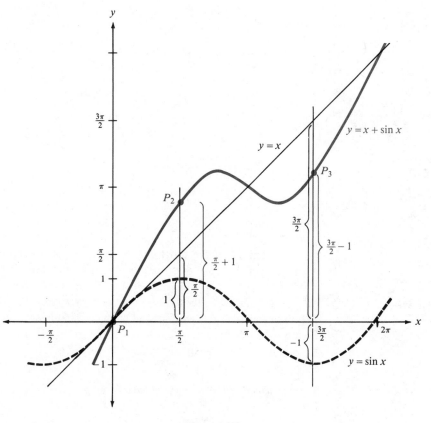

Figure 4.25

As shown on the graph of Figure 4.25, we actually treat the ordinates as line segments. For example, the ordinate of P_2 is found by adding the lengths of the two line segments which represent the ordinates of $\sin x$ and x at $\pi/2$. The same is true for the ordinate of P_3 as well as for each of the other ordinates.

EXAMPLE 2 Graph $y = \cos x - \tan x$.

First graph $y = \cos x$ and $y = \tan x$ on the same axes, as in Figure 4.26. At $x = 0$, the ordinates are 1 and 0, so the ordinate of $y = \cos x - \tan x$ is $1 - 0 = 1$, and the point $(0, 1)$ is on the graph. At any point where the graphs of $\cos x$ and $\tan x$ cross, the ordinates are the same. Therefore the ordinate of $y = \cos x - \tan x$ is 0. See P_1 and P_2 on the graph in Figure 4.26, for example.

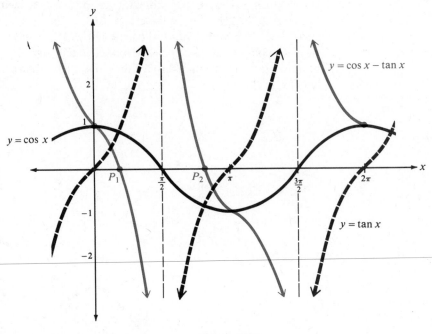

Figure 4.26

The domain of the function $y = \cos x - \tan x$ excludes $\pi/2 + k\pi$, where k is any integer, because these points are not in the domain of $\tan x$. Thus, the lines $x = \pi/2 + k\pi$ are asymptotes, so that, as x approaches $\pi/2$ and $3\pi/2$ from the right, y gets larger and larger. Also, when x approaches $\pi/2$ and $3\pi/2$ from the left, the value of y gets smaller and smaller. The finished graph is shown in color in Figure 4.26 ●

4.4 EXERCISES *Use the method of addition of ordinates to graph each of the following. See Examples 1 and 2.*

1. $y = x + \cos x$

2. $y = \sin x - 2x$

3. $y = 3x - \cos 2x$

4. $y = x + 2 - \sin x$

5. $y = \frac{1}{4}x^2 + \sin x$

6. $y = |x + \cos x|$
(Hint: first find $y = x + \cos x$)

7. $y = \sin x + \sin 2x$

8. $y = \cos x - \cos \frac{1}{2}x$

9. $y = \sin x + \tan x$

10. $y = \sin x + \csc x$

11. $y = 2 \cos x - \sec x$

12. $y = 2 \sec x + \sin x$

13. $y = \cos x + \cot x$

14. $y = \sin x - 2 \cos x$

15. $y = \sec x - x$

16. $y = \csc x + x$

17. The function $y = (6 \cos x)(\cos 8x)$ can come up in AM radio transmissions, as mentioned in Section 4.1. Graph this function on an interval from 0 to 2π. (Hint: first graph $y = 6 \cos x$ and $y = \cos 8x$ as dashed lines.)

18. Graph $y = \sin 8x + \sin 9x$. The period of this function is very long. By placing two engines side by side that are running at almost the same speed, we get an effect of "beats." See the caption below.

The top two sine waves represent pure tones, such as those put out by a tuning fork or an electronic oscillator. When two such pure tones, having slightly different periods, are played side-by-side, the amplitudes add algebraically, instant by instant, producing a result such as shown in the bottom graph. The peaks here are called beats. *Beats result, for example, from engines on an airplane that are running at almost, but not quite, the same speeds. Blowers in different apartments can also cause such beats; these can be quite annoying.*

In this section we discuss applications of the graphs of trigonometric functions, especially the sine wave.

Biorhythm. According to a theory called biorhythm, everyone has three inner rhythms that start at birth: a 23-day physical cycle, a 28-day emotional cycle, and a 33-day intellectual cycle. Each cycle consists of a high period, a low period, and a critical transition day when a person moves from one period to the other. These three cycles can be graphed so that a person can determine in advance when "good" and "bad" days will occur.

The graph of each biorhythm cycle is a sine wave. Figure 4.27 shows a typical biorhythm chart for the month of March. The three sine graphs, representing the physical, emotional, and intellectual cycles, have different periods (of 23, 28, and 33 days), different amplitudes, and different phase shifts.

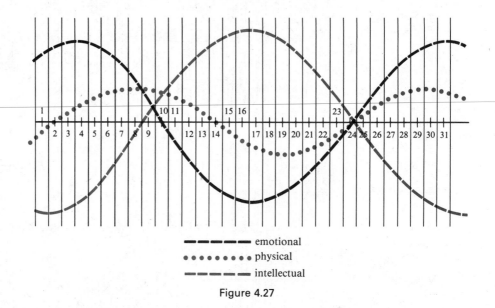

----- emotional
••••••••• physical
----- intellectual

Figure 4.27

EXAMPLE 1 Suppose you were born on January 1, 1962, and today is February 10, 1982. Calculate your biorhythm chart.

First, calculate the total number of days you have lived. That is 20 years at 365 days per year, plus 5 days for the 5 leap year days. Add also the number of days from your last birthday through today, in this example, 41 days.

$$20(365) + 5 + 41 = 7346 \text{ days}$$

Now divide 7346 by the lengths of the three cycles: 23, 28, and 33. We have

$$\frac{7346}{23} = 319 \text{ with 9 days left over}$$

$$\frac{7346}{28} = 262 \text{ with 10 days left over}$$

$$\frac{7346}{33} = 222 \text{ with 20 days left over.}$$

This means that you are in the 9*th* day of your physical cycle (having completed 319 physical cycles since birth), the 10*th* day of your emotional cycle, and the 20*th* day of your intellectual cycle.

The physical cycle, which has a period of 23 days, will start on February 2 (since February 10 is the 9*th* day of the cycle) and end on February 24, which is 23 days later. If you were to graph this, remember that each sine curve starts at the horizontal axis, goes up, then down, then up again to the horizontal axis by the end of its period. The amplitudes are arbitrary.   ●

It is claimed that many industrial firms use biorhythm for accident prevention. In the United States, United Airlines is perhaps the largest firm using this theory. George Thommen, who founded the study of biorhythm in the United States, gives a full explanation of the theory and history of biorhythm in his book *Is This Your Day?* (New York: Crown Publishers, 1973). A more scientific view of biorhythm is given by Gay Gaer Luce, in *Biological Rhythms in Human and Animal Physiology* (New York: Dover Publications, 1971). Luce feels that there is much to be said about biorhythms, but finds the formulas of Thommen and others are of little use.

Sound Waves.   A sound wave is made up of vibrations. Our eardrum picks up these vibrations and transfers them to our brain as electrical impulses. An *oscilloscope* is an electronic instrument with a television-like screen that converts sound waves into electrical impulses. Everyday sounds make very complex patterns on the screen of an oscilloscope. For example, the photograph on the left is an oscilloscope pattern of Helen Reddy singing ''I Am Woman.'' On the right is an oscilloscope photograph of Roy Clark singing ''Thank God and Greyhound She's Gone.'' While the sounds appear very complex in the photographs, it is shown in more advanced courses that they are composed of sums of a large number of sine waves.

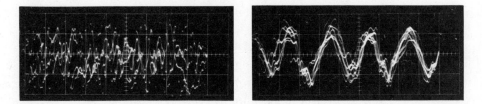

Temperature.   Sine waves are used to describe many of the periodic relationships that occur in nature. For example, scientists now believe that the average annual temperature in a given location is periodic. The overall temperature at a given place during a given season fluctuates as time goes on, from colder to warmer, and back to colder. The graph of Figure 4.28 shows an idealized description of the temperature for the last few thousand years of a location at the same latitude as Anchorage.

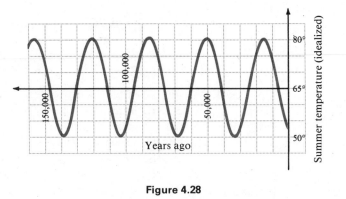

Figure 4.28

EXAMPLE 2   Suppose that the waterwheel in Figure 4.29 rotates at 6 revolutions per minute (rpm). You start your stopwatch. Two seconds later, point P on the rim of the wheel is at its greatest height. You are to find an equation for the distance d of point P from the surface of the water in terms of the number of seconds t the stopwatch reads.

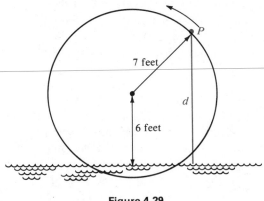

Figure 4.29

Assuming that d varies sinusoidally (as a sine wave) with t, you can sketch a graph as in Figure 4.30. Your thought process should be:

1. The sinusoidal axis is 6 units above the t-axis, because the center of the waterwheel is 6 feet above the surface of the water.

2. The amplitude is 7 units, since the point P goes 7 feet above and 7 feet below the center of the wheel.

3. Therefore, the upper and lower bounds of the graph are $6 + 7 = 13$, and $6 - 7 = -1$.

4. The point P was at its highest when the stopwatch read 2 seconds. Thus, the phase shift (for the cosine) is 2 units.

5. The period is 10 seconds, since the waterwheel makes 6 complete revolutions every 60 seconds (1 minute).

6. Therefore, the sinusoid reaches its next high point at $2 + 10 = 12$ units on the t-axis.

7. Halfway between two high points there is a low point at $t = (1/2)(2 + 12) = 7$; halfway between each high and low point the graph crosses the sinusoidal axis.

8. With the points from part 7 you can sketch the graph.

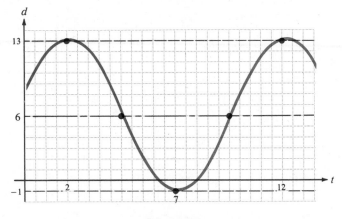

Figure 4.30

From the graph, the four constants in the sinusoidal equation are

$$a = 7,$$
$$b = 2\pi/\text{period} = 2\pi/10 = \pi/5,$$
$$c = 6,$$
$$d = 2.$$

The equation is therefore

$$d = 6 + 7 \cos \frac{\pi}{5} (t - 2). \qquad \bullet$$

4.5 EXERCISES   *Biorhythm*

1. Graph your own biorhythm cycle. Follow the steps in Example 1.

Sound Waves   Pure sounds produce single sine waves on an oscilloscope. Find the amplitude and period of each sine wave in the following photographs. On the vertical scale, each square represents .5, and on the horizontal scale each square represents 30°.

2.   **3.**

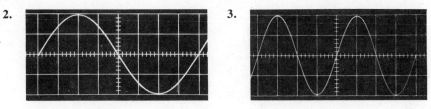

Temperature

4. See Figure 4.28 to find the highest temperature recorded.

5. Find the lowest temperature recorded.

6. Use these two numbers to find the amplitude. (Hint: an alternate definition of the amplitude is half the difference of the highest and lowest points on the graph.)

7. Find the period of the graph.

8. What is the trend of the temperature now?

Living Organisms   Many of the activities of living organisms are periodic. For example, the graph below shows the time that flying squirrels begin their evening activity.

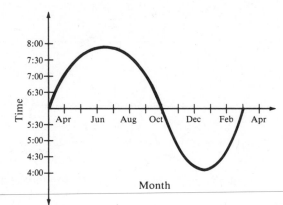

9. Find the amplitude of this graph.

10. Find the period.

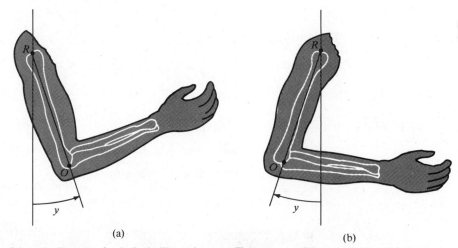

Schematic diagrams of a rhythmically moving arm. The upper arm *RO* rotates back and forth about the point *R*; the position of the arm is measured by the angle *y* between the actual position and the downward vertical position. See Exercises 11–12.*

―――――――――

*From *Calculus for the Life Science*, by Rodolfo De Sapio. W. H. Freeman and Company. Copyright © 1978.

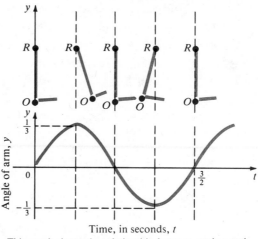

Time, in seconds, t

This graph shows the relationship between angle y and time t in seconds.

11. Find an equation of the form $y = a \sin kt$ for the graph above.

12. How long does it take for a complete movement of the arm?

13. When a spaceship is fired into orbit from a site such as Cape Kennedy, which is not on the equator, it goes into an orbit that takes it alternately north and south of the equator. Its distance from the equator is approximately a sinusoidal function of time.

Suppose that a spaceship is fired into orbit from Cape Kennedy. Ten minutes after it leaves the Cape, it reaches its farthest distance north of the equator, 4000 kilometers. Half a cycle later it reaches its farthest distance south of the equator (On the other side of the Earth, of course!), also 4000 kilometers. The spaceship completes an orbit once every 90 minutes.

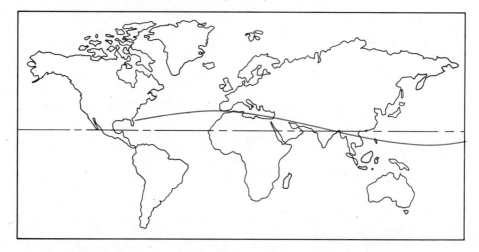

Let y be the number of kilometers the spaceship is north of the equator (you may consider distances south of the equator to be negative). Let t be the number of minutes that have elapsed since liftoff.

    a. Sketch a complete cycle of the graph with t on the horizontal axis.

    b. Write an equation expressing y in terms of t.

    c. Use your equation to predict the distance of the spaceship from the equator when

        (i) $t = 25$ **(ii)** $t = 41$ **(iii)** $t = 163$.

    d. Calculate the distance of Cape Kennedy from the equator by calculating y when $t = 0$.

14. For several hundred years, astronomers have kept track of a number of solar flares, or "sunspots," which occur on the surface of the Sun. The number of sunspots counted in a given year varies periodically from a minimum of about 10 per year to a maximum of about 110 per year. Between the maximums that occurred in the years 1750 and 1948, there were 18 complete cycles.

    a. What is the period of the sunspot cycle?

    b. Assume that the number of sunspots counted in a year varies sinusoidally with the year. Sketch a graph of two sunspot cycles, starting in 1948.

    c. Write an equation expressing the number of sunspots per year in terms of the year. Use an appropriate value for the phase shift.

    d. How many sunspots would you expect in the year 2000? In this year?

    e. What is the first year after 2000 in which the number of sunspots will be about 35? A maximum?

Chapter 4 Test

[4.1–4.3] *For each of the following trigonometric functions, give the amplitude, period, and phase shift, as applicable.*

1. $y = 2 \sin x$ **2.** $y = \tan 3x$

3. $y = 3 \cos \left(x + \dfrac{\pi}{2} \right)$ **4.** $y = \dfrac{1}{2} \csc \left(2x - \dfrac{\pi}{4} \right)$

5. $y = \dfrac{1}{3} \sec \left(3x - \dfrac{\pi}{3} \right)$ **6.** $2y = \cot \left(\dfrac{x}{2} + \dfrac{3\pi}{4} \right)$

Graph the following functions over a one-period interval.

7. $y = 3 \sin x$ **8.** $y = \dfrac{1}{2} \sec x$ **9.** $y = -\tan x$

10. $y = -2 \cos x$ **11.** $y = \cot x + 2$ **12.** $y = \csc x - 1$

13. $y = \sin 2x$ **14.** $y = \tan 3x$ **15.** $y = 3 \cos 2x$

16. $y = \dfrac{1}{2} \cot 3x$ **17.** $y = \cos \left(x - \dfrac{\pi}{4} \right)$ **18.** $y = \tan \left(x - \dfrac{\pi}{2} \right)$

19. $y = \sec \left(2x + \dfrac{\pi}{3} \right)$ **20.** $y = \sin \left(3x + \dfrac{\pi}{2} \right)$

[4.4] *Graph each of the following using the method of addition of ordinates.*

21. $y = \tan x - x$ **22.** $y = \cos x + \dfrac{1}{2} x$

23. $y = \sin x + \cos x$ **24.** $y = \tan x + \cot x$

5

Trigonometric Identities

A *conditional equation*, such as $2x + 1 = 9$, or $m^2 - 2m = 3$, is true for *certain* values in its domain; $2x + 1 = 9$ is true only for $x = 4$, and $m^2 - 2m = 3$ is true only for $m = 3$ and $m = -1$, for example. On the other hand, an **identity** is an equation which is true for *every* value in its domain. Examples of identities include

$$5(x + 3) = 5x + 15, \qquad (a + b)^2 = a^2 + 2ab + b^2, \text{ and } \qquad p^0 = 1.$$

In this chapter we discuss identities which involve trigonometric functions. The variables in the trigonometric functions represent either angles or real numbers. The domain is assumed to be all values for which a given function is defined.

5.1 Fundamental Identities

In this section, we review the fundamental trigonometric identities and discuss some of their uses.* For convenience, the definitions of the six trigonometric functions are restated here. If x, y, r, and θ are defined as shown in Figure 5.1, then

$$\sin \theta = \frac{y}{r} \qquad \tan \theta = \frac{y}{x} \qquad \sec \theta = \frac{r}{x}$$

$$\cos \theta = \frac{x}{r} \qquad \cot \theta = \frac{x}{y} \qquad \csc \theta = \frac{r}{y}.$$

---

*All the identities of this chapter are summarized in the appendix.

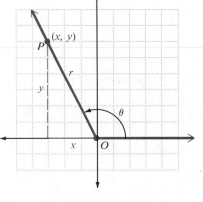

Figure 5.1

In Chapter 1 we used these definitions of the trigonometric functions to derive the following relationships. Since they are true for all suitable replacements of the variable, they are trigonometric identities.

$$\cot \theta = \frac{1}{\tan \theta}$$

$$\csc \theta = \frac{1}{\sin \theta} \qquad \sec \theta = \frac{1}{\cos \theta}$$

Each of these identities leads to another identity. For example, from $\csc \theta = 1/\sin \theta$, we have $\sin \theta = 1/\csc \theta$.

From the definitions above,

$$\tan \theta = \frac{y}{x} = \frac{\dfrac{y}{r}}{\dfrac{x}{r}} = \frac{\sin \theta}{\cos \theta}$$

or

$$\tan \theta = \frac{\sin \theta}{\cos \theta}.$$

In the same way,

$$\cot \theta = \frac{\cos \theta}{\sin \theta}.$$

These last two identities are sometimes called the **quotient identities**.

In the definitions of the trigonometric functions, x, y, and r are the lengths of the sides of a right triangle. Thus, by the Pythagorean theorem,

$$x^2 + y^2 = r^2.$$

Dividing both sides of this equation by r^2 and rearranging terms gives

$$\frac{y^2}{r^2} + \frac{x^2}{r^2} = \frac{r^2}{r^2},$$

or
$$\left(\frac{y}{r}\right)^2 + \left(\frac{x}{r}\right)^2 = 1.$$

Substituting $\sin \theta$ for y/r and $\cos \theta$ for x/r gives
$$(\sin \theta)^2 + (\cos \theta)^2 = 1.$$

It is customary to write $\sin^2 \theta$ for $(\sin \theta)^2$ and $\cos^2 \theta$ for $(\cos \theta)^2$. (This is done with all powers of the trigonometric functions except -1. We define the notation $\sin^{-1} \theta$ in Chapter 6.) Making this change gives the identity
$$\sin^2 \theta + \cos^2 \theta = 1.$$

This identity can also be written as
$$\sin^2 \theta = 1 - \cos^2 \theta \quad \text{or} \quad \cos^2 \theta = 1 - \sin^2 \theta.$$

A little algebraic manipulation of the identity $\sin^2 \theta + \cos^2 \theta = 1$ results in two more identities. First, divide both sides of this identity by $\cos^2 \theta$ (noting the necessary restrictions on θ).
$$\frac{\sin^2 \theta}{\cos^2 \theta} + \frac{\cos^2 \theta}{\cos^2 \theta} = \frac{1}{\cos^2 \theta} \quad (\cos \theta \neq 0)$$

Now simplify and substitute in $\tan \theta$ and $\sec \theta$.
$$\tan^2 \theta + 1 = \sec^2 \theta$$

An alternate form of this identity comes from adding -1 to both sides.
$$\tan^2 \theta = \sec^2 \theta - 1.$$

In the same way, we can divide both sides of $\sin^2 \theta + \cos^2 \theta = 1$ by $\sin^2 \theta$ to get
$$1 + \cot^2 \theta = \csc^2 \theta \quad \text{or} \quad \cot^2 \theta = \csc^2 \theta - 1.$$

The identities
$$\sin^2 \theta + \cos^2 \theta = 1, \quad \tan^2 \theta + 1 = \sec^2 \theta$$
and
$$1 + \cot^2 \theta = \csc^2 \theta$$

are often called the **Pythagorean identities** since they are derived using the Pythagorean theorem.

As suggested by the circle of Figure 5.2, for any angle θ with a point (x, y) on its terminal side, there is a corresponding angle $-\theta$ with a point $(x, -y)$ on its terminal side. From the definition of sine,
$$\sin (-\theta) = \frac{-y}{r} \quad \text{and} \quad \sin \theta = \frac{y}{r},$$

so that sin $(-\theta)$ and sin θ are negatives of each other, or

$$\sin (-\theta) = -\sin \theta.$$

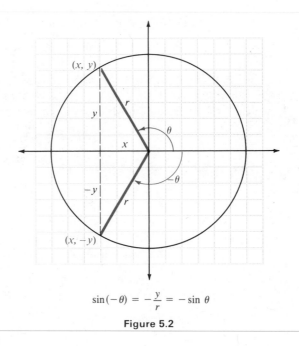

$$\sin(-\theta) = -\frac{y}{r} = -\sin \theta$$

Figure 5.2

Similarly,

$$\cos (-\theta) = \frac{x}{r} \quad \text{and} \quad \cos \theta = \frac{x}{r},$$

so that

$$\cos (-\theta) = \cos \theta.$$

Using these formulas for sin $(-\theta)$ and cos $(-\theta)$, we can find tan $(-\theta)$ in terms of tan θ.

$$\tan (-\theta) = \frac{\sin (-\theta)}{\cos (-\theta)}$$

$$= \frac{-\sin \theta}{\cos \theta}$$

$$\tan (-\theta) = -\tan \theta.$$

We can now summarize the identities of this section; as a group they are called the **fundamental identities**.

Fundamental identities

Reciprocal identities

$$\cot \theta = \frac{1}{\tan \theta} \qquad \sec \theta = \frac{1}{\cos \theta} \qquad \csc \theta = \frac{1}{\sin \theta}$$

Quotient identities

$$\tan \theta = \frac{\sin \theta}{\cos \theta} \qquad \cot \theta = \frac{\cos \theta}{\sin \theta}$$

Pythagorean identities

$$\sin^2 \theta + \cos^2 \theta = 1 \qquad \tan^2 \theta + 1 = \sec^2 \theta \qquad 1 + \cot^2 \theta = \csc^2 \theta$$

Identities for negative angles

$$\sin (-\theta) = -\sin \theta \qquad \cos (-\theta) = \cos \theta \qquad \tan (-\theta) = -\tan \theta$$

Trigonometric identities are useful in several ways. One use for trigonometric identities is finding the value of the other trigonometric functions from the value of a given trigonometric function. For example, given a value of $\tan \theta$, we can find the value of $\cot \theta$ by using the identity $\cot \theta = 1/\tan \theta$. In fact, given $\tan \theta$ and the quadrant in which θ lies, we can find the values of all the other trigonometric functions by using identities, as shown in the following example.

EXAMPLE 1   If $\tan \theta = -5/3$ and θ is in quadrant II, find the values of the other trigonometric functions.

We know $\cot \theta = 1/\tan \theta$, so that $\cot \theta = -3/5$. Also, $\tan^2 \theta + 1 = \sec^2 \theta$. Thus,

$$\left(-\frac{5}{3}\right)^2 + 1 = \sec^2 \theta$$

$$\frac{25}{9} + 1 = \sec^2 \theta$$

$$\frac{34}{9} = \sec^2 \theta$$

$$-\sqrt{\frac{34}{9}} = \sec \theta$$

$$-\frac{\sqrt{34}}{3} = \sec \theta.$$

Choose the negative square root since sec θ is negative in quadrant II. Since cos θ is the reciprocal of sec θ,

$$\cos \theta = \frac{-3}{\sqrt{34}} = \frac{-3\sqrt{34}}{34},$$

after rationalizing the denominator. Now find sin θ by using the identity $\sin^2 \theta + \cos^2 \theta = 1$.

$$\sin^2 \theta + \left(\frac{-3\sqrt{34}}{34}\right)^2 = 1$$

$$\sin^2 \theta = 1 - \frac{9}{34}$$

$$\sin^2 \theta = \frac{25}{34}$$

$$\sin \theta = \frac{5}{\sqrt{34}} \quad \text{or} \quad \sin \theta = \frac{5\sqrt{34}}{34}.$$

Here we choose the positive square root because sin θ is positive in quadrant II. Finally, since csc θ is the reciprocal of sin θ,

$$\csc \theta = \frac{\sqrt{34}}{5}. \quad \bullet$$

Another use of identities is to simplify trigonometric expressions by substituting one half of an identity for the other half. For example, the expression $\sin^2 \theta + \cos^2 \theta$ can be replaced by 1, as in the following example.

EXAMPLE 2   Use the fundamental identities to write tan θ + cot θ in terms of sin θ and cos θ and then simplify the expression.
From the fundamental identities,

$$\tan \theta + \cot \theta = \frac{\sin \theta}{\cos \theta} + \frac{\cos \theta}{\sin \theta}.$$

To simplify this expression, add the two fractions on the right side, using the common denominator of cos θ sin θ.

$$= \frac{\sin^2 \theta}{\cos \theta \sin \theta} + \frac{\cos^2 \theta}{\cos \theta \sin \theta}$$

$$= \frac{\sin^2 \theta + \cos^2 \theta}{\cos \theta \sin \theta}$$

Now substitute 1 for $\sin^2 \theta + \cos^2 \theta$, to get

$$\tan \theta + \cot \theta = \frac{1}{\cos \theta \sin \theta}. \quad \bullet$$

EXAMPLE 3   Express $\cos x$ in terms of $\tan x$.

Start with $\tan^2 x + 1 = \sec^2 x$. Then

$$\frac{1}{\tan^2 x + 1} = \frac{1}{\sec^2 x}$$

or

$$\frac{1}{\tan^2 x + 1} = \cos^2 x.$$

$$\pm \sqrt{\frac{1}{\tan^2 x + 1}} = \cos x \qquad \text{Take the square root of both sides.}$$

or

$$\cos x = \frac{\pm 1}{\sqrt{\tan^2 x + 1}}.$$

Rationalize the denominator to get

$$\cos x = \frac{\pm \sqrt{\tan^2 x + 1}}{\tan^2 x + 1}.$$

Here, the $+$ or the $-$ sign is chosen, depending on the quadrant of x.   ●

5.1 EXERCISES

Find $\sin s$ for each of the following.

1. $\cos s = 3/4$, s in quadrant I

2. $\cot s = -\dfrac{1}{3}$, s in quadrant IV

3. $\cos s = \sqrt{5}/5$, $\tan s < 0$

4. $\tan s = -\sqrt{7}/2$, $\sec s > 0$

5. Find $\tan \theta$ if $\cos \theta = -2/5$, and $\sin \theta < 0$.

6. Find $\csc \alpha$ if $\tan \alpha = 6$, and $\cos \alpha > 0$.

Use the fundamental identities to find the remaining five trigonometric functions of θ. See Example 1.

7. $\sin \theta = \dfrac{2}{3}$, θ in quadrant II

8. $\cos \theta = \dfrac{1}{5}$, θ in quadrant I

9. $\tan \theta = -\dfrac{1}{4}$, θ in quadrant IV

10. $\tan \theta = \dfrac{2}{3}$, θ in quadrant III

11. $\sec \theta = -3$, θ in quadrant II

12. $\csc \theta = -\dfrac{5}{2}$, θ in quadrant III

13. $\cot \theta = \dfrac{4}{3}$, $\sin \theta > 0$

14. $\sin \theta = -\dfrac{4}{5}$, $\cos \theta < 0$

15. $\sec \theta = \dfrac{4}{3}$, $\sin \theta < 0$

16. $\cos \theta = -\dfrac{1}{4}$, $\sin \theta > 0$

For each trigonometric expression in Column I, choose the expression from Column II which completes a fundamental identity.

Column I   Column II

17. $\dfrac{\cos x}{\sin x}$ **(a)** $\sin^2 x + \cos^2 x$

18. $\tan x$ **(b)** $\cot x$

19. $\cos(-x)$ **(c)** $\sec^2 x$

20. $\tan^2 x + 1$ **(d)** $\dfrac{\sin x}{\cos x}$

21. 1 **(e)** $\cos x$

For each expression in Column I, choose the expression from Column II which completes an identity. You will have to rewrite one or both expressions, using a fundamental identity, to recognize the matches.

Column I   Column II

22. $-\tan x \cos x$ **(a)** $\dfrac{\sin^2 x}{\cos^2 x}$

23. $\sec^2 x - 1$ **(b)** $\dfrac{1}{\sec^2 x}$

24. $\dfrac{\sec x}{\csc x}$ **(c)** $\sin(-x)$

25. $1 + \sin^2 x$ **(d)** $\csc^2 x - \cot^2 x + \sin^2 x$

26. $\cos^2 x$ **(e)** $\tan x$

In each of the following, use the fundamental identities to get an equivalent expression involving only sines and cosines and then simplify it. See Example 2.

27. $\csc^2 \beta - \cot^2 \beta$

28. $\dfrac{\tan(-\theta)}{\sec \theta}$

29. $\tan(-\alpha) \cos(-\alpha)$

30. $\cot^2 x (1 + \tan^2 x)$

31. $\tan^2 \theta - \dfrac{\sec^2 \theta}{\csc^2 \theta}$

32. $\dfrac{\tan x \csc x}{\sec x}$

33. $\sec \theta + \tan \theta$

34. $\dfrac{\sec \alpha}{\tan \alpha + \cot \alpha}$

35. $\sec^2 t - \tan^2 t$

36. $\csc^2 \gamma + \sec^2 \gamma$

37. $\cot^2 \beta - \csc^2 \beta$

38. $1 + \cot^2 \alpha$

39. $\dfrac{1 + \tan^2 \theta}{\cot^2 \theta}$

40. $\dfrac{1 - \sin^2 t}{\csc^2 t}$

41. $\cot^2 \beta \sin^2 \beta + \tan^2 \beta \cos^2 \beta$
          42. $\sec^2 x + \cos^2 x$

43. $\dfrac{\cot^2 \alpha + \csc^2 \alpha}{\cos^2 \alpha}$
          44. $1 - \tan^4 \theta$

45. $1 - \cot^4 s$
          46. $\tan^4 \gamma - \cot^4 \gamma$

Write all the trigonometric functions in terms of

47. $\sin x$

48. $\cos x$

49. Write $\tan x$ in terms of $\csc x$.

50. Write $\sec \alpha$ in terms of $\tan \alpha$.

51. Express $\cot s$ in terms of $\sec s$.

52. Express $\csc t$ in terms of $\tan t$.

53. Suppose $\cos \theta = x/(x + 1)$. Find $\sin \theta$.

54. Find $\tan \alpha$ if $\sec \alpha = (p + 4)/p$.

Show that each of the following is not *an identity.*

55. $(\sin s + \cos s)^2 = 1$
          56. $(\tan s + 1)^2 = \sec^2 s$

57. $2 \sin s = \sin 2s$
          58. $\sin x = \sqrt{1 - \cos^2 x}$

5.2 Verifying Trigonometric Identities

One of the skills required for more advanced work in mathematics (and especially in calculus) is the ability to use the trigonometric identities to write trigonometric expressions in alternate forms. To develop this skill, we use the fundamental identities to verify that a trigonometric equation is an identity (for those values of the variable for which it is defined). This process is a skill that must be learned with practice. Here are some hints that may help you get started.

1. Memorize the fundamental identities given in the last section. Whenever you see either half of a fundamental identity, the other half should come to mind.

2. Try to rewrite the more complicated side of the equation so that it is identical to the simpler side.

3. It is often helpful to express all other trigonometric functions in the equation in terms of sine and cosine and then simplify the result.

4. You should usually perform any factoring or indicated algebraic operations. For example, the expression $\sin^2 x + 2 \sin x + 1$ can be factored as $(\sin x + 1)^2$. The sum or difference of two trigonometric expressions, such as

$$\frac{1}{\sin \theta} + \frac{1}{\cos \theta}$$

can be added or subtracted in the same way as any other rational expression. For example.

$$\frac{1}{\sin \theta} + \frac{1}{\cos \theta} = \frac{\cos \theta}{\sin \theta \cos \theta} + \frac{\sin \theta}{\sin \theta \cos \theta}$$

$$= \frac{\cos \theta + \sin \theta}{\sin \theta \cos \theta}$$

5. Keep in mind the side you are not changing as you select substitutions. It represents your goal. For example, if you are to verify the identity

$$\tan^2 x + 1 = \frac{1}{\cos^2 x},$$

try to think of an identity that relates $\tan x$ to $\cos x$. Here, since $\sec x = 1/\cos x$ and $\sec^2 x = \tan^2 x + 1$, the secant function is the best link between the two sides of the equation.

We use these hints in the following examples. (A word of warning: verifying identities is *not* the same as solving equations. Techniques used in solving equations, such as adding the same terms to both sides, are not valid when working with identities.)

EXAMPLE 1 Verify that

$$\cot s + 1 = \csc s(\cos s + \sin s)$$

is an identity.

We use the fundamental identities to rewrite one side of the equation so that it is identical to the other side. Since the right side is more complicated, we work with it. Here we use the method of changing all the trigonometric functions to sine or cosine.

$$\csc s(\cos s + \sin s) = \frac{1}{\sin s} (\cos s + \sin s)$$

$$= \frac{\cos s}{\sin s} + \frac{\sin s}{\sin s}$$

$$= \cot s + 1.$$

The equation is an identity because the right side equals the left side, for any value of s. ●

EXAMPLE 2 Verify that

$$\tan^2 \alpha (1 + \cot^2 \alpha) = \frac{1}{1 - \sin^2 \alpha}$$

is an identity.

Working with the left side gives

$$\tan^2 \alpha \,(1 + \cot^2 \alpha) = \tan^2 \alpha + \tan^2 \alpha \cot^2 \alpha$$

$$= \tan^2 \alpha + \tan^2 \alpha \cdot \frac{1}{\tan^2 \alpha}$$

$$= \tan^2 \alpha + 1$$

$$= \sec^2 \alpha$$

$$= \frac{1}{\cos^2 \alpha}$$

$$= \frac{1}{1 - \sin^2 \alpha} \quad \bullet$$

EXAMPLE 3 Show that

$$\frac{\tan t - \cot t}{\sin t \cos t} = \sec^2 t - \csc^2 t.$$

Work with the left side.

$$\frac{\tan t - \cot t}{\sin t \cos t} = \frac{\tan t}{\sin t \cos t} - \frac{\cot t}{\sin t \cos t}$$

$$= \tan t \cdot \frac{1}{\sin t \cos t} - \cot t \cdot \frac{1}{\sin t \cos t}$$

$$= \frac{\sin t}{\cos t} \cdot \frac{1}{\sin t \cdot \cos t} - \frac{\cos t}{\sin t} \cdot \frac{1}{\sin t \cos t}$$

$$= \frac{1}{\cos^2 t} - \frac{1}{\sin^2 t}$$

$$= \sec^2 t - \csc^2 t. \quad \bullet$$

5.2 EXERCISES   *For each of the following, perform the indicated operations and simplify the result.*

1. $\tan \theta + \dfrac{1}{\tan \theta}$ 2. $\dfrac{\cos x}{\sin x} + \dfrac{\sin x}{\cos x}$

3. $\cot s(\tan s + \sin s)$ 4. $\sec \beta(\cos \beta + \sin \beta)$

5. $\dfrac{1}{\csc^2 \theta} + \dfrac{1}{\sec^2 \theta}$ 6. $\dfrac{1}{\sin \alpha - 1} - \dfrac{1}{\sin \alpha + 1}$

7. $\dfrac{\cos x}{\sec x} + \dfrac{\sin x}{\csc x}$ 8. $\dfrac{\cos \gamma}{\sin \gamma} + \dfrac{\sin \gamma}{1 + \cos \gamma}$

9. $(1 + \sin t)^2 + \cos^2 t$ 10. $(1 + \tan s)^2 - 2 \tan s$

Factor each of the following trigonometric expressions.

11. $\sin^2 \gamma - 1$ 12. $\sec^2 \theta - 1$

13. $(\sin x + 1)^2 - (\sin x - 1)^2$ 14. $(\tan x + \cot x)^2 - (\tan x - \cot x)^2$

15. $2 \sin^2 x + 3 \sin x + 1$

16. $4 \tan^2 \beta + \tan \beta - 3$

17. $4 \sec^2 x + 3 \sec x - 1$

18. $2 \csc^2 x + 7 \csc x - 30$

19. $\cos^4 x + 2 \cos^2 x + 1$

20. $\cot^4 x + 3 \cot^2 s + 2$

Use the fundamental identities to simplify each of the given expressions.

21. $\tan \theta \cos \theta$

22. $\cot \alpha \sin \alpha$

23. $\sec r \cos r$

24. $\cot t \tan t$

25. $\dfrac{\sin \beta \tan \beta}{\cos \beta}$

26. $\dfrac{\csc \theta \sec \theta}{\cot \theta}$

27. $\sec^2 x - 1$

28. $\csc^2 t - 1$

29. $\dfrac{\sin^2 x}{\cos^2 x} + \sin x \csc x$

30. $\dfrac{1}{\tan^2 \alpha} + \cot \alpha \tan \alpha$

Verify each of the following trigonometric identities. See Examples 1–3.

31. $1 - \sec \alpha \cos \alpha = \tan \alpha \cot \alpha - 1$

32. $\csc^4 \theta = \cot^4 \theta + 2 \cot^2 \theta + 1$

33. $\dfrac{\sin^2 \theta}{\cos^2 \theta} = \sec^2 \theta - 1$

34. $\cot \beta \sin \beta = \cos \beta$

35. $\sin^2 \alpha + \tan^2 \alpha + \cos^2 \alpha = \sec^2 \alpha$

36. $\sin^2 s - 1 = -\cos^2 s$

37. $\dfrac{\sin^2 \gamma}{\cos \gamma} = \sec \gamma - \cos \gamma$

38. $(1 + \tan^2 x) \cos^2 x = 1$

39. $\cot s + \tan s = \sec s \csc s$

40. $\dfrac{\cos \alpha}{\sec \alpha} + \dfrac{\sin \alpha}{\csc \alpha} = \sec^2 \alpha - \tan^2 \alpha$

41. $\dfrac{\cos \alpha}{\sin \alpha \cot \alpha} = 1$

42. $\sin^4 \theta - \cos^4 \theta = 2 \sin^2 \theta - 1$

43. $\dfrac{1 + \sin x}{\cos x} = \dfrac{\cos x}{1 - \sin x}$ (Hint: rationalize the denominator on the right.)

44. $(1 - \cos^2 \alpha)(1 + \cos^2 \alpha) = 2 \sin^2 \alpha - \sin^4 \alpha$

45. $\dfrac{(\sec \theta - \tan \theta)^2 + 1}{\sec \theta \csc \theta - \tan \theta \csc \theta} = 2 \tan \theta$

46. $\dfrac{\cos \theta + 1}{\tan^2 \theta} = \dfrac{\cos \theta}{\sec \theta - 1}.$

47. $\dfrac{1}{\sec \alpha - \tan \alpha} = \sec \alpha + \tan \alpha$

48. $\dfrac{1}{1 - \sin \theta} + \dfrac{1}{1 + \sin \theta} = 2 \sec^2 \theta$

49. $\dfrac{1 - \cos x}{1 + \cos x} = (\cot x - \csc x)^2$

50. $\dfrac{\tan s}{1 + \cos s} + \dfrac{\sin s}{1 - \cos s} = \cot s + \sec s \csc s$

51. $\dfrac{1}{\tan \alpha - \sec \alpha} + \dfrac{1}{\tan \alpha + \sec \alpha} = -2 \tan \alpha$

52. $\dfrac{\cot \alpha + 1}{\cot \alpha - 1} = \dfrac{1 + \tan \alpha}{1 - \tan \alpha}$

53. $\dfrac{\csc \theta + \cot \theta}{\tan \theta + \sin \theta} = \cot \theta \csc \theta$

54. $\sin^2 \alpha \sec^2 \alpha + \sin^2 \alpha \csc^2 \alpha = \sec^2 \alpha$

55. $\sec^4 x - \sec^2 x = \tan^4 x + \tan^2 x$

56. $\dfrac{1 - \sin \theta}{1 + \sin \theta} = \sec^2 \theta - 2 \sec \theta \tan \theta + \tan^2 \theta$

57. $\sin \theta + \cos \theta = \dfrac{\sin \theta}{1 - \dfrac{\cos \theta}{\sin \theta}} + \dfrac{\cos \theta}{1 - \dfrac{\sin \theta}{\cos \theta}}$

58. $\dfrac{\sin \theta}{1 - \cos \theta} - \dfrac{\sin \theta \cos \theta}{1 + \cos \theta} = \csc \theta + \csc \theta \cos^2 \theta$

59. $\dfrac{\sec^4 s - \tan^4 s}{\sec^2 s + \tan^2 s} = \sec^2 s - \tan^2 s$

60. $\dfrac{\cot^2 t - 1}{1 + \cot^2 t} = 1 - 2 \sin^2 t$

61. $\dfrac{\tan^2 t - 1}{\sec^2 t} = \dfrac{\tan t - \cot t}{\tan t + \cot t}$

62. $(1 + \sin x + \cos x)^2 = 2(1 + \sin x)(1 + \cos x)$

63. $(\sin s + \cos s)^2 \cdot \csc s = 2 \cos s + \dfrac{1}{\sin s}$

64. $\dfrac{\sin^3 t - \cos^3 t}{\sin t - \cos t} = 1 + \sin t \cos t$

65. $\dfrac{1 + \cos x}{1 - \cos x} - \dfrac{1 - \cos x}{1 + \cos x} = 4 \cot x \csc x$

66. $(\sec \alpha - \tan \alpha)^2 = \dfrac{1 - \sin \alpha}{1 + \sin \alpha}$

67. $(\sec \alpha + \csc \alpha)(\cos \alpha - \sin \alpha) = \cot \alpha - \tan \alpha$

68. $\dfrac{\sin^4 \alpha - \cos^4 \alpha}{\sin^2 \alpha - \cos^2 \alpha} = 1$

69. $\dfrac{\cot^2 x + \sec^2 x + 1}{\cot^2 x} = \sec^4 x$

70. $\dfrac{\cos x - (\sin x - 1)}{\cos x + (\sin x - 1)} = \dfrac{\sin x}{1 - \cos x}$ (Hint: multiply numerator and denominator on the left by $\cos x - (\sin x - 1)$.)

Given a complicated equation involving trigonometric functions, it is a good idea to decide whether it really is an identity before trying to prove that it is. Substitute $s = 1$ and $s = 2$ into each of the following (with the calculator set on **radian** *mode). If you get the same results on both sides of the equation, it* may *be an identity. Then prove that it is.*

71. $\dfrac{2 + 5 \cos s}{\sin s} = 2 \csc s + 5 \cot s$

72. $1 + \cot^2 s = \dfrac{\sec^2 s}{\sec^2 s - 1}$

73. $\dfrac{\tan s - \cot s}{\tan s + \cot s} = 2 \sin^2 s$

74. $\dfrac{1}{1 + \sin s} + \dfrac{1}{1 - \sin s} = \sec^2 s$

75. $\dfrac{1 - \tan^2 s}{1 + \tan^2 s} = \cos^2 s - \sin s$

76. $\dfrac{\sin^3 s - \cos^3 s}{\sin s - \cos s} = \sin^2 s + 2 \sin s \cos s + \cos^2 s$

77. $\sin^2 s + \cos^2 s = \dfrac{1}{2}(1 - \cos 4 s)$

78. $\cos 3 s = 3 \cos s + 4 \cos^3 s$

Show that the following are not *identities for real numbers s and t.*

79. $\sin(\csc s) = 1$

80. $\sqrt{\cos^2 s} = \cos s$

81. $\csc t = \sqrt{1 + \cot^2 t}$

82. $\sin t = \sqrt{1 - \cos^2 t}$

5.3   Sum and Difference Identities for Cosine

It is sometimes useful to rewrite a trigonometric function of the sum of two angles in terms of the trigonometric functions of each angle. For example, we can rewrite $\cos(A - B)$ in terms of functions of angles A and B.

To get a formula for $\cos(A - B)$, locate angles A and B in standard position on a unit circle, with $B < A$. Let S and Q be the points where angles A and B, respectively, cut the unit circle. Locate point R on the unit circle so that angle POR equals the difference $A - B$. See Figure 5.3.

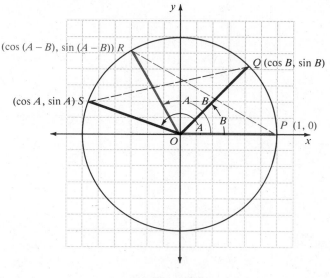

Figure 5.3

Since point Q is on the unit circle, its x-coordinate is given by the cosine of angle B, while the y-coordinate of Q is given by the sine of angle B. Thus,

Q has coordinates $(\cos B, \sin B)$.

In the same way, S has coordinates $(\cos A, \sin A)$, and R has coordinates $(\cos (A - B), \sin (A - B))$.

Angle SOQ also equals $A - B$. Since the central angles SOQ and POR are equal, chords PR and SQ are equal. By the distance formula, since $PR = SQ$,

$$\sqrt{[\cos (A - B) - 1]^2 + [\sin (A - B)]^2}$$
$$= \sqrt{(\cos A - \cos B)^2 + (\sin A - \sin B)^2}.$$

Squaring both sides and clearing parentheses gives

$$\cos^2 (A - B) - 2 \cos (A - B) + 1 + \sin^2 (A - B)$$
$$= \cos^2 A - 2 \cos A \cos B + \cos^2 B + \sin^2 A - 2 \sin A \sin B + \sin^2 B.$$

Since $\sin^2 x + \cos^2 x = 1$ for any value of x, rewrite the equation as

$$2 - 2 \cos (A - B) = 2 - 2 \cos A \cos B - 2 \sin A \sin B$$
$$\cos (A - B) = \cos A \cos B + \sin A \sin B.$$

This is the identity we wanted. Although Figure 5.3 shows angles A and B in the second and first quadrants respectively, it can be shown that this result is the same for any values of these angles.

To find a similar expression for $\cos (A + B)$, write $A + B = A - (-B)$ and use the identity for $\cos (A - B)$ that was found above, along with the fact that $\cos (-B) = \cos B$ and $\sin (-B) = -\sin B$.

$$\cos (A + B) = \cos [A - (-B)]$$
$$= \cos A \cos (-B) + \sin A \sin (-B)$$
$$= \cos A \cos B + \sin A (-\sin B)$$
$$\cos (A + B) = \cos A \cos B - \sin A \sin B$$

The two formulas we have just derived are useful in determining certain values of the cosine function without using a calculator or tables. This is shown in the following examples.

EXAMPLE 1   Use identities to find the value of each of the following.

(a) $\cos 15°$

To find $\cos 15°$, write $15°$ as the sum or difference of two angles which have known function values. Since we know the trigonometric function values of both $45°$ and $30°$, write $15°$ as $45° - 30°$. Then use the identity for the cosine of the difference of two angles.

$$\cos 15° = \cos (45° - 30°)$$
$$= \cos 45° \cos 30° + \sin 45° \sin 30°$$
$$= \frac{\sqrt{2}}{2} \cdot \frac{\sqrt{3}}{2} + \frac{\sqrt{2}}{2} \cdot \frac{1}{2}$$
$$\cos 15° = \frac{\sqrt{6} + \sqrt{2}}{4}$$

(b) $\cos \dfrac{5}{12}\,\pi = \cos\left(\dfrac{\pi}{6} + \dfrac{\pi}{4}\right)$

$$= \cos\frac{\pi}{6}\cos\frac{\pi}{4} - \sin\frac{\pi}{6}\sin\frac{\pi}{4}$$

$$= \frac{\sqrt{3}}{2}\cdot\frac{\sqrt{2}}{2} - \frac{1}{2}\cdot\frac{\sqrt{2}}{2}$$

$$\cos\frac{5}{12}\,\pi = \frac{\sqrt{6} - \sqrt{2}}{4} \qquad \bullet$$

EXAMPLE 2   Suppose $\sin x = 1/2$, $\cos y = -12/13$, and both x and y are in quadrant II. Find $\cos (x + y)$.

We know that $\cos (x + y) = \cos x \cos y - \sin x \sin y$. We are given the values of $\sin x$ and $\cos y$. To use the formula for $\cos (x + y)$, we need to find $\cos x$ and $\sin y$.

To find $\cos x$, use the fact that $\sin^2 x + \cos^2 x = 1$, and then substitute $1/2$ for $\sin x$.

$$\sin^2 x + \cos^2 x = 1$$

$$\left(\frac{1}{2}\right)^2 + \cos^2 x = 1$$

$$\frac{1}{4} + \cos^2 x = 1$$

$$\cos^2 x = \frac{3}{4}$$

$$\cos x = \pm\frac{\sqrt{3}}{2}$$

Since x is in quadrant II, $\cos x$ is negative, so $\cos x = -\sqrt{3}/2$.
Find $\sin y$ as follows.

$$\sin^2 y + \cos^2 y = 1$$

$$\sin^2 y + \left(-\frac{12}{13}\right)^2 = 1$$

$$\sin^2 y + \frac{144}{169} = 1$$

$$\sin y = \pm\frac{5}{13}$$

Since y is in quadrant II, $\sin y = 5/13$.
Now find $\cos (x + y)$.

$$\cos (x + y) = \cos x \cos y - \sin x \sin y$$

$$= -\frac{\sqrt{3}}{2} \cdot \left(-\frac{12}{13}\right) - \frac{1}{2} \cdot \frac{5}{13}$$

$$= \frac{12\sqrt{3}}{26} - \frac{5}{26}$$

$$\cos (x + y) = \frac{12\sqrt{3} - 5}{26} \quad \bullet$$

We can also use the identities for the cosine of the sum and difference of two angles to derive other identities. Recall the **cofunction identities** which were presented earlier for values of θ where $0° \le \theta \le 90°$.

$$\cos (90° - \theta) = \sin \theta \qquad \cot (90° - \theta) = \tan \theta$$
$$\sin (90° - \theta) = \cos \theta \qquad \sec (90° - \theta) = \csc \theta$$
$$\tan (90° - \theta) = \cot \theta \qquad \csc (90° - \theta) = \sec \theta$$

These identities can now be generalized to any angle θ, not just those between $0°$ and $90°$. For example, if we substitute $90°$ for A and θ for B in the identity for $\cos (A - B)$, we get

$$\cos (90° - \theta) = \cos 90° \cos \theta + \sin 90° \sin \theta$$
$$= 0 \cdot \cos \theta + 1 \cdot \sin \theta$$
$$\cos (90° - \theta) = \sin \theta.$$

This result is true for *any* value of θ since the identity for $\cos (A - B)$ is true for any values of A and B. For the derivations of other cofunction identities, see Exercises 63 and 64.

EXAMPLE 3   Find an angle θ which satisfies each of the following.

(a) $\cot \theta = \tan 25°$

Since tangent and cotangent are cofunctions,

$$\cot \theta = \tan (90° - \theta).$$

Thus, $90° - \theta = 25°$, and $\theta = 65°$.

(b) $\sin \theta = \cos (-30°)$

In the same way,

$$\sin \theta = \cos (90° - \theta) = \cos (-30°).$$

Thus,

$$90° - \theta = -30°$$
$$\theta = 120°. \quad \bullet$$

EXAMPLE 4   Write $\cos(180° - \theta)$ as a trigonometric function of θ.
Use the difference identity. Replace A with $180°$ and B with θ.

$$\cos(180° - \theta) = \cos 180° \cos \theta + \sin 180° \sin \theta$$
$$= (-1)\cos \theta + (0)\sin \theta$$
$$\cos(180° - \theta) = -\cos \theta. \quad \bullet$$

Cofunctions can be related in an even more general way. We know that $\cos(0° - \theta) = \cos(-\theta) = \cos \theta$, and $\cos(90° - \theta) = \sin \theta$. From Example 4, $\cos(180° - \theta) = -\cos \theta$. In the Exercises, you are asked to show that $\cos(270° - \theta) = -\sin \theta$. Similar results can be shown for $\tan \theta$ and $\cot \theta$, and for $\sec \theta$ and $\csc \theta$.

5.3 EXERCISES   *Write each of the following in terms of the cofunction of a complementary angle.*

1. $\tan 87°$
2. $\sin 15°$
3. $\cos \pi/12$
4. $\sin 2\pi/5$
5. $\csc(-14° 24')$
6. $\sin 142° 14'$
7. $\sin 5\pi/8$
8. $\cot 9\pi/10$
9. $\sec 146° 42'$
10. $\tan 174° 3'$

Use the cofunction identities to fill in each of the following blanks with the appropriate trigonometric function name.

11. $\cot \dfrac{\pi}{4} = \underline{\hspace{1cm}} \dfrac{\pi}{4}$
12. $\sin \dfrac{2\pi}{3} = \underline{\hspace{1cm}} \left(-\dfrac{\pi}{6}\right)$
13. $\underline{\hspace{1cm}} 33° = \sin 57°$
14. $\underline{\hspace{1cm}} 72° = \cot 18°$
15. $\cos 70° = \dfrac{1}{\underline{\hspace{1cm}} 20°}$
16. $\tan 24° = \dfrac{1}{\underline{\hspace{1cm}} 66°}$

Identify each of the following as true *or* false.

17. $\cos 42° = \cos(30° + 12°)$
18. $\cos(-24°) = \cos 16° - \cos 40°$
19. $\cos 74° = \cos 60° \cos 14° + \sin 60° \sin 14°$
20. $\cos 140° = \cos 60° \cos 80° - \sin 60° \sin 80°$
21. $\cos 10° = \cos 90° \cos 80° + \sin 90° \sin 80°$
22. $\cos(-10°) = \cos 90° \cos 80° + \sin 90° \sin 80°$

Use the cofunction identities to find the angle θ which makes each of the following true.

23. $\tan \theta = \cot(45° + 2\theta)$
24. $\sin \theta = \cos(2\theta - 10°)$
25. $\sec \theta = \csc(\theta/2 + 20°)$
26. $\cos \theta = \sin(3\theta + 10°)$
27. $\sin(3\theta - 15°) = \cos(\theta + 25°)$
28. $\cot(\theta - 10°) = \tan(2\theta + 20°)$

Use the sum and difference identities for cosine to find the value of each of the following without using calculators or tables. See Example 1.

29. $\cos 285°$

30. $\cos (-15°)$

31. $\cos (-105°)$

32. $\cos 75°$

33. $\cos \dfrac{7\pi}{12}$

34. $\cos \left(-\dfrac{5\pi}{12}\right)$

35. $\cos 40° \cos 50° - \sin 40° \sin 50°$

36. $\cos 80° \cos 35° + \sin 80° \sin 35°$

37. $\cos (-10°) \cos 35° + \sin (-10°) \sin 35°$

Write as a function of θ or x. See Example 4.

38. $\cos (30° + \theta)$

39. $\cos (45° - \theta)$

40. $\cos (60° + \theta)$

41. $\cos (\theta - 30°)$

42. $\cos \left(\dfrac{3\pi}{2} - x\right)$

43. $\cos \left(x + \dfrac{\pi}{4}\right)$

For each of the following, find $\cos (s + t)$ and $\cos (s - t)$. See Example 2.

44. $\cos s = 3/5$ and $\sin t = 5/13$, s and t in quadrant I

45. $\cos s = -1/5$ and $\sin t = 3/5$, s and t in quadrant II

46. $\sin s = 2/3$ and $\sin t = -1/3$, s in quadrant II and t in IV

47. $\sin s = 3/5$ and $\sin t = -12/13$, s in quadrant I and t in III

48. $\cos s = -8/17$ and $\cos t = -3/5$, s and t in quadrant III

49. $\cos s = -15/17$ and $\sin t = 4/5$, s in quadrant II and t in I

50. $\sin s = -4/5$ and $\cos t = 12/13$, s in quadrant IV and t in I

51. $\sin s = -5/13$ and $\sin t = 3/5$, s in quadrant III and t in II

52. $\sin s = -8/17$ and $\cos t = -8/17$, s and t in quadrant III

53. $\sin s = 2/3$ and $\sin t = 2/5$, s and t in quadrant I

Verify each of the following identities.

54. $\cos (\pi/2 + x) = -\sin x$

55. $\sec (\pi - x) = -\sec x$

56. $\cos 2x = \cos^2 x - \sin^2 x$ (Hint: $\cos 2x = \cos (x + x)$)

57. $\cos (x + y) + \cos (x - y) = 2 \cos x \cos y$

58. $\dfrac{\cos (\alpha - \theta) - \cos (\alpha + \theta)}{\cos (\alpha - \theta) + \cos (\alpha + \theta)} = \tan \theta \tan \alpha$

59. $1 + \cos 2x - \cos^2 x = \cos^2 x$ (Hint: use the result in Exercise 56.)

60. $\cos (\pi + s - t) = -\sin s \sin t - \cos s \cos t$

61. $\cos (\pi/2 + s - t) = \sin (t - s)$

62. Use the identity for cosine of the sum and difference of two angles to complete each of the following. See Example 4.

$\cos (0° - \theta) =$
$\cos (90° - \theta) =$
$\cos (180° - \theta) =$
$\cos (270° - \theta) =$
$\cos (0° + \theta) =$
$\cos (90° + \theta) =$
$\cos (180° + \theta) =$
$\cos (270° + \theta) =$

63. Use the identity $\cos (90° - \theta) = \sin \theta$, and replace θ with $90° - A$, to derive the identity $\cos A = \sin (90° - A)$.

64. Use the results of Exercise 63 and derive the identity $\tan \theta = \cot (90° - \theta)$.

Let $\sin s = -0.09463$ and $\cos t = 0.83499$, where s terminates in quadrant III and t in quadrant IV. Find each of the following.

65. $\cos (s - t)$ 66. $\cos (s + t)$

67. $\cos 2s$ 68. $\cos 2t$

69. Let $f(x) = \cos x$. Prove that

$$\frac{f(x + h) - f(x)}{h} = \cos x \left(\frac{\cos h - 1}{h} \right) - \sin x \left(\frac{\sin h}{h} \right)$$

5.4 Sum and Difference Identities for Sine and Tangent

Formulas for $\sin (A + B)$ and $\sin (A - B)$ can be developed from the results of Section 5.3. The cofunction relationship gives

$$\sin \theta = \cos (90° - \theta).$$

Replace θ with $A + B$.

$$\sin (A + B) = \cos [90° - (A + B)]$$
$$= \cos [(90° - A) - B].$$

Using the formula for $\cos (A - B)$ from the previous section gives

$$= \cos (90° - A) \cos B + \sin (90° - A) \sin B$$

$$\sin (A + B) = \sin A \cos B + \cos A \sin B.$$

(In the last step we substituted from the cofunction relationships.)

If we now write $\sin (A - B)$ as $\sin [A + (-B)]$ and use the identity for $\sin (A + B)$ we have

$$\sin (A - B) = \sin A \cos B - \cos A \sin B.$$

Using the identities for $\sin (A + B)$, $\cos (A + B)$, $\sin (A - B)$, and $\cos (A - B)$, and the identity $\tan \theta = \sin \theta/\cos \theta$, we get the following identities.

$$\tan (A + B) = \frac{\tan A + \tan B}{1 - \tan A \tan B}$$

$$\tan (A - B) = \frac{\tan A - \tan B}{1 + \tan A \tan B}$$

We show the proof for the first of these two identities. The proof for the other is very similar.

$$\tan (A + B) = \frac{\sin (A + B)}{\cos (A + B)}$$

$$= \frac{\sin A \cos B + \cos A \sin B}{\cos A \cos B - \sin A \sin B}$$

To express this result in terms of the tangent function, multiply both numerator and denominator by $1/(\cos A \cos B)$.

$$= \frac{\dfrac{\sin A \cos B + \cos A \sin B}{1}}{\dfrac{\cos A \cos B - \sin A \sin B}{1}} \cdot \frac{\dfrac{1}{\cos A \cos B}}{\dfrac{1}{\cos A \cos B}}$$

$$= \frac{\dfrac{\sin A \cos B}{\cos A \cos B} + \dfrac{\cos A \sin B}{\cos A \cos B}}{\dfrac{\cos A \cos B}{\cos A \cos B} - \dfrac{\sin A \sin B}{\cos A \cos B}}$$

$$= \frac{\dfrac{\sin A}{\cos A} + \dfrac{\sin B}{\cos B}}{1 - \dfrac{\sin A}{\cos A} \cdot \dfrac{\sin B}{\cos B}}$$

Using the identity $\tan \theta = \sin \theta / \cos \theta$,

$$\tan (A + B) = \frac{\tan A + \tan B}{1 - \tan A \tan B}$$

Similar formulas can be found for the remaining trigonometric functions. However, they are seldom used, so we do not give them here.

EXAMPLE 1   Find each of the following.

(a) $\sin 75° = \sin (45° + 30°)$

$$= \sin 45° \cos 30° + \cos 45° \sin 30°$$

$$= \frac{\sqrt{2}}{2} \cdot \frac{\sqrt{3}}{2} + \frac{\sqrt{2}}{2} \cdot \frac{1}{2}$$

$$\sin 75° = \frac{\sqrt{6}}{4} + \frac{\sqrt{2}}{4} = \frac{\sqrt{6} + \sqrt{2}}{4}$$

(b) $\tan 105° = \tan (60° + 45°)$

$$= \frac{\tan 60° + \tan 45°}{1 - \tan 60° \tan 45°}$$

$$= \frac{\sqrt{3} + 1}{1 - \sqrt{3} \cdot 1}$$

To simplify this result, rationalize the denominator by multiplying numerator and denominator by $1 + \sqrt{3}$.

$$= \frac{\sqrt{3} + 1}{1 - \sqrt{3}} \cdot \frac{1 + \sqrt{3}}{1 + \sqrt{3}}$$

$$= \frac{\sqrt{3} + 3 + 1 + \sqrt{3}}{1 - 3}$$

$$= \frac{4 + 2\sqrt{3}}{-2}$$

$$\tan 105° = -2 - \sqrt{3} \qquad \bullet$$

EXAMPLE 2 If $\sin A = 4/5$ and $\cos B = -5/13$, where A is in quadrant II and B is in quadrant III, find each of the following.

(a) $\sin (A + B)$

Use the identity for the sine of the sum of two angles,

$$\sin (A + B) = \sin A \cos B + \cos A \sin B.$$

To find $\cos A$ and $\sin B$, use the identity $\sin^2 x + \cos^2 x = 1$. Let us first find $\cos A$.

$$\sin^2 A + \cos^2 A = 1$$

$$\frac{16}{25} + \cos^2 A = 1$$

$$\cos^2 A = \frac{9}{25}$$

$$\cos A = -\frac{3}{5} \qquad A \text{ is in quadrant II.}$$

In the same way, check that $\sin B = -12/13$. Now

$$\sin (A + B) = \frac{4}{5}\left(-\frac{5}{13}\right) + \left(-\frac{3}{5}\right)\left(-\frac{12}{13}\right)$$

$$= \frac{-20}{65} + \frac{36}{65}$$

$$\sin (A + B) = \frac{16}{65}.$$

(b) $\tan (A + B)$

Use the identity

$$\tan (A + B) = \frac{\tan A + \tan B}{1 - \tan A \tan B}.$$

Here we have $\tan A = -4/3$ and $\tan B = 12/5$ (where did we get these values?), so

$$\tan (A + B) = \frac{-\dfrac{4}{3} + \dfrac{12}{5}}{1 - \left(-\dfrac{4}{3}\right)\left(\dfrac{12}{5}\right)} = \frac{\dfrac{16}{15}}{1 + \dfrac{48}{15}} = \frac{\dfrac{16}{15}}{\dfrac{63}{15}} = \frac{16}{63} \quad \bullet$$

EXAMPLE 3   Write each of the following as a function of θ.

(a) $\sin (30° + \theta)$

Using the identity for $\sin (A + B)$,

$$\sin (30° + \theta) = \sin 30° \cos \theta + \cos 30° \sin \theta$$

$$\sin (30° + \theta) = \frac{1}{2} \cos \theta + \frac{\sqrt{3}}{2} \sin \theta$$

(b) $\tan (45° - \theta) = \dfrac{\tan 45° - \tan \theta}{1 + \tan 45° \tan \theta}$

$$\tan (45° - \theta) = \frac{1 - \tan \theta}{1 + \tan \theta}. \quad \bullet$$

5.4 EXERCISES   *Use the identities of this section to find the value of each of the following without using calculators or tables. See Example* 1.

1. $\sin 15°$

2. $\sin 105°$

3. $\tan 15°$

4. $\tan (-105°)$

5. $\sin (-105°)$

6. $\tan \dfrac{5\pi}{12}$

7. $\sin \dfrac{5\pi}{12}$

8. $\sin 285°$

9. $\sin 76° \cos 31° - \cos 76° \sin 31°$

10. $\sin 40° \cos 50° + \cos 40° \sin 50°$

11. $\dfrac{\tan 80° + \tan 55°}{1 - \tan 80° \tan 55°}$

12. $\dfrac{\tan 80° - \tan (-55°)}{1 + \tan 80° \tan (-55°)}$

13. $\dfrac{\tan 100° + \tan 80°}{1 - \tan 100° \tan 80°}$

14. $\sin 100° \cos 10° - \cos 100° \sin 10°$

15. $\sin 80° \cos (-55°) - \cos 80° \sin (-55°)$

16. $\dfrac{\tan 40° + \tan 5°}{1 - \tan 40° \tan 5°}$

Write each of the following as a function of θ. See Example 3.

17. $\sin (45° + \theta)$ **18.** $\sin (\theta - 30°)$

19. $\tan (\theta + 30°)$ **20.** $\tan (60° - \theta)$

21. $\sin (180° - \theta)$ **22.** $\sin (270° - \theta)$

23. $\tan (180° + \theta)$ **24.** $\tan (0° - \theta)$

25. $\sin (180° + \theta)$ **26.** $\tan (180° - \theta)$

For each of the following, find sin (s + t), sin (s − t), tan (s + t), and tan (s − t). See Example 2.

27. $\cos s = 3/5$ and $\sin t = 5/13$, s and t in quadrant I

28. $\cos s = -1/5$ and $\sin t = 3/5$, s and t in quadrant II

29. $\sin s = 2/3$ and $\sin t = -1/3$, s in quadrant II and t in quadrant IV

30. $\sin s = 3/5$ and $\sin t = -12/13$, s in quadrant I and t in quadrant III

31. $\cos s = -8/17$ and $\cos t = -3/5$, s and t in quadrant III

32. $\cos s = -15/17$ and $\sin t = 4/5$, s in quadrant II and t in quadrant I

33. $\sin s = -4/5$ and $\cos t = 12/13$, s in quadrant III and t in quadrant IV

34. $\sin s = -5/13$ and $\sin t = 3/5$, s in quadrant III and t in quadrant II

35. $\sin s = -8/17$ and $\cos t = -8/17$, s and t in quadrant III

36. $\sin s = 2/3$ and $\sin t = 2/5$, s and t in quadrant I

Verify that each of the following are identities.

37. $\sin \left(\dfrac{\pi}{2} + x\right) = \cos x$ **38.** $\sin \left(\dfrac{3\pi}{2} + x\right) = -\cos x$

39. $\tan \left(\dfrac{\pi}{2} + x\right) = -\cot x$ $\left(\text{Hint: } \tan \theta = \dfrac{\sin \theta}{\cos \theta}\right)$ **40.** $\tan \left(\dfrac{\pi}{4} + x\right) = \dfrac{1 + \tan x}{1 - \tan x}$

41. $\sin 2x = 2 \sin x \cos x$ (Hint: $\sin 2x = \sin (x + x)$)

42. $\sin (x + y) + \sin (x - y) = 2 \sin x \cos y$

43. $\sin (x + y) - \sin (x - y) = 2 \cos x \sin y$

44. $\tan (x - y) - \tan (y - x) = \dfrac{2(\tan x - \tan y)}{1 + \tan x \tan y}$

45. $\sin (30° + \alpha) + \cos (60° + \alpha) = \cos \alpha$

46. $\sin (210° + x) - \cos (120° + x) = 0$

47. $\dfrac{\cos (\alpha - \beta)}{\cos \alpha \sin \beta} = \tan \alpha + \cot \beta$

48. $\dfrac{\sin (s + t)}{\cos s \cos t} = \tan s + \tan t$

Let $\sin s = 0.599832$, *where s terminates in quadrant II. Let* $\sin t = -0.845992$, *where t terminates in quadrant III. Find each of the following.*

49. $\sin (s + t)$

50. $\sin (s - t)$

51. $\tan (s + t)$

52. $\sin 2s$

53. $\tan 2t$

54. $\sin 2t$

5.5   Reduction of *a* sin θ ± *b* cos θ to *k* sin (θ ± α)   (Optional)

The expressions $a \sin \theta + b \cos \theta$ and $a \sin \theta - b \cos \theta$ occur so frequently that it is useful to have a way of rewriting them in a simpler form. To find this simpler form, rewrite $a \sin \theta + b \cos \theta$ as follows.

$$a \sin \theta + b \cos \theta = \frac{\sqrt{a^2 + b^2}}{\sqrt{a^2 + b^2}} (a \sin \theta + b \cos \theta)$$

$$= \sqrt{a^2 + b^2} \left(\frac{a}{\sqrt{a^2 + b^2}} \sin \theta + \frac{b}{\sqrt{a^2 + b^2}} \cos \theta \right)$$

$$= \sqrt{a^2 + b^2} \left(\sin \theta \frac{a}{\sqrt{a^2 + b^2}} + \cos \theta \frac{b}{\sqrt{a^2 + b^2}} \right). \quad (1)$$

Now choose angle α so that

$$\sin \alpha = \frac{b}{\sqrt{a^2 + b^2}} \quad \text{and} \quad \cos \alpha = \frac{a}{\sqrt{a^2 + b^2}}.$$

See Figure 5.4.

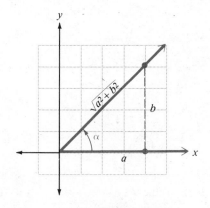

Figure 5.4

Substitute the values of $\sin \alpha$ and $\cos \alpha$ into equation (1).

$$a \sin \theta + b \cos \theta = \sqrt{a^2 + b^2} (\sin \theta \cos \alpha + \cos \theta \sin \alpha)$$

Using the identity for $\sin (A + B)$,

$$a \sin \theta + b \cos \theta = \sqrt{a^2 + b^2} \sin (\theta + \alpha).$$

This identity is called a **reduction identity**.

EXAMPLE 1 Simplify $\frac{1}{2} \sin \theta + \frac{\sqrt{3}}{2} \cos \theta$ using the reduction identity given above.

From the identity above, $a = \frac{1}{2}$ and $b = \frac{\sqrt{3}}{2}$, so that

$$a \sin \theta + b \cos \theta = \sqrt{a^2 + b^2} \sin (\theta + \alpha)$$

becomes

$$\frac{1}{2} \sin \theta + \frac{\sqrt{3}}{2} \cos \theta = 1 \cdot \sin (\theta + \alpha),$$

where angle α satisfies the conditions

$$\sin \alpha = \frac{b}{\sqrt{a^2 + b^2}} = \frac{\sqrt{3}}{2} \quad \text{and} \quad \cos \alpha = \frac{a}{\sqrt{a^2 + b^2}} = \frac{1}{2}.$$

The smallest possible positive value of α that satisfies both of these conditions is $\alpha = 60°$. Thus,

$$\frac{1}{2} \sin \theta + \frac{\sqrt{3}}{2} \cos \theta = \sin (\theta + 60°). \qquad \bullet$$

EXAMPLE 2 Express $2 \sin (\theta - 60°)$ as $a \sin \theta + b \cos \theta$, where a and b are constants.

First write

$$2 \sin (\theta - 60°) = 2 \sin [\theta + (-60°)].$$

From the reduction identity,

$$\sin (-60°) = \frac{b}{\sqrt{a^2 + b^2}} = \frac{b}{2},$$

and

$$\cos (-60°) = \frac{a}{\sqrt{a^2 + b^2}} = \frac{a}{2}.$$

Since $\sin (-60°) = b/2$, and since $\sin (-60°) = -\sin 60°$,

$$\sin 60° = -\frac{b}{2}$$

$$\frac{\sqrt{3}}{2} = -\frac{b}{2}$$

$$b = -\sqrt{3}.$$

In the same way, verify that $a = 1$. Thus,

$$2 \sin (\theta - 60°) = \sin \theta - \sqrt{3} \cos \theta. \qquad \bullet$$

The method of Example 2 is not the best method of working this problem; using the identity for $\sin (A - B)$ would have been faster. However, we show this method to illustrate the reduction identity.

The reduction identity of this section is useful when graphing functions which are sums of sine and cosine functions. It can be used instead of the method of addition of ordinates that we discussed in Chapter 4.

EXAMPLE 3   Graph $y = \sin x + \cos x$.

Reduce $\sin x + \cos x$ as follows. Since $a = b = 1$, we have $\sqrt{a^2 + b^2} = \sqrt{2}$, and

$$\sin x + \cos x = \sqrt{2} \sin (x + \alpha).$$

To find α, let

$$\sin \alpha = \frac{b}{\sqrt{a^2 + b^2}} = \frac{1}{\sqrt{2}} \quad \text{and} \quad \cos \alpha = \frac{a}{\sqrt{a^2 + b^2}} = \frac{1}{\sqrt{2}}$$

Thus, $\alpha = \pi/4$ and

$$y = \sin x + \cos x = \sqrt{2} \sin \left(x + \frac{\pi}{4} \right).$$

The graph of this function has an amplitude of $\sqrt{2}$, a period of 2π, and a phase shift of $\pi/4$ to the left, as shown in Figure 5.5.   ●

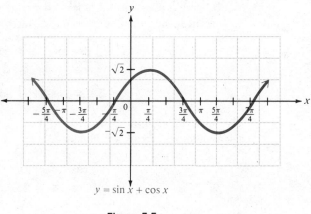

$y = \sin x + \cos x$

Figure 5.5

5.5 EXERCISES   *Use the reduction identity to simplify each of the following for angles between $0°$ and $360°$. Use a calculator or Table II to find angles to the nearest degree. Choose the smallest possible positive value of α. See Example 1.*

1. $-\sin x + \cos x$ 2. $\sqrt{3} \sin x - \cos x$

3. $5 \sin \theta - 12 \cos \theta$ 4. $12 \sin A + 5 \cos A$

5. $-15 \sin x + 8 \cos x$ 6. $15 \sin B - 8 \cos B$

7. $-7 \sin \theta - 24 \cos \theta$ 8. $24 \cos t - 7 \sin t$

9. $3 \sin x + 4 \cos x$ 10. $-4 \sin x + 3 \cos x$

Use the reduction identity to express each of the following as $a \sin \theta \pm b \cos \theta$. See Example 2.

11. $2 \sin (\theta + 120°)$ 12. $2 \sin (\theta - 30°)$

13. $\sqrt{2} \sin \left(\theta - \frac{\pi}{4} \right)$ 14. $\sqrt{2} \sin \left(\theta + \frac{3\pi}{4} \right)$

15. $\sin (\theta + 90°)$ **16.** $\sin (\theta - 90°)$

Graph each of the following by first changing the function to a sine function. See Example 3.

17. $y = \sqrt{3} \sin x + \cos x$ **18.** $y = \sin x - \sqrt{3} \cos x$

19. $y = -\sin x + \cos x$ **20.** $y = -\sin x - \cos x$

5.6 Double-Angle Identities

Some special cases of the identities for the sum of two angles are used often enough to be expressed as separate identities. These are the identities that result from the addition identities when $A = B$, so that $A + B = 2A$. These identities, called the **double-angle identities,** are derived in this section.

In the identity for $\cos (A + B)$, we let $B = A$ to derive an expression for $\cos 2A$.

$$\cos 2A = \cos (A + A)$$
$$= \cos A \cos A - \sin A \sin A$$
$$\mathbf{\cos 2A = \cos^2 A - \sin^2 A}$$

By substitution from either $\cos^2 A = 1 - \sin^2 A$ or $\sin^2 A = 1 - \cos^2 A$, two useful alternate forms are obtained.

$$\mathbf{\cos 2A = 1 - 2 \sin^2 A}$$
$$\mathbf{\cos 2A = 2 \cos^2 A - 1}$$

We can do the same thing with $\sin (A + B)$.

$$\sin 2A = \sin (A + A)$$
$$= \sin A \cos A + \cos A \sin A$$
$$\mathbf{\sin 2A = 2 \sin A \cos A.}$$

Find $\tan 2A$ from the identity for $\tan (A + B)$.

$$\tan 2A = \tan (A + A)$$
$$= \frac{\tan A + \tan A}{1 - \tan A \tan A}$$
$$\mathbf{\tan 2A = \frac{2 \tan A}{1 - \tan^2 A}}$$

These identities, together with the addition identities, allow us to rewrite trigonometric functions of multiple angles of A in terms of A, as show in the next example.

EXAMPLE 1   Write sin $3s$ in terms of sin s.

$$\sin 3s = \sin (2s + s)$$
$$= \sin 2s \cos s + \cos 2s \sin s$$
$$= (2 \sin s \cos s)\cos s + (\cos^2 s - \sin^2 s)\sin s$$
$$= 2 \sin s \cos^2 s + \cos^2 s \sin s - \sin^3 s$$
$$= 2 \sin s(1 - \sin^2 s) + (1 - \sin^2 s)\sin s - \sin^3 s$$
$$= 2 \sin s - 2 \sin^3 s + \sin s - \sin^3 s - \sin^3 s$$
$$\sin 3s = 3 \sin s - 4 \sin^3 s \quad \bullet$$

The double-angle identities for $2A$ can be used to find values of the trigonometric functions of A. The following example shows this use.

EXAMPLE 2   Find the values of the six trigonometric functions of θ if cos $2\theta = 4/5$ and θ terminates in quadrant II.
Use one of the double-angle identities for cosine.

$$\cos 2\theta = 1 - 2 \sin^2 \theta$$

$$\frac{4}{5} = 1 - 2 \sin^2 \theta$$

$$-\frac{1}{5} = -2 \sin^2 \theta$$

$$\frac{1}{10} = \sin^2 \theta$$

$$\sin \theta = \frac{\sqrt{10}}{10}.$$

Use the positive square root since θ terminates in quadrant II. Values of cos θ and tan θ can now be found using the fundamental identities.

$$\sin^2 \theta + \cos^2 \theta = 1$$

$$\frac{1}{10} + \cos^2 \theta = 1$$

$$\cos^2 \theta = \frac{9}{10}$$

$$\cos \theta = \frac{-3}{\sqrt{10}}$$

$$\cos \theta = \frac{-3\sqrt{10}}{10}$$

Verify that tan θ = sin θ/cos θ = $-1/3$. Find the other three functions using reciprocals.

$$\csc \theta = \frac{1}{\sin \theta} = \sqrt{10} \qquad \sec \theta = \frac{1}{\cos \theta} = \frac{-\sqrt{10}}{3} \qquad \cot \theta = \frac{1}{\tan \theta} = -3 \quad \bullet$$

EXAMPLE 3   Given $\cos \theta = 3/5$, where $3\pi/2 < \theta < 2\pi$, find $\cos 2\theta$, $\sin 2\theta$, and $\tan 2\theta$.

Since $\cos \theta = 3/5$, we can show that $\sin \theta = \pm 4/5$ by using the identity $\sin^2 \theta + \cos^2 \theta = 1$. Since θ terminates in quadrant IV, choose $\sin \theta = -4/5$. Then, using the double-angle identities,

$$\sin 2\theta = 2 \sin \theta \cos \theta = 2\left(-\frac{4}{5}\right)\left(\frac{3}{5}\right) = -\frac{24}{25}$$

$$\cos 2\theta = \cos^2 \theta - \sin^2 \theta = \frac{9}{25} - \frac{16}{25} = -\frac{7}{25}$$

$$\tan 2\theta = \frac{\sin 2\theta}{\cos 2\theta} = \frac{-24/25}{-7/25} = \frac{24}{7}.$$

We can also find $\tan 2\theta$ by noting that $\tan \theta = -4/3$, so that

$$\tan 2\theta = \frac{2 \tan \theta}{1 - \tan^2 \theta} = \frac{2\left(-\frac{4}{3}\right)}{1 - \frac{16}{9}} = \frac{-\frac{8}{3}}{-\frac{7}{9}} = \frac{24}{7}. \quad \bullet$$

5.6 EXERCISES   *Use the identities of this section to complete the following equations.*

1. $2 \sin \dfrac{\pi}{5} \cos \dfrac{\pi}{5} = \sin \underline{\hspace{1cm}}$

2. $\cos^2 10° - \sin^2 10° = \cos \underline{\hspace{1cm}}$

3. $4 \cos^2 x - 2 = 2\,(\underline{\hspace{1cm}})$

4. $\dfrac{2 \tan \dfrac{\pi}{3}}{1 - \tan^2 \dfrac{\pi}{3}} = \tan \underline{\hspace{1cm}}$

5. $\sin 320° = 2 \sin \underline{\hspace{1cm}} \cos \underline{\hspace{1cm}}$

6. $\sin 2(\underline{\hspace{1cm}}) = 2 \sin 37° \cos \underline{\hspace{1cm}}$

7. $\tan 8k = \dfrac{2 \tan \underline{\hspace{1cm}}}{1 - \underline{\hspace{1cm}}}$

8. $\sin 4p = \underline{\hspace{1cm}} 2p \underline{\hspace{1cm}} 2p$

9. $\cos 6x = \underline{\hspace{1cm}} 3x - \underline{\hspace{1cm}} 3x$

10. $\tan 10x = \dfrac{\underline{\hspace{1cm}} 5x}{1 - \underline{\hspace{1cm}}}$

Use the identities of this section to find values of the six trigonometric functions for each of the following. See Examples 2 and 3.

11. θ, given $\cos 2\theta = 3/5$ and θ terminates in quadrant I

12. α, given $\cos 2\alpha = 3/4$ and α terminates in quadrant III

13. x, given $\cos 2x = -5/12$, with $\pi/2 < x < \pi$

14. t, given $\cos 2t = 2/3$ and $\pi/2 < t < \pi$

15. 2θ, given $\sin \theta = 2/5$ and $\cos \theta < 0$

16. 2β, given $\cos \beta = -12/13$ and $\sin \beta > 0$

17. $2x$, given $\tan x = 2$ and $\cos x > 0$

18. $2x$, given $\tan x = 5/3$ and $\sin x < 0$

Express each of the following as trigonometric functions of x. See Example 1.

19. $\tan^2 2x$ **20.** $\cos^2 2x$ **21.** $\cos 3x$

22. $\sin 4x$ **23.** $\cos 4x$ **24.** $\tan 4x$

Verify each of the following identities.

25. $(\sin \gamma + \cos \gamma)^2 = \sin 2\gamma + 1$

26. $\cos 2s = \cos^4 s - \sin^4 s$

27. $\sec 2x = \dfrac{\sec^2 x + \sec^4 x}{2 + \sec^2 x - \sec^4 x}$

28. $\sin 2\theta = \dfrac{4 \tan \theta \cos^2 \theta - 2 \tan \theta}{1 - \tan^2 \theta}$

29. $\cot 2\beta = \dfrac{\cot^2 \beta - 1}{2 \cot \beta}$

30. $\tan 8k - \tan 8k \cdot \tan^2 4k = 2 \tan 4k$

31. $\sin 2\gamma = \dfrac{2 \tan \gamma}{1 + \tan^2 \gamma}$

32. $-\tan 2\theta = \dfrac{2 \tan \theta}{\sec^2 \theta - 2}$

33. $\cos 2y = \dfrac{2 - \sec^2 y}{\sec^2 y}$

34. $\cot s + \tan s = 2 \csc 2s$

35. $\sin 4\alpha = 4 \sin \alpha \cos \alpha \cos 2\alpha$

36. $\dfrac{1 + \cos 2x}{\sin 2x} = \cot x$

37. $\tan (\theta - 45°) + \tan (\theta + 45°) = 2 \tan 2\theta$

38. $\cot 4\theta = \dfrac{1 - \tan^2 2\theta}{2 \tan 2\theta}$

39. $\dfrac{2 \cos 2\alpha}{\sin 2\alpha} = \cot \alpha - \tan \alpha$

40. $\sin 4\gamma = 4 \sin \gamma \cos \gamma - 8 \sin^3 \gamma \cos \gamma$

41. $\sin 2\alpha \cos 2\alpha = \sin 2\alpha - 4 \sin^3 \alpha \cos \alpha$

42. $\dfrac{\sin^3 t - \cos^3 t}{\sin t - \cos t} = \dfrac{2 + \sin 2t}{2}$

Let sin s = −0.481143, with 3π/2 < s < 2π. Find each of the following.

43. $\sin 2s$ **44.** $\cos 2s$ **45.** $\tan 2s$ **46.** $\sec 2s$

5.7 Half-Angle Identities

From the alternate forms of the double-angle identity for cosine, we can derive three additional identities. These **half-angle identities**, listed below, are quite useful in the study of calculus.

$$\cos \frac{A}{2} = \pm \sqrt{\frac{1 + \cos A}{2}}$$

$$\sin \frac{A}{2} = \pm \sqrt{\frac{1 - \cos A}{2}}$$

$$\tan \frac{A}{2} = \pm \sqrt{\frac{1 - \cos A}{1 + \cos A}}$$

There are two alternate forms for the last identity which are sometimes preferred.

$$\tan \frac{A}{2} = \frac{\sin A}{1 + \cos A}$$

$$\tan \frac{A}{2} = \frac{1 - \cos A}{\sin A}$$

In these identities, the plus or minus sign is selected according to the quadrant in which $A/2$ terminates. For example, if A represents an angle of 324°, then $A/2 = 162°$, which lies in quadrant II. Thus, $\cos A/2$ and $\tan A/2$ would be negative, while $\sin A/2$ would be positive.

To derive the identity for $\sin A/2$, start with the following double-angle identity for cosine.

$$\cos 2x = 1 - 2 \sin^2 x$$

$$2 \sin^2 x = 1 - \cos 2x$$

$$\sin x = \pm \sqrt{\frac{1 - \cos 2x}{2}}$$

Now let $2x = A$, so that $x = A/2$, and substitute into this last expression.

$$\sin \frac{A}{2} = \pm \sqrt{\frac{1 - \cos A}{2}}$$

The identity for $\cos A/2$ is derived in exactly the same way, starting with the double-angle identity $\cos 2x = 2 \cos^2 x - 1$. Finally, the identity for $\tan A/2$ comes from the half-angle identities for sine and cosine.

$$\tan \frac{A}{2} = \frac{\pm \sqrt{\dfrac{1 - \cos A}{2}}}{\pm \sqrt{\dfrac{1 + \cos A}{2}}}$$

$$\tan \frac{A}{2} = \pm \sqrt{\frac{1 - \cos A}{1 + \cos A}}$$

The following examples show the use of these identities.

EXAMPLE 1   Find tan 22.5°.

Since 22.5° = 45°/2, we can use the half-angle identity for tangent.

$$\tan 22.5° = \tan \frac{45°}{2}$$

$$= \sqrt{\frac{1 - \cos 45°}{1 + \cos 45°}}$$

$$= \sqrt{\frac{1 - \dfrac{\sqrt{2}}{2}}{1 + \dfrac{\sqrt{2}}{2}}}$$

$$= \sqrt{\frac{2 - \sqrt{2}}{2 + \sqrt{2}}}$$

$$\tan 22.5° = \sqrt{3 - 2\sqrt{2}}$$

In the last step we rationalized the denominator under the radical sign, using the positive value of the radical since 22.5° is in quadrant I.   ●

EXAMPLE 2   Given cos s = 2/3, with s terminating in quadrant IV, find cos $s/2$, sin $s/2$, and tan $s/2$.

Since s terminates in quadrant IV, we have $3\pi/2 < s < 2\pi$, so that $3\pi/4 < s/2 < \pi$. Thus, $s/2$ terminates in quadrant II and cos $s/2$ and tan $s/2$ are negative, while sin $s/2$ is positive. Using the half-angle identities gives

$$\sin \frac{s}{2} = \sqrt{\frac{1 - \dfrac{2}{3}}{2}} = \sqrt{\frac{1}{6}} = \frac{\sqrt{6}}{6}$$

$$\cos \frac{s}{2} = -\sqrt{\frac{1 + \dfrac{2}{3}}{2}} = -\sqrt{\frac{5}{6}} = -\frac{\sqrt{30}}{6}$$

$$\tan \frac{s}{2} = \frac{\dfrac{\sqrt{6}}{6}}{-\dfrac{\sqrt{30}}{6}} = \frac{-\sqrt{5}}{5}.$$ ●

5.7 EXERCISES   *Use the identities of this section to complete the following.*

1. $\sin \underline{\qquad} = \sqrt{\dfrac{1 - \cos 18°}{2}}$

2. $\sin 42° = \sqrt{\dfrac{1 - \cos \underline{\qquad}}{2}}$

3. $\cos \underline{\qquad} = -\sqrt{\dfrac{1 + \cos 388°}{2}}$

4. $\cos \underline{\hspace{1cm}} = \sqrt{\dfrac{\underline{\hspace{1cm}}\cos 44°}{2}}$

5. $\underline{\hspace{2cm}} = -\sqrt{\dfrac{1 - \cos 340°}{1 + \cos 340°}}$

6. $\underline{\hspace{2cm}} = \sqrt{\dfrac{1 + \cos 40°}{2}}$

For each of the following, determine whether the positive or negative square root should be selected.

7. $\sin 195° = \pm \sqrt{\dfrac{1 - \cos 390°}{2}}$

8. $\cos 58° = \pm \sqrt{\dfrac{1 + \cos 116°}{2}}$

9. $\tan 225° = \pm \sqrt{\dfrac{1 - \cos 450°}{1 + \cos 450°}}$

10. $\sin(-10°) = \pm \sqrt{\dfrac{1 - \cos(-20°)}{2}}$

Use the identities of this section to find the sine, cosine, and tangent for each of the following. See Examples 1 and 2.

11. $\theta = 22\frac{1}{2}°$ **12.** $\theta = 15°$ **13.** $\theta = 195°$ **14.** $\theta = 67\frac{1}{2}°$

15. $x = -\pi/8$ **16.** $x = -5\pi/6$ **17.** $x = 5\pi/2$ **18.** $x = 3\pi/2$

Find each of the following. See Example 2.

19. $\sin \theta$, given $\cos 2\theta = 3/5$ and θ terminates in quadrant I

20. $\cos \theta$, given $\cos 2\theta = 1/2$ and θ terminates in quadrant II

21. $\cos x$, given $\cos 2x = -5/12$ and $\pi/2 < x < \pi$

22. $\sin x$, given $\cos 2x = 2/3$ and $\pi < x < 3\pi/2$

Verify that each of the following equations is an identity.

23. $\sec^2 \dfrac{x}{2} = \dfrac{2}{1 + \cos x}$

24. $\cot^2 \dfrac{x}{2} = \dfrac{(1 + \cos x)^2}{\sin^2 x}$

25. $\sin^2 \dfrac{x}{2} = \dfrac{\tan x - \sin x}{2 \tan x}$

26. $\dfrac{\sin 2x}{2 \sin x} = \cos^2 \dfrac{x}{2} - \sin^2 \dfrac{x}{2}$

27. $\dfrac{2}{1 + \cos x} - \tan^2 \dfrac{x}{2} = 1$

28. $\tan \dfrac{\theta}{2} = \dfrac{\sin \theta}{1 + \cos \theta}$

29. $\tan \dfrac{\alpha}{2} = \dfrac{1 - \cos \alpha}{\sin \alpha}$

30. $\tan \dfrac{\gamma}{2} = \csc \gamma - \cot \gamma$

31. $\dfrac{\tan \dfrac{x}{2} + \cot \dfrac{x}{2}}{\cot \dfrac{x}{2} - \tan \dfrac{x}{2}} = \sec x$

32. $1 - \tan^2 \dfrac{\theta}{2} = \dfrac{2 \cos \theta}{1 + \cos \theta}$

33. $\cos x = \dfrac{1 - \tan^2 \dfrac{x}{2}}{1 + \tan^2 \dfrac{x}{2}}$

34. $\dfrac{\sin 2\alpha - 2 \sin \alpha}{2 \sin \alpha + \sin 2\alpha} = -\tan^2 \dfrac{\alpha}{2}$

35. $8 \sin^2 \dfrac{\gamma}{2} \cos^2 \dfrac{\gamma}{2} = 1 - \cos 2\gamma$

36. $\cos^2 \dfrac{x}{2} = \dfrac{1 + \sec x}{2 \sec x}$

An airplane flying faster than sound sends out sound waves that form a cone, as shown in the figure. The cone intersects the ground to form a hyperbola. As this hyperbola passes over a particular point on the ground, a sonic boom is heard at that point.

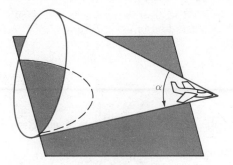

If α is the angle at the vertex of the cone, then

$$\sin \frac{\alpha}{2} = \frac{1}{m}$$

where m is the mach number of the plane. (We assume m > 1.) The mach number is the ratio of the speed of the plane and the speed of sound. Thus, a speed of mach 1.4 means that the plane is flying 1.4 times the speed of sound. Find α or m, as necessary, for each of the following.

37. $m = 3/2$ **38.** $m = 5/4$ **39.** $m = 2$ **40.** $m = 5/2$

41. $\alpha = 30°$ **42.** $\alpha = 60°$

Let cos s = −0.592147, with $\pi < s < 3\pi/2$. Use the identities of this section to find each of the following.

43. $\sin \frac{1}{2} s$ **44.** $\cos \frac{1}{2} s$ **45.** $\tan \frac{1}{2} s$ **46.** $\csc \frac{1}{2} s$

In Example 1, we used the identity

$$\tan s/2 = \pm \sqrt{(1 - \cos s)/(1 + \cos s)}$$

to find that $\tan 22.5° = \sqrt{3 - 2\sqrt{2}}$.

47. Find $\tan 22.5°$ with the identity $\tan s/2 = \sin s/(1 + \cos s)$.

48. Show that both answers are the same.

5.8   Sum and Product Identities   (Optional)

The identities given in this section are used less frequently than those in the preceding sections of this chapter. Yet they are important in further work in mathematics. One group of identities can be used to rewrite a product of two functions as a sum or difference. The other group can be used to rewrite a sum or difference of two functions as a product. Some of these identities can also be used to rewrite an expression involving both sine and cosine functions as an expression with only one of these functions. In Sections 6.3 and 6.4 on conditional equations, the need for this kind of change will become clear.

All of the identities that we discuss in this section result from the sum and difference identities for sine and cosine. For example, adding the two addition identities for $\sin(A + B)$ and $\sin(A - B)$ gives

$$\sin(A + B) = \sin A \cos B + \cos A \sin B$$
$$\underline{\sin(A - B) = \sin A \cos B - \cos A \sin B}$$
$$\sin(A + B) + \sin(A - B) = 2 \sin A \cos B,$$

or

$$\sin A \cos B = \frac{1}{2}[\sin(A + B) + \sin(A - B)].$$

If we subtract $\sin(A - B)$ from $\sin(A + B)$, the result is

$$\cos A \sin B = \frac{1}{2}[\sin(A + B) - \sin(A - B)].$$

Use the identities for $\cos(A + B)$ and $\cos(A - B)$ in a similar manner to get

$$\cos A \cos B = \frac{1}{2}[\cos(A + B) + \cos(A - B)]$$

$$\sin A \sin B = \frac{1}{2}[\cos(A - B) - \cos(A + B)].$$

EXAMPLE 1 Rewrite $\cos 2\theta \sin \theta$ as the sum or difference of two functions.
Use the identity for $\cos A \sin B$.

$$\cos 2\theta \sin \theta = \frac{1}{2}(\sin 3\theta - \sin \theta)$$

$$\cos 2\theta \sin \theta = \frac{1}{2}\sin 3\theta - \frac{1}{2}\sin \theta. \quad \bullet$$

EXAMPLE 2 Evaluate $\cos 15° \cos 45°$.
Use the identity for $\cos A \cos B$.

$$\cos 15° \cos 45° = \frac{1}{2}[\cos(15° + 45°) + \cos(15° - 45°)]$$

$$= \frac{1}{2}[\cos 60° + \cos(-30°)]$$

$$= \frac{1}{2}(\cos 60° + \cos 30°)$$

$$= \frac{1}{2}\left(\frac{1}{2} + \frac{\sqrt{3}}{2}\right)$$

$$\cos 15° \cos 45° = \frac{1 + \sqrt{3}}{4} \quad \bullet$$

Now we can use the identities from above to obtain identities that are used in calculus when we need to rewrite a sum of trigonometric functions as a product. To begin, let $A + B = x$, and let $A - B = y$. Then

$$A = \frac{x + y}{2} \quad \text{and} \quad B = \frac{x - y}{2}.$$

(To get these results, add x and y, then subtract x and y.) With these results, the identity

$$\sin A \cos B = \frac{1}{2} \left[\sin (A + B) + \sin (A - B) \right]$$

becomes

$$\sin \left(\frac{x + y}{2} \right) \cos \left(\frac{x - y}{2} \right) = \frac{1}{2} (\sin x + \sin y),$$

or

$$\sin x + \sin y = 2 \sin \left(\frac{x + y}{2} \right) \cos \left(\frac{x - y}{2} \right).$$

Three other identities can be obtained in a very similar way.

$$\sin x - \sin y = 2 \cos \left(\frac{x + y}{2} \right) \sin \left(\frac{x - y}{2} \right)$$

$$\cos x + \cos y = 2 \cos \left(\frac{x + y}{2} \right) \cos \left(\frac{x - y}{2} \right)$$

$$\cos x - \cos y = -2 \sin \left(\frac{x + y}{2} \right) \sin \left(\frac{x - y}{2} \right)$$

EXAMPLE 3   Write $\sin 2\gamma - \sin 4\gamma$ as a product of two functions.
Use the identity for $\sin x - \sin y$.

$$\sin 2\gamma - \sin 4\gamma = 2 \cos \left(\frac{2\gamma + 4\gamma}{2} \right) \sin \left(\frac{2\gamma - 4\gamma}{2} \right)$$

$$= 2 \cos \frac{6\gamma}{2} \sin \frac{-2\gamma}{2}$$

$$= 2 \cos 3\gamma \sin (-\gamma)$$

$$\sin 2\gamma - \sin 4\gamma = -2 \cos 3\gamma \sin \gamma. \quad \bullet$$

EXAMPLE 4   Verify that the equation $\dfrac{\sin 3s + \sin s}{\cos s + \cos 3s} = \tan 2s$ is an identity.
Work as follows.

$$\frac{\sin 3s + \sin s}{\cos s + \cos 3s} = \frac{2 \sin \left(\dfrac{3s + s}{2} \right) \cos \left(\dfrac{3s - s}{2} \right)}{2 \cos \left(\dfrac{s + 3s}{2} \right) \cos \left(\dfrac{s - 3s}{2} \right)}$$

$$= \frac{\sin 2s \cos s}{\cos 2s \cos (-s)}$$

$$= \frac{\sin 2s}{\cos 2s}$$

$$= \tan 2s. \quad \bullet$$

5.8 EXERCISES *Rewrite each of the following as a sum or difference of trigonometric functions.*

1. $\cos 45° \sin 25°$

2. $2 \sin 74° \cos 114°$

3. $3 \cos 5x \cos 3x$

4. $2 \sin 2x \sin 4x$

5. $\sin (-\theta) \sin (-3\theta)$

6. $4 \cos 8\alpha \sin (-4\alpha)$

7. $-8 \cos 4y \cos 5y$

8. $2 \sin 3k \sin 14k$

Rewrite each of the following as a product of trigonometric functions.

9. $\sin 60° - \sin 30°$

10. $\sin 28° + \sin (-18°)$

11. $\cos 42° + \cos 148°$

12. $\cos 2x - \cos 8x$

13. $\sin 12\beta - \sin 3\beta$

14. $\cos 5x + \cos 10x$

15. $-3 \sin 2x + 3 \sin 5x$

16. $-\cos 8s + \cos 14s$

Verify that each of the following is an identity.

17. $\tan x = \dfrac{\sin 3x - \sin x}{\cos 3x + \cos x}$

18. $\dfrac{\sin 5t + \sin 3t}{\cos 3t - \cos 5t} = \cot t$

19. $\dfrac{\cot 2\theta}{\tan 3\theta} = \dfrac{\cos 5\theta + \cos \theta}{\cos \theta - \cos 5\theta}$

20. $\dfrac{\cos \alpha + \cos \beta}{\cos \alpha - \cos \beta} = -\cot \left(\dfrac{\alpha + \beta}{2}\right) \cot \left(\dfrac{\alpha - \beta}{2}\right)$

21. $\dfrac{1}{\tan 2s} = \dfrac{\sin 3s - \sin s}{\cos s - \cos 3s}$

22. $\dfrac{\sin^2 5\alpha - 2 \sin 5\alpha \sin 3\alpha + \sin^2 3\alpha}{\sin^2 5\alpha - \sin^2 3\alpha} = \dfrac{\tan \alpha}{\tan 4\alpha}$

23. $\sin 6\theta \cos 4\theta - \sin 3\theta \cos 7\theta = \sin 3\theta \cos \theta$

24. $\sin 8\beta \sin 4\beta + \cos 10\beta \cos 2\beta = \cos 6\beta \cos 2\beta$

25. $\sin^2 u - \sin^2 v = \sin (u + v) \sin (u - v)$

26. $\cos^2 u - \cos^2 v = -\sin (u + v) \sin (u - v)$

27. Show that the double-angle identity for sine can be considered a special case of the identity $\sin s \cos t = (1/2)[\sin (s + t) + \sin (s - t)]$.

28. Show that the double-angle identity $\cos 2s = 2 \cos^2 s - 1$ is a special case of the identity $\cos s \cos t = \dfrac{1}{2} [\cos (s + t) + \cos (s - t)]$.

ADDITIONAL EXERCISES *Show that each of the following is an identity.*

1. $\dfrac{\sin 2x}{\sin x} = \dfrac{2}{\sec x}$

2. $2 \cos A - \sec A = \cos A - \dfrac{\tan A}{\csc A}$

3. $\dfrac{2 \tan B}{\sin 2B} = \sec^2 B$

4. $\tan \beta = \dfrac{1 - \cos 2\beta}{\sin 2\beta}$

5. $1 + \tan^2 \alpha = 2 \tan \alpha \csc 2\alpha$

6. $-\dfrac{\sin (A - B)}{\sin (A + B)} = \dfrac{\cot A - \cot B}{\cot A + \cot B}$

7. $\dfrac{\sin t}{1 - \cos t} = \cot \dfrac{t}{2}$

8. $2 \cos (A + B) \sin (A + B) = \sin 2A \cos 2B + \sin 2B \cos 2A$

9. $\dfrac{2 \cot x}{\tan 2x} = \csc^2 x - 2$

10. $\sin t = \dfrac{\cos t \sin 2t}{1 + \cos 2t}$

11. $\tan \theta \sin 2\theta = 2 - 2 \cos^2 \theta$

12. $\csc A \sin 2A - \sec A = \cos 2A \sec A$

13. $2 \tan x \csc 2x - \tan^2 x = 1$

14. $2 \cos^2 \theta - 1 = \dfrac{1 - \tan^2 \theta}{1 + \tan^2 \theta}$

15. $\tan \theta \cos^2 \theta = \dfrac{2 \tan \theta \cos^2 \theta - \tan \theta}{1 - \tan^2 \theta}$ **16.** $-\cot \dfrac{x}{2} = \dfrac{\sin 2x + \sin x}{\cos 2x - \cos x}$

17. $2 \cos^3 x - \cos x = \dfrac{\cos^2 x - \sin^2 x}{\sec x}$ **18.** $\sin^3 \theta = \sin \theta - \cos^2 \theta \sin \theta$

19. $\cos^4 \theta = \dfrac{3}{8} + \dfrac{1}{2} \cos 2\theta + \dfrac{1}{8} \cos 4\theta$ **20.** $\tan \dfrac{7}{2} x = \dfrac{2 \tan \dfrac{7}{4} x}{1 - \tan^2 \dfrac{7}{4} x}$

21. $\sec^2 \alpha - 1 = \dfrac{\sec 2\alpha - 1}{\sec 2\alpha + 1}$ **22.** $\dfrac{\sin 3t + \sin 2t}{\sin 3t - \sin 2t} = \dfrac{\tan \dfrac{5t}{2}}{\tan \dfrac{t}{2}}$

23. $\tan 4\theta = \dfrac{2 \tan 2\theta}{2 - \sec^2 2\theta}$ **24.** $\sin 2\alpha = \dfrac{2(\sin \alpha - \sin^3 \alpha)}{\cos \alpha}$

Chapter 5 Test

1. Use the trigonometric identities to find the remaining five trigonometric functions of x, given that $\cos x = 3/5$ and x is in quadrant IV.

2. Given $\tan x = -5/4$, where $\pi/2 < x < \pi$, use trigonometric identities to find the other trigonometric functions of x.

3. Given $\sin x = -1/4$, $\cos y = -4/5$, and both x and y are in quadrant III, find $\sin (x + y)$ and $\cos (x - y)$.

4. Given $\sin 2\theta = \sqrt{3}/2$ and 2θ terminates in quadrant II, use trigonometric identities to find $\tan \theta$.

5. Given $x = \pi/8$, use trigonometric identities to find $\sin x$, $\cos x$, and $\tan x$.

For each item in Column I give the letter of the item in Column II which completes an identity.

Column I

6. $\sin 35°$

7. $\tan (-35°)$

8. $-\sin 35°$

9. $\cos 35°$

10. $\cos 75°$

11. $\sin 75°$

12. $\sin 300°$

13. $\cos 300°$

Column II

(a) $\sin (-35°)$

(b) $\cos 55°$

(c) $\sqrt{\dfrac{1 + \cos 150°}{2}}$

(d) $2 \sin 150° \cos 150°$

(e) $\cos 150° \cos 60° - \sin 150° \sin 60°$

(f) $\cot (-35°)$

(g) $\cos^2 150° - \sin^2 150°$

(h) $\sin 15° \cos 60° + \cos 15° \sin 60°$

(i) $\cos (-35°)$

(j) $\cot 125°$

For each item in Column I give the letter of the item in Column II which completes an identity.

Column I

14. $\sec x$

15. $\csc x$

16. $\tan x$

17. $\cot x$

18. $\sin^2 x$

19. $\tan^2 x + 1$

20. $\tan^2 x$

Column II

(a) $\dfrac{1}{\sin x}$

(b) $\dfrac{1}{\cos x}$

(c) $\dfrac{\sin x}{\cos x}$

(d) $\dfrac{1}{\cot^2 x}$

(e) $\dfrac{1}{\cos^2 x}$

(f) $\dfrac{\cos x}{\sin x}$

(g) $\dfrac{1}{\sin^2 x}$

(h) $1 - \cos^2 x$

Use identities to express each of the following in terms of $\sin \theta$ and $\cos \theta$, and simplify.

21. $\sec^2 \theta - \tan^2 \theta$

22. $\dfrac{\cot \theta}{\sec \theta}$

23. $\tan^2 \theta (1 + \cot^2 \theta)$

24. $\csc \theta + \cot \theta$

25. $\csc^2 \theta + \sec^2 \theta$

26. $\tan \theta - \sec \theta \csc \theta$

Verify that each of the following equations is an identity.

27. $\sin^2 x - \sin^2 y = \cos^2 y - \cos^2 x$

28. $2 \cos^3 x - \cos x = \dfrac{\cos^2 x - \sin^2 x}{\sec x}$

29. $-\cot \dfrac{x}{2} = \dfrac{\sin 2x + \sin x}{\cos 2x - \cos x}$

30. $\dfrac{\sin^2 x}{2 - 2 \cos x} = \cos^2 \dfrac{x}{2}$

6

Inverse Trigonometric Functions and Trigonometric Equations

In many applications of trigonometry, it is necessary to find an angle given its sine, or some other trigonometric function. To do this, we need an inverse trigonometric function. The first two sections of this chapter introduce these functions, then the last three sections explain how to solve *conditional* equations in which the variable is a trigonometric function or an inverse trigonometric function.

6.1 Inverse Functions

As we know, a function is a relation in which each value of x leads to exactly one value of y. In the function $y = 5x + 4$, two different values of x lead to two *different* values of y. But in the function $y = x^2$, two different values of x can lead to the *same* value of y. For example, $x = 4$ leads to $y = 4^2 = 16$, and $x = -4$ leads to $y = (-4)^2 = 16$. The different x-values, 4 and -4, lead to the same y-value, 16.

A function such as $y = 5x + 4$, where different x-values lead to different y-values, is called a **one-to-one function**.

EXAMPLE 1 Decide whether or not the following are one-to-one functions.

(a) $y = 4x + 12$ If we choose two different values of x, we always get two different values of y. Thus, $y = 4x + 12$ is a one-to-one function.

(b) $y = \sqrt{25 - x^2}$ If $x = 3$, then $y = \sqrt{25 - 3^2} = \sqrt{25 - 9} = \sqrt{16} = 4$. Also, if $x = -3$, then $y = 4$. Thus, two different values of x lead to the same value of y, and $y = \sqrt{25 - x^2}$ is not a one-to-one function.   ●

There is a useful graphical test which tells whether or not a function is one-to-one. Figure 6.1 shows the graph of a function cut by a horizontal line. Each point where the horizontal line cuts the graph has the same y-value, but a different x-value. In this graph three different values of x lead to the same value of y. Thus the function is not one-to-one.

This idea gives us the **horizontal line test**:

If it is possible to draw a horizontal line that cuts the graph of a function in more than one point, then the function is not one-to-one.

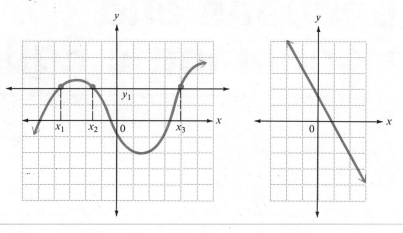

Figure 6.1   Figure 6.2

EXAMPLE 2   Is the function graphed in Figure 6.2, one-to-one?

A horizontal line never cuts this graph in more than one point. Therefore the function is one-to-one.   ●

One-to-one functions are important because, given a one-to-one function f, we can define another useful function from f, the *inverse function* of f. By definition, the inverse function of the one-to-one function f is found by interchanging the elements of the ordered pairs of f. That is, the **inverse function f^{-1}** (read "f inverse") is defined as

$$f^{-1} = \{(y, x) \mid (x, y) \text{ belongs to} f\}.$$

Suppose $f = \{(x, y) \mid y = 3x + 1\}$. If $x = 2$, then $y = 7$, so the ordered pair $(2, 7)$ belongs to f. Similarly $(4, 13)$ and $(-2, -5)$ belong to f. By the definition of an inverse function, $(7, 2)$, $(13, 4)$, and $(-5, -2)$ belong to f^{-1}.

To get the equation of the inverse function, use the definition and exchange x and y in the equation for f. If $f = \{(x, y) \mid y = 3x + 1\}$, then we can find f^{-1} by exchanging x and y in the equation $y = 3x + 1$. Doing this gives $x = 3y + 1$. We now solve for y.

$$x - 1 = 3y$$

$$\frac{x - 1}{3} = y$$

Since this is the equation of the inverse function, $f^{-1}(x)$ can be used to represent y, or

$$f^{-1}(x) = \frac{x-1}{3}.$$

EXAMPLE 3   For each of the following functions that is one-to-one, find the equation of its inverse function.

(a) $f(x) = \dfrac{4x+6}{5}$

This function is one-to-one and thus has an inverse. Let $f(x) = y$ and then exchange x and y. Finally, solve for y.

$$y = \frac{4x+6}{5}$$

$$x = \frac{4y+6}{5}$$

$$5x = 4y+6$$

$$y = \frac{5x-6}{4}$$

Replace y with $f^{-1}(x)$. Thus, $f^{-1}(x) = \dfrac{5x-6}{4}$.

(b) $f(x) = x^3 - 1$

This function is one-to-one and thus has an inverse. Begin with the equation $y = x^3 - 1$ and exchange x and y, to get $x = y^3 - 1$. Solving for y gives $y = \sqrt[3]{x+1}$, or $f^{-1}(x) = \sqrt[3]{x+1}$.

(c) $f(x) = x^2$

This function is not one-to-one, so it has no inverse function.   ●

The graph of an inverse can be obtained from the graph of a function. To see how, suppose that a point (a, b), shown in Figure 6.3, is on the graph of a function f. Then, the point (b, a) would belong to f^{-1}. The figure shows that the line

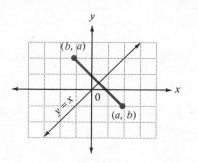

Figure 6.3

segment connecting (a, b) and (b, a) is cut in half by the line $y = x$. Because of this, (a, b) and (b, a) are "mirror images" of each other with respect to the line $y = x$.

If we are given the graph of a function f, the graph of f^{-1} can be found by locating the mirror image of each point of f with respect to the line $y = x$. Figure 6.4 shows the graph of f and f^{-1} from Example 3(a) above, while Figure 6.5 shows the graph of the function and its inverse from Example 3(b) above. In each case, f and f^{-1} are mirror images of each other with respect to the line $y = x$.

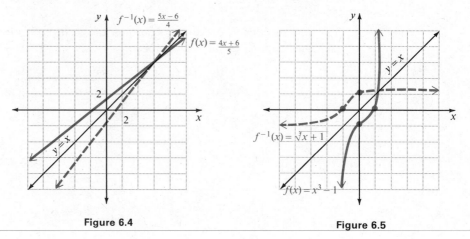

Figure 6.4   **Figure 6.5**

6.1 EXERCISES

Which of the following functions are one-to-one? See Example 2.

1.   **2.**   **3.**

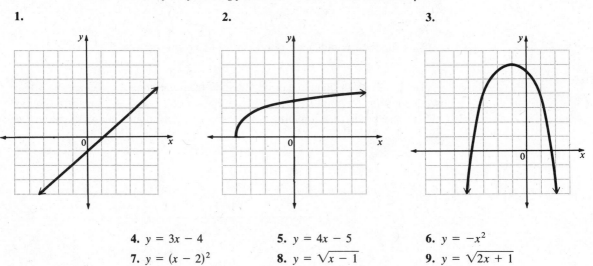

4. $y = 3x - 4$ **5.** $y = 4x - 5$ **6.** $y = -x^2$

7. $y = (x - 2)^2$ **8.** $y = \sqrt{x - 1}$ **9.** $y = \sqrt{2x + 1}$

10. $y = \dfrac{2}{x}$

Sketch the graph of the inverse of the following functions which are one-to-one.

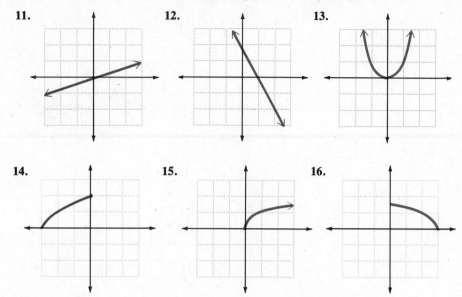

11.   **12.**   **13.**

14.   **15.**   **16.**

Sketch the graph of each of the following on the indicated interval, using a solid line. Then sketch the graph of the inverse, using a dashed line.

17. $y = \sin \theta, -\pi/2 \le \theta \le \pi/2$ **18.** $y = \cos \theta, 0 \le \theta \le \pi$

19. $y = \tan \theta, -\pi/2 < \theta < \pi/2$ **20.** $y = 2 \sin \theta, -\pi/2 \le \theta \le \pi/2$

For each of the following that is a one-to-one function, find an equation for its inverse. See Example 3.

21. $y = 2x$ **22.** $y + 1 = 3x$

23. $2y + 1 = 3x$ **24.** $5y + 6x = 30$

25. $y = 2x^2$ **26.** $2y - 1 = x^2$

27. $y + 1 = \sqrt[3]{x}$ **28.** $x = 2$

For a one-to-one function, f, and its inverse function, f^{-1}, it is always true that

$$f[f^{-1}(x)] = x \text{ and } f^{-1}[f(x)] = x.$$

Use this fact to decide if the following pairs of functions are inverses of each other.

EXAMPLE   Decide if $f(x) = 3x - 1$ and $g(x) = (x + 1)/3$ are inverses of each other.

Find $f[g(x)]$. $f[g(x)] = f\left(\dfrac{x + 1}{3}\right)$

$$= 3\left(\frac{x + 1}{3}\right) - 1$$

$$= x + 1 - 1$$

$$= x$$

Find $g[f(x)]$. $\quad g[f(x)] = g(3x - 1)$

$$= \frac{(3x - 1) + 1}{3}$$

$$= \frac{3x}{3}$$

$$= x$$

Since both $f[g(x)]$ and $g[f(x)]$ equal x, the functions are inverses of each other. ●

29. $f(x) = -8x$ and $g(x) = -\dfrac{1}{8}x$

30. $f(x) = 2x + 4$ and $g(x) = \dfrac{1}{2}x - 2$

31. $f(x) = \dfrac{1}{x + 1}$ and $g(x) = \dfrac{x - 9}{12}$

32. $f(x) = \dfrac{1}{x + 1}$ and $g(x) = \dfrac{1 - x}{x}$

33. $f(x) = \dfrac{1}{x}$ and $g(x) = \dfrac{1}{x}$

34. $f(x) = 4x$ and $g(x) = \dfrac{4}{x}$

6.2 Inverse Trigonometric Functions

In the last section we defined the inverse of a one-to-one function; in this section we consider inverses of the trigonometric functions.

We begin with $y = \sin x$. A function must be one-to-one to have an inverse, but from the graph of $y = \sin x$ in Figure 6.6, it is clear that $y = \sin x$ is not a one-to-one function. However, by suitably restricting the domain of the sine function, we can define a one-to-one function. The domain of $y = \sin x$ is restricted to $-\pi/2 \leq x \leq \pi/2$, the solid part of the graph in Figure 6.6. We will call this function with restricted domain $y = \text{Sin } x$ to distinguish it from $y = \sin x$, which has the real numbers as domain. Reflecting the graph of $y = \text{Sin } x$ about the line $y = x$ gives the graph of the inverse function, shown in Figure 6.7.

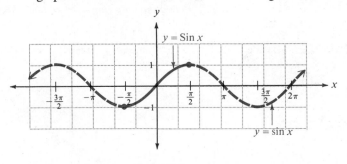

Figure 6.6

The equation of the inverse function of $y = \text{Sin } x$ is found by exchanging the x and y in $y = \text{Sin } x$ to get $x = \text{Sin } y$. This equation is solved for y by writing $y = \textbf{Arcsin } x$.* As Figure 6.7 shows, the domain of $y = \text{Arcsin } x$ is $-1 \leq x \leq 1$, while the range is $-\pi/2 \leq x \leq \pi/2$. The function $y = \text{Arcsin } x$ has all real numbers in its range. Thus, by definition,

$$y = \text{Arcsin } x \qquad \text{means} \qquad x = \text{Sin } y, \quad \text{for } -\pi/2 \leq y \leq \pi/2.$$

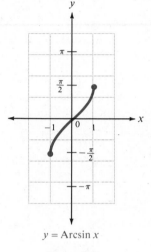

$$y = \text{Arcsin } x$$

Figure 6.7

EXAMPLE 1 Find y in radians for each of the following.

(a) $y = \text{Arcsin } \dfrac{1}{2}$

Rewrite the expression as $\text{Sin } y = 1/2$. Since $\sin \pi/6 = 1/2$ and $\pi/6$ is in the range of the Arcsin function, $y = \pi/6$.

(b) $y = \text{Arcsin } (-1)$.

By writing the alternate equation, $\text{Sin } y = -1$, we see that $y = -\pi/2$. (The value $y = 3\pi/2$ is incorrect, since $3\pi/2$ is not in the range of the Arcsin function.)

For each of the other trigonometric functions, we can define an inverse function by a suitable restriction on the range, just as we did with sine. The **inverse trigonometric functions** and their ranges are:

---

*An alternate notation for Arcsin x is $\text{Sin}^{-1} x$.

Function	Range
$y = \text{Arcsin } x,$	$-\pi/2 \le y \le \pi/2$
$y = \text{Arccos } x,$	$0 \le y \le \pi$
$y = \text{Arctan } x,$	$-\pi/2 < y < \pi/2$
$y = \text{Arccot } x,$	$0 < y < \pi$
$y = \text{Arcsec } x,$	$0 \le y < \pi/2 \text{ or } \pi \le y < 3\pi/2*$
$y = \text{Arccsc } x,$	$0 < y \le \pi/2 \text{ or } \pi < y \le 3\pi/2*$

The graphs of $y = \text{Arccos } x$ and $y = \text{Arctan } x$ are shown in Figures 6.8 and 6.9. Arccot x, Arcsec x, and Arccsc x are less important, since they can be expressed in terms of Arctan, Arccos, or Arcsin.

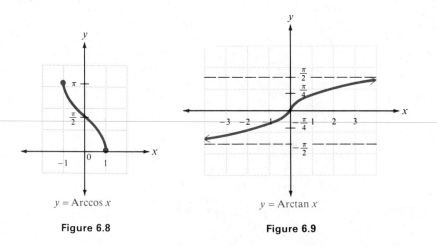

Figure 6.8 $\quad y = \text{Arccos } x$

Figure 6.9 $\quad y = \text{Arctan } x$

EXAMPLE 2 Find θ in degrees for each of the following.

(a) $\theta = \text{Arccos}\left(-\dfrac{1}{\sqrt{2}}\right)$

The values for Arccos are in quadrants I and II. (Why?) Since $-1/\sqrt{2}$ is negative, we are restricted to values in quadrant II. Write the equation as Cos $\theta = -1/\sqrt{2}$. In quadrant II, cos $135° = -1/\sqrt{2}$, so $\theta = 135°$.

(b) $\theta = \text{Arctan } 1$.

By writing the alternate equation, Tan $\theta = 1$, we see that $\theta = 45°$. Note that θ must be in quadrant I here.

---

*Arcsec and Arccsc are sometimes defined with a different range. The definition we have given is the most useful in calculus.

(c) $\theta = \text{Arccot}\,(-.3541)$

From a calculator or Table II, we see that $\cot 70° 30' = .3541$. We need a second quadrant angle. Thus,

$$\theta = 180° - 70° 30' = 109° 30'. \quad \bullet$$

EXAMPLE 3 Evaluate each of the following without a calculator or tables.

(a) $\sin\left(\text{Arctan}\,\dfrac{3}{2}\right)$

Let $y = \text{Arctan}\,3/2$, so that $\text{Tan}\,y = 3/2$. Since Arctan is defined only in quadrants I and IV, and since $3/2$ is positive, we are interested in quadrant I. Sketch y in quadrant I, and label a triangle as shown in Figure 6.10. The hypotenuse is $\sqrt{13}$, so

$$\sin\left(\text{Arctan}\,\dfrac{3}{2}\right) = \sin y = \dfrac{3}{\sqrt{13}} = \dfrac{3\sqrt{13}}{13}.$$

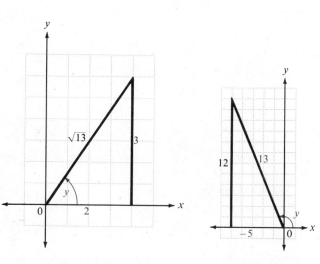

Figure 6.10   Figure 6.11

(b) $\tan\left(\text{Arccos}\,\dfrac{-5}{13}\right)$

Let $y = \text{Arccos}\,(-5/13)$. Then $\text{Cos}\,y = -5/13$. Sketch y in quadrant II. (Why?) See Figure 6.11. From the triangle in Figure 6.11,

$$\tan\left(\text{Arccos}\,\dfrac{-5}{13}\right) = \tan y = -\dfrac{12}{5}.$$

(c) $\cos(\text{Arctan}\,\sqrt{3} + \text{Arcsin}\,1/3)$

Let $A = \text{Arctan}\,\sqrt{3}$ and $B = \text{Arcsin}\,1/3$. Then $\text{Tan}\,A = \sqrt{3}$ and $\text{Sin}\,B = 1/3$. Sketch both A and B in quadrant I, as shown in Figure 6.12.

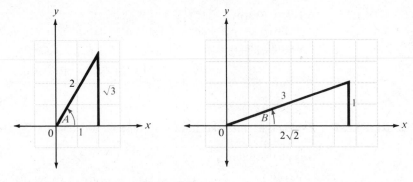

Figure 6.12

Now use the identity for cos $(A + B)$.

$$\cos (A + B) = \cos A \cos B - \sin A \sin B$$
$$\cos(\text{Arctan } \sqrt{3} + \text{Arcsin } 1/3) = \cos(\text{Arctan } \sqrt{3})\cos(\text{Arcsin } 1/3)$$
$$- \sin(\text{Arctan } \sqrt{3})\sin(\text{Arcsin } 1/3) \qquad (*)$$

From Figure 6.12

$$\cos(\text{Arctan } \sqrt{3}) = \cos A = \frac{1}{2},$$

$$\sin(\text{Arctan } \sqrt{3}) = \sin A = \frac{\sqrt{3}}{2},$$

$$\cos\left(\text{Arcsin } \frac{1}{3}\right) = \cos B = \frac{2\sqrt{2}}{3},$$

$$\sin\left(\text{Arcsin } \frac{1}{3}\right) = \sin B = \frac{1}{3}.$$

Substitute these values into equation (*) to get

$$\cos\left(\text{Arctan } \sqrt{3} + \text{Arcsin } \frac{1}{3}\right) = \frac{1}{2} \cdot \frac{2\sqrt{2}}{3} - \frac{\sqrt{3}}{2} \cdot \frac{1}{3}$$

$$= \frac{2\sqrt{2}}{6} - \frac{\sqrt{3}}{6}$$

$$= \frac{2\sqrt{2} - \sqrt{3}}{6}. \qquad \bullet$$

6.2 EXERCISES   *For each of the following give the value of y in radians without using a calculator or tables. See Example 1.*

1. $y = \text{Arcsin } \left(\dfrac{-\sqrt{3}}{2}\right)$ **2.** $y = \text{Arccos } \dfrac{\sqrt{3}}{2}$ **3.** $y = \text{Arctan } 1$

4. $y = \text{Arccot } (-1)$ **5.** $y = \text{Arcsin } (-1)$ **6.** $y = \text{Arccos } (-1)$

7. $y = \text{Arccos } \dfrac{1}{2}$ **8.** $y = \text{Arcsin } \left(\dfrac{-1}{\sqrt{2}}\right)$ **9.** $y = \text{Arcsec } (-\sqrt{2})$

10. $y = \text{Arccsc } (-2)$ **11.** $y = \text{Arccot } (-\sqrt{3})$ **12.** $y = \text{Arccos } \left(\dfrac{-1}{2}\right)$

For each of the following give the value in degrees to the nearest ten minutes.

13. $\text{Arcsin } (-.1334)$ **14.** $\text{Arccos } (-.1334)$

15. $\text{Arccos } (-.3987)$ **16.** $\text{Arcsin } .7790$

17. $\text{Arccsc } 1.942$ **18.** $\text{Arccot } 1.767$

For each of the following give the value in radians.

19. $\text{Arctan } 1.111$ **20.** $\text{Arcsin } .8192$

21. $\text{Arccot } (-.9217)$ **22.** $\text{Arcsec } (-1.287)$

23. $\text{Arcsin } .9283$ **24.** $\text{Arccos } .4462$

For each of the following give the value without using a calculator or tables. See Example 3.

25. $\tan \left(\text{Arccos } \dfrac{2}{3} \right)$ **26.** $\sin \left(\text{Arccos } \dfrac{1}{4} \right)$

27. $\cos (\text{Arctan } (-2))$ **28.** $\sec \left(\text{Arcsin } \left(-\dfrac{1}{3} \right) \right)$

29. $\cot \left(\text{Arcsin } \left(\dfrac{-2}{5} \right) \right)$ **30.** $\cos \left(\text{Arctan } \dfrac{8}{5} \right)$

31. $\sec \left(\text{Arccot } \dfrac{3}{5} \right)$ **32.** $\csc \left(\text{Arcsin } \dfrac{12}{13} \right)$

33. $\sin \left(2 \text{ Arctan } \dfrac{12}{5} \right)$ **34.** $\cos \left(2 \text{ Arcsin } \dfrac{1}{4} \right)$

    (Hint: use the identity for $\sin 2\theta$)

35. $\cos \left(2 \text{ Arctan } \dfrac{4}{3} \right)$ **36.** $\sin \left(\text{Arcsin } \dfrac{1}{2} + \text{Arctan } (-3) \right)$

37. $\cos \left(\text{Arctan } \dfrac{5}{12} - \text{Arccot } \dfrac{4}{3} \right)$ **38.** $\cos \left(\text{Arcsin } \dfrac{3}{5} + \text{Arccos } \dfrac{5}{13} \right)$

 Use the inverse key of your calculator together with the trigonometric function keys to find each of the following in radians to six decimal places.

39. $\cos (\text{Arctan } .3)$ **40.** $\sin (\text{Arccos } .75)$

41. $\tan (\text{Arcsin } .1225)$ **42.** $\cot (\text{Arccos } .5823)$

Write each of the following as an algebraic expression. (Hint: write x as $x/1$.)

43. $\sin (\text{Arccos } x)$ **44.** $\tan (\text{Arccos } x)$

45. $\sec (\text{Arccot } x)$ **46.** $\csc (\text{Arcsec } x)$

47. $\cot (\text{Arcsin } x)$ **48.** $\cos (\text{Arcsin } x)$

Graph each of the following and give the domain and range.

49. $y = \text{Arccot } x$ **50.** $y = \text{Arctan } 2x$

51. $y = 2 \text{ Arccos } x$

52. $y = \text{Arcsin } \dfrac{x}{2}$

53. Enter 1.003 in your calculator and press the keys for inverse sine. The response will indicate that something is wrong. What is wrong?

54. Enter 1.003 in your calculator and push the keys for inverse tangent. This time, unlike in Exercise 53, you get an answer. What is different?

55. We know that Arcsin $(\sin x) = x$. Enter 1.74283 in your calculator (set for radians), and press the sine key. Then press the keys for inverse sine. You get 1.398763 instead of 1.74283. What happened?

Suppose an airplane flying faster than sound goes directly over you. Assume that the plane is flying level. At the instant that you feel the sonic boom from the plane, the angle of elevation to the plane is given by

$$\alpha = 2 \text{ Arcsin } \frac{1}{m},$$

where m is the mach number of the plane's speed. See the exercises at the end of Section 5.7. Find α for each of the following values of m to the nearest degree.

56. $m = 1.2$

57. $m = 1.5$

58. $m = 2$

59. $m = 2.5$

A painting 1 meter high and 3 meters from the floor will cut off an angle θ to an observer, where

$$\theta = \text{Arctan } \left(\frac{x}{x^2 + 2} \right).$$

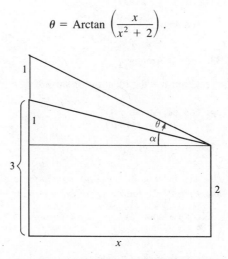

Assume that the observer is x meters from the wall displaying the painting and that the eyes of the observer are 2 meters above the ground. See the figure. Find the value of θ for the following values of x. Round to the nearest degree.

60. 1

61. 2

62. 3

63. Derive the formula given above. (Hint: use the identity for tan $(\theta + \alpha)$. Use right triangles.)

A **conditional equation** is an equation in which some replacements for the variable make the statement true, while others make it false. For example,

$$2x + 3 = 5, \qquad x^2 - 5x = 10, \qquad \text{and} \qquad 2x = 8$$

are conditional equations. We are interested here in conditional equations which involve trigonometric functions.

Conditional equations with trigonometric functions can usually be solved by using algebraic methods and trigonometric identities to simplify the equation. The next examples illustrate the methods used in solving a trigonometric equation.

EXAMPLE 1   Solve $3 \sin x = \sqrt{3} + \sin x$.

Treat $\sin x$ as the variable. Collect all terms with $\sin x$ on one side of the equation. Solve for $\sin x$, then for x.

$$3 \sin x = \sqrt{3} + \sin x$$
$$2 \sin x = \sqrt{3}$$
$$\sin x = \frac{\sqrt{3}}{2}$$
$$x = \arcsin \frac{\sqrt{3}}{2}$$

Since we are not concerned with the Arcsin *function* here, the range need not be restricted. To indicate this, we write arcsin $\sqrt{3}/2$ rather than Arcsin $\sqrt{3}/2$.

We know that $\sin 60° = \sqrt{3}/2$; so does $\sin 120°$, $\sin 420°$, and so on. There are an infinite number of values of x which satisfy this equation. We can express the infinite number of solutions as

$$x = 60° + 360° \cdot n \qquad \text{or} \qquad x = 120° + 360° \cdot n,$$

where n is any integer. Usually, we need the solutions of a trigonometric equation only for some particular interval, as in the next example.   ●

EXAMPLE 2   Solve $\tan^2 x + \tan x - 2 = 0$ for $0 \le x < 2\pi$.

If we let $y = \tan x$, the equation becomes $y^2 + y - 2 = 0$, which factors as $(y - 1)(y + 2) = 0$. Substituting $\tan x$ back for y, gives

$$(\tan x - 1)(\tan x + 2) = 0$$
$$\tan x - 1 = 0 \qquad \tan x + 2 = 0$$
$$\tan x = 1 \qquad \tan x = -2$$
$$x = \arctan 1 \qquad x = \arctan (-2).$$

If $x = \arctan 1$, then for the interval $0 \le x < 2\pi$ we get $x = \pi/4$ or $x = 5\pi/4$.

If $x = \arctan(-2)$, then by interpolating in Table II, or using a calculator, we find that $x = 2.0344$ or 5.1760 (approximately). The solutions are

$$\frac{\pi}{4}, \quad \frac{5\pi}{4}, \quad 2.0344, \quad \text{and} \quad 5.1760. \quad \bullet$$

When an equation involves more than one trigonometric function, it is often helpful to use a suitable identity to rewrite the equation in terms of just one trigonometric function, as in the following example.

EXAMPLE 3   Solve $\sin x + \cos x = 0$ for $0° \le x < 360°$.

One way to solve this equation is to divide both sides by $\cos x$. (Remember that we can only do this if we assume $\cos x$ cannot equal 0.)

$$\frac{\sin x}{\cos x} + \frac{\cos x}{\cos x} = \frac{0}{\cos x}$$

$$\tan x + 1 = 0$$

$$\tan x = -1$$

$$x = \arctan(-1)$$

The solutions in the given interval are $135°$ and $315°$ $\bullet$

EXAMPLE 4   Solve $\sin x \tan x = \sin x$ for $0° \le x < 360°$.

Subtract $\sin x$ from both sides, then factor on the left.

$$\sin x \tan x = \sin x$$

$$\sin x \tan x - \sin x = 0$$

$$\sin x (\tan x - 1) = 0$$

Now set each factor equal to 0.

$$\sin x = 0 \quad \text{or} \quad \tan x - 1 = 0$$

$$x = \arcsin 0 \qquad\qquad x = \arctan 1$$

$$x = 0° \quad \text{or} \quad x = 180° \qquad x = 45° \quad \text{or} \quad x = 225° \quad \bullet$$

There are four solutions to Example 4. If we tried to solve the equation by dividing both sides by $\sin x$, we would have $\tan x = 1$, which would give $x = 45°$ or $x = 225°$. The other two solutions would not appear. The missing solutions are the ones which make the divisor, $\sin x$, equal 0. Thus, when dividing by a variable expression, it is necessary to check to see if the numbers which make that expression 0 are solutions. We should have done this in Example 3. There we divided by $\cos x$. If $\cos x = 0$, $x = 90°$ or $x = 270°$. However, neither of these values satisfies the equation of Example 3.

Sometimes we can solve a trigonometric equation by first squaring both sides, then using a trigonometric identity. When we square both sides of an equation, we must remember to check for any numbers which satisfy the squared equation, but not the given equation.

EXAMPLE 5   Solve $\tan x + \sqrt{3} = \sec x$ for $0 \le x < 2\pi$.

Square both sides, then express $\sec^2 x$ in terms of $\tan^2 x$.

$$\tan x + \sqrt{3} = \sec x$$

$$\tan^2 x + 2\sqrt{3} \tan x + 3 = \sec^2 x$$

$$\tan^2 x + 2\sqrt{3} \tan x + 3 = 1 + \tan^2 x$$

$$2\sqrt{3} \tan x = -2$$

$$\tan x = -\frac{1}{\sqrt{3}}$$

$$x = \arctan\left(-\frac{1}{\sqrt{3}}\right)$$

The possible solutions in the given interval are $5\pi/6$ and $11\pi/6$. Now check the possible solutions. Try $5\pi/6$ first.

$$\tan x + \sqrt{3} = \tan \frac{5\pi}{6} + \sqrt{3} = \frac{-\sqrt{3}}{3} + \sqrt{3} = \frac{2\sqrt{3}}{3}$$

$$\sec x = \sec \frac{5\pi}{6} = \frac{-2\sqrt{3}}{3}$$

Thus $5\pi/6$ is not a solution.

$$\tan \frac{11\pi}{6} + \sqrt{3} = \frac{-\sqrt{3}}{3} + \sqrt{3} = \frac{2\sqrt{3}}{3}$$

$$\sec \frac{11\pi}{6} = \frac{2\sqrt{3}}{3}$$

So $11\pi/6$ is the only solution to the given equation.   ●

When a trigonometric equation which is quadratic in form cannot be factored, the quadratic theorem can be used to solve the equation.

EXAMPLE 6   Solve $\cot^2 x + 3 \cot x = 1$ for $0° \le x < 360°$.

Write the equation in quadratic form with 0 on one side.

$$\cot^2 x + 3 \cot x - 1 = 0$$

Since this equation cannot be factored, use the quadratic formula with $a = 1$, $b = 3$, $c = -1$, and $\cot x$ as the variable.

$$\cot x = \frac{-3 \pm \sqrt{9 + 4}}{2} = \frac{-3 \pm \sqrt{13}}{2} = \frac{-3 \pm 3.606}{2}$$

$$\cot x = .303 \quad \text{or} \quad \cot x = -3.303$$

$$x = \text{arccot} \ .303 \quad \text{or} \quad x = \text{arccot} \ (-3.303)$$

Use Table II or a calculator to find x to the nearest ten minutes:

$$x = 73°\ 10',\ 253°\ 10',\ 163°\ 10',\ \text{or}\ 343°\ 10'.$$ ●

The methods for solving trigonometric equations illustrated in the examples can be summarized as follows.

---

1. If only one trigonometric function is present, first solve the equation for that function.

2. If more than one trigonometric function is present, rearrange the equation so that one side equals 0. Then try to factor and set each factor equal to zero to solve.

3. If Step 2 does not work, try using identities to change the form of the equation. It may be helpful to square the equation first.

4. If the equation is quadratic in form, but not factorable, use the quadratic formula.

6.3 EXERCISES

Solve each of the following equations for $0 \le x < 2\pi$. Use 3.1416 as an approximation for π when you need values from Table II or a calculator. See Examples 1 and 2.

1. $3 \tan x + 5 = 2$

2. $\tan x + 1 = 2$

3. $2 \sin x + 3 = 4$

4. $2 \sec x + 1 = \sec x + 3$

5. $\tan^2 x - 1 = 0$

6. $\sec^2 x + 1 = 0$

7. $(\cot x - \sqrt{3})(2 \sin x + \sqrt{3}) = 0$

8. $(\tan x - 1)(\cos x - 1) = 0$

9. $(\sec x - 2)(\sqrt{3} \sec x - 2) = 0$

10. $(2 \sin x + 1)(\sqrt{2} \cos x + 1) = 0$

11. $\cos^2 x + 2 \cos x + 1 = 0$

12. $2 \cos^2 x - \sqrt{3} \cos x = 0$

13. $-2 \sin^2 x = 3 \sin x + 1$

14. $3 \sin^2 x - \sin x = 2$

15. $\cos^2 x - \sin^2 x = 0$

16. $\dfrac{2 \tan x}{3 - \tan^2 x} = 1$

Solve each of the following equations for $0° \le \theta < 360°$. Find θ to the nearest ten minutes. See Examples 3, 4, and 5.

17. $\tan \theta + 6 \cot \theta = 5$

18. $\csc \theta = 2 \sin \theta + 1$

19. $\tan \theta - \cot \theta = 0$

20. $\sec^2 \theta = 2 \tan \theta + 4$

21. $\cos^2 \theta = \sin^2 \theta + 1$

22. $\csc^2 \theta - 2 \cot \theta = 0$

23. $3 \cot^3 \theta = \cot \theta$

24. $2 \cos^4 \theta = \cos^2 \theta$

25. $\sin^2 \theta \cos \theta = \cos \theta$

26. $2 \tan^2 \theta \sin \theta - \tan^2 \theta = 0$

27. $5 \sec^2 \theta = 6 \sec \theta$

28. $3 \cot^2 \theta = \cot \theta$

29. $\sin^2 \theta \cos^2 \theta = 0$

30. $\sec^2 \theta \tan \theta = 2 \tan \theta$

31. $4(1 + \sin \theta) = \dfrac{3}{1 - \sin \theta}$

32. $\tan \theta = 4 \sin \theta$

33. $\sin \theta + \cos \theta = 1$

34. $\sec \theta - \tan \theta = 1$

To solve the following equations, you will need the quadratic formula. Find all solutions in the interval $0° \le x < 360°$. Give solutions to the nearest ten minutes. See Example 6.

35. $9 \sin^2 x - 6 \sin x = 1$

36. $4 \cos^2 x + 4 \cos x = 1$

37. $\tan^2 x + 4 \tan x + 2 = 0$

38. $3 \cot^2 x - 3 \cot x - 1 = 0$

39. $\sin^2 x - 2 \sin x + 3 = 0$

40. $2 \cos^2 x + 2 \cos x - 1 = 0$

41. $\cot x + 2 \csc x = 3$

42. $2 \sin x = 1 - 2 \cos x$

In an electric circuit, let V represent the electromotive force in volts at t seconds. Assume $V = \cos 2\pi t$. Find the smallest positive value of t where $0 \le t \le 1/2$ for each of the following values of V.

43. $V = 0$

44. $V = .5$

A coil of wire rotating in a magnetic field induces a voltage given by

$$e = 20 \sin \left(\frac{\pi t}{4} - \frac{\pi}{2} \right),$$

where t is time in seconds. Find the smallest positive time to produce the following voltages.

45. 0

46. $10 \sqrt{3}$

6.4 Trigonometric Equations With Multiple Angles

Conditional trigonometric equations where a half angle or multiple angle is given, such as $2 \sin (x/2) = 1$, often require an additional step to solve. This is shown in the following example.

EXAMPLE 1 Solve $2 \sin (x/2) = 1$ for $0° \le x < 360°$.

We begin by solving for the trigonometric function.

$$2 \sin \frac{x}{2} = 1$$

$$\sin \frac{x}{2} = \frac{1}{2}$$

If we let $x/2 = \theta$, then

$$\sin \theta = \frac{1}{2}$$

$$\theta = \arcsin \frac{1}{2}$$

$$\theta = 30° \quad \text{or} \quad \theta = 150°$$

$$\frac{x}{2} = 30° \qquad\qquad \frac{x}{2} = 150°$$

$$x = 60° \qquad\qquad x = 300° \quad \bullet$$

Sometimes equations with multiple angles which cannot be solved as shown above can be solved by using an appropriate identity, as in the next examples.

EXAMPLE 2 Solve $\cos 2x = \cos x$ for $0 \le x < 2\pi$.
Use the identity $\cos 2x = 2 \cos^2 x - 1$.

$$\cos 2x = \cos x$$
$$2 \cos^2 x - 1 = \cos x$$
$$2 \cos^2 x - \cos x - 1 = 0$$
$$(2 \cos x + 1)(\cos x - 1) = 0$$
$$2 \cos x + 1 = 0 \qquad \cos x - 1 = 0$$

$$\cos x = -\frac{1}{2} \qquad\qquad \cos x = 1$$

$$x = \arccos \left(-\frac{1}{2} \right) \qquad x = \arccos 1$$

$$x = \frac{2\pi}{3} \quad \text{or} \quad \frac{4\pi}{3} \qquad x = 0$$

The solutions are 0, $2\pi/3$, and $4\pi/3$. $\bullet$

EXAMPLE 3 Solve $4 \sin x \cos x = \sqrt{3}$ for $0° \le x < 360°$.
The identity $2 \sin x \cos x = \sin 2x$ is useful here.

$$4 \sin x \cos x = \sqrt{3}$$
$$2(2 \sin x \cos x) = \sqrt{3}$$
$$2 \sin 2x = \sqrt{3}$$
$$\sin 2x = \frac{\sqrt{3}}{2}$$

$$2x = \arcsin \frac{\sqrt{3}}{2}$$

$$2x = 60°, \ 120°, \ 420°, \ \text{or} \ 480°$$
$$x = 30°, \ 60°, \ 210°, \ \text{or} \ 240°$$

In this case the domain $0° \leq x < 360°$ implies $0° \leq 2x < 720°$, which allows four solutions for x.   ●

6.4 EXERCISES   *Solve each of the following equations for $0 \leq x < 2\pi$. See Examples 1–3.*

1. $\sin 2x = 0$ **2.** $\sin 2x = 1$

3. $\cos 2x = 0$ **4.** $\cos 2x = 1$

5. $3 \tan 2x = \sqrt{3}$ **6.** $\cot 2x = \sqrt{3}$

7. $\sqrt{2} \cos 2x = -1$ **8.** $2\sqrt{3} \sin 2x = -3$

9. $\sin \dfrac{x}{2} = \sqrt{2} - \sin \dfrac{x}{2}$ **10.** $\sin x = \sin 2x$

11. $\tan 2x = 0$ **12.** $\cos 2x - \cos x = 0$

13. $\sec^4 2x = 4$ **14.** $\tan^2 2x - 1 = 0$

15. $\sin \dfrac{x}{2} = \cos \dfrac{x}{2}$ **16.** $\sec \dfrac{x}{2} = \cos \dfrac{x}{2}$

17. $\cos 2x + \cos x = 0$ **18.** $\sin x \cos x = \dfrac{1}{4}$

Solve each of the following equations for $0° \leq \theta < 360°$. Use Table II or a calculator to find solutions to the nearest ten minutes as necessary. See Examples 1–3.

19. $2 \sin 2\theta = \sqrt{3}$ **20.** $2 \cos 2\theta = \sqrt{2}$

21. $\cos \dfrac{\theta}{2} = 1$ **22.** $\sin \dfrac{\theta}{2} = 1$

23. $2\sqrt{3} \sin \dfrac{\theta}{2} = 3$ **24.** $2\sqrt{3} \cos \dfrac{\theta}{2} = -3$

25. $2 \sin \theta = 2 \cos 2\theta$ **26.** $\cos \theta - 1 = \cos 2\theta$

27. $1 - \sin \theta = \cos 2\theta$ **28.** $\sin 2\theta = 2 \cos^2 \theta$

29. $\csc^2 \dfrac{\theta}{2} = 2 \sec \theta$ **30.** $\cos \theta = \sin^2 \dfrac{\theta}{2}$

31. $2 - \sin 2\theta = 4 \sin 2\theta$ **32.** $4 \cos 2\theta = 8 \sin \theta \cos \theta$

33. $2 \cos^2 2\theta = 1 - \cos 2\theta$ **34.** $\sin \theta = \cos \dfrac{\theta}{2}$

For the following equations, use the sum and product identities for Section 5.8. Give all solutions in the interval $0 \leq x < 2\pi$.

35. $\sin x + \sin 3x = \cos x$ **36.** $\cos 4x - \cos 2x = \sin x$

37. $\sin 3x - \sin x = 0$ **38.** $\cos 2x + \cos x = 0$

39. $\sin 4x + \sin 2x = 2 \cos x$ **40.** $\cos 5x + \cos 3x = 2 \cos 4x$

41. A spacecraft is in an elliptical orbit around the earth. See the figure. Its distance (in kilometers) from the earth varies with time (in minutes) according to the function

$$d = 550 + 450 \cos \frac{\pi}{50} t.$$

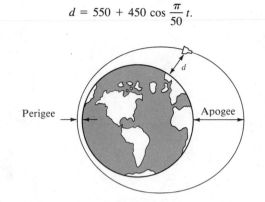

(a) At time $t = 0$ it is at its apogee (highest point). Fifty minutes later (at $t = 50$), it is at its perigee (lowest point. Find d at the apogee and perigee. (Hint: use radian measure.)

(b) Find the first three positive values of t when the spacecraft is 200 kilometers from the surface.

(c) To transmit information back to earth, the spacecraft must be within 700 kilometers of the surface. For how many consecutive minutes will the spacecraft be able to transmit?

42. At a certain point on the beach, a post sticks out of the sand. The top of the post is 76 centimeters above the sand. See the figure. The depth of the water at the

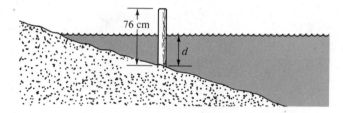

post varies with time in hours (with $t = 0$ corresponding to midnight), due to the motion of the tides, according to the function

$$d = 40 + 60 \cos \frac{\pi}{6} (t - 2).$$

(a) What is the earliest time of day at which the water level is just at the top of the post?

(b) At the time you calculated in part (a), is the post just going under water or just emerging from the water? Explain your answer.

(c) When d is negative, the tide is completely out and there is no water at the post. Between what times will the entire post be out of the water? (Hint: Graph the function.)

The study of alternating current in electricity requires the solution of equations of the form $i = I_{max} \sin 2\pi ft$, for time t in seconds, where i is instantaneous current in amps, I_{max} is maximum current in amps, and f is the number of cycles per second.* *Find the smallest positive value of t, given the following data.*

43. $i = 40, I_{max} = 100, f = 60$

44. $i = 50, I_{max} = 100, f = 120$

45. $i = I_{max}, f = 60$

46. $i = \dfrac{1}{2} I_{max}, f = 60$

6.5 Inverse Trigonometric Equations   (Optional)

The solutions to the equations in the last two sections could have been found without using the inverse trigonometric function notation. However, sometimes it is necessary to solve a trigonometric equation with more than one variable. Then we must use an inverse trigonometric function, as shown in the next example.

EXAMPLE 1   Solve $y = 3 \cos 2x$ for x.

We want $\cos 2x$ alone on one side of the equation. First, divide both sides of the equation by 3.

$$y = 3 \cos 2x$$

$$\frac{y}{3} = \cos 2x$$

Now write the statement in the alternate form

$$\arccos \frac{y}{3} = 2x.$$

Finally, multiply both sides by 1/2.

$$x = \frac{1}{2} \arccos \frac{y}{3}. \quad \bullet$$

The next examples show how to solve equations involving inverse trigonometric functions.

---

*Basic Technical Mathematics With Calculus, Ralph H. Hannon, W. B. Saunders Co., 1978, p. 300–302.

EXAMPLE 2   Solve $2 \text{ Arcsin } x = \pi$.

First solve for Arcsin x.

$$2 \text{ Arcsin } x = \pi$$

$$\text{Arcsin } x = \frac{\pi}{2}$$

$$x = \sin \frac{\pi}{2}$$

$$x = 1$$

Verify that the solution satisfies the given equation.   ●

EXAMPLE 3   Solve $\text{Arccos } x = \text{Arcsin } \frac{1}{2}$.

Let Arcsin $1/2 = u$. Then Sin $u = 1/2$ and the equation becomes

$$\text{Arccos } x = u,$$

for u in quadrant I. This can be written as

$$\text{Cos } u = x.$$

Sketch a triangle and label it using the facts that u is in quadrant I and sin $u = 1/2$. See Figure 6.13.

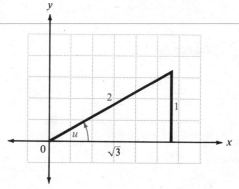

Since $x = \cos u$,

Figure 6.13

$$x = \frac{\sqrt{3}}{2}.$$ ●

Some equations with inverse trigonometric functions require the use of identities.

EXAMPLE 4   Solve $\text{Arcsin } x - \text{Arccos } x = \pi/6$.

Begin by adding Arccos x to both sides of the equation so that one inverse function is alone on one side of the equation.

$$\text{Arcsin } x = \text{Arccos } x + \frac{\pi}{6}.$$

Write this statement as

$$\sin\left(\text{Arccos } x + \frac{\pi}{6}\right) = x.$$

Let $u = \text{Arccos } x$. Then

$$\sin\left(u + \frac{\pi}{6}\right) = x.$$

Now use the identity for $\sin(A + B)$.

$$\sin\left(u + \frac{\pi}{6}\right) = \sin u \cos \frac{\pi}{6} + \cos u \sin \frac{\pi}{6}$$

and

$$\sin u \cos \frac{\pi}{6} + \cos u \sin \frac{\pi}{6} = x \qquad (*)$$

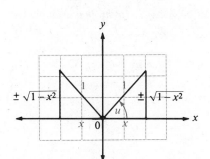

u can be in either quadrant I or II

Figure 6.14

Since $u = \text{Arccos } x$, $\text{Cos } u = x$. Sketch a triangle and label it as shown in Figure 6.14. Since we don't know what quadrant u is in, we use $\pm\sqrt{1 - x^2}$ for the third side of the triangle. From the triangle, we see that $\sin u = \pm\sqrt{1 - x^2}$. Now substitute into equation (*) using $\sin u = \pm\sqrt{1 - x^2}$, $\sin \pi/6 = 1/2$, $\cos \pi/6 = \sqrt{3}/2$, and $\cos u = x$

$$(\pm\sqrt{1 - x^2})\frac{\sqrt{3}}{2} + x \cdot \frac{1}{2} = x$$

$$(\pm\sqrt{1 - x^2})\sqrt{3} + x = 2x$$

$$(\pm\sqrt{3})\sqrt{1 - x^2} = x.$$

Squaring both sides, we get

$$3(1 - x^2) = x^2$$

$$3 - 3x^2 = x^2$$

$$3 = 4x^2$$

$$x = \pm\sqrt{\frac{3}{4}} = \pm\frac{\sqrt{3}}{2}.$$

To check, if $x = \sqrt{3}/2$, we have

$$\text{Arcsin } \frac{\sqrt{3}}{2} - \text{Arccos } \frac{\sqrt{3}}{2} = \frac{\pi}{3} - \frac{\pi}{6} = \frac{\pi}{6}$$

as required. However, if $x = -\sqrt{3}/2$,

$$\text{Arcsin } \left(-\frac{\sqrt{3}}{2}\right) - \text{Arccos } \left(-\frac{\sqrt{3}}{2}\right) = \frac{-\pi}{3} - \frac{5\pi}{6} = \frac{-7\pi}{6} \neq \frac{\pi}{6}.$$

Thus, only $x = \sqrt{3}/2$ satisfies the original equation. We checked each proposed solution since we squared both sides of the equation. ●

6.5 EXERCISES   *Solve each of the following equations for x. See Example 1.*

1. $y = 4 \sin x$ **2.** $3y = \cos x$

3. $2y = \tan 2x$ **4.** $y = \dfrac{1}{2} \tan x$

5. $y = 5 \cot 2x$ **6.** $y = 3 \sin \dfrac{x}{2}$

7. $y = 6 \cos \dfrac{x}{4}$ **8.** $y = -\sin \dfrac{x}{3}$

9. $y = -2 \cos 5x$ **10.** $y = 3 \cot 5x$

11. $y = \sin (x + 2)$ **12.** $y = \tan (2x - 1)$

13. $y = \cos x - 3$ **14.** $y = \cot x + 1$

15. $y = 2 \sin x - 4$ **16.** $y = \pi + 3 \cos x$

Solve each of the following equations. See Examples 2 and 3.

17. $\dfrac{4}{3} \text{Arcsin } \dfrac{y}{4} = \pi$ **18.** $4\pi + 4 \text{ Arctan } y = \pi$

19. $2 \text{ Arccos } \left(\dfrac{y - \pi}{3}\right) = 2\pi$ **20.** $\text{Arccos } \left(y - \dfrac{\pi}{3}\right) = \dfrac{\pi}{6}$

21. $\text{Arcsin } x = \text{Arctan } \dfrac{3}{4}$ **22.** $\text{Arctan } x = \text{Arccos } \dfrac{5}{13}$

23. $\text{Arccos } x = \text{Arcsin } \dfrac{3}{5}$ **24.** $\text{Arccot } x = \text{Arctan } \dfrac{4}{3}$

Solve each of the following equations. See Example 4.

25. $\text{Arcsin } x - \text{Arctan } 1 = -\dfrac{\pi}{4}$ **26.** $\text{Arcsin } x + \text{Arctan } \sqrt{3} = \dfrac{2\pi}{3}$

27. $\text{Arccos } x + 2 \text{ Arcsin } \dfrac{\sqrt{3}}{2} = \pi$ **28.** $\text{Arccos } x + 2 \text{ Arcsin } \dfrac{\sqrt{3}}{2} = \dfrac{\pi}{3}$

29. $\text{Arcsin } 2x + \text{Arccos } x = \dfrac{\pi}{6}$

30. $\text{Arcsin } 2x + \text{Arcsin } x = \dfrac{\pi}{2}$

31. $\text{Arccos } x + \text{Arctan } x = \dfrac{\pi}{2}$

32. $\text{Arctan } x + \text{Arccos } x = \dfrac{\pi}{2}$

33. Solve $d = 550 + 450 \cos \dfrac{\pi}{50} t$ for t in terms of d. See Exercise 41, Section 6.4.

34. Solve $d = 40 + 60 \cos \dfrac{\pi}{6} (t - 2)$ for t in terms of d. See Exercise 42, Section 6.4.

35. In the study of alternating current in electricity, instantaneous voltage in amps is given by

$$e = E_{max} \sin 2\pi ft,$$

where f is the number of cycles per second, E_{max} is the maximum voltage in amps, and t is time in seconds.

(a) Solve the equation for t.

(b) Find the smallest positive value of t in radians if $E_{max} = 12$, $e = 5$, and $f = 100$.

36. The highway department is planning a new freeway. The road will involve a tunnel and a bridge as shown in the figure. The vertical distance y (in meters) from the

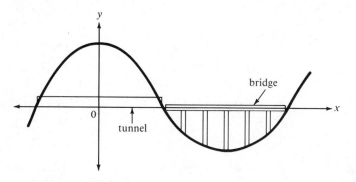

surface of the mountain or valley is related to the horizontal distance x (in meters) from the center of the tunnel by the equation

$$\text{arccos} \left(\dfrac{y - 100}{150} \right) = \dfrac{\pi}{700} x.$$

(a) Solve the equation for y.

(b) The horizontal distance, x, from the center of the mountain to the center of the valley is 700 m. How long will the longest bridge support be?

37. Many computer languages such as BASIC and FORTRAN have only the Arctan function available. To use the other inverse trigonometric functions, it is necessary to express them in terms of Arctangent. This can be done as follows.

(a) Let $u = \text{Arcsin } x$. Solve the equation for x in terms of u.

(b) Use the result of part (a) to label the three sides of the triangle of the figure on the next page in terms of x.

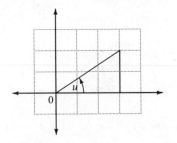

(c) Use the triangle from part (b) to write an equation for tan u in terms of x.

(d) Solve the equation from part (c) for u.

(e) Use your equation from part (d) to calculate Arcsin $(1/2)$. Compare the answer with the actual value of Arcsin $(1/2)$.

Chapter 6   Test

Find the equation of the inverse for each of the following which is one-to-one. Solve each for y.

1. $2x + 3y = 6$

2. $5x - 7y = 30$

3. $x = y^2$

4. $x + 5 = \sqrt[3]{y}$

Solve each of the following for y in radians. Use Table II or a calculator for Exercises 9 and 10, with 3.1416 as an approximation for π.

5. $y = \text{Arctan } 1$

6. $y = \text{Arcsin } \dfrac{\sqrt{2}}{2}$

7. $y = \text{Arccot } \dfrac{-\sqrt{3}}{3}$

8. $y = \text{Arccos } \dfrac{-\sqrt{3}}{2}$

9. $y = \text{Arccot } 1.804$

10. $y = \text{Arccos } -.3090$

11. $y = \tan \left(\text{Arcsin } \dfrac{-3}{5} \right)$

12. $y = \cos \left(\text{Arccot } \dfrac{12}{5} \right)$

13. $y = \sin \left(\text{Arccos } \dfrac{2}{3} + \text{Arctan } 1 \right)$

14. $y = \cos \left(\text{Arcsin } \dfrac{1}{2} + \text{Arcsin } \dfrac{2}{3} \right)$

Solve each of the following equations for $0° \le \theta < 360°$.

15. $2 \cos \theta = 1$

16. $(\tan \theta + 1) \left(\sec \theta - \dfrac{1}{2} \right) = 0$

17. $\sin^2 \theta + 3 \sin \theta + 2 = 0$

18. $\dfrac{\sin \theta}{\cos \theta} = \tan^2 \theta$

19. $\sin 2\theta = \cos 2\theta + 1$

20. $4 \sin \theta \cos \theta = 1$

Solve each of the following for x.

21. $3y = 2 \cos x + 1$

22. $2y = \tan (x + 3)$

23. $\text{Arctan } x = \text{Arccot } 1$

24. $\text{Arcsin } x - \text{Arccos } 1 = \dfrac{\pi}{3}$

7

Triangles and Vectors

Trigonometry goes back to the ancient Egyptians' survey of land and the Babylonians' study of the stars. Over the years, uses of trigonometry have led to ways of *solving triangles,* that is, ways of finding the measure of all sides and all angles of the triangle. A triangle has three sides and three angles. We see in this chapter that knowing any three of these six measures (if at least one measure is of a side) leads to the measure of the others.

7.1 Review of Right Triangles

In Chapter 2, we discussed solving right triangles. The angles we used had simple degree measures. In this section we will work with right triangles whose angles are measured more accurately in degrees and minutes (which is more realistic in applications of trigonometry).

First, recall that the values of the trigonometric functions can be found from the length of the sides of a right triangle as follows. If a right triangle has an acute angle A, then

$$\sin A = \frac{\text{side opposite}}{\text{hypotenuse}} \qquad \cos A = \frac{\text{side adjacent}}{\text{hypotenuse}}$$

$$\tan A = \frac{\text{side opposite}}{\text{side adjacent}}$$

where "side opposite" represents the length of the side of the triangle that is opposite angle A, and "side adjacent" represents the length of the side adjacent to A. The hypotenuse of a right triangle is the longest side of the right triangle.

The values of cot A, sec A, and csc A can be found by using the reciprocal identities: cot $A = 1/\tan A$, sec $A = 1/\cos A$, and csc $A = 1/\sin A$ for all acceptable values of A.

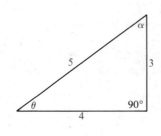

Figure 7.1

EXAMPLE 1 The right triangle of Figure 7.1 has sides of lengths 3, 4, and 5. Find each of the following.

(a) $\sin \theta$, $\cos \theta$, and $\tan \theta$.
Use the results given above.

$$\sin \theta = \frac{\text{side opposite}}{\text{hypotenuse}} = \frac{3}{5} \qquad \cos \theta = \frac{\text{side adjacent}}{\text{hypotenuse}} = \frac{4}{5}$$

$$\tan \theta = \frac{\text{side opposite}}{\text{side adjacent}} = \frac{3}{4}$$

(b) The degree measure of angle θ, to the nearest minute.
We know that $\sin \theta = 3/5 = .6000$. Using a calculator or interpolating in Table II, we have

$$\theta = 36° \, 52'.$$

(c) $\sin \alpha$, $\cos \alpha$, and $\tan \alpha$.

$$\sin \alpha = \frac{4}{5}, \qquad \cos \alpha = \frac{3}{5} \qquad \text{and} \qquad \tan \alpha = \frac{4}{3}$$

(d) The degree measure of angle α.
We know that $\theta = 36° \, 52'$, and that $\alpha + \theta = 90°$. Thus,

$$\begin{aligned}
\alpha &= 90° - \theta \\
&= 90° - 36° \, 52' \\
&= 89° \, 60' - 36° \, 52' \\
\alpha &= 53° \, 08'. \quad \bullet
\end{aligned}$$

In using trigonometry to solve triangles or to find the measures of all sides and all angles, it is convenient to use a to represent the length of the side opposite angle A, b for the length of the side opposite angle B, and so on. The letter c is used for the hypotenuse in a right triangle.

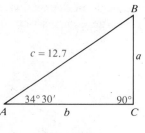

Figure 7.2

EXAMPLE 2   Solve right triangle ABC, with $A = 34° \ 30'$ and $c = 12.7$. See Figure 7.2.

To solve the triangle, we must find the measures of the remaining sides and angles. By the definitions given above, $\sin A = a/c$, where $A = 34° \ 30'$ and $c = 12.7$. Thus,

$$\sin A = \frac{a}{c}$$

$$\sin 34° \ 30' = \frac{a}{12.7}$$

or, upon multiplying both sides by 12.7,

$$a = 12.7 \sin 34° \ 30'.$$
$$a = 7.19.$$

We could use the Pythagorean theorem to find b. However, it is best to use the given information of the problem rather than a result just calculated. If a mistake is made in finding a, then b would also be wrong. Using $\cos A$ gives

$$\cos A = \frac{b}{c}$$

$$\cos 34° \ 30' = \frac{b}{12.7}$$

$$b = 12.7 \cos 34° \ 30'.$$
$$b = 10.5.$$

The Pythagorean theorem could be used as a check, once b is found. All that remains to solve triangle ABC is to find B. We know that $A + B = 90°$ and $A = 34° \ 30'$. Thus,

$$A + B = 90°$$
$$B = 90° - A$$
$$= 89° \ 60' - 34° \ 30'$$
$$B = 55° \ 30'. \quad ●$$

In Figure 7.3 we show an angle of elevation and an angle of depression. For the **angle of elevation**, assume you are standing at point X and looking *up* at point

Y. For the **angle of depression**, you are standing at point *X* and are looking *down* at point *Y*. (These angles were first discussed in Section 2.6.)

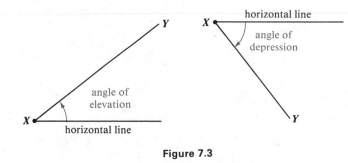

Figure 7.3

EXAMPLE 3   On the way to breakfast at Fort Secret, Private Spence was told that when she stands 123 ft from the base of a flagpole, the angle of elevation to the top is 26° 40′. If her eyes are 5.3 ft above the ground, find the height of the flagpole.

We know the length of the side adjacent to Private Spence and we want to find the length of the side opposite her. See Figure 7.4. The ratio that involves these two values is the tangent. Thus,

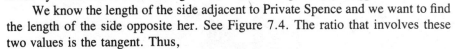

$$\tan A = \frac{\text{side opposite}}{\text{side adjacent}}$$

$$\tan 26° 40′ = \frac{a}{123}$$

$$a = 123 \tan 26° 40′.$$

$$a = 61.8 \text{ ft}$$

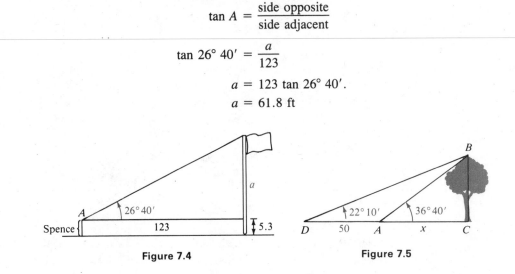

Figure 7.4   **Figure 7.5**

Since Spence's eyes are 5.3 ft above the ground, the height of the flagpole is

$$61.8 + 5.3 = 67.1 \text{ ft.}   \bullet$$

EXAMPLE 4   Francisco needs to know the height of a tree. From a given point on the ground he finds that the angle of elevation to the top of the tree is 36° 40′. He then moves back 50 ft. From the second point, the angle of elevation to the top of the tree is 22° 10′. See Figure 7.5. Find the height of the tree.

Here we have two unknowns, x, the distance from the center of the trunk of the tree to the point where the first observation was made, and h, the height of the tree. Since we know nothing about the length of the hypotenuse of either triangle ABC or triangle BCD, we use a ratio which doesn't involve the hypoteneuse, that is, the tangent. We have

in triangle ABC $\quad \tan 36° 40' = \dfrac{h}{x}\quad$ or $\quad h = x \tan 36° 40'$

in triangle BCD $\quad \tan 22° 10' = \dfrac{h}{50 + x}\quad$ or $\quad h = (50 + x) \tan 22° 10'$.

Since we have two expressions equaling h, these expressions must be equal.

$$x \tan 36° 40' = (50 + x) \tan 22° 10'$$

Now use algebra to solve for x.

$$x \tan 36° 40' = 50 \tan 22° 10' + x \tan 22° 10'$$
$$x \tan 36° 40' - x \tan 22° 10' = 50 \tan 22° 10'$$
$$x(\tan 36° 40' - \tan 22° 10') = 50 \tan 22° 10'$$
$$x = \frac{50 \tan 22° 10'}{\tan 36° 40' - \tan 22° 10'}$$

We saw above that $h = x \tan 36° 40'$. Substituting for x,

$$h = \left(\frac{50 \tan 22° 10'}{\tan 36° 40' - \tan 22° 10'} \right) (\tan 36° 40').$$

From Table II, or using a calculator,

$$\tan 36° 40' = .7445$$
$$\tan 22° 10' = .4074.$$

Thus, $\quad \tan 36° 40' - \tan 22° 10' = .7445 - .4074 = .3371,$

and

$$h = \left(\frac{50(.4074)}{.3371} \right) (.7445) = 45 \text{ ft.} \quad \bullet$$

7.1 EXERCISES

Solve each of the following right triangles. Angle C is the right angle. Use a calculator or interpolate as necessary. See Example 2.

1. $A = 28° 00'$, $c = 17.4$ ft

2. $B = 46° 00'$, $c = 29.7$ m

3. $B = 73° 00'$, $b = 128$ in

4. $A = 61° 00'$, $b = 39.2$ cm

5. $A = 48° 20'$, $b = 78.9$ mi

6. $B = 23° 50'$, $b = 698$ mm

7. $a = 76.4$ yd, $b = 39.3$ yd

8. $a = 958$ m, $b = 489$ m

9. $a = 18.9$ cm, $c = 46.3$ cm

10. $b = 219$ m, $c = 647$ m

11. $A = 53° 24'$, $c = 387.1$ ft   **12.** $A = 13° 47'$, $c = 1285$ m

13. $B = 39° 09'$, $c = .6231$ m   **14.** $B = 82° 51'$, $c = 4.825$ cm

Solve each of the following. See Example 2.

15. A 39.4 m fire-truck ladder is leaning against a wall. Find the distance the ladder goes up the wall if it makes an angle of 42° 30′ with the ground.

16. A swimming pool is 50.0 ft long and 4.00 ft deep at one end. If it is 12.0 ft deep at the other end, find the total distance along the bottom.

17. A guy wire 87.4 m long is attached to the top of a tower that is 69.4 m high. Find the angle that the wire makes with the ground.

18. Find the length of a guy wire that makes an angle of 42° 10′ with the ground if the wire is attached to the top of a tower 79.6 m high.

Work the following problems involving angles of elevation or depression. See Example 3.

19. Suppose the angle of elevation of the sun is 28.4°. Find the length of the shadow cast by a man 6.00 ft tall.

20. The shadow of a vertical tower is 58.2 m long when the angle of elevation of the sun is 36.51°. Find the height of the tower.

21. Find the angle of elevation of the sun if a 53.9 ft flagpole casts a shadow 74.6 ft long.

22. The angle of depression from the top of a building to a point on the ground is 34° 50′. How far is the point on the ground from the top of the building if the building is 368 m high?

23. An airplane is flying at an altitude of 10,000 ft. The angle of depression from the plane to a tree is 13° 50′. How far horizontally must the plane fly to be directly over the tree?

24. The angle of elevation from the top of a small building to the top of a nearby taller building is 46° 40′, while the angle of depression to the bottom is 14° 10′. If the smaller building is 28.0 m high, find the height of the taller building.

25. Priscilla drives her Peterbilt up a straight road inclined at an angle of 4° 12′ with the horizontal. She starts at an elevation of 684 ft above sea level, and drives 12,400 ft along the road. Find her final altitude.

26. The road into Death Valley is straight; it makes an angle of 4° 08′ with the horizontal. Starting at sea level, the road descends to −121 ft. Find the distance it is necessary to travel along the road to reach bottom.

Solve each of the following.

27. Find h.   **28.** Find h.

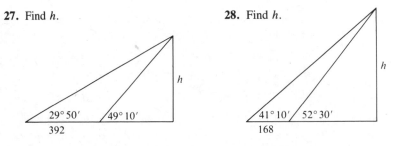

29. The angle of elevation from a point on the ground to the top of a pyramid is 35° 30′. The angle of elevation from a point 135 ft further back to the top of the pyramid is 21° 10′. Find the height of the pyramid.

30. A lighthouse keeper is watching a boat approach directly to the lighthouse. When she first begins watching the boat, the angle of depression of the boat is 15° 50′. Just as the boat turns away from the lighthouse, the angle of depression is 35° 40′. If the height of the lighthouse is 68.7 m, find the distance traveled by the boat as it approaches the lighthouse.

31. A television antenna is on top of the center of a house. The angle of elevation from a point 28.0 m from the center of the house to the top of the antenna is 27° 10′, and the angle of elevation to the bottom of the antenna is 18° 10′. Find the height of the antenna.

32. The angle of elevation from Lone Pine to the top of Mt. Whitney is 10° 50′. If I drive 7.00 km along a straight level road toward Mt. Whitney, I find the angle of elevation to be 22° 40′. Find the height of the top of Mt. Whitney above the level of the road.

Recall from Section 2.6 that bearing *is defined as the degree measure of the angle between due north and the line representing the direction of travel. This angle is measured in a clockwise direction. Use the idea of bearing to solve each of the following.*

33. A ship leaves port and sails on a bearing of 28° 10′. Another ship leaves the same port at the same time and sails on a bearing of 118° 10′. If the first ship sails at 20.0 mi per hour and the second sails at 24.0 mi per hour, find the distance between the two ships after five hours.

34. Radio direction finders are set up at points *A* and *B*, which are 2.00 mi apart on an east-west line. From *A* it is found that the bearing of the signal from a radio transmitter is 36° 20′, while from *B* the bearing of the same signal is 306° 20′. Find the distance of the transmitter from *B*.

35. Atoms in metals can be arranged in patterns called **unit cells**. One such unit cell, called a **primitive cell**, is a cube with an atom at each corner. A right triangle can be formed from one edge of the cell, a face diagonal and a body diagonal as shown in the figure. If each cell edge is 3×10^{-8} cm and the face diagonal is 4.24×10^{-8} cm, what is the angle between the cell edge and a body diagonal?

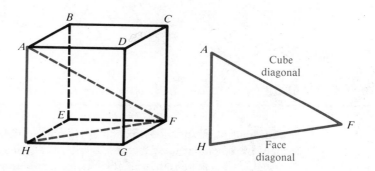

36. To determine the diameter of the sun, an astronomer might sight with a transit (a device used by surveyors for measuring angles) first to one edge of the sun and

then to the other, finding that the included angle equals $1° 4'$. Assuming that the distance from the earth to the sun is 92,919,800 mi, calculate the diameter of the sun.

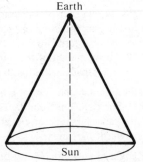

Earth

Sun

 37. The distance from the earth to a nearby star is determined by the method of triangulation, as shown in the figure (not drawn to scale). When the earth is on opposite sides of the sun (see the figure), the angle between lines joining the two positions of earth and the star is measured. For the star Alpha Centauri, the angle of elevation is $89° 59' 59''$. Calculate the distance from the earth to Alpha Centauri.

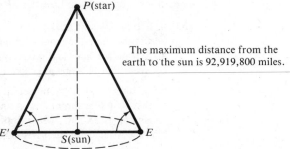

P(star)

The maximum distance from the earth to the sun is 92,919,800 miles.

E' E

S(sun)

38. The figure shows a magnified view of the threads of a bolt. Find x if d is 2.894 mm.

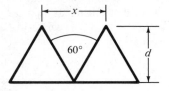

7.2   Oblique Angles and the Law of Sines

The methods of the previous section apply only to right triangles. In the next few sections we generalize these methods to include all triangles, not just right triangles. A triangle that is not a right triangle is called an **oblique triangle**. The measures of the three sides and the three angles of a triangle can be found if at least one side and any other two measures are known. There are four possible cases.

1. One side and two angles are known.

2. Two sides and one angle (not included between the two sides) are known. (This case may lead to more than one triangle.)

3. Three sides are known.

4. Two sides and the angle included between the two sides are known.

The first two cases require the *law of sines*, which is discussed in this section and the next. The last two cases require the *law of cosines*, discussed in Section 7.4.

To get the law of sines, start with a general oblique triangle, such as the one shown in Figure 7.6.

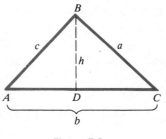

Figure 7.6

First, construct the perpendicular from B to side AC. Let h be the length of this perpendicular. Let c be the hypotenuse of right triangle ADB, and let a be the hypotenuse of right triangle BDC. By the definitions from the last section,

$$\text{in triangle } ADB \qquad \sin A = \frac{h}{c} \qquad \text{or} \qquad h = c \sin A,$$

$$\text{in triangle } BDC \qquad \sin C = \frac{h}{a} \qquad \text{or} \qquad h = a \sin C.$$

Since $h = c \sin A$, and $h = a \sin C$,

$$a \sin C = c \sin A$$

or, upon dividing both sides by $\sin A \sin C$,

$$\frac{a}{\sin A} = \frac{c}{\sin C}.$$

In a similar way,

$$\frac{a}{\sin A} = \frac{b}{\sin B} \qquad \text{and} \qquad \frac{b}{\sin B} = \frac{c}{\sin C}.$$

We have now proved the following theorem.

THEOREM 7.1   *(The Law of Sines)*   In any triangle ABC, with sides a, b, and c,

$$\frac{a}{\sin A} = \frac{b}{\sin B} \qquad \frac{a}{\sin A} = \frac{c}{\sin C} \qquad \text{and} \qquad \frac{b}{\sin B} = \frac{c}{\sin C}.$$

The three formulas of the law of sines can be written in a more compact form as

$$\frac{a}{\sin A} = \frac{b}{\sin B} = \frac{c}{\sin C}.$$

If two angles and one side of a triangle are known, the law of sines can always be used to solve the triangle.

EXAMPLE 1   Solve triangle ABC if $A = 32°\ 00'$, $B = 81°\ 50'$, and $a = 42.9$ cm. See Figure 7.7.
     Since we know A, B, and a, use the part of the law of sines that involves these variables.

$$\frac{a}{\sin A} = \frac{b}{\sin B}$$

Substituting the known values gives

$$\frac{42.9}{\sin 32°\ 00'} = \frac{b}{\sin 81°\ 50'}$$

or

$$b = \frac{42.9 \sin 81°\ 50'}{\sin 32°\ 00'}$$

$$b = 80.1 \text{ cm.}$$

Use the fact that the sum of the angles of any triangle is $180°$ to find C.

$$A + B + C = 180°$$
$$C = 180° - A - B$$
$$= 180° - 32°\ 00' - 81°\ 50'$$
$$C = 66°\ 10'$$

Now we can use the law of sines again to find c. (Why shouldn't we use the Pythagorean theorem?) We have

$$\frac{a}{\sin A} = \frac{c}{\sin C}$$

$$\frac{42.9}{\sin 32°\ 00'} = \frac{c}{\sin 66°\ 10'}$$

$$c = \frac{42.9 \sin 66°\ 10'}{\sin 32°\ 00'}.$$

$$c = 74.1 \text{ cm.} \quad \bullet$$

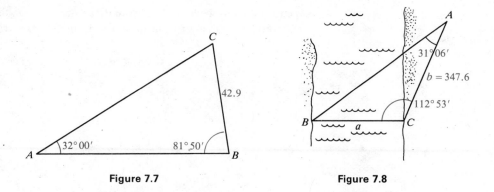

Figure 7.7   Figure 7.8

EXAMPLE 2   Shawn wishes to measure the distance across the Big Muddy River. See Figure 7.8. She finds that $C = 112° 53'$, $A = 31° 06'$, and $b = 347.6$ ft. Find the required distance.

Before we can use the law of sines to find a, we must first find angle B.

$$B = 180° - A - C$$
$$= 180° - 31° 06' - 112° 53'$$
$$B = 36° 01'.$$

Use the part of the law of sines involving A, B, and b.

$$\frac{a}{\sin A} = \frac{b}{\sin B}$$

Substitute the known values.

$$\frac{a}{\sin 31° 06'} = \frac{347.6}{\sin 36° 01'}$$

$$a \doteq \frac{347.6 \sin 31° 06'}{\sin 36° 01'}$$

$$a = 305.3 \text{ ft} \quad \bullet$$

The method we used to derive the law of sines can also be used to derive a useful formula for the area of a triangle. The standard formula for the area of a triangle is $K = \frac{1}{2}bh$, where K represents the area, b the base, and h the height. This formula cannot always be used, since in practice h is often unknown. To find a more useful formula, refer to triangle ABC in Figure 7.9.

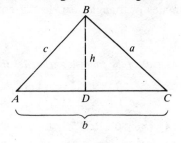

Figure 7.9

A perpendicular has been drawn from B to the base of the triangle. This perpendicular forms two smaller right triangles. Using triangle ABD,

$$\sin A = \frac{h}{c},$$

or

$$h = c \sin A.$$

Substituting into the formula $K = \frac{1}{2}bh$,

$$K = \frac{1}{2}b(c \sin A)$$

$$K = \frac{1}{2}bc \sin A.$$

We could have used any other pair of sides and the angle between them, as stated in the next theorem.

THEOREM 7.2   The area of any triangle is given by half the product of the lengths of two sides and the sine of the angle between the two sides.

EXAMPLE 3   Find the area of triangle MNP if $m = 29.7$ m, $n = 53.9$ m, and $P = 28° \, 40'$. By Theorem 7.2, the area of the triangle is

$$\frac{1}{2}(29.7)(53.9)\sin 28° \, 40' = 384 \text{ m}^2 \quad \bullet$$

EXAMPLE 4   Find the area of triangle ABC if $A = 24° \, 40'$, $b = 27.3$ cm, and $C = 52° \, 40'$. Before we can use the formula of Theorem 7.2, we must use the law of sines to find either a or c. Let us find a.

$$\frac{a}{\sin 24° \, 40'} = \frac{27.3}{\sin 102° \, 40'}$$

(Where did we get $102° \, 40'$?) Solve for a to verify that $a = 11.7$ cm. Now find the area, K.

$$K = \frac{1}{2}ab \sin C = \frac{1}{2}(11.7)(27.3)\sin 52° \, 40' = 127 \text{ cm}^2.$$

The area of triangle ABC is 127 cm^2. $\bullet$

7.2 EXERCISES

Solve each of the following triangles that exist. See Example 1.

1. $A = 51°$, $B = 46°$, $c = 14$ m

2. $B = 57°$, $C = 38°$, $a = 32$ cm

3. $A = 46° \, 30'$, $B = 52° \, 50'$, $b = 87.3$ mm

4. $A = 59° \, 30'$, $B = 48° \, 20'$, $b = 32.9$ m

5. $A = 27° 10'$, $C = 115° 30'$, $c = 76.0$ ft

6. $B = 124° 10'$, $C = 18° 40'$, $c = 94.6$ m

7. $A = 68.41°$, $B = 54.23°$, $a = 12.75$ ft

8. $C = 74.08°$, $B = 69.38°$, $c = 45.38$ m

9. $A = 87° 10'$, $b = 75.9$ yd, $C = 74° 20'$

10. $B = 38° 40'$, $a = 19.7$ cm, $C = 91° 40'$

11. $B = 20° 50'$, $C = 103° 10'$, $AC = 132$ ft

12. $A = 35° 20'$, $B = 52° 50'$, $AC = 675$ ft (See the photograph below.)

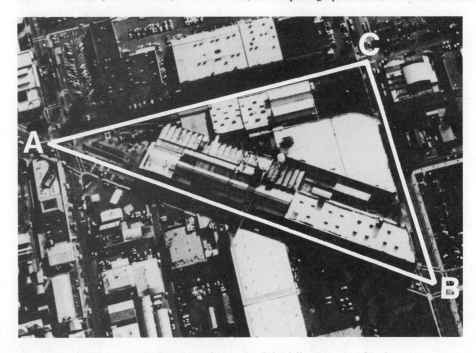

Use interpolation or a calculator to solve each of the following triangles that exist.

13. $A = 39° 42'$, $C = 30° 21'$, $b = 39.74$ m

14. $C = 71° 50'$, $B = 42° 34'$, $a = 2.614$ cm

15. $B = 42° 53'$, $C = 102° 24'$, $b = 3974$ ft

16. $A = 18° 45'$, $B = 51° 32'$, $c = 2798$ yd

17. $A = 39° 54'$, $a = 268.7$ m, $B = 42° 32'$

18. $C = 79° 18'$, $c = 39.81$ mm, $A = 32° 57'$

Solve each of the following exercises. Recall that bearing was discussed in Section 2.6. Use a calculator or interpolate as necessary. See Example 2.

19. To find the distance AB across a river, a distance $BC = 354$ m is laid off on one side of the river. It is found that $B = 112° 10'$ and $C = 15° 20'$. Find AB.

20. To determine the distance RS across a deep canyon, Joanna lays off a distance $TR = 582$ yd. She then finds that $T = 32° 50'$ and $R = 102° 20'$. Find RS.

21. Radio direction finders are placed at points *A* and *B*, which are 3.46 mi apart on an east-west line, with *A* west of *B*. From *A* the bearing of a certain radio transmitter is 47° 40′, while from *B* the bearing is 302° 30′. Find the distance of the transmitter from *A*.

22. A ship is sailing due north. Captain Odjakjian notices that the bearing of a lighthouse 12.5 km distant is 38° 50′. Later on, the captain notices that the bearing of the lighthouse has become 135° 48′. How far did the ship travel between the two observations of the lighthouse?

23. A hill slopes at an angle of 12° 28′ with the horizontal. The angle of elevation from the base of the hill to the top of a 457 ft tower at the top of the hill is 35° 59′. Find the distance from the base of the hill to the base of the tower.

24. Mark notices that the bearing of a tree on the opposite bank of a river is 115° 27′. Lisa is on the same bank as Mark, but 428.3 m away. She notices that the bearing of the tree is 45° 28′. The river is flowing north between parallel banks. What is the distance across the river?

25. Three gears are arranged as shown in the figure. Find angle θ.

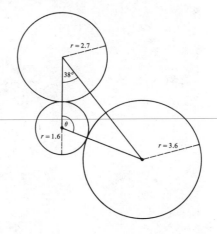

26. Three atoms with atomic radii of 2, 3, and 4.5 are arranged as in the figure. Find the distance between the centers of atoms *A* and *C*.

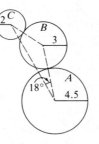

 Find the area of each of the following triangles. Use a calculator or interpolate as necessary. See Examples 3 and 4.

27. *A* = 46° 30′, *b* = 12.7 ft, *c* = 8.90 ft

28. *C* = 67° 40′, *b* = 46.7 m, *a* = 38.2 m

29. $B = 124.5°$, $a = 30.4$ cm, $c = 28.4$ cm

30. $C = 142.7°$, $a = 21.9$ km, $b = 24.6$ km

31. $A = 56° 48'$, $b = 32.67$ in, $c = 52.89$ in

32. $A = 34° 58'$, $b = 35.29$ m, $c = 28.67$ m

33. $A = 24° 25'$, $B = 56° 20'$, $c = 78.40$ cm

34. $B = 48° 30'$, $C = 74° 20'$, $a = 462$ km

35. A painter is going to apply a special coating to a triangular metal plate on a new building. Two sides measure 16.1 and 15.2 m. She knows that the angle between these sides is 125°. How many m^2 should she plan to cover?

36. A real estate salesman wants to find the area of a triangular lot. A surveyor friend takes measurements for him. He finds that two sides are 52.1 and 21.3 m, and the angle between them is 42° 10'. What is the area of the lot?

7.3 The Ambiguous Case of the Law of Sines

The law of sines can be used with any two sides of a triangle and the two angles opposite them. We have seen that if two angles and one side are known, we can solve the triangle. What about the case where two sides and an angle opposite one of them is known? We should be able to use the law of sines to find the missing angle.

EXAMPLE 1 Solve triangle ABC if $C = 55° 40'$, $c = 8.94$ m, and $b = 25.1$ m.
Let us look first for angle B. We have

$$\frac{b}{\sin B} = \frac{c}{\sin C}$$

$$\frac{25.1}{\sin B} = \frac{8.94}{\sin 55° 40'}$$

$$\sin B = \frac{25.1 \sin 55° 40'}{8.94}$$

$$\sin B = 2.3184.$$

Sin B is greater than 1. This is impossible, since $-1 \leq \sin B \leq 1$, for any angle B. Therefore, triangle ABC does not exist. This is shown in Figure 7.10.   ●

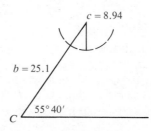

Figure 7.10

From Example 1, we see that when two sides and the angle opposite one of them are given, the information does not necessarily determine a triangle. To see all the possible outcomes in this case, look at Figures 7.11 and 7.12.

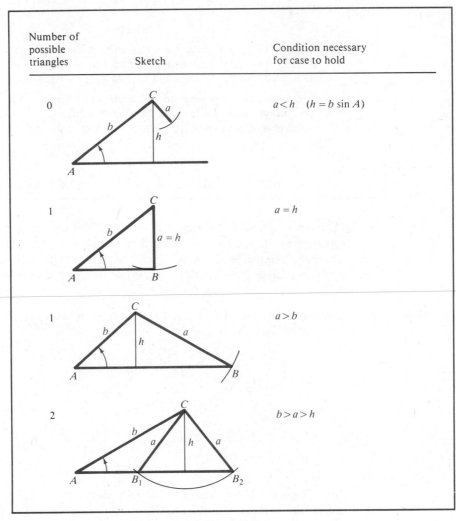

Figure 7.11

In a triangle ABC, suppose we know the measure of acute angle A, the length of side a, and the length of side b. To show this information, we draw angle A having a terminal side of length b. Now we draw a side of length a opposite angle A. Figure 7.11 shows that there might be more than one possible outcome. This situation is called the **ambiguous case of the law of sines**.

If angle A is obtuse, there are two possible outcomes, as shown in Figure 7.12.

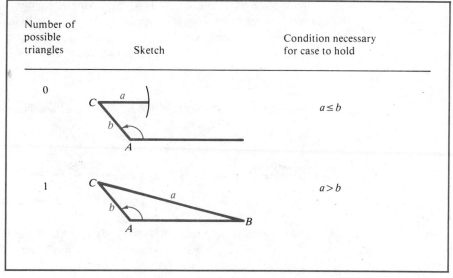

Number of possible triangles	Sketch	Condition necessary for case to hold
0		$a \le b$
1		$a > b$

Figure 7.12

It is possible to derive formulas that show which of the various cases exist for a particular set of numerical data. However, this work is unnecessary if we use the law of sines. For example, if we use the law of sines and find that sin B is greater than 1, there is no triangle at all. (Why?) The case where we get two different triangles is illustrated in the next example.

EXAMPLE 2   Solve triangle ABC if $A = 55° 20'$, $a = 22.8$, and $b = 24.9$.

To begin, let us use the law of sines to find angle B.

$$\frac{a}{\sin A} = \frac{b}{\sin B}$$

$$\frac{22.8}{\sin 55° 20'} = \frac{24.9}{\sin B}$$

$$\sin B = \frac{24.9 \sin 55° 20'}{22.8}$$

$$\sin B = .8982$$

Figure 7.13

Since $\sin B < 1$, there is at least one triangle. Figure 7.13 shows the case if there are two triangles. We will assume there are two triangles and find the two values of B.

Since $\sin B = .8982$, we find that one value of B is

$$B = 64° \, 00'.$$

We know that $\sin (180° - B) = \sin B$. Therefore, another value of B is

$$B = 180° - 64° \, 00'$$
$$B = 116° \, 00'.$$

To keep track of these two different values of B, let

$$B_1 = 116° \, 00' \qquad \text{and} \qquad B_2 = 64° \, 00'.$$

We must now separately solve triangles AB_1C_1 and AB_2C_2 shown in Figure 7.14.

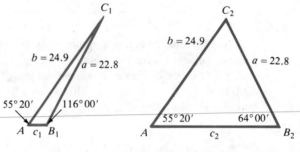

Figure 7.14

Since B_1 is the larger of the two values of B, we find C_1 next.

$$C_1 = 180° - A - B_1$$
$$C_1 = 8° \, 40'.$$

Had this answer come out negative, there would have been only one triangle. This is why we used the larger angle first. Now, use the law of sines to find c_1.

We have
$$\frac{a}{\sin A} = \frac{c_1}{\sin C_1}$$

$$\frac{22.8}{\sin 55° \, 20'} = \frac{c_1}{\sin 8° \, 40'}$$

$$c_1 = \frac{22.8 \sin 8° \, 40'}{\sin 55° \, 20'}$$

$$c_1 = 4.18.$$

To solve triangle AB_2C_2, first find C_2.

$$C_2 = 180° - A - B_2$$
$$C_2 = 60° \, 40'.$$

By the law of sines,

$$\frac{22.8}{\sin 55° 20'} = \frac{c_2}{\sin 60° 40'}$$

$$c_2 = \frac{22.8 \sin 60° 40'}{\sin 55° 20'}$$

$$c_2 = 24.2 \quad \bullet$$

7.3 EXERCISES

Sketch all possible triangles satisfying each of the following conditions. Do not try to solve.

1. $A = 47°$, $b = 29$, $a = 32$
2. $A = 53°$, $b = 58$, $a = 48$
3. $C = 70°$, $b = 96$, $c = 93$
4. $B = 33°$, $b = 14$, $a = 18$
5. $A = 128°$, $a = 18$, $c = 12$
6. $C = 114°$, $a = 39$, $c = 20$

Find the missing angles in each of the following triangles. Use a calculator or interpolate as necessary. See Example 1.

7. $B = 29° 40'$, $a = 39.6$ ft, $b = 28.4$ ft
8. $A = 52° 10'$, $b = 980$ cm, $a = 796$ cm
9. $C = 41° 20'$, $b = 25.9$ m, $c = 38.4$ m
10. $B = 48° 50'$, $a = 3850$ in, $b = 4730$ in
11. $B = 74° 20'$, $a = 859$ m, $b = 783$ m
12. $C = 82° 10'$, $a = 10.9$ km, $c = 7.62$ km
13. $A = 142.13°$, $b = 5.432$ ft, $a = 7.297$ ft
14. $B = 113.72°$, $a = 189.6$ yd, $b = 243.8$ yd
15. $C = 129° 18'$, $a = 372.9$ cm, $c = 416.7$ cm
16. $A = 132° 07'$, $b = 7.481$ mi, $a = 8.219$ mi

Solve each of the following triangles. Use a calculator or interpolate as necessary. See Example 1.

17. $A = 42° 30'$, $a = 15.6$ ft, $b = 8.14$ ft
18. $C = 52° 20'$, $a = 32.5$ yd, $c = 59.8$ yd
19. $B = 72° 10'$, $b = 78.3$ m, $c = 145$ m
20. $C = 68° 30'$, $c = 258$ cm, $b = 386$ cm
21. $A = 38° 40'$, $a = 9.72$ km, $b = 11.8$ km
22. $C = 29° 50'$, $a = 8.61$ m, $c = 5.21$ m
23. $B = 32° 50'$, $a = 7540$ cm, $b = 5180$ cm
24. $C = 22° 50'$, $b = 159$ mm, $c = 132$ mm
25. $A = 96.80°$, $b = 3.589$ ft, $a = 5.818$ ft
26. $C = 88.70°$, $b = 56.87$ yd, $c = 112.4$ yd
27. $B = 39° 41'$, $a = 29.81$ m, $b = 23.76$ m
28. $A = 51° 12'$, $c = 7986$ cm, $a = 7208$ cm

29. A surveyor reported the following data about a piece of property: "The property is triangular in shape, with dimensions as shown in the figure." Use the law of sines to see if such a piece of property could exist.

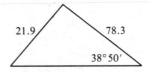

30. The surveyor tries again: "A second triangular piece of property has dimensions as shown." This time it turns out that the surveyor did not consider every possible case. Use the law of sines to show why.

7.4 The Law of Cosines

The law of sines cannot always be used. For example, if two sides and the angle between the two sides are given, the law of sines cannot be used. (Try it.) Also, if all three of the sides of a triangle are given, the law of sines again cannot be used to find the unknown angles. For both these cases we need the law of cosines.

To get this law, let *ABC* be any oblique triangle. Choose a coordinate system so that the origin is at vertex *B* and side *BC* is along the positive *x*-axis. See Figure 7.15.

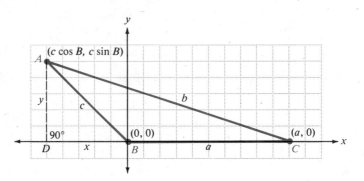

Figure 7.15

Let (x, y) be the coordinates of vertex *A* of the triangle. Verify that for angle *B*, whether obtuse or acute,

$$\sin B = \frac{y}{c} \quad \text{and} \quad \cos B = \frac{x}{c}.$$

(Here we assume x is negative if *B* is obtuse.) From these results

$$y = c \sin B \quad \text{and} \quad x = c \cos B,$$

so that the coordinates of point A become

$$(c \cos B, c \sin B).$$

Point C has coordinates $(a, 0)$, and AC has length b. By the distance formula

$$b = \sqrt{(c \cos B - a)^2 + (c \sin B)^2}.$$

Squaring both sides and simplifying gives

$$\begin{aligned} b^2 &= (c \cos B - a)^2 + (c \sin B)^2 \\ &= c^2 \cos^2 B - 2ac \cos B + a^2 + c^2 \sin^2 B \\ &= a^2 + c^2 (\cos^2 B + \sin^2 B) - 2ac \cos B \\ &= a^2 + c^2(1) - 2ac \cos B \\ b^2 &= a^2 + c^2 - 2ac \cos B. \end{aligned}$$

This result is one form of the law of cosines. In the work above, we could just as easily have placed A or C at the origin. This would have given the same result, but one which is different in appearance. These various forms are summarized in the following theorem.

THEOREM 7.3   *(The Law of Cosines).*   In any triangle ABC, with sides a, b, and c,

$$\begin{aligned} a^2 &= b^2 + c^2 - 2bc \cos A \\ b^2 &= a^2 + c^2 - 2ac \cos B \\ c^2 &= a^2 + b^2 - 2ab \cos C. \end{aligned}$$

EXAMPLE 1   Solve triangle ABC if $A = 42° \, 20'$, $b = 12.9$, and $c = 15.4$. See Figure 7.16. We can find a by using the law of cosines.

$$\begin{aligned} a^2 &= b^2 + c^2 - 2bc \cos A \\ a^2 &= (12.9)^2 + (15.4)^2 - 2(12.9)(15.4) \cos 42° \, 20' \\ &= 166.41 + 237.16 - (397.32)(.7392) \\ &= 403.57 - 293.70 \\ a^2 &= 109.87 \\ a &= 10.5. \end{aligned}$$

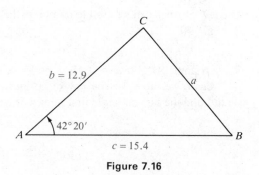

Figure 7.16

Now we know a, b, c, and A. We can use the law of sines to find either angle B or angle C next. If there is an obtuse angle in the triangle, it will be the larger of B and C. Since we can't tell from the sine of the angle whether it is acute or obtuse, it is a good idea to find the smaller angle (which will be acute) first. We know $B < C$ because $b < c$, so we use the law of sines to find B.

$$\frac{10.5}{\sin 42° \ 20'} = \frac{12.9}{\sin B}$$

$$\sin B = \frac{12.9 \ \sin 42° \ 20'}{10.5}$$

$$\sin B = .8274$$

$$B = 55° \ 50'.$$

Finally, we can find C.

$$C = 180° - A - B$$

$$C = 81° \ 50' \qquad \bullet$$

EXAMPLE 2 Solve triangle ABC if $C = 132° \ 40'$, $b = 259$, and $a = 423$.

Here we use the form of the law of cosines $c^2 = a^2 + b^2 - 2ab \cos C$. Inserting the given data gives

$$c^2 = a^2 + b^2 - 2ab \cos C$$
$$c^2 = (423)^2 + (259)^2 - 2(423)(259) \cos 132° \ 40'.$$

To find $\cos 132° \ 40'$, recall that $\cos C = -\cos (180° - C)$. Thus,

$$\cos 132° \ 40' = -\cos 47° \ 20' = -.6777.$$

Now we can finish finding c.

$$c^2 = (423)^2 + (259)^2 - 2(423)(259)(-.6777)$$
$$= 178{,}929 + 67{,}081 + 148{,}494$$
$$c^2 = 394{,}504$$

and

$$c = 628.$$

The law of sines can be used to complete the solution. Check that $A = 29° \ 40'$ and $B = 17° \ 40'$. $\bullet$

EXAMPLE 3 Solve triangle ABC if $a = 9.47$, $b = 15.9$, and $c = 21.1$.

Again we must use the law of cosines. When we use the law of cosines, we should find the largest angle first in case it is obtuse, so let us look for C. We have

$$c^2 = a^2 + b^2 - 2ab \cos C$$

or

$$\cos C = \frac{a^2 + b^2 - c^2}{2ab}.$$

Inserting the given values leads to

$$\cos C = \frac{(9.47)^2 + (15.9)^2 - (21.1)^2}{2(9.47)(15.9)}$$

$$= \frac{-102.7191}{301.146}$$

$$\cos C = -.3411.$$

From this last result,

$$C = 110° \, 00'.$$

(We know that C is obtuse since $\cos C$ is negative.) Use the law of sines to find B. Verify that $B = 45° \, 00'$. Since $A = 180° - B - C$,

$$A = 25° \, 00'. \quad \bullet$$

The law of cosines can be used to find a formula for the area of a triangle when only the lengths of the three sides of the triangle are known. This formula is given as the next theorem.

THEOREM 7.4   ***(Heron's Area Formula).***   If a triangle has sides of lengths a, b, and c, and if

$$s = \frac{1}{2} (a + b + c),$$

then, the area of the triangle is

$$K = \sqrt{s(s - a)(s - b)(s - c)}.$$

EXAMPLE 4   Find the area of the triangle having sides of lengths $a = 29.7$ ft, $b = 42.3$ ft, and $c = 38.4$ ft.

To use Heron's area formula, first find s.

$$s = \frac{1}{2} (a + b + c)$$

$$s = \frac{1}{2} (29.7 + 42.3 + 38.4)$$

$$s = 55.2$$

The area is then given by

$$K = \sqrt{s(s - a)(s - b)(s - c)}$$

$$= \sqrt{55.2(55.2 - 29.7)(55.2 - 42.3)(55.2 - 38.4)}$$

$$K = \sqrt{55.2(25.5)(12.9)(16.8)}$$

$$K = 552 \text{ ft}^2. \quad \bullet$$

As we have seen, there are four possible cases that can come up in solving an oblique triangle. These cases are summarized as follows. (The first two cases require the law of sines, while the second two require the law of cosines. In all four cases, we assume that the given information actually produces a triangle.)

Case	Abbreviation	Example
One side and two angles are known	SAA	a, B, A known, find b $b = \frac{a \sin B}{\sin A}$
two sides and one angle (not included between the two sides) are known	SSA	b, c, B known, find C $\sin C = \frac{c \sin B}{b}$ (watch for the ambiguous case—there may be two triangles)
three sides are known	SSS	a, b, c, known, find A $\cos A = \frac{b^2 + c^2 - a^2}{2bc}$
two sides and the angle included between the two sides are known	SAS	a, B, c known, find b $b^2 = a^2 + c^2 - 2ac \cos B$

7.4 EXERCISES

Solve each of the following triangles. Use a calculator or interpolate as necessary. See Examples 1 and 2.

1. $A = 39° 50'$, $b = 6.74$ in, $c = 5.92$ in
2. $B = 35° 10'$, $a = 5.78$ yd, $c = 4.87$ yd
3. $C = 45° 40'$, $b = 8.94$ m, $a = 7.23$ m
4. $A = 67° 20'$, $b = 37.9$ km, $c = 40.8$ km
5. $A = 80° 40'$, $b = 143$ cm, $c = 89.6$ cm
6. $C = 72° 40'$, $a = 327$ ft, $b = 251$ ft

7. $B = 74.80°$, $a = 8.919$ in, $c = 6.427$ in

8. $C = 59.70°$, $a = 3.725$ mi, $b = 4.698$ mi

9. $A = 112° 50'$, $b = 6.28$ m, $c = 12.2$ m

10. $B = 168° 10'$, $a = 15.1$ cm, $c = 19.2$ cm

11. $C = 24° 49'$, $a = 251.3$ m, $b = 318.7$ m

12. $B = 52° 28'$, $a = 7598$ in, $c = 6973$ in

Find all the angles in each of the following triangles. Round answers to the nearest ten minutes. See Example 3.

13. $a = 2$ ft, $b = 3$ ft, $c = 4$ ft

14. $a = 3$ m, $b = 4$ m, $c = 6$ m

15. $a = 9.3$ cm, $b = 5.7$ cm, $c = 8.2$ cm

16. $a = 28$ ft, $b = 47$ ft, $c = 58$ ft

17. $a = 42.9$ m, $b = 37.6$ m, $c = 62.7$ m

18. $a = 189$ yd, $b = 214$ yd, $c = 325$ yd

19. $AB = 1240$ ft, $AC = 876$ ft, $BC = 918$ ft

20. $AB = 298$ m, $AC = 421$ m, $BC = 324$ m

 Use a calculator or interpolation to find all the angles in each of the following triangles to the nearest minute.

21. $a = 18.92$ in, $b = 24.35$ in, $c = 22.16$ in

22. $a = 250.8$ ft, $b = 212.7$ ft, $c = 324.1$ ft

23. $a = 7.095$ m, $b = 5.613$ m, $c = 11.53$ m

24. $a = 15,250$ m, $b = 17,890$ m, $c = 27,840$ m

Solve each of the following problems. Use the laws of this chapter as necessary.

25. Points A and B are on opposite sides of Lake Yankee. From a third point, C, the angle between the lines of sight to A and B is $46° 20'$. If AC is 350 m long and BC is 286 m long, find AB.

26. The sides of a parallelogram are 4.0 cm and 6.0 cm. One angle is $58°$ while another is $122°$. Find the lengths of the diagonals of the figure.

27. Airports A and B are 450 km apart, on an east-west line. Tom flies in a northeast direction from A to airport C. From C he flies 359 km on a bearing of $128° 40'$ to B. How far is C from A?

28. Two ships leave a harbor together, traveling on courses that have an angle of $135° 40'$ between them. If they each travel 402 mi, how far apart are they?

29. Pearl took a plane from A to B, a distance of 350 mi. Then her plane continued from B to C, a distance of 400 mi. Finally, she returned to A, a distance of 300 mi. If A and B are on an east-west line, find the bearing from A to C. (Assume C is north of the line through A and B.)

30. A hill slopes at an angle of $12° 28'$ with the horizontal. From the base of the hill, the angle of inclination of a 459.0 ft tower at the top of the hill is $35° 59'$. How much rope would be required to reach from the top of the tower to the bottom of the hill?

31. A crane with a counterweight is shown in the figure. Find the distance between points *A* and *B*.

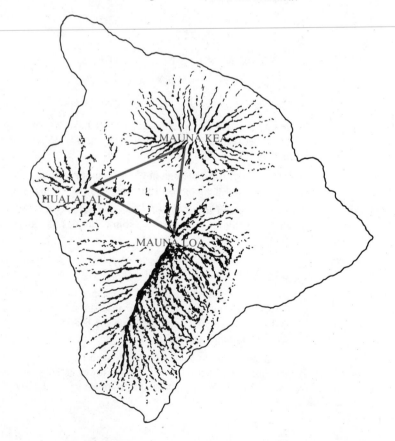

32. A weight is supported by cables attached to both ends of a balance beam. See the figure. What angles are formed between the beams and the cables?

To help predict eruptions from the volcano Mauna Loa on the island of Hawaii, scientists keep track of the volcano's movement by using a "super triangle" with vertices on the three volcanos shown on the map below. (For example, in a recent year, Mauna Loa moved six inches north and northwest—a result of increasing internal pressure.) The data in the following exercises has been rounded.

33. $AB = 22.47928$ mi, $AC = 28.14276$ mi, $A = 58.56989°$; find BC

34. $AB = 22.47928$ mi, $BC = 25.24983$ mi, $A = 58.56989°$; find B

Find the area of each of the following triangles. See Example 4.

35. $a = 15$ in, $b = 19$ in, $c = 24$ in

36. $a = 27$ m, $b = 40$ m, $c = 34$ m

37. $a = 154$ cm, $b = 179$ cm, $c = 183$ cm

38. $a = 25.4$ yd, $b = 38.2$ yd, $c = 19.8$ yd

39. $a = 76.3$ ft, $b = 109$ ft, $c = 98.8$ ft

40. $a = 15.89$ in, $b = 21.74$ in, $c = 10.92$ in

41. $a = 74.14$ ft, $b = 89.99$ ft, $c = 51.82$ ft

42. $a = 1.096$ km, $b = 1.142$ km, $c = 1.253$ km

43. Sam wants to paint a triangular region 75 by 68 by 85 m. A can of paint covers 75 m^2 of area. How many cans (to the next higher can) will he need?

44. How many cans would be needed if the region were 8.2 by 9.4 by 3.8 m?

7.5 Vectors

With what we have learned so far in this chapter, we can find the measure of all six of the parts of a triangle, given at least one side and any two other measures. In the next two sections, we look at applications of this work to **vectors**. In this section, we look at the basic ideas of vectors and then apply the law of sines and the law of cosines to vector problems.

Many of the quantities that we deal with in mathematics involve magnitudes. For example, we have seen magnitudes such as 45 pounds or 60 miles per hour. These quantities are often called **scalars**. We sometimes need to work with quantities involving both magnitude and direction, called **vector quantities**. Typical vector quantities include velocities, accelerations, and forces, such as a force of 40 lb acting from the north.

Vector quantities are often represented with vectors. A **vector** is a directed line segment, that is, a line segment pointing in a particular direction. The length of the vector represents the magnitude of the vector quantity. The direction of the vector, indicated with an arrowhead, represents the direction of the quantity. For example, the vector in Figure 7.17 represents a force of 10 pounds applied at an angle of 30° from the horizontal.

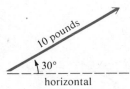

Figure 7.17

Vectors are often printed in boldface type. When writing vectors by hand, it is customary to use an arrow over the letter or letters. Thus **OP** and $\overrightarrow{OP}$ both represent vector OP. They may be named by using either one lowercase or uppercase letter, or two uppercase letters. When two letters are used, the first indicates the *initial point* and the second indicates the *terminal point*. Knowing these points gives the direction of the vector. For example, vectors **OP** and **PO** of Figure 7.18 are not the same vectors. They have the same magnitudes, but opposite directions. The magnitude of vector **OP** is written $|\mathbf{OP}|$.

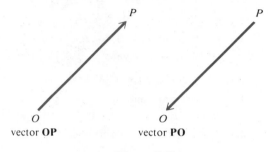

vector **OP**   vector **PO**

Figure 7.18

Two vectors are *equal* if and only if they both have the same directions and the same magnitudes. In Figure 7.19, vectors **A** and **B** are equal, as are vectors **C** and **D**.

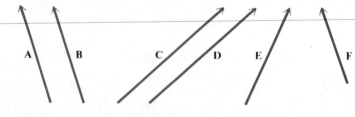

Figure 7.19

As Figure 7.19 shows, equal vectors need not coincide, but they must be parallel. Note that $\mathbf{A} \neq \mathbf{E}$ because they do not have the same direction, while $\mathbf{A} \neq \mathbf{F}$ because they have different magnitudes, as indicated by their different lengths.

To find the *sum* of two vectors **A** and **B**, written $\mathbf{A} + \mathbf{B}$, place the initial point of vector **B** at the terminal point of vector **A**, as shown in Figure 7.20. The vector with the same initial point as **A** and the same terminal point as **B** is the sum $\mathbf{A} + \mathbf{B}$. The sum of two vectors is again a vector.

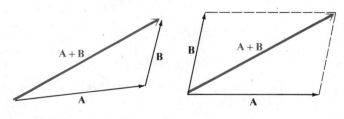

Figure 7.20   Figure 7.21

Another way to find the sum of two vectors is to use the **parallelogram rule**. Place vectors **A** and **B** so that their initial points coincide. Then complete a parallelogram which has **A** and **B** as two sides. The diagonal of the parallelogram with the same initial point as **A** and **B** is the same vector sum **A** + **B** that we found by the definition. See Figure 7.21.

Parallelograms can be used to show that vector **B** + **A** is the same as vector **A** + **B**, or that

$$\mathbf{A} + \mathbf{B} = \mathbf{B} + \mathbf{A}.$$

Thus, vector addition is **commutative**.

The vector sum **A** + **B** is called the **resultant** of vectors **A** and **B**. Each of the vectors **A** and **B** is called a **component** of vector **A** + **B**. In many practical applications, such as surveying, it is necessary to break a vector into its **vertical** and **horizontal components**. These components are two vectors, one vertical and one horizontal, whose resultant is the original vector. As shown in Figure 7.22, vector **OR** is the vertical component and vector **OS** is the horizontal component of **OP**.

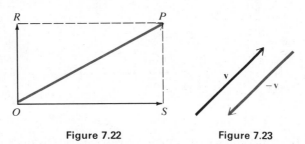

Figure 7.22   Figure 7.23

For every vector **v** there is a vector −**v**, which has the same magnitude as **v** but opposite direction. Vector −**v** is called the **opposite** of **v**. See Figure 7.23. The sum of **v** and −**v** has magnitude 0 and is called a **zero vector**. As with real numbers, to *subtract* vector **B** from vector **A**, find the vector sum **A** + (−**B**). See Figure 7.24.

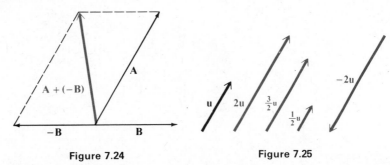

Figure 7.24   Figure 7.25

The **scalar product** of a real number (or scalar)k and a vector **u** is the vector $k \cdot \mathbf{u}$ which has magnitude $|k|$ times the magnitude of **u**. As shown in Figure 7.25, $k \cdot \mathbf{u}$ has the same direction as **u** if $k > 0$, and the opposite direction if $k < 0$.

EXAMPLE 1   Vector **w** has magnitude 25.0 and is inclined at an angle of 40° from the horizontal. Find the magnitudes of the horizontal and vertical components of the vector.

In Figure 7.26, the vertical component is labeled **v** and the horizontal component is labeled **u**. Vectors **u**, **v**, and **w** form a right triangle. In this right triangle, $\sin 40° = |\mathbf{v}|/|\mathbf{w}| = |\mathbf{v}|/25.0$, from which

$$|\mathbf{v}| = 25.0 \sin 40° = 25.0(.6428) = 16.1$$

In the same way, $\cos 40° = |\mathbf{u}|/25.0$, and

$$|\mathbf{u}| = 25.0 \cos 40° = 19.2. \quad \bullet$$

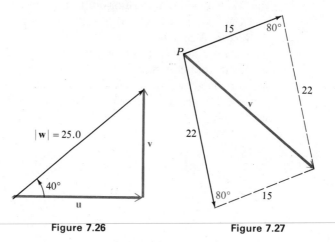

Figure 7.26   Figure 7.27

EXAMPLE 2   Two forces of 15 and 22 newtons (a newton is a unit of force used in physics) act on a point in the plane. If the angle between the forces is 100°, find the magnitude of the resultant force.

As shown in Figure 7.27, we can form a parallelogram with the forces as adjacent sides. The angles of the parallelogram adjacent to angle P each measure 80°, and the opposite sides of the parallelogram are equal in length. The resultant force divides the parallelogram into two triangles. Now we can use the law of cosines to get

$$|\mathbf{v}|^2 = 15^2 + 22^2 - 2(15)(22)\cos 80°$$
$$= 225 + 484 - 115$$
$$|\mathbf{v}|^2 = 594$$
$$|\mathbf{v}| = 24. \quad \bullet$$

7.5 EXERCISES   *In Exercises 1–4 refer to the following vectors.*

Name all pairs of vectors

1. which appear to be equal.

2. which are opposites.

3. where the first is a scalar multiple of the other, with the scalar positive.

4. where the scalar is negative.

In Exercises 5–22 refer to the vectors pictured here.

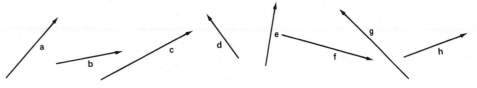

Draw a sketch to represent each of the following vectors.

EXAMPLE   **a + e**

Place **a** and **e** so that their initial points coincide. Then use the parallelogram rule to find the resultant.   ●

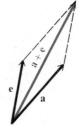

5. −**b**	**6.** −**g**	**7.** 3**a**	**8.** 2**h**
9. **a** + **c**	**10.** **a** + **b**	**11.** **h** + **g**	**12.** **e** + **f**
13. **a** + **h**	**14.** **b** + **d**	**15.** **h** + **d**	**16.** **a** + **f**
17. **a** − **c**	**18.** **d** − **e**	**19.** **a** + (**b** + **c**)	**20.** (**a** + **b**) + **c**
21. **h** + (**e** + **g**)	**22.** (**h** + **e**) + **g**		

23. From the results of Exercises 19–22, do you think that vector addition is associative?

*For each of the following forces, represented by **u** and **w** with angle θ between the forces, sketch the resultant.*

EXAMPLE $|\mathbf{u}| = 8$, $|\mathbf{v}| = 6$, $\theta = 45°$

Sketch the two vectors, as shown. Then use the parallelogram rule to find the resultant. The resultant is in color in the sketch.   ●

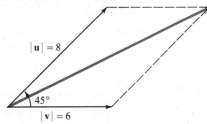

24. $|\mathbf{u}| = 15$, $|\mathbf{w}| = 20$, $\theta = 50°$ **25.** $|\mathbf{u}| = 10$, $|\mathbf{w}| = 18$, $\theta = 25°$

26. $|\mathbf{u}| = 8$, $|\mathbf{w}| = 12$, $\theta = 20°$ **27.** $|\mathbf{u}| = 20$, $|\mathbf{w}| = 30$, $\theta = 30°$

28. $|\mathbf{u}| = 27$, $|\mathbf{w}| = 50$, $\theta = 12°$ **29.** $|\mathbf{u}| = 50$, $|\mathbf{w}| = 70$, $\theta = 40°$

For each of the following, vector **v** *has the given magnitude and direction. See the figure. Find the magnitude of the horizontal and vertical components of* **v**. *See Example 1.*

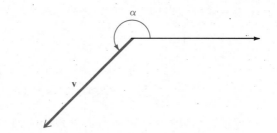

30. $\alpha = 30°$, $|\mathbf{v}| = 40$ **31.** $\alpha = 45°$, $|\mathbf{v}| = 20$

32. $\alpha = 75°$, $|\mathbf{v}| = 100$ **33.** $\alpha = 60° \ 10'$, $|\mathbf{v}| = 28.6$

34. $\alpha = 35° \ 50'$, $|\mathbf{v}| = 47.8$ **35.** $\alpha = 27° \ 30'$, $|\mathbf{v}| = 15.4$

36. $\alpha = 59° \ 40'$. $|\mathbf{v}| = 78.9$ **37.** $\alpha = 128.5°$, $|\mathbf{v}| = 198$

38. $\alpha = 146.3°$, $|\mathbf{v}| = 238$ **39.** $\alpha = 251° \ 10'$, $|\mathbf{v}| = 69.1$

40. $\alpha = 302° \ 40'$, $|\mathbf{v}| = 7890$

In each of the following, two forces act on a point in the plane. The angle between the two forces is given. Find the magnitude of the resultant force. See Example 2.

41. forces of 300 and 500 newtons, forming an angle of 95°

42. forces of 25 and 40 newtons, forming an angle of 120°

43. forces of 17.9 and 25.8 lb, forming an angle of 105° 30′

44. forces of 75.6 and 98.2 lb, forming an angle of 82° 50′

45. forces of 116 and 139 lb, forming an angle of 140° 50′

46. forces of 37.8 and 53.7 lb, forming an angle of 68° 30′

47. *When an airplane is in flight, the air pressure creates a force vector, called the "lift," perpendicular to the wings. When the plane banks for a turn, this lift vector may be resolved into horizontal and vertical components. The vertical component has magnitude equal to the plane's weight (this is what holds the plane up), and the horizontal component "pushes" the plane into its curved path. Suppose that a jet plane weighing 500,000 lb banks at an angle θ (figure).*

(a) Find the magnitude of the lift and the horizontal component if (i) $\theta = 10°$, (ii) $\theta = 20°$, (iii) $\theta = 30°$, (iv) $\theta = 0°$.

(b) Based on your answers to part (a), why do you suppose a plane can turn in a smaller circle when it banks at a greater angle?

(c) Why do you suppose a plane flies straight when it is not banking?

(d) If the maximum lift the wings can sustain is 600,000 lb, what is the maximum angle at which the plane can bank?

(e) What two things might happen if the plane tried to bank at an angle steeper than this maximum?

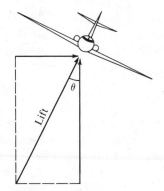

 48. Paula and Steve are pulling their daughter Jessie on a sled. Steve pulls with a force of 18 lb at an angle of 10°. Paula pulls with a force of 12 lb at an angle of 15°. What is the weight of Jessie and the sled? See the figure. (Hint: find the resultant.)

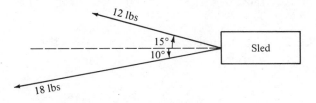

7.6   Application of Vectors

Vectors are useful in solving problems which involve forces, velocities, or accelerations. In this section, we discuss some of the typical applications of vectors.

In the last section, we discussed methods for finding the resultant of two forces. If the resultant of two forces is **u**, then **−u** is called the equilibrant of the two forces. The **equilibrant** is the force necessary to counterbalance the joint action of the two forces.

EXAMPLE 1   Find the magnitude of the equilibrant of forces of 48 and 60 newtons acting on a point A, if the angle between the forces is 50°. Then find the angle between the equilibrant and the 48 newton force.

In Figure 7.28, the equilibrant is **−v**. The magnitude of **v**, and hence of **−v**, is found by using triangle ABC and the law of cosines.

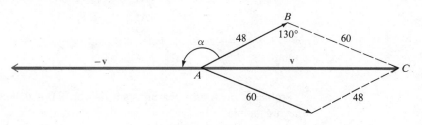

Figure 7.28

$$|\mathbf{v}|^2 = 48^2 + 60^2 - 2(48)(60) \cos 130°$$
$$= 2304 + 3600 - 5760(-.6428)$$
$$|\mathbf{v}|^2 = 9606.5,$$

or

$$|\mathbf{v}| = 98,$$

to two significant digits.

The angle we wish to find, labeled α in Figure 7.28, can be found by subtracting angle CAB from 180°. Using the law of sines to find angle CAB, we have

$$\frac{98}{\sin 130°} = \frac{60}{\sin CAB}$$

$$\sin CAB = .4690$$

$$\text{angle } CAB = 28° \ 00'.$$

Thus, $\alpha = 180° - 28° \ 00' = 152° \ 00'.$ ●

EXAMPLE 2   Find the force required to pull a 50 lb weight up a ramp inclined at 20° to the horizontal.

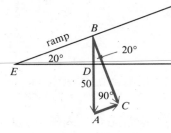

Figure 7.29

In Figure 7.29, the vertical 50 lb force represents the force due to gravity. The component **BC** represents the force with which the body pushes against the ramp, while the component **AC** represents the force that would pull the body up the ramp. The angle between AB and BC is 20° since triangles ABC and DEB are similar triangles. Thus, in right triangle ABC,

$$\sin 20° = \frac{|\mathbf{AC}|}{50}$$

$$|\mathbf{AC}| = 50 \sin 20°$$

$$|\mathbf{AC}| = 17.1.$$

Thus, 17 lb of force, to the nearest pound, will be required to pull the weight up the ramp.   ●

Problems involving bearing can also be worked with vectors, as shown in the next example.

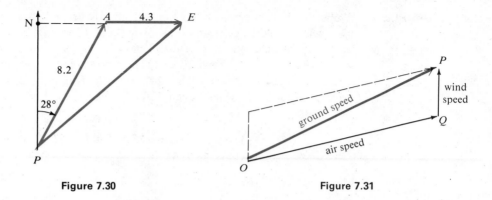

Figure 7.30   **Figure 7.31**

EXAMPLE 3   A ship leaves port on a bearing of 28° and travels 8.2 mi. The ship then turns due east and travels 4.3 mi. How far is the ship from port? What is its bearing from port?

In Figure 7.30, vectors **PA** and **AE** represent the ship's line of travel. We need to find the magnitude and bearing of the resultant **PE**. Triangle *PNA* is a right triangle, so angle *NAP* = 90° − 28° = 62°. Then angle *PAE* = 180° − 62° = 118°. Using the law of cosines, we can find $|\mathbf{PE}|$, the magnitude of vector **PE**.

$$|\mathbf{PE}|^2 = 8.2^2 + 4.3^2 - 2(8.2)(4.3) \cos 118°$$
$$= 67.24 + 18.49 - 70.52(-.4695)$$
$$|\mathbf{PE}|^2 = 118.84$$

Therefore,

$$|\mathbf{PE}| = 10.9.$$

To find the bearing of the ship from port, we need to find angle *APE*. Using the law of sines, we have

$$\frac{4.3}{\sin APE} = \frac{10.9}{\sin 118°}$$

$$\sin APE = \frac{4.3 \sin 118°}{10.9}$$

$$\text{angle } APE = 20° \ 20'$$

The ship is 10.9 mi from port on a bearing of 28° + 20° 20′ = 48° 20′.   ●

In air navigation, the airspeed of a plane is its speed relative to the air, while the ground speed is its speed relative to the ground. Because of the wind, these two speeds are usually different. The ground speed of the plane is represented by the vector sum of the air speed and wind speed vectors. In Figure 7.31, **OQ** represents the airspeed, **QP** the wind speed, and **OP** the ground speed.

EXAMPLE 4 A plane with an airspeed of 190 mi per hour is headed on a bearing of 120°. A north wind is blowing (from north to south) at 15 mi per hour. Find the ground speed and the actual bearing of the plane.

In Figure 7.32 the ground speed is represented by $|\mathbf{x}|$. We must find the angle α to find the bearing, which will be $120° + \alpha$. From Figure 7.32, we have angle BCO equal to angle AOC, which equals 120°. We can find $|\mathbf{x}|$ by the law of cosines.

$$|\mathbf{x}|^2 = 190^2 + 15^2 - 2(190)(15)\cos 120°$$
$$= 36{,}100 + 225 - 5700(-.5)$$
$$|\mathbf{x}|^2 = 39{,}175$$

Therefore,

$$|\mathbf{x}| = 198.$$

Now find α by using the law of sines.

$$\frac{15}{\sin \alpha} = \frac{198}{\sin 120°}$$
$$\sin \alpha = .0656$$
$$\alpha = 3° \; 50'$$

The ground speed is about 198 mi per hour, at a bearing of 123° 50'. ●

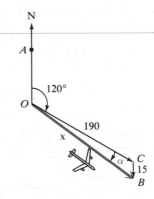

Figure 7.32

7.6 EXERCISES *Solve each of the following problems. See Examples 1–4.*

1. Two forces of 692 and 423 newtons act on a point. The resultant force is 786 newtons. Find the angle between the forces.

2. Two forces of 128 and 253 lb act on a point. The equilibrant force is 320 lb. Find the angle between the forces.

3. Find the force required to push a 100-lb box up a ramp inclined 10° with the horizontal.

4. Find the force required to keep a 3000-lb car parked on a hill which makes an angle of 15° with the horizontal.

5. A force of 25 lb is required to push an 80-lb lawn mower up a hill. What angle does the hill make with the horizontal?

6. A force of 500 lb is required to pull a boat up a ramp inclined at 18° with the horizontal. How much does the boat weigh?

7. Anna and Kerry are little dogs. Anna pulls on a rope attached to their doggie dish with a force of 3.89 lb. Kerry pulls on another rope with a force of 4.72 lb. The angle between the forces is 142.8°. Find the direction and magnitude of the equilibrant.

8. Two people are carrying a box. One person exerts a force of 150 lb at an angle of 62.4° with the horizontal. The other person exerts a force of 114 lb at an angle of 54.9°. Find the weight of the box.

9. A crate is supported by two ropes. One rope makes an angle of 46° 20′ with the horizontal and has a tension of 89.6 lb on it. The other rope is horizontal. Find the weight of the crate and the tension in the horizontal rope.

10. Three forces acting at a point are in equilibrium. The forces are 980 lb, 760 lb, and 1220 lb. Find the angles between the directions of the forces. (Hint: arrange the forces to form the sides of a triangle.)

11. A force of 176 lb makes an angle of 78° 50′ with a second force. The resultant of the two forces makes an angle of 41° 10′ with the first force. Find the magnitude of the second force and of the resultant.

12. A force of 28.7 lb makes an angle of 42° 10′ with a second force. The resultant of the two forces makes an angle of 32° 40′ with the first force. Find the magnitude of the second force and of the resultant.

13. A plane flies 650 mi per hour at a bearing of 175.3°. A 25 mi per hour wind, bearing 86.6°, blows against the plane. Find the resulting bearing of the plane.

14. A pilot wants to fly at a bearing of 74.9°. By flying due east, he finds that a 42 mi per hour wind, blowing from the south, puts him on course. Find the airspeed and the ground speed.

15. Starting at point *A*, a ship sails 18.5 km on a bearing of 189°, then turns and sails 47.8 km on a bearing of 317°. Find the distance of the ship from point *A*.

16. The distance between points *A* and *B* is 1.7 mi. In between *A* and *B* is a dark forest, containing a big woolly bear. To avoid the bear, John walks from *A* a distance of 1.1 mi on a bearing of 325°, and then turns and walks 1.4 mi to *B*. Find the bearing of *B* from *A*.

17. The airline route from San Francisco to Honolulu is on a bearing of 233°. A jet flying at 450 mi per hour on that bearing runs into a wind blowing at 39 mi per hour from a direction 114°. Find the resulting bearing and ground speed of the plane.

18. The bearing of the Evergreen Ranch from Galt is 57° 40′. Harriet is flying there to visit her sister, a wrangler. She flies at 168 mi per hour. A wind is blowing at 27.1 mi per hour from the south. Find the bearing she should fly and her ground speed.

19. What bearing and airspeed are required for a plane to fly 400 mi due north in 2.5 hours, if the wind is blowing from a direction 328° at 11 mi per hour?

20. A plane is headed due south with an airspeed of 192 mi per hour. A wind from a direction 78° is blowing at 23 mi per hour. Find the ground speed and resulting bearing of the plane.

21. An airplane is heading on a bearing of 174° at an airspeed of 240 km per hour. A 30 km per hour wind is blowing from a bearing of 245°. Find the ground speed and resulting bearing of the plane.

22. A pilot of a commerical airliner finds it necessary to detour around a group of thundershowers. She turns at an angle of 21° from the original path, flies for a while, turns, and intercepts the original path at an angle of 35°, 70 km from where she left it. See the figure. How much further did the plane have to go because of the detour?

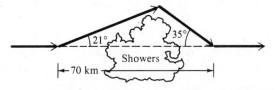

23. A submarine crew is conducting torpedo practice off the Florida coast. The target is 7200 m away on a bearing of 276° and is steaming on a course of 68°. See the figure. The submarine has long-range torpedos that will go 6400 m, and short-range torpedos that will go 3200 m. Between what two bearings can the crew fire torpedos. that will reach the target's path if they use

(a) long-range torpedos;

(b) short-range torpedos.

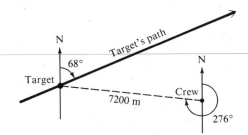

As a jet plane takes off, its path makes a fairly steep angle to the ground. The plane itself makes an even steeper angle. Its velocity vector may be resolved into two components, as shown in the figure. The axial component (the one directed along the plane's axis) is the plane's velocity ignoring the action of gravity. The vertical component is the velocity at which the plane is "falling" under the influence of gravity.

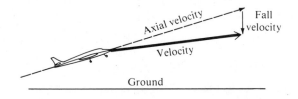

24. A plane's velocity vector is 250 kph at an angle of 10° to the ground. The plane's axis makes an angle of 15° with the ground.

(a) Find the speed of the axial direction.

(b) Find the speed at which the plane is falling.

25. If the plane maintains an angle of 15° with the ground and the fall vector stays the same as in Exercise 24:

(a) What is the minimum speed the plane can go without going downward? (That is, the velocity vector must be horizontal.)

(b) At this minimum speed, what will the axial velocity vector equal?

Chapter 7   Test

Find the indicated parts in each of the following right triangles. Assume that the right angle is at C.

1. $A = 47° 20'$, $b = 39.6$ cm, find B and c

2. $B = 34° 40'$, $b = 9820$ yd, find A and a

3. $A = 15° 29'$, $c = 301.4$ m, find B

Find the indicated parts of each of the following triangles.

4. $C = 74° 10'$, $c = 96.3$ m, $B = 39° 30'$, find b

5. $A = 129° 40'$, $a = 127$ ft, $b = 69.8$ ft, find B

6. $C = 51° 20'$, $c = 68.3$ m, $b = 58.2$ m, find B

7. $a = 86.14$ in, $b = 253.2$ in, $c = 241.9$ in, find A

8. Solve the triangle having $A = 61.7°$, $a = 78.9$ m, $b = 86.4$ m

Find the area of each of the following triangles.

9. $a = .913$ km, $b = .816$ km, $c = .582$ km

10. $b = 840.6$ m, $c = 715.9$ m, $A = 149° 18'$

[7.1–7.4]   *Solve each of the following problems.*

11. The angle of elevation from the top of a cliff to the top of a second cliff 290 ft away is 68°, while the angle of depression from the top of the first cliff to the bottom of the second cliff is 63°. Find the height of the second cliff.

12. A tree leans at an angle of 8° from the vertical. From a point 7 m from the bottom of the tree, the angle of elevation to the top of the tree is 68°. How tall is the tree?

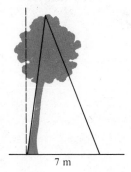

7 m

13. Two boats leave a dock together. They travel in straight line courses with a difference of 54° 10′ between their courses. One boat travels 36 km per hour, while the other goes 45 km per hour. How far apart will they be after 3 hours?

14. Raoul plans to paint a triangular wall in his A-frame cabin. Two sides measure 7 m each and the third side measures 6 m. How much paint will he need if a can of paint covers 7.5 m²?

In Exercises 15–17 use the vectors pictured here.

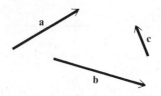

Find each of the following.

15. a + b   **16. a − b**   **17. a + 3c**

Find the horizontal and vertical components of each of the following vectors.

18. $\alpha = 45°$, magnitude 50

19. $\alpha = 75°$, magnitude 69.2

20. $\alpha = 154° \ 20′$, magnitude 964

Solve each of the following problems.

21. Forces of 475 and 586 lb act on an object. The angle between the forces is 78° 20′. Find the magnitude of the resultant.

22. A force of 186 lb just keeps a 2800-lb Toyota from rolling down a hill. What angle does the hill make with the horizontal?

23. A box of chickens is supported above the ground to keep the foxes out. The box hangs from two ropes. One makes an angle of 52° 40′ with the horizontal. The tension in this rope is 89.6 lb. The second rope makes an angle of 82° 30′ with the first rope, and has a tension of 61.7 lb. The box weighs 10 lb. Find the weight of the chickens. (Hint: add the vertical components of each tension vector.)

24. A long-distance swimmer starts out swimming a steady 3.2 mi per hour due north. A 5.1 mi per hour current is flowing on a bearing of 12°. What is the swimmer's resultant bearing and speed?

8

Complex Numbers

So far in this text, we have dealt only with real numbers. However, the set of real numbers does not include enough numbers for our needs. For example, there is no real number solution of the equation $x^2 + 1 = 0$. In this chapter we discuss a set of numbers having the real numbers as a subset, that is, the set of **complex** numbers.

8.1 Operations on Complex Numbers

The number i is defined to be a square root of -1, so that

$$i = \sqrt{-1}$$

This means that $i^2 = -1$. Higher powers of i can be found as follows:

$$i^3 = i^2 \cdot i = -1 \cdot i = -i,$$
$$i^4 = i^2 \cdot i^2 = (-1)(-1) = 1,$$
$$i^5 = i^4 \cdot i = 1 \cdot i = i,$$
$$i^6 = i^4 \cdot i^2 = 1(-1) = -1,$$

and so on. If you find further powers of i, you will see they keep repeating the four values i, -1, $-i$, and 1.

EXAMPLE 1 Simplify each of the following.

(a) $i^{25} = i^{24} \cdot i = (i^4)^6 \cdot i = 1^6 \cdot i = i$

(b) $i^{18} = (i^4)^4 \cdot i^2 = 1^4 \cdot -1 = -1$ ●

In general, $\sqrt{-a}$, where $a > 0$, is defined as

$$\sqrt{-a} = i\sqrt{a} \qquad (a > 0).$$

Thus, $\sqrt{-16} = 4i$, $\sqrt{-75} = 5i\sqrt{3}$, and so on. We write $5i\sqrt{3}$ instead of $5\sqrt{3}i$ to avoid any confusion with $5\sqrt{3i}$ where i is under the radical.

EXAMPLE 2   Write each of the following as a multiple of i.
(a) $\sqrt{-5} = \sqrt{5(-1)} = \sqrt{5} \cdot \sqrt{-1} = i\sqrt{5}$
(b) $\sqrt{-25} = \sqrt{25} \cdot \sqrt{-1} = 5i$
(c) $\sqrt{-24} = \sqrt{24} \cdot \sqrt{-1} = \sqrt{4} \cdot \sqrt{6}\, i = 2i\sqrt{6}$ ●

The number $a + bi$, where a and b are real numbers, is a **complex number**. If $a = 0$ and $b \neq 0$, then the complex number is a nonzero multiple of i and is called an **imaginary number.** If $b = 0$, the complex number is of the form $a + 0i$, or just a, which is a real number. Therefore, every real number is a complex number with both the real numbers and the imaginary numbers subsets of the set of complex numbers. When a complex number is written in the form $a + bi$ (or, with radicals, $a + ib$), where a and b are real numbers, the number is said to be written in **standard form**.

Equality for complex numbers is defined as

$$a + bi = c + di \quad \text{if and only if} \quad a = c \text{ and } b = d.$$

Thus, $2 + mi = k + 3i$ if and only if $2 = k$ and $m = 3$. **Addition** of complex numbers is defined as

$$(a + bi) + (c + di) = (a + c) + (b + d)i.$$

EXAMPLE 3   Add $3 - 4i$ and $-2 + 6i$.
$$(3 - 4i) + (-2 + 6i) = [3 + (-2)] + (-4 + 6)i$$
$$= 1 + 2i \quad ●$$

Subtraction of complex numbers is defined in much the same way as subtraction of real numbers.

$$(a + bi) - (c + di) = (a - c) + (b - d)i.$$

EXAMPLE 4   Subtract $(-2 + 6i)$ from $(3 - 4i)$.
$$(3 - 4i) - (-2 + 6i) = [3 - (-2)] + (-4 - 6)i$$
$$= 5 - 10i \quad ●$$

The **product** of two complex numbers can be found by multiplying them as we do binomials to get
$$(a + bi)(c + di) = ac + adi + bci + bidi$$
$$= ac + (ad + bc)i + bdi^2$$
$$= ac + (ad + bc)i + bd(-1)$$
$$(a + bi)(c + di) = (ac - bd) + (ad + bc)i.$$

EXAMPLE 5 Multiply $(2 - 3i)$ and $(3 + 4i)$.

$$(2 - 3i)(3 + 4i) = 2(3) + 2(4i) + (-3i)(3) + (-3i)(4i)$$
$$= 6 + 8i - 9i - 12i^2$$
$$= 6 + (-1)i - 12(-1)$$
$$(2 - 3i)(3 + 4i) = 18 - i \quad \bullet$$

The **conjugate** of the complex number $a + bi$ is defined to be the complex number $a - bi$. The conjugate is used to find the **quotient** of two complex numbers. For example, to divide $3 - 2i$ by $-4 + 3i$, multiply both numerator and denominator of the quotient

$$\frac{3 - 2i}{-4 + 3i}$$

by $-4 - 3i$, the conjugate of $-4 + 3i$.

$$\frac{(3 - 2i)}{(-4 + 3i)} \cdot \frac{(-4 - 3i)}{(-4 - 3i)} = \frac{-12 - 9i + 8i + 6i^2}{(-4)^2 - (3i)^2}$$
$$= \frac{-12 - i - 6}{16 - (-9)}$$
$$= \frac{-18 - i}{25}$$
$$\frac{3 - 2i}{-4 + 3i} = -\frac{18}{25} - \frac{1}{25}i.$$

The last step expresses the result in standard form.

EXAMPLE 6 Divide $3 - 4i$ by $2 - i$ and write the result in standard form.

Multiply both numerator and denominator by the conjugate of $2 - i$, which is $2 + i$.

$$\frac{(3 - 4i)}{(2 - i)} \cdot \frac{(2 + i)}{(2 + i)} = \frac{6 + 3i - 8i - 4i^2}{4 - i^2}$$
$$= \frac{10 - 5i}{5}$$
$$\frac{3 - 4i}{2 - i} = 2 - i \quad \bullet$$

EXAMPLE 7 Solve $3x - 4yi = (2 + 4i)(3 - 5i)$.

First, find the product on the right side of the equation.

$$(2 + 4i)(3 - 5i) = 6 - 10i + 12i - 20i^2$$
$$= 26 + 2i$$

Then

$$3x - 4yi = 26 + 2i.$$

Now, by the definition of equality,

$$3x = 26 \quad \text{and} \quad -4yi = 2i$$

$$x = \frac{26}{3} \quad \text{and} \quad y = -\frac{1}{2}. \quad \bullet$$

8.1 EXERCISES

Write each of the following as a multiple of i. See Example 2.

1. $\sqrt{-9}$ **2.** $\sqrt{-25}$ **3.** $\sqrt{-64}$ **4.** $\sqrt{-100}$

5. $\sqrt{-\frac{4}{9}}$ **6.** $\sqrt{-\frac{1}{16}}$ **7.** $\sqrt{-18}$ **8.** $\sqrt{-45}$

9. $\sqrt{-150}$ **10.** $\sqrt{-180}$ **11.** $\sqrt{-27}$ **12.** $\sqrt{-48}$

13. $\sqrt{-80}$ **14.** $\sqrt{-72}$

Simplify each of the following. See Example 1.

15. i^6 **16.** i^7 **17.** i^8

18. i^{19} **19.** i^{85} **20.** i^{78}

Perform the following operations and express all results in standard form. See Examples 3–6.

21. $(3 + 2i) + (4 - 3i)$ **22.** $(4 - i) + (2 + 5i)$ **23.** $(6 - 4i) - (3 + 2i)$

24. $(5 - 2i) - (5 + 3i)$ **25.** $(-2 + 3i) - (-4 + 2i)$ **26.** $(-3 + 5i) - (-4 + 3i)$

27. $(2 + i)(3 - 2i)$ **28.** $(-2 + 3i)(4 - 2i)$ **29.** $(2 + 4i)(-1 + 3i)$

30. $(1 + 3i)(2 - 5i)$ **31.** $(5 + 2i)(5 - 3i)$ **32.** $(-3 + 2i)^2$

33. $(2 + i)^2$ **34.** $(\sqrt{6} - i)(\sqrt{6} + i)$ **35.** $(2 - i)(2 + i)$

36. $(5 + 4i)(5 - 4i)$ **37.** $i(3 - 4i)(3 + 4i)$ **38.** $i(2 + 5i)(2 - 5i)$

39. $i(3 - 4i)^2$ **40.** $i(2 + 6i)^2$ **41.** $\dfrac{1 + i}{1 - i}$

42. $\dfrac{2 - i}{2 + i}$ **43.** $\dfrac{4 - 3i}{4 + 3i}$ **44.** $\dfrac{5 + 6i}{5 - 6i}$

45. $\dfrac{4 + i}{6 + 2i}$ **46.** $\dfrac{3 - 2i}{5 + 3i}$ **47.** $\dfrac{5 - 2i}{6 - i}$

48. $\dfrac{3 - 4i}{2 - 5i}$ **49.** $\dfrac{1 - 3i}{1 + i}$ **50.** $\dfrac{-3 + 4i}{2 - i}$

Solve each of the following equations for x and y. See Example 7.

51. $x + yi = 4 + 2i$ **52.** $x + yi = 3 - 5i$

53. $2x + yi = 4 - 3i$ **54.** $x + 3yi = 5 + 2i$

55. $7 - 2yi = 14x - 30i$ **56.** $-5 + yi = x + 6i$

57. $x + yi = (2 + 3i)(4 - 2i)$ **58.** $x + yi = (5 - 7i)(1 + i)$

59. $x + 2i = (3 + yi)(2 - yi)$ **60.** $8 + yi = (x - i)(x + i)$

*In work with alternating current, complex numbers are used to describe current, E, voltage, I, and **impedance,** Z (the opposition to current). These three quantities are related by the equation E = IZ. Thus, if any two of these quantities are known, the third can be found. In each of the following problems, solve the equation E = IZ for the missing variable.*

61. $I = 8 + 6i$, $Z = 6 + 3i$ **62.** $I = 10 + 6i$, $Z = 8 + 5i$

63. $I = 7 + 5i$, $E = 28 + 54i$ **64.** $E = 35 + 55i$, $Z = 6 + 4i$

8.2 Trigonometric Form of Complex Numbers

It is not possible to graph complex numbers on the coordinate system used throughout this text. To graph a complex number such as $2 - 3i$ we must modify the coordinate system. One way to do this is to call the horizontal axis the **real axis** and the vertical axis the **imaginary axis**. Then complex numbers can be graphed as shown in Figure 8.1.

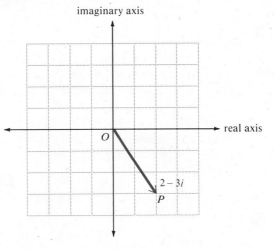

Figure 8.1

Each complex number graphed in this way determines a unique directed line segment, the segment from the origin to the point representing the complex number. Recall from Chapter 7 that such directed line segments (like **OP** of Figure 8.1) are called vectors.

We know from the previous section how to find the sum of the two complex numbers $4 + i$ and $1 + 3i$.

$$(4 + i) + (1 + 3i) = 5 + 4i$$

Graphically, the sum of two complex numbers is represented by the vector which is the resultant of the vectors corresponding to the two numbers. The vectors representing the complex numbers $4 + i$ and $1 + 3i$, and the resultant vector which represents their sum, $5 + 4i$, are shown in Figure 8.2.

EXAMPLE 1 Find the resultant of $6 - 2i$ and $-4 - 3i$. Graph both complex numbers and their resultant.

The resultant is found by adding the two numbers.

$$(6 - 2i) + (-4 - 3i) = 2 - 5i$$

The graphs are shown in Figure 8.3. ●

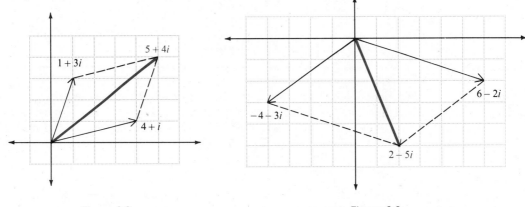

Figure 8.2   Figure 8.3

Figure 8.4 shows a complex number $x + yi$ which determines a vector **OP**. Let $r(r \geq 0)$ represent the length of vector **OP**, and let θ be the smallest positive angle (measured in a counterclockwise direction) between the positive real axis and **OP**. Point P can be located uniquely if we know r and θ. Therefore, we can use r and θ as coordinates of point P. The ordered pair (r, θ) gives the **polar coordinates** of point P. The following relationships between r, θ, x, and y can be verified from Figure 8.4.

$$x = r \cos \theta \qquad r = \sqrt{x^2 + y^2}$$
$$y = r \sin \theta \qquad \theta = \arctan y/x$$

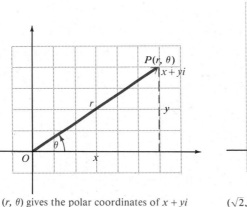

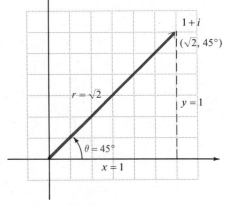

(r, θ) gives the polar coordinates of $x + yi$ $(\sqrt{2}, 45°)$ gives the polar coordinates of $1 + i$

Figure 8.4   Figure 8.5

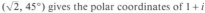

EXAMPLE 2 Find the polar coordinates of the complex number $1 + i$.

Here $x = 1$ and $y = 1$. Thus, $r = \sqrt{1^2 + 1^2} = \sqrt{2}$, and $\theta = \arctan 1/1 = \arctan 1$, so that $\theta = 45°$. (Angle θ cannot be $225°$ because the complex number lies in quadrant I.) Hence the polar coordinates of $1 + i$ are $(\sqrt{2}, 45°)$, as shown in Figure 8.5.   ●

We know $x = r \cos \theta$ and $y = r \sin \theta$. Substituting these results into $x + yi$ gives

$$x + yi = r \cos \theta + (r \sin \theta)i$$

or

$$x + yi = r(\cos \theta + i \sin \theta)$$

The expression $r(\cos \theta + i \sin \theta)$ is called the **trigonometric form** or **polar form** of the complex number $x + yi$. The number r is called the **modulus** or **absolute value** of $x + yi$, while θ is called the **argument** of $x + yi$. Using the work from Example 2 above, we can express $1 + i$ in trigonometric form by writing

$$1 + i = \sqrt{2}(\cos 45° + i \sin 45°).$$

EXAMPLE 3 Express $2(\cos 300° + i \sin 300°)$ in standard form.

We know $\cos 300° = 1/2$, while $\sin 300° = -\sqrt{3}/2$. Hence

$$2(\cos 300° + i \sin 300°) = 2\left(\frac{1}{2} - i\frac{\sqrt{3}}{2}\right)$$

$$= 1 - i\sqrt{3}.   ●$$

EXAMPLE 4 Write the following complex numbers in trigonometric form.

(a) $-\sqrt{3} + i$

Since $x = -\sqrt{3}$ and $y = 1$,

$$r = \sqrt{x^2 + y^2} = \sqrt{3 + 1} = 2,$$

$$\theta = \arctan \frac{y}{x} = \arctan \left(\frac{1}{-\sqrt{3}}\right) = \arctan \left(-\frac{\sqrt{3}}{3}\right).$$

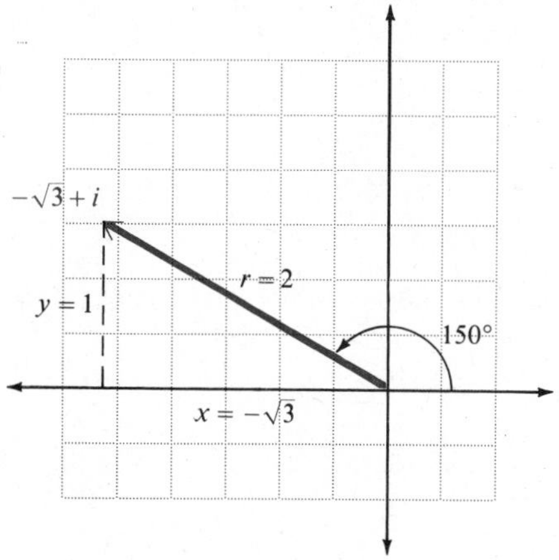

Figure 8.6

As shown in Figure 8.6, θ is in quadrant II, so that $\theta = 150°$. In trigonometric form,

$$x + yi = r(\cos \theta + i \sin \theta)$$
$$-\sqrt{3} + i = 2(\cos 150° + i \sin 150°).$$

(b) $-2 - 2i$

First find r and θ.

$$r = \sqrt{x^2 + y^2} = \sqrt{4 + 4} = 2\sqrt{2}$$

$$\theta = \arctan \frac{y}{x} = \arctan \left(\frac{-2}{-2} \right) = \arctan 1$$

Since θ is in quadrant III, $\theta = 225°$. Thus, the trigonometric form of $-2 - 2i$ is

$$2\sqrt{2}(\cos 225° + i \sin 225°). \quad \bullet$$

8.2 EXERCISES

Graph each of the following complex numbers.

1. $-2 + 3i$ 2. $-4 + 5i$ 3. $8 - 5i$ 4. $6 - 5i$
5. $2 - 2\sqrt{3}i$ 6. $4\sqrt{2} + 4\sqrt{2}i$ 7. $-4i$ 8. $3i$
9. -8 10. 2

Find the resultant of each of the following pairs of complex numbers. See Example 1.

11. $2 - 3i, -1 + 4i$ 12. $-4 - 5i, 2 + i$
13. $-5 + 6i, 3 - 4i$ 14. $8 - 5i, -6 + 3i$
15. $-2, 4i$ 16. $5, -4i$
17. $2 + 6i, -2i$ 18. $4 - 2i, 5$
19. $7 + 6i, 3i$ 20. $-5 - 8i, -1$

Find the polar coordinates of each of the following complex numbers. See Example 2.

21. $2 - 2i$ 22. $-1 - i$
23. $3i$ 24. $-2i$
25. 5 26. -3
27. $\sqrt{3} + i$ 28. $-\sqrt{2} - \sqrt{2}i$
29. $1 + \sqrt{3}i$ 30. $-2 + 2\sqrt{3}i$

Rewrite in standard form the complex numbers whose polar coordinates are given. Graph each complex number.

31. $(2, 45°)$ 32. $(3, 60°)$
33. $(1, 135°)$ 34. $(2, 300°)$
35. $(3, 90°)$ 36. $(2, 180°)$
37. $(4, 240°)$ 38. $(5, 270°)$
39. $(1, -30°)$ 40. $(4, -60°)$

Rewrite the following complex numbers in standard form. See Example 3.

41. $2(\cos 45° + i \sin 45°)$ **42.** $4(\cos 60° + i \sin 60°)$

43. $10(\cos 90° + i \sin 90°)$ **44.** $8(\cos 270° + i \sin 270°)$

45. $4(\cos 240° + i \sin 240°)$ **46.** $2(\cos 330° + i \sin 330°)$

47. $(\cos 30° + i \sin 30°)$ **48.** $3(\cos 150° + i \sin 150°)$

49. $5(\cos 300° + i \sin 300°)$ **50.** $6(\cos 135° + i \sin 135°)$

Rewrite each of the following complex numbers in trigonometric form. See Example 4.

51. $3 - 3i$ **52.** $-2 + 2\sqrt{3}i$

53. $-3 - 3\sqrt{3}i$ **54.** $1 + \sqrt{3}i$

55. $\sqrt{3} - i$ **56.** $4\sqrt{3} + 4i$

57. $-5 - 5i$ **58.** $-\sqrt{2} + \sqrt{2}i$

Using a calculator or Table II, complete the following chart to the nearest ten minutes.

	Standard Form	Polar Coordinates	Trigonometric Form
59.	$2 + 3i$	_____	_____
60.	_____	$(1, 35°)$	_____
61.	_____	_____	$3(\cos 250° 10' + i \sin 250° 10')$
62.	$-4 + i$	_____	_____
63.	_____	$(2, 160°)$	_____
64.	_____	_____	$2(\cos 310° 20' + i \sin 310° 20')$

65. Suppose that the gravity of the earth, the sun, and the moon are pulling on a spaceship, as shown in the figure. The force vectors are

Earth: (120 lb, 27°)
Sun: (50 lb, 142°)
Moon: (20 lb, 243°).

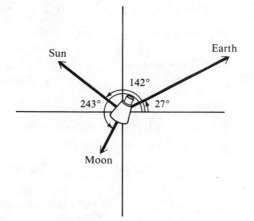

(a) Write each vector in standard form.

(b) To the nearest pound and the nearest degree, what is the resultant of these three forces?

66. A neutron escaping from a nuclear reactor enters the surrounding shielding at an angle of 27°. See the figure. It goes 20 cm along this path before colliding with an atom in the shielding. Then it goes 31 cm at an angle of −118° before colliding with another shielding atom. If the neutron goes 53 cm further in the direction 54°,

    (a) What is its displacement vector from the point at which it entered the shielding? (Hint: add the three vectors.)

    (b) The shielding is 27 cm thick. Has it gone all the way through the shielding? Explain.

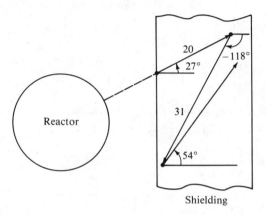

Shielding

8.3 De Moivre's Theorem

We can find the product of the two complex numbers $1 + i\sqrt{3}$ and $-2\sqrt{3} + 2i$ as shown in Section 8.1.

$$(1 + i\sqrt{3})(-2\sqrt{3} + 2i) = -2\sqrt{3} + 2i - 2i(3) + 2i^2\sqrt{3}$$
$$= -2\sqrt{3} + 2i - 6i - 2\sqrt{3}$$
$$(1 + i\sqrt{3})(-2\sqrt{3} + 2i) = -4\sqrt{3} - 4i$$

We can also obtain this same product by first converting the complex numbers $1 + \sqrt{3}i$ and $-2\sqrt{3} + 2i$ to trigonometric form. Using the method explained in the previous section,

$$1 + i\sqrt{3} = 2(\cos 60° + i \sin 60°)$$

and
$$-2\sqrt{3} + 2i = 4(\cos 150° + i \sin 150°).$$

If we now multiply the trigonometric forms together and use the trigonometric identities for the cosine and the sine of the sum of two angles, we have

$$[2(\cos 60° + i \sin 60°)][4(\cos 150° + i \sin 150°)]$$
$$= 2 \cdot 4(\cos 60° \cdot \cos 150° + i \sin 60° \cdot \cos 150°$$
$$+ i \cos 60° \cdot \sin 150° + i^2 \sin 60° \cdot \sin 150°)$$
$$= 8[(\cos 60° \cdot \cos 150° - \sin 60° \cdot \sin 150°)$$
$$+ i(\sin 60° \cdot \cos 150° + \cos 60° \cdot \sin 150°)]$$
$$= 8[\cos(60° + 150°) + i \sin(60° + 150°)]$$
$$= 8(\cos 210° + i \sin 210°).$$

The modulus of the product, 8, is equal to the *product* of the moduli of the factors, $2 \cdot 4$, while the argument of the product, $210°$, is the *sum* of the arguments of the factors, $60° + 150°$. In general, we have the following result.

THEOREM 8.1   If $r_1(\cos \theta_1 + i \sin \theta_1)$ and $r_2(\cos \theta_2 + i \sin \theta_2)$ are any two complex numbers, then

$$[r_1(\cos \theta_1 + i \sin \theta_1)][r_2(\cos \theta_2 + i \sin \theta_2)]$$
$$= r_1 r_2[\cos(\theta_1 + \theta_2) + i \sin (\theta_1 + \theta_2)].$$

EXAMPLE 1   Find the product of $3(\cos 45° + i \sin 45°)$ and $2(\cos 135° + i \sin 135°)$.
Use Theorem 8.1,

$$[3(\cos 45° + i \sin 45°)][2(\cos 135° + i \sin 135°)]$$
$$= 3 \cdot 2[\cos (45° + 135°) + i \sin (45° + 135°)]$$
$$= 6(\cos 180° + i \sin 180°),$$

which can be expressed as $6(-1 + i \cdot 0) = 6(-1) = -6$. The two complex numbers of this example are complex factors of -6.   ●

We can use the results of Theorem 8.1 to find the square of a complex number. We have

$$[r(\cos \theta + i \sin \theta)]^2 = [r(\cos \theta + i \sin \theta)][r(\cos \theta + i \sin \theta)]$$
$$= r \cdot r[\cos (\theta + \theta) + i \sin (\theta + \theta)]$$
$$[r(\cos \theta + i \sin \theta)]^2 = r^2(\cos 2\theta + i \sin 2\theta).$$

In the same way,

$$[r(\cos \theta + i \sin \theta)]^3 = r^3(\cos 3\theta + i \sin 3\theta).$$

These results suggest the plausibility of the following theorem for positive integer values of n. Although the following theorem can be proved for all n, we will use it only for positive integer values of n and their reciprocals.

THEOREM 8.2   *(De Moivre's Theorem)*   If $r(\cos \theta + i \sin \theta)$ is a complex number and if n is any real number, then

$$[r(\cos \theta + i \sin \theta)]^n = r^n(\cos n\theta + i \sin n\theta).$$

EXAMPLE 2   Find $(1 + i\sqrt{3})^8$.
We can use De Moivre's theorem if we first convert $1 + i\sqrt{3}$ into trigonometric form, as shown below.

$$1 + i\sqrt{3} = 2(\cos 60° + i \sin 60°)$$

Now apply De Moivre's theorem.

$$(1 + i\sqrt{3})^8 = [2(\cos 60° + i \sin 60°)]^8$$
$$= 2^8[\cos (8 \cdot 60°) + i \sin (8 \cdot 60°)]$$
$$= 256(\cos 480° + i \sin 480°)$$
$$= 256(\cos 120° + i \sin 120°)$$
$$= 256 \left(-\frac{1}{2} + i \frac{\sqrt{3}}{2}\right)$$
$$(1 + i\sqrt{3})^8 = -128 + 128i\sqrt{3} \quad \bullet$$

Now let's consider the quotient of two complex numbers. In standard form, the quotient of the complex numbers $1 + i\sqrt{3}$ and $-2\sqrt{3} + 2i$ is

$$\frac{(1 + i\sqrt{3})(-2\sqrt{3} - 2i)}{(-2\sqrt{3} + 2i)(-2\sqrt{3} - 2i)} = \frac{-2\sqrt{3} - 2i - 6i - 2i^2\sqrt{3}}{12 - 4i^2}$$
$$= \frac{-8i}{16}$$
$$\frac{1 + i\sqrt{3}}{-2\sqrt{3} + 2i} = -\frac{1}{2}i.$$

If we write $1 + i\sqrt{3}$, $-2\sqrt{3} + 2i$, and $-\frac{1}{2}i$ in trigonometric form, we have

$$1 + i\sqrt{3} = 2(\cos 60° + i \sin 60°)$$
$$-2\sqrt{3} + 2i = 4(\cos 150° + i \sin 150°)$$
$$-\frac{1}{2}i = \frac{1}{2}[(\cos (-90°) + i \sin (-90°))]$$

The modulus of the quotient, 1/2, is the quotient of the two moduli, 2 and 4. The argument of the quotient, $-90°$, is the difference of the two arguments, $60° - 150° = -90°$. It was easier to find the quotient of these two complex numbers in trigonometric form than in standard form. Generalizing from this example leads to Theorem 8.3.

THEOREM 8.3   If $r_1(\cos \theta_1 + i \sin \theta_1)$ and $r_2(\cos \theta_2 + i \sin \theta_2)$ are complex numbers, where $r_2(\cos \theta_2 + i \sin \theta_2) \neq 0$, then

$$\frac{r_1(\cos \theta_1 + i \sin \theta_1)}{r_2(\cos \theta_2 + i \sin \theta_2)} = \frac{r_1}{r_2}[\cos (\theta_1 - \theta_2) + i \sin (\theta_1 - \theta_2)].$$

EXAMPLE 3   Find the quotient of $10(\cos (-60°) + i \sin (-60°))$ and $5(\cos 150° + i \sin 150°)$. Write the result in standard form.

By Theorem 8.3,

$$\frac{10(\cos{(-60°)} + i\sin{(-60°)})}{5(\cos{150°} + i\sin{150°})}$$

$$= \frac{10}{5}\left[(\cos{(-60° - 150°)} + i\sin{(-60° - 150°)}\right]$$

$$= \frac{10}{5}(\cos{(-210°)} + i\sin{(-210°)}).$$

$$= 2(\cos{150°} + i\sin{150°}).$$

Since $\cos{150°} = -\sqrt{3}/2$ and $\sin{150°} = 1/2$,

$$2(\cos{150°} + i\sin{150°}) = 2\left(\frac{-\sqrt{3}}{2} + i \cdot \frac{1}{2}\right)$$

$$= -\sqrt{3} + i.$$

The quotient in standard form is $-\sqrt{3} + i$.   ●

8.3 EXERCISES

Find each of the following products. Write each product in standard form. See Example 1.

1. $[2(\cos{30°} + i\sin{30°})][3(\cos{60°} + i\sin{60°})]$

2. $[3(\cos{60°} + i\sin{60°})][4(\cos{150°} + i\sin{150°})]$

3. $[2(\cos{135°} + i\sin{135°})][2(\cos{225°} + i\sin{225°})]$

4. $[6(\cos{240°} + i\sin{240°})][8(\cos{300°} + i\sin{300°})]$

5. $[4(\cos{60°} + i\sin{60°})][6(\cos{330°} + i\sin{330°})]$

6. $[8(\cos{210°} + i\sin{210°})][2(\cos{330°} + i\sin{330°})]$

7. $[5(\cos{90°} + i\sin{90°})][3(\cos{45°} + i\sin{45°})]$

8. $[6(\cos{120°} + i\sin{120°})][5(\cos{(-30°)} + i\sin{(-30°)})]$

9. $[\sqrt{3}(\cos{45°} + i\sin{45°})][\sqrt{3}(\cos{225°} + i\sin{225°})]$

10. $[\sqrt{2}(\cos{300°} + i\sin{300°})][\sqrt{2}(\cos{270°} + i\sin{270°})]$

Find each of the following powers. Write each answer in standard form. See Example 2.

11. $[2(\cos{60°} + i\sin{60°})]^3$

12. $[3(\cos{120°} + i\sin{120°})]^4$

13. $(\cos{45°} + i\sin{45°})^8$

14. $[2(\cos{120°} + i\sin{120°})]^3$

15. $[3(\cos{100°} + i\sin{100°})]^3$

16. $[3(\cos{40°} + i\sin{40°})]^3$

17. $(\sqrt{3} + i)^5$

18. $(2\sqrt{2} - 2i\sqrt{2})^6$

19. $(2 - 2i\sqrt{3})^4$

20. $\left(\frac{\sqrt{2}}{2} - \frac{\sqrt{2}}{2}i\right)^8$

21. $(-2 - 2i)^5$

22. $(-1 + i)^7$

Find each of the following quotients. Write each answer in standard form. See Example 3.

23. $\dfrac{3(\cos{60°} + i\sin{60°})}{(\cos{30°} + i\sin{30°})}$

24. $\dfrac{9(\cos{135°} + i\sin{135°})}{3(\cos{45°} + i\sin{45°})}$

25. $\dfrac{16(\cos 300° + i \sin 300°)}{8(\cos 60° + i \sin 60°)}$

26. $\dfrac{24(\cos 150° + i \sin 150°)}{2(\cos 30° + i \sin 30°)}$

27. $\dfrac{3(\cos 305° + i \sin 305°)}{9(\cos 65° + i \sin 65°)}$

28. $\dfrac{12(\cos 293° + i \sin 293°)}{6(\cos 23° + i \sin 23°)}$

29. $\dfrac{8}{(\sqrt{3} + i)}$

30. $\dfrac{2i}{-1 - i\sqrt{3}}$

31. $\dfrac{-i}{1 + i}$

32. $\dfrac{1}{2 - 2i}$

33. $\dfrac{2\sqrt{6} - 2i\sqrt{2}}{\sqrt{2} - i\sqrt{6}}$

34. $\dfrac{4 + 4i}{2 - 2i}$

Use your calculator to work each of the following problems. Leave your answers in standard form.

35. $[3.7(\cos 27° 15' + i \sin 27° 15')][4.1(\cos 53° 42' + i \sin 53° 42')]$

36. $[2.81(\cos 54° 12' + i \sin 54° 12')][5.8(\cos 82° 53' + i \sin 82° 53')]$

37. $\dfrac{45.3(\cos 127° 25' + i \sin 127° 25')}{12.8(\cos 43° 32' + i \sin 43° 32')}$

38. $\dfrac{2.94(\cos 1.5032 + i \sin 1.5032)}{10.5(\cos 4.6528 + i \sin 4.6528)}$

39. $\left[1.86\left(\cos \dfrac{5\pi}{9} + i \sin \dfrac{5\pi}{9}\right)\right]^{15}$

40. $\left[24.3\left(\cos \dfrac{7\pi}{12} + i \sin \dfrac{7\pi}{12}\right)\right]^{3}$

8.4 Roots of Complex Numbers

The complex number $a + bi$ is an **nth root** of the complex number $x + yi$ if

$$(a + bi)^n = x + yi.$$

We can use De Moivre's theorem to find nth roots of complex numbers. For example, to find the cube roots of the complex number $8(\cos 135° + i \sin 135°)$, we look for a complex number, say $r(\cos \alpha + i \sin \alpha)$, that will satisfy

$$[r(\cos \alpha + i \sin \alpha)]^3 = 8(\cos 135° + i \sin 135°).$$

By De Moivre's theorem, this equation becomes

$$r^3(\cos 3\alpha + i \sin 3\alpha) = 8(\cos 135° + i \sin 135°).$$

One way to satisfy this equation is to set $r^3 = 8$ and also $\cos 3\alpha + i \sin 3\alpha = \cos 135° + i \sin 135°$. The first of these conditions implies that $r = 2$, and the second implies that

$$\cos 3\alpha = \cos 135° \quad \text{and} \quad \sin 3\alpha = \sin 135°.$$

These equations can only be satisfied if

$$3\alpha = 135° + 360° \cdot k, \qquad k \text{ any integer,}$$

or

$$\alpha = \frac{135° + 360° \cdot k}{3}, \qquad k \text{ any integer.}$$

If $k = 0$,

$$\alpha = \frac{135° + 0}{3} = 45°.$$

For $k = 1$, we get

$$\alpha = \frac{135° + 360°}{3} = \frac{495°}{3} = 165°.$$

When $k = 2$,

$$\alpha = \frac{135° + 720°}{3} = \frac{855°}{3} = 285°.$$

In the same way, $\alpha = 405°$ when $k = 3$. But $\sin 405° = \sin 45°$ and $\cos 405° = \cos 45°$. Hence, we get all of the cube roots (3 of them) by letting $k = 0$, 1, and 2. When $k = 0$ we get the root

$$2(\cos 45° + i \sin 45°).$$

When $k = 1$ we have $2(\cos 165° + i \sin 165°)$, and when $k = 2$ we have $2(\cos 285° + i \sin 285°)$. In summary, $2(\cos 45° + i \sin 45°)$, $2(\cos 165° + i \sin 165°)$, and $2(\cos 285° + i \sin 285°)$ are the three cube roots of $8(\cos 135° + i \sin 135°)$.

We generalize this result in the following theorem.

THEOREM 8.4 If n is any positive integer and r is a positive real number, then the complex number $r(\cos \theta + i \sin \theta)$ has exactly n distinct nth roots, given by

$$r^{1/n}(\cos \alpha + i \sin \alpha),$$

where

$$\alpha = \frac{\theta + 360° \cdot k}{n}, \qquad k = 0, 1, 2, \ldots, n - 1.$$

EXAMPLE 1 Find all 4th roots of $-8 + 8i\sqrt{3}$.

First write $-8 + 8i\sqrt{3}$ in trigonometric form as

$$-8 + 8i\sqrt{3} = 16(\cos 120° + i \sin 120°).$$

Here $r = 16$ and $\theta = 120°$. The 4th roots of this number have modulus $16^{1/4} = 2$ and arguments given as follows.

$$\text{If } k = 0, \qquad \frac{120° + 360° \cdot 0}{4} = 30°,$$

$$\text{if } k = 1, \qquad \frac{120° + 360° \cdot 1}{4} = 120°,$$

$$\text{if } k = 2, \qquad \frac{120° + 360° \cdot 2}{4} = 210°,$$

$$\text{if } k = 3, \qquad \frac{120° + 360° \cdot 3}{4} = 300°.$$

Using these angles, the 4th roots are

$$2(\cos 30° + i \sin 30°)$$
$$2(\cos 120° + i \sin 120°)$$
$$2(\cos 210° + i \sin 210°)$$
$$2(\cos 300° + i \sin 300°).$$

We can also write these four roots in standard form as $\sqrt{3} + i$, $-1 + i\sqrt{3}$, $-\sqrt{3} - i$, and $1 - i\sqrt{3}$. ●

The graphs of these roots are all on a circle which has center at the origin and radius 2, as shown in Figure 8.7.

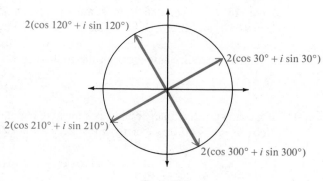

Figure 8.7

EXAMPLE 2   Find all 5th roots of 1.
We can write 1 in trigonometric form as

$$1 = 1 + 0i = 1(\cos 0° + i \sin 0°).$$

The modulus of the 5th roots is $1^{1/5} = 1$, while the arguments are given by

$$\frac{0° + 360° \cdot k}{5}, \qquad k = 0, 1, 2, 3, \text{ or } 4.$$

Using these arguments the 5th roots become

$$1(\cos 0° + i \sin 0°)$$
$$1(\cos 72° + i \sin 72°)$$
$$1(\cos 144° + i \sin 144°)$$
$$1(\cos 216° + i \sin 216°)$$
$$1(\cos 288° + i \sin 288°).$$

The first of these roots equals 1, but the others cannot easily be expressed in standard form. The five 5th roots all lie on a unit circle and are equally spaced around it, as shown in Figure 8.8.

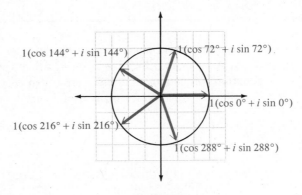

Figure 8.8

8.4 EXERCISES   *Find and graph all cube roots of each of the following complex numbers. In Exercises 1–28, leave answers in trigonometric form. See Example 1.*

1. 1   **2.** i **3.** $-8i$

4. $27i$ **5.** -64 **6.** 27

7. $1 + i\sqrt{3}$ **8.** $2 - 2i\sqrt{3}$ **9.** $-2\sqrt{3} + 2i$

10. $\sqrt{3} - i$

Find and graph all the following roots of 1. *See Example 2.*

11. 2nd   **12.** 4th

13. 6th   **14.** 8th

Find and graph all the following roots of i.

15. 2nd   **16.** 4th

Find all solutions of each of the following equations.

17. $x^3 - 1 = 0$ **18.** $x^3 + 1 = 0$
    (Hint: write this equation as $x^3 = 1$)   **19.** $x^3 + i = 0$

20. $x^4 + i = 0$ **21.** $x^3 - 8 = 0$

22. $x^3 + 27 = 0$ **23.** $x^4 + 1 = 0$

24. $x^4 + 16 = 0$ **25.** $x^4 - i = 0$

26. $x^5 - i = 0$ **27.** $x^3 - (4 + 4i\sqrt{3}) = 0$

28. $x^4 - (8 + 8i\sqrt{3}) = 0$

Use your calculator to find all solutions of each of the following equations.

29. $x^3 + 4 - 5i = 0$ **30.** $x^5 + 2 + 3i = 0$

31. $x^2 + (3.72 + 8.24i) = 0$ **32.** $x^4 - (5.13 - 4.27i) = 0$

8.5   Polar Equations

In Section 2 of this chapter, we saw how to graph a point given its polar coordinates, (r, θ). An equation, like $r = 3 \sin \theta$, where r and θ are the variables, is a **polar equation**. (Equations in x and y are called **rectangular** or **Cartesian** equations.) The simplest equation for many useful curves turns out to be a polar equation.

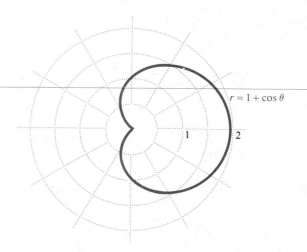

Figure 8.9

Graphing a polar equation is much the same as graphing a Cartesian equation—we obtain representative ordered pairs, (r, θ), belonging to the relation, and then sketch the graph. For example, to graph $r = 1 + \cos \theta$, we first find and graph some ordered pairs, and then connect the points in order—from $(2, 0°)$ to $(1.9, 30°)$ to $(1.7, 45°)$ and so on. The graph is shown in Figure 8.9. This curve is called a **cardioid** because of its heart shape.

θ	0°	30°	45°	60°	90°	120°	135°	150°	180°	270°	315°
$\cos \theta$	1	.9	.7	.5	0	−.5	−.7	−.9	−1	0	.7
$r = 1 + \cos \theta$	2	1.9	1.7	1.5	1	.5	.3	.1	0	1	1.7

Once the pattern of values of r becomes clear, it is not necessary to find more ordered pairs. That is why we stopped with the ordered pair (1.7, 315°). From the pattern in the table, we see that the pair (1.9, 330°) would also satisfy the relation.

EXAMPLE 1 Graph $r^2 = \cos 2\theta$.

First, we complete a table of ordered pairs as shown, and then sketch the graph, as in Figure 8.10. The point $(-1, 0°)$, with r negative, is plotted as $(1, 180°)$. Also, $(-2, 30°)$ is plotted as $(2, 210°)$, $(-5, 45°)$ as $(5, 225°)$, and so on. This curve is called a **lemniscate**.

θ	0°	30°	45°	135°	150°	180°
2θ	0	60	90	270	300	360
$\cos 2\theta$	1	.5	0	0	.5	1
$r = \pm\sqrt{\cos 2\theta}$	±1	±.7	0	0	±.7	±1

Values of θ for $45° < \theta < 135°$ are not included in the table because the corresponding values of $\cos 2\theta$ are negative (quadrants II and III) and so do not have real square roots. Values of θ larger than 180° give 2θ larger than 360°, so we would repeat the points we already have. ●

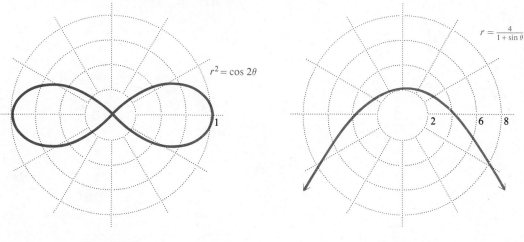

Figure 8.10

Figure 8.11

EXAMPLE 2 Graph $r = \dfrac{4}{1 + \sin\theta}$.

We can again complete a table of ordered pairs, which leads to the graph shown in Figure 8.11.

θ	0°	30°	45°	60°	90°	120°	135°	150°	180°	210°	225°
$\sin\theta$	0	.5	.7	.9	1	.9	.7	.5	0	−.5	−.7
$r = \dfrac{4}{1 + \sin\theta}$	4	2.7	2.3	2.1	2.0	2.1	2.3	2.7	4.0	8.0	13.3

With the points given in the table, the pattern of the graph should be clear. If it is not, you should continue to find additional points.   ●

We can convert the equation of Example 2,

$$r = \frac{4}{1 + \sin \theta},$$

to rectangular coordinates (x, y), using the results of Section 8.2. Work as follows.

$$r = \frac{4}{1 + \sin \theta}$$
$$r + r \sin \theta = 4$$
$$\sqrt{x^2 + y^2} + y = 4$$
$$\sqrt{x^2 + y^2} = 4 - y$$
$$x^2 + y^2 = (4 - y)^2$$
$$x^2 + y^2 = 16 - 8y + y^2$$
$$x^2 = -8y + 16$$
$$x^2 = -8(y - 2)$$

The final equation represents a parabola and can be graphed using rectangular coordinates.

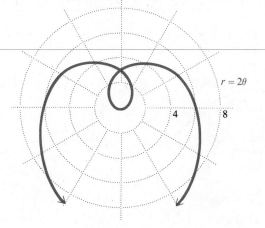

Figure 8.12

EXAMPLE 3   Graph $r = 2\theta$ (θ measured in radians).

Some ordered pairs are shown below. Since $r = 2\theta$, rather than a trigonometric function of θ, it is also necessary to consider negative values of θ. The radian measures have been rounded for simplicity.

θ(degrees)	−180	−90	−45	0	30	60	90	180	270	360
θ(radians)	−3.1	−1.6	−.8	0	.5	1	1.6	3	4.7	6.3
$r = 2\theta$	−6.2	−3.2	−1.6	0	1	2	3.2	6	9.4	12.6

Figure 8.12 shows this graph, called a **spiral of Archimedes**.   ●

EXAMPLE 4   Note the use of polar coordinates in the following example, taken with permission from *Calculus and Analytic Geometry,* fifth edition, by George Thomas and Ross Finney (Addison-Wesley, 1979).

Karl von Frisch has advanced the following theory about how bees communicate information about newly discovered sources of food. A scout returning to the hive from a flower bed gives away samples of the food and then, if the bed is more than about a hundred yards away, performs a dance to show where the flowers are. The bee runs straight ahead for a centimeter or so, waggling from side to side, and circles back to the starting place. The bee then repeats the straight run, circling back in the opposite direction (See Figure 8.13). The dance continues this way in regular alternation. Exceptionally excited bees have been observed to dance for more than three and a half hours.

If the dance is performed inside, it is performed on the vertical wall of a honeycomb, with gravity substituting for the sun's position. A vertical straight run means that the food is in the direction of the sun. A run 30° to the right of vertical means that the food is 30° to the right of the sun, and so on. Distance (more accurately, the amount of energy required to reach the food) is communicated by the duration of the straight-run portions of the dance. Straight runs lasting three seconds each are typical for distances of about a half-mile from the hive. Straight runs that last five seconds each mean about two miles.   ●

The waggle dance of a scout bee.

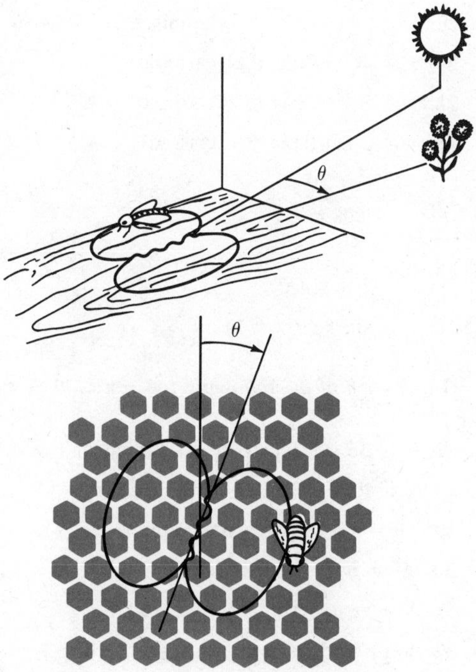

Figure 8.13

8.5 EXERCISES *For each of the following equations, find an equivalent equation in rectangular coordinates and graph. See Example 2.*

1. $r = 2 \sin \theta$ **2.** $r = 2 \cos \theta$

3. $r = \dfrac{2}{1 - \cos \theta}$ **4.** $r = \dfrac{3}{1 - \sin \theta}$

5. $r = 2 \cos \theta - 2 \sin \theta$ **6.** $r = \dfrac{3}{4 \cos \theta - \sin \theta}$

7. $r = 2 \sec \theta$ **8.** $r = -5 \csc \theta$

9. $r(\cos \theta + \sin \theta) = 2$ **10.** $r(2 \cos \theta + \sin \theta) = 2$

11. $r \sin \theta + 2 = 0$ **12.** $r \sec \theta = 5$

Graph each of the following for $0° \le \theta \le 180°$, unless other domains are specified. See Examples 1 and 2.

13. $r = 2 + 2 \cos \theta$

14. $r = 2(4 + 3 \cos \theta)$

15. $r = 3 + \cos \theta$ (limaçon)

16. $r = 2 - \cos \theta$ (limaçon)

17. $r = \sin 2\theta$ (four-leaved rose)
(Hint: use $0° \le \theta < 360°$ every 15°.)

18. $r = 3 \cos 5\theta$ (five-leaved rose) $0° \le \theta < 360°$

19. $r^2 = 4 \cos 2\theta$ (lemniscate)

20. $r^2 = 4 \sin 2\theta$ (lemniscate) $0° \le \theta < 360°$

21. $r = 4(1 - \cos \theta)$ (cardioid)

22. $r = 3(2 - \cos \theta)$ (cardioid)

23. $r = 2 \sin \theta \tan \theta$ (cissoid)

24. $r = \dfrac{\cos 2\theta}{\cos \theta}$

25. $r = \dfrac{3}{2 + \sin \theta}$

26. $r = \sin \theta \cos^2 \theta$

Graph each of the following for $-\pi \le \theta \le \pi$, measuring θ in radians.

27. $r = 5\theta$ (spiral of Archimedes)

28. $r = \theta$ (spiral of Archimedes)

29. $r\theta = \pi$ (hyperbolic spiral)

30. $r^2 = \theta$ (parabolic spiral)

31. $\ln r = \theta$ (logarithmic spiral)

32. $\log r = \theta$ (logarithmic spiral)

Chapter 8 Test

Write Exercises 1–3 as a multiple of i.

1. $\sqrt{-9}$

2. $\sqrt{-12}$

3. $\sqrt{-\dfrac{4}{5}}$

4. Simplify i^{25}.

5. Solve $3x - 2yi = (i + 5)(2i - 1)$ for x and y.

6. Find the resultant of $7 + 3i$ and $-2 + i$.

Graph each of the following.

7. $-4 + 2i$ 8. $5i$ 9. -4

Complete the following chart.

Standard Form	Polar Coordinates	Trigonometric Form
10. $-2 + 2i$	_____	_____
11. _____	$(3, 90°)$	_____
12. _____	_____	$2(\cos 315° + i \sin 315°)$

Perform the indicated operations and write your answers in standard form.

13. $(6 + 3i) + (4 - 5i)$

14. $(-3 - 2i) - (1 - i)$

15. $(4 - 3i)^2$

16. $(2 + i)(2 - i)$

17. $(4 + i)(-3 - i)$

18. $2i(4 - i)(3 + 2i)$

19. $\dfrac{1 - i}{2 + i}$

20. $3(\cos 135° + i \sin 135°) \cdot 2(\cos 105° + i \sin 105°)$

21. $[2(\cos 60° + i \sin 60°)]^4$

22. $\dfrac{4(\cos 270° + i \sin 270°)}{2(\cos 90° + i \sin 90°)}$

23. $(2 - 2i)^5$

24. Find the cube roots of $1 - i$. Leave all results in trigonometric form.

25. Write the following equation using rectangular coordinates.

$$r = \frac{1}{2 - \sin \theta}$$

26. Graph $r = 2 + 3 \sin \theta$.

9

Logarithms

Until several hundred years ago, numerical calculations had to be done by long and tedious hand work. About 1650, Henry Briggs and John Napier of England developed *logarithms* to simplify this work. By the use of logarithms, problems of multiplication and division are replaced by problems of addition and subtraction. Also, problems of exponents and roots become problems of multiplication and division.

Logarithmic functions are the inverses of exponential functions. In the first section of this chapter, we discuss exponential functions. Then, in the second section, we see how logarithmic functions are obtained from exponential functions. This discussion is followed by a look at how logarithms are used in numerical work.

9.1 Exponential Functions

Exponential functions are written with exponents. Thus, before looking at exponential functions, let us review exponents.

Repeated products, such as $3 \cdot 3 \cdot 3 \cdot 3$, can be written with *exponents*. In $3 \cdot 3 \cdot 3 \cdot 3$, written 3^4, the number 4 means that 3 is to be written 4 times in the product. In general for a real number a and a natural number n,

$$a^n = \underbrace{a \cdot a \cdot a \cdots a}_{a \text{ appears } n \text{ times}}.$$

The expression a^n is called an **exponential**. The number n is the **exponent** and a is the **base**.

To extend our work with exponents to negative integers, we have the following definition.

If a is a nonzero real number, then

$$a^{-n} = \frac{1}{a^n}.$$

Futhermore, we define rational number exponents as follows.

For all integers m and n, and all numbers a for which the roots exist,
$$a^{m/n} = \sqrt[n]{a^m} = (\sqrt[n]{a})^m.$$

It is shown in more advanced courses that the exponential a^n can be given meaning for any real value of n.

The basic properties of exponents are given below.

For any real numbers a and b and any real numbers m and n, where no denominators are zero,

$$a^m \cdot a^n = a^{m+n} \qquad (ab)^m = a^m b^m$$

$$\frac{a^m}{a^n} = a^{m-n} \qquad (a^m)^n = a^{mn}$$

$$a^0 = 1 \quad (\text{if } a \neq 0).$$

EXAMPLE 1   Use the properties of exponents listed above to simplify each of the following.

(a) $2^5 \cdot 2^9 \cdot 2^7 = 2^{5+9+7} = 2^{21}$

(b) $3^{-2} = \frac{1}{3^2} = \frac{1}{9}$

(c) $5^{-4} = \frac{1}{625}$

(d) $\frac{4^9}{4^{-2}} = 4^{9-(-2)} = 4^{11}$

(e) $(7^3 \cdot 3^4)^2 = 7^6 \cdot 3^8$

(f) $2^0 + (-5)^0 - 3^0 = 1 + 1 - 1 = 1$

(g) $4^{3/2} = (4^{1/2})^3 = (\sqrt{4})^3 = 2^3 = 8.$ ●

To solve equations with exponentials, we sometimes use the following property: For $a > 0$, $a \neq 1$, if $a^x = a^y$, then $x = y$.

EXAMPLE 2   Find the value of x that makes each of the following true.

(a) $2^x = 8$

Since $8 = 2^3$, we have

$$2^x = 2^3,$$

from which $x = 3$.

(b) $32^x = 64$

Write both 32 and 64 as powers of the same base, 2.

$$32 = 2^5 \quad \text{and} \quad 64 = 2^6$$

Thus, $32^x = 64$ becomes

$$(2^5)^x = 2^6$$
$$2^{5x} = 2^6,$$

from which

$$5x = 6$$

or

$$x = \frac{6}{5}. \quad \bullet$$

An **exponential function** is a function of the form

$$y = a^x,$$

where a is a fixed number, $a > 0$ and $a \neq 1$.

The equation

$$y = 2^x$$

is a typical exponential function. To graph this function, we first make a table of values of x and y, as follows.

x	-3	-2	-1	0	1	2	3	4
2^x	$\frac{1}{8}$	$\frac{1}{4}$	$\frac{1}{2}$	1	2	4	8	16

If we plot these points and draw a smooth curve through them, we get the graph shown in Figure 9.1. This graph is typical of the graphs of exponential functions of the form $y = a^x$, where $a > 1$. The larger the value of a, the faster the graph rises.

Since neither horizontal nor vertical lines cut the graph of $y = 2^x$ in more than one point, $y = 2^x$ is a one-to-one function. For this reason, the inverse of $y = 2^x$, whose equation is $x = 2^y$, is a function. (To get the equation of the inverse, we exchanged x and y, as in Section 6.1.) The equation $x = 2^y$ leads to a logarithmic function, as we show in the next section.

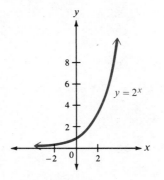

Figure 9.1

EXAMPLE 3   Graph $y = (1/2)^x$.

Again, we find typical points of the graph.

x	-3	-2	-1	0	1	2	3	4
$\left(\frac{1}{2}\right)^x$	8	4	2	1	$\frac{1}{2}$	$\frac{1}{4}$	$\frac{1}{8}$	$\frac{1}{16}$

This graph, shown in Figure 9.2, represents a one-to-one function. It is typical of the graphs of exponential functions of the form $y = a^x$, where $0 < a < 1$.   ●

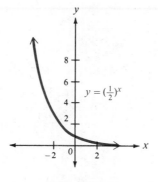

Figure 9.2

Exponential functions have many practical applications. In many situations involving growth or decay of a quantity, the amount or number present at time t can be closely approximated by a function of the form

$$y = y_0 a^{kt},$$

where y_0 is the amount or number present at time $t = 0$, and k is a constant.

EXAMPLE 4   The amount in grams of a radioactive substance present at time t is

$$y = 250 \left(\frac{1}{2}\right)^{.03t},$$

where t is time in days. Find the amount present initially, and after 100 days.

The initial amount (when $t = 0$) is given by

$$y = 250 \left(\frac{1}{2}\right)^{(.03)(0)} = 250,$$

since $(1/2)^0 = 1$. Thus, there were 250 grams present initially.

After 100 days,

$$y = 250 \left(\frac{1}{2}\right)^{(.03)(100)}$$

$$= 250 \left(\frac{1}{2}\right)^3$$

$$\approx 31.$$

After 100 days, about 31 grams remain.   ●

9.1 EXERCISES   *Use the properties of exponents to simplify each of the following. Leave answers in exponential form. See Example 1.*

1. $3^4 \cdot 3^7$ **2.** $4^5 \cdot 4^8$ **3.** $\dfrac{7^4}{7^3}$ **4.** $\dfrac{9^5}{9^2}$

5. $\dfrac{6^4 \cdot 6^5}{6^6}$ **6.** $\dfrac{9^{12} \cdot 9^4}{9^{11}}$ **7.** $(8^9)^2$ **8.** $(3^4)^3$

9. $\dfrac{(2^5)^2 \cdot 2^4}{2^6}$ **10.** $\dfrac{(3^6)^3 \cdot 3^7}{3^8}$ **11.** 2^{-3} **12.** 4^{-2}

13. $3^{-7} \cdot 3^8$ **14.** $5^{-9} \cdot 5^6$ **15.** $\dfrac{9^{-8} \cdot 9^2}{(9^2)^{-2}}$ **16.** $\dfrac{(4^{-3})^2 \cdot 4^5}{(4^3)^{-3}}$

17. $25^{1/2}$ **18.** $8^{2/3}$ **19.** $16^{3/4}$ **20.** $9^{3/2}$

Solve each of the following equations. See Example 2.

21. $5^x = 125$ **22.** $3^x = 81$ **23.** $8^x = 32$ **24.** $9^x = 27$

25. $3^x = \dfrac{1}{9}$ **26.** $2^x = \dfrac{1}{16}$ **27.** $\left(\dfrac{5}{2}\right)^x = \dfrac{4}{25}$ **28.** $\left(\dfrac{3}{4}\right)^x = \dfrac{16}{9}$

29. $\left(\dfrac{1}{2}\right)^x = 8$ **30.** $\left(\dfrac{1}{3}\right)^x = 9$ **31.** $16^{-x+1} = 8$ **32.** $25^{-2x} = 3125$

Graph each of the following exponential functions. See Example 3.

33. $y = 3^x$ **34.** $y = 4^x$

35. $y = \left(\dfrac{1}{3}\right)^x$ **36.** $y = \left(\dfrac{1}{4}\right)^x$

37. $y = 2^{x+1}$ **38.** $y = 3^{x+1}$

39. $y = 2^{-x}$ **40.** $y = 3^{-x}$

41. $y = 3^x - 3$ **42.** $y = 2^x - 2$

Suppose the population of a city is

$$P = 1{,}000{,}000(2^{.02t}),$$

where t represents time measured in months. Find the population at the following times.

43. $t = 0$ **44.** $t = 50$ **45.** $t = 100$

Suppose the quantity in grams of a radioactive substance present at time t is

$$y = 500(3^{-.05t}),$$

where t is measured in days. Find the amount present at each of the following times.

46. $t = 0$ **47.** $t = 10$ **48.** $t = 20$

If P dollars is deposited into an account paying a rate of interest i compounded m times a year, with the money left on deposit for n years, the account will end up with

$$A = P\left(1 + \dfrac{i}{m}\right)^{nm}$$

dollars. Find the final amount on deposit for each of the following.

49. $1000 at 6% compounded annually for 3 years. (Write 6% as .06.)

50. $1000 at 6% compounded semi-annually for 3 years.

51. $1000 at 6% compounded monthly for 3 years.

52. $1000 at 6% compounded daily (365 days per year) for 3 years.

9.2   Definition of Logarithm

The graph of the exponential function $y = 2^x$ is the solid curve shown in Figure 9.3. The figure also shows the inverse function, $x = 2^y$, as a dashed line. As explained in Chapter 6, we get the graph of the inverse by reflecting the graph of the given function about the line $y = x$. The inverse function, $x = 2^y$, is found by exchanging x and y in the given function $y = 2^x$.

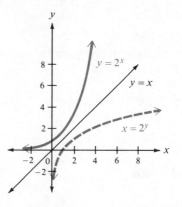

Figure 9.3

At this point, we cannot solve $x = 2^y$ for y. To do this, we introduce a new definition. For all positive numbers a, where $a \neq 1$,

$$x = a^y \qquad \text{means the same as} \qquad y = \log_a x.$$

We use *log* to mean **logarithm**. For example, the exponential statement

$$32 = 2^5 \qquad \text{means the same as} \qquad 5 = \log_2 32$$

(read "5 is the logarithm of 32 to the base 2"). Here 5 is the exponent on 2 that gives a result of 32.

By the definition given here, exponential statements can be turned into logarithmic statements, and logarithmic statements into exponential statements.

EXAMPLE 1   The following list shows the same statement, written in both exponential and logarithmic form.

Exponential Form	Logarithmic Form
$3^4 = 81$	$4 = \log_3 81$
$5^3 = 125$	$3 = \log_5 125$
$2^{-4} = \dfrac{1}{16}$	$-4 = \log_2 \dfrac{1}{16}$
$5^{-1} = \dfrac{1}{5}$	$-1 = \log_5 \dfrac{1}{5}$
$\left(\dfrac{3}{4}\right)^{-2} = \dfrac{16}{9}$	$-2 = \log_{3/4} \dfrac{16}{9}$ ●

EXAMPLE 2   Find the value of the variable in each of the following.

(a) $\log_3 81 = x$

Write the given statement in exponential form as

$$3^x = 81.$$

Since $81 = 3^4$, $3^x = 3^4$ and $x = 4$.

(b) $\log_8 16 = y$

Begin by writing the exponential statement

$$8^y = 16.$$

Both 8 and 16 are powers of 2. Rewrite $8^y = 16$ as

$$(2^3)^y = 2^4,$$

or $2^{3y} = 2^4$,

from which $3y = 4$

and $y = \dfrac{4}{3}.$ ●

For all positive numbers b, we know that $b^0 = 1$ and $b^1 = b$. Therefore, writing these statements in logarithmic form,

$$\log_b b = 1 \quad \text{and} \quad \log_b 1 = 0.$$

EXAMPLE 3   (a) $\log_7 1 = 0$

(b) $\log_{2/3} 1 = 0$

(c) $\log_8 8 = 1$

(d) $\log_{4/3} \dfrac{4}{3} = 1$ ●

By the definition of $y = \log_a x$ given above, a must be a positive real number not equal to 1, and x must be a positive number, while y can be any real number.

Because of this,

The domain of a logarithm function is the set of all positive real numbers, while the range is the set of all real numbers.

The basic properties of logarithms needed for work in trigonometry are summarized in the following theorem.

THEOREM 9.1   For any positive real number a, with $a \neq 1$, for any positive real numbers x and y, and for any real number r,

(a) $\log_a xy = \log_a x + \log_a y$

(b) $\log_a \dfrac{x}{y} = \log_a x - \log_a y$

(c) $\log_a x^r = r \cdot \log_a x$.

To prove part (a) of the theorem, let $\log_a x = M$ and $\log_a y = N$. By the definition of logarithm,

$$a^M = x \quad \text{and} \quad a^N = y.$$

Thus, $$(a^M)(a^N) = xy,$$

or $$a^{M+N} = xy$$

and $$\log_a xy = M + N.$$

Substituting for M and N gives the desired result

$$\log_a xy = \log_a x + \log_a y.$$

The proof of part (b) is saved for the exercises below. To prove part (c), let $\log_a x = M$, so that $a^M = x$. Thus,

$$(a^M)^r = x^r,$$

or $$x^r = a^{Mr}$$

and $$\log_a x^r = Mr,$$

by the definition of logarithm. Substituting for M gives

$$\log_a x^r = r \cdot \log_a x,$$

as required.

EXAMPLE 4   Rewrite each of the following using the three properties given in Theorem 9.1.

(a) $\log_6 9 \cdot 4 = \log_6 9 + \log_6 4$

(b) $\log_{12} \dfrac{17}{18} = \log_{12} 17 - \log_{12} 18$

(c) $\log_5 9^8 = 8 \cdot \log_5 9$

(d) $\log_7 \sqrt{19} = \log_7 19^{1/2} = \dfrac{1}{2} \cdot \log_7 19$ ●

EXAMPLE 5 Assume that

$$\log_{10} 2 = .3010 \quad \text{and} \quad \log_{10} 3 = .4771.$$

Find the base 10 logarithms of 4, 5, 6, and 12.
Use the properties of logarithms.

(a) $\log_{10} 4 = \log_{10} 2^2 = 2 \cdot \log_{10} 2 = 2(.3010) = .6020$

(b) $\log_{10} 5 = \log_{10} \dfrac{10}{2} = \log_{10} 10 - \log_{10} 2$

$$= 1 - .3010 = .6990$$

(c) $\log_{10} 6 = \log_{10} 2 \cdot 3 = \log_{10} 2 + \log_{10} 3$

$$= .3010 + .4771 = .7781$$

(d) $\log_{10} 12 = \log_{10} 4 \cdot 3 = \log_{10} 4 + \log_{10} 3$

$$= .6020 + .4771 = 1.0791 \quad \bullet$$

9.2 EXERCISES   *Convert each of the following to logarithmic form. See Example 1.*

1. $3^5 = 243$ 2. $2^7 = 128$

3. $10^4 = 10,000$ 4. $8^2 = 64$

5. $6^{-2} = \dfrac{1}{36}$ 6. $2^{-3} = \dfrac{1}{8}$

7. $\left(\dfrac{2}{3}\right)^{-2} = \dfrac{9}{4}$ 8. $\left(\dfrac{3}{8}\right)^{-1} = \dfrac{8}{3}$

Write each of the following in exponential form. See Example 1.

9. $\log_4 16 = 2$ 10. $\log_5 25 = 2$

11. $\log_{10} 1000 = 3$ 12. $\log_7 2401 = 4$

13. $\log_7 7 = 1$ 14. $\log_{15} 1 = 0$

15. $\log_{3/4} \dfrac{9}{16} = 2$ 16. $\log_{5/8} \dfrac{125}{512} = 3$

17. $\log_4 \dfrac{1}{16} = -2$ 18. $\log_5 \dfrac{1}{125} = -3$

Find the value of the variable in each of the following. See Example 2.

19. $\log_2 x = 4$ 20. $\log_2 m = 2$

21. $\log_3 27 = k$ 22. $\log_5 625 = z$

23. $\log_m 27 = 3$ 24. $\log_z 32 = 5$

25. $\log_{3/2} k = 2$ 26. $\log_{2/3} m = -2$

27. $\log_{32} m = \dfrac{4}{5}$ 28. $\log_{64} a = \dfrac{2}{3}$

29. $\log_{16} 32 = y$ 30. $\log_{36} 216 = p$

Simplify each of the following using the properties of logarithms given in Theorem 9.1. See Example 4.

31. $\log_6 9 + \log_6 5$

32. $\log_2 7 + \log_2 3$

33. $\log_5 12 - \log_5 7$

34. $\log_9 17 - \log_9 23$

35. $\log_2 7 + \log_2 4 - \log_2 5$

36. $\log_7 8 + \log_7 16 - \log_7 3$

37. $4 \cdot \log_3 2$

38. $3 \cdot \log_5 2$

39. $\dfrac{1}{2} \cdot \log_8 7$

40. $\dfrac{1}{2} \cdot \log_2 14$

41. $4 \cdot \log_2 3 - 2 \cdot \log_2 5$

42. $3 \cdot \log_4 5 - 4 \cdot \log_4 2$

Assume that

$$\log_{10} 2 = .3010 \qquad \log_{10} 7 = .8451$$
$$\log_{10} 3 = .4771 \qquad \log_{10} 11 = 1.0414.$$

Use the properties of logarithms to find each of the following. See Example 5.

43. $\log_{10} 14$

44. $\log_{10} 22$

45. $\log_{10} 28$

46. $\log_{10} 63$

47. $\log_{10} 2^8$

48. $\log_{10} 3^7$

49. $\log_{10} 11^3$

50. $\log_{10} \sqrt{3}$

51. $\log_{10} \sqrt[3]{11}$

52. $\log_{10} \sqrt[4]{3}$

Graph each of the following. See Figure 9.3.

53. $y = \log_4 x$

54. $y = \log_{1/4} x$

55. Prove part (b) of Theorem 9.1. (Hint: the proof is very similar to that of part (a).)

56. *The population of an animal species that is introduced into an area may grow rapidly at first, but then grow more slowly as time goes on. A logarithmic function can provide an excellent description of such growth. Suppose that the population of foxes, y in an area t months after the species is introduced into the area is*

$$y = 500 \log_{10} (2t + 2).$$

Find the population of foxes at the following times:

(a) when they are first released into the area ($t = 0$). Use the value of $\log_{10} 2$ given above.

(b) after 4 months

(c) after 49 months

9.3 Common Logarithms

Two systems of logarithms are in general use today. Logarithms to base 10 are used for numerical calculation, since our number system is base 10. This use of logarithms has been almost entirely replaced by calculators. However, since many calculators do not have an exponential key, common logarithms are still useful for finding powers and roots of numbers.

The other useful system of logarithms, natural logarithms, has assumed greater importance and is used in both applications and theoretical work, such as calculus. We discuss natural logarithms briefly in Section 5 of this chapter.

Base 10 logarithms are called **common logarithms**. For convenience, $\log_{10} x$ is written as $\log x$. Thus, $\log_{10} 100$ is written as $\log 100$. Since non-scientific calculators do not have a logarithm key, in this section we briefly explain the use of the table of common logarithms in the back of this book, Table IV. The table gives the common logarithm of the numbers between 1 and 10. Any number can be written in scientific notation as a number between 1 and 10 times a power of 10. This fact plus the properties of logarithms can be used to find the common logarithm of any number with the tables.

EXAMPLE 1   Find $\log 5.74$.

Look down the left column of Table IV to find the first two digits of 5.74, which are 5.7. Read across that row until you reach the column having 4 at the top. You should find the digits .7589. Thus,

$$\log 5.74 = .7589. \qquad \bullet$$

All the numbers in Table IV are approximations, but we shall use the equals sign for convenience.

To find the logarithm of a number greater than 10 or less than 1, first write the number in scientific notation and then apply Theorem 9.1(a).

EXAMPLE 2   Find $\log 596$.

Write the number 596 in scientific notation as

$$596 = 5.96 \times 10^2.$$

Then

$$\begin{aligned}
\log 596 &= \log (5.96 \times 10^2). \\
&= \log 5.96 + \log 10^2 \quad \text{(Theorem 9.1(a))} \\
&= \log 5.96 + 2. \qquad (\log_{10} 10^2 = 2)
\end{aligned}$$

From Table IV, $\log 5.96 = .7752$. Thus,

$$\log 596 = .7752 + 2 = 2.7752. \qquad \bullet$$

The integer part of this logarithm, 2, is called the **characteristic**, while the decimal part, .7752, is called the **mantissa**. The mantissa is always a positive number. The characteristic may be a positive or negative integer.

EXAMPLE 3   Find $\log .000421$.

$$\begin{aligned}
\log .000421 &= \log (4.21 \times 10^{-4}) \\
&= \log 4.21 + \log 10^{-4} \\
&= \log 4.21 + (-4)
\end{aligned}$$

From Table IV,

$$\log .000421 = .6243 + (-4) \qquad \text{or} \qquad .6243 - 4. \qquad \bullet$$

If you use a calculator with a logarithm key to find log .000421, the display will show -3.3757, which is the algebraic sum $.6243 - 4$.

EXAMPLE 4   Find the value of N that makes log $N = 1.6955$.

Since we are given the logarithm and must find the number, we reverse the process used above. On a calculator, this is done by pressing the inverse key, then the logarithm key. To use Table IV, work in the opposite direction from the way we used the table before. First find the mantissa, .6955, in the body of the table. Then look at the left of the row containing .6955 for the first two digits of the answer. The first two digits are 4.9. Then find the third digit by looking at the top (or bottom) of the column containing .6955. The third digit is 6. Thus, the *digits* of N are 4.96. Since the characteristic is 1,

$$N = 4.96 \times 10^1 = 49.6.$$

49.6 is called the **antilogarithm** of 1.6955.   ●

EXAMPLE 5   Find the antilogarithm of each of the following.

(a) $.8785 - 3$.

We want to find a number N such that log $N = .8785 - 3$. If using a calculator, first write the logarithm as -2.1215 (found by adding .8785 and -3). Then use the inverse and logarithm keys. If we use Table IV, we find the digits of N are 7.56. The characteristic is -3. Thus,

$$N = 7.56 \times 10^{-3} = .00756,$$

and .00756 is the antilogarithm of $.8785 - 3$.

(b) 4.7774.

From Table IV or a calculator, the antilogarithm is

$$5.99 \times 10^4 = 59,900.   ●$$

Table IV gives the logarithms of numbers with three significant digits. For greater accuracy when finding the logarithms of numbers with more significant digits, we can use interpolation.

EXAMPLE 6   Use Table IV to find log 8.874.

First, find two numbers in Table IV that are closest to 8.874, and then note their logarithms.

$$.010\left\{.004\left\{\begin{array}{l} \log 8.870 = .9479 \\ \log 8.874 = \quad ? \\ \log 8.880 = .9484 \end{array}\right\}d\right\}.0005$$

We can approximate d by setting the ratios on each side equal.

$$\frac{.004}{.010} = \frac{d}{.0005}$$

$$d \approx .0002$$

Thus, $\log 8.874 \approx .9479 + .0002 = .9481.$ ●

Interpolation can also be used to find the antilogarithm of a given logarithm.

EXAMPLE 7   Find the antilogarithm of 3.4042.

Locate the two numbers in the body of the logarithm table that are closest to the mantissa, .4042. Then set up an array as above.

$$10 \left\{ d \begin{cases} \log 2530 = 3.4031 \\ \log \ \ ? \ \ = 3.4042 \end{cases} .0011 \\ \log 2540 = 3.4048 \right\} .0017$$

Equate the two ratios and solve for d.

$$\frac{d}{10} = \frac{.0011}{.0017}$$

$$d \approx 6$$

Then the antilogarithm of 3.4042 is

$$2530 + 6 = 2536. \quad ●$$

The properties of logarithms can be used to simplify numerical calculations. Logarithms are particularly useful for finding powers and roots since they make it possible to use the simpler operations of multiplication and division.

EXAMPLE 8   Find $(.0839)^{2/3}$.

Let $R = (.0839)^{2/3}$. Then

$$\log R = \log (.0839)^{2/3}$$

$$= \frac{2}{3} \log .0839$$

$$\log R = \frac{2}{3} (.9238 - 2).$$

To simplify the computation, change the characteristic, -2, to a number which is a multiple of 3. One way to do this is to write the characteristic as $1 - 3$. Adding the positive part of $1 - 3$ to the mantissa gives

$$\log R = \frac{2}{3} (1.9238 - 3).$$

Now, multiply 2/3 times 1.9238, and then times -3 to get

$$\log R = 1.2825 - 2$$

$$= .2825 - 1$$

from which $R = .192$ to three significant digits.   ●

EXAMPLE 9   Find M if $M = \dfrac{\sqrt{29.8}}{.00972}$.

By the properties of logarithms,

$$\log M = \log \frac{\sqrt{29.8}}{.00972}$$

$$= \log \sqrt{29.8} - \log .00972$$

$$= \log (29.8)^{1/2} - \log .00972$$

$$= \frac{1}{2} \log 29.8 - \log .00972.$$

Now use Table IV or a calculator.

$$\log M = \frac{1}{2} (1.4742) - (.9877 - 3)$$

$$= .7371 - .9877 + 3$$

Now add these three terms.

$$\log M = 2.7494$$

From Table IV, $M = 562$ to three significant digits.   ●

9.3 EXERCISES

Find the logarithm of each of the following numbers. See Examples 1–3.

1. 2.79   **2.** 794

3. 98,300   **4.** 59.2

5. 749,000   **6.** .000976

7. .00591   **8.** .0105

Find the antilogarithm of each of the following. See Examples 4 and 5.

9. 2.8585   **10.** 5.7945

11. 3.3674   **12.** .7767 − 3

13. .0569 − 1   **14.** .9991 − 2

15. .7566 − 3   **16.** .6821

Use interpolation or a calculator to find each of the following. See Example 6.

17. log 4.897   **18.** log 358.7

19. log 37,990   **20.** log .8276

21. log .02913   **22.** log .0009744

Use interpolation or a calculator to find the antilogarithm of each of the following. See Example 7.

23. .4383   **24.** 1.4691

25. 3.4207

26. .2745 − 1

27. .7060 − 3

28. .9678 − 4

Use logarithms to find each of the following to three significant digits. See Examples 8 and 9.

29. $(.00432)^2$

30. $(21.9)^{3.1}$

31. $\sqrt{91.7}$

32. $\sqrt[4]{39{,}900}$

33. $(596)^{2/3}$

34. $(1.74)^{4/3}$

35. $(9.81)^{-2}$

36. $\dfrac{(7.18)^3(2.41)}{(59.8)^2}$

37. $\dfrac{(38.4)^2(5.17)^3}{(98.6)^5}$

38. $\left(\dfrac{7.19}{2.43}\right)^5$

Use logarithms with interpolation or a calculator to find the value of each of the following to four significant digits.

39. $(98.71)^{2.5}$

40. $(3.125)^3$

41. $\sqrt[3]{.005352}$

42. $87.64\sqrt{29.83}$

43. $\sqrt[4]{\dfrac{.7162}{.04763}}$

44. $\dfrac{(49.71)^{2/3}}{.09813}$

In chemistry, the pH of a solution is defined as

$$pH = -\log\,[H_3O^+],$$

where $[H_3O^+]$ is the hydronium ion concentration in moles per liter. Find the pH of each of the following hydronium ion concentrations.

45. Grapefruit, 6.3×10^{-4}

46. Crackers, 3.9×10^{-9}

47. Limes, 1.6×10^{-2}

48. Sodium hydroxide (lye), 3.2×10^{-14}

Find $[H_3O^+]$ for each of the following, given its pH.

49. Soda pop, 2.7

50. Wine, 3.4

51. Beer, 4.8

52. Drinking water, 6.5

Sound is measured in decibels (db) and the number of decibels in a sound is defined as

$$db = \log\left(\frac{P_2}{P_1}\right)^{10},$$

where P_1 is the output power and P_2 is input power. Find the decibels for each of the following.

53. $P_1 = 2.61, P_2 = 3.402$

54. $P_1 = 5.629, P_2 = 6.403$

9.4 Logarithmic Equations

Equations involving variable exponents are called **exponential equations**. Equations involving logarithms are called **logarithmic equations**. We see how to solve both these types of equations in this section. The solution of these equations depends on the following two properties.

If a is a positive number, $a \neq 1$, and x and y are real numbers, then

1. $a^x = a^y$ if and only if $x = y$.

In addition, if x and y are both positive, then

2. $x = y$ if and only if $\log_a x = \log_a y$.

We used the first of these properties to solve one type of exponential equation in Sections 9.1 and 9.2. The next example illustrates this type of exponential equation.

EXAMPLE 1 Solve the exponential equation $9^x = 27$.
Write 9 as 3^2 and 27 as 3^3. Then, $9^x = 27$ becomes

$$(3^2)^x = 3^3$$
$$3^{2x} = 3^3.$$

By Property 1 from above,

$$2x = 3$$
$$x = \frac{3}{2}. \quad \bullet$$

Other methods of using these properties to solve exponential and logarithmic equations are shown in the following examples.

EXAMPLE 2 Solve $5^x = 15$.
Here we cannot write both sides as powers of the same base. Use Property 2 from above and take common logarithms of both sides of the equation.

$$\log 5^x = \log 15$$
$$x \cdot \log 5 = \log 15 \qquad \text{use a property of logarithms}$$
$$x = \frac{\log 15}{\log 5}$$

The exact solution is $x = \log 15/\log 5$. We can find a decimal approximation by finding $\log 15$ and $\log 5$ in Table IV or with a calculator.

$$x = \frac{\log 15}{\log 5}$$

$$\approx \frac{1.1761}{.6990}$$

$$x \approx 1.68. \quad \bullet$$

EXAMPLE 3   Solve $\log (x - 3) + \log x = 1$.
By properties of logarithms,

$$\log (x - 3) + \log x = \log x(x - 3).$$

Also, $1 = \log 10$. Thus, the original equation becomes

$$\log x(x - 3) = \log 10.$$

Then, by Property 2 above,

$$x(x - 3) = 10$$
$$x^2 - 3x = 10$$
$$x^2 - 3x - 10 = 0$$
$$(x - 5)(x + 2) = 0$$
$$x = 5 \text{ or } x = -2.$$

The domain of the common logarithm function does not include negative numbers, so the only solution here is

$$x = 5. \quad \bullet$$

EXAMPLE 4   Solve $\log_y 7 = 2$.
Convert this equation from logarithmic form to exponential form, using the definition of logarithms. We have

$$y^2 = 7.$$

Take the square root of both sides.

$$y = \pm \sqrt{7}$$

Since the base of a logarithm must be positive,

$$y = \sqrt{7}. \quad \bullet$$

9.4 EXERCISES   *Solve each of the following equations. Do not use any tables or a calculator. See Example 1.*

1. $5^x = 125$ **2.** $3^p = 81$ **3.** $32^k = 2$

4. $64^z = 4$ **5.** $100^r = 1000$ **6.** $32^m = 16$

7. $27^z = 81$ **8.** $49^r = 343$ **9.** $2^{5x} = 16^{x+2}$

10. $3^{6x} = 9^{2x+1}$ **11.** $25^{2k} = 125^{k+1}$ **12.** $36^{2p+1} = 6^{3p-2}$

Solve each of the following equations. Express all answers with three significant digits. See Examples 2–4.

13. $10^p = 3$ **14.** $10^m = 7$

15. $10^{r+2} = 15$ **16.** $10^{m-3} = 28$

17. $6^k = 10$ **18.** $12^x = 10$

19. $14^z = 28$ **20.** $21^p = 63$

21. $7^a = 32$ **22.** $12^b = 70$

23. $15^x = 8^{2x+1}$ **24.** $21^{y+1} = 32^{2y}$

25. $16^{z+3} = 28^{2z-1}$ **26.** $40^{r-3} = 32^{3r+1}$

27. $\log x - \log (x - 14) = \log 8$ **28.** $\log (k - 3) = 1 + \log (k - 21)$

29. $\log z = 1 - \log (3z - 13)$ **30.** $\log x + \log (x + 2) = 0$

31. $\log_x 10 = 3$ **32.** $\log_k 25 = 5$

33. $2 + \log x = 0$ **34.** $-6 + \log 2k = 0$

35. The amount of a radioactive specimen present at time t (measured in seconds) is

$$A(t) = 5000(10)^{-.02t},$$

where $A(t)$ is measured in grams. Find the half-life of the specimen, that is, the time when only half of the specimen remains.

A large cloud of radioactive debris from a nuclear explosion has floated over the Pacific Northwest, contaminating much of the hay supply. Consequently, farmers in the area are concerned that the cows eating this hay will give contaminated milk. (The tolerance level for radioactive iodine in milk is 0.) The percent of the initial amount of radioactive iodine still present in the hay after t days is approximated by

$$y = 100(2.7)^{-.1t},$$

where t is time measured in days.

36. Some scientists feel that the hay is safe after the percent of radioactive iodine has declined to 10% of the original amount. Find the number of days before the hay can be used.

37. Other scientists believe that the hay is not safe until the level of radioactive iodine has declined to only 1% of the original level. Find the number of days this would take.

9.5 Change of Base

We said earlier in this chapter that there are two bases for logarithms in common use today. Common logarithms, or logarithms to base 10, are used primarily in numerical calculations. **Natural logarithms**, which are logarithms to base e, are used in applications and in theoretical work, such as in calculus. The number e is irrational, like π. To nine decimal places,

$$e = 2.718281828.$$

To find the value of natural logarithms, we need a new theorem. To obtain this theorem, let $\log_a N = x$ for positive real numbers a and N, $a \neq 1$, and any real number x. Since

$$\log_a N = x,$$

we can use the definition of logarithms to write

$$a^x = N.$$

Let b represent a positive number, $b \neq 1$. Take base b logarithms of both sides of this last equation:

$$\log_b a^x = \log_b N,$$

from which

$$x \cdot \log_b a = \log_b N,$$

$$x = \frac{\log_b N}{\log_b a}.$$

Since we know that $x = \log_a N$, we finally have

$$\log_a N = \frac{\log_b N}{\log_b a}.$$

This result is given below in the **change of base theorem**.

THEOREM 9.2   If a, b, and N are positive numbers, with $a \neq 1$ and $b \neq 1$, then

$$\log_a N = \frac{\log_b N}{\log_b a}.$$

EXAMPLE 1   Find $\log_5 15$.

We can find the value of logarithms to bases other than 10 by using the change of base theorem with $b = 10$. Here we have

$$a = 5, \qquad N = 15, \qquad \text{and} \qquad b = 10.$$

Thus,

$$\log_5 15 = \frac{\log 15}{\log 5} \quad (\text{recall: } \log 15 = \log_{10} 15)$$

$$\approx \frac{1.1761}{.6990}$$

$$\log_5 15 \approx 1.683. \qquad \bullet$$

EXAMPLE 2   Find $\log_e 20$.

Let $a = e = 2.718$ (to three decimal places), $N = 20$, and $b = 10$. Thus,

$$\log_e 20 = \frac{\log 20}{\log e}$$

$$\approx \frac{1.3010}{.4343}$$

$$\log_e 20 \approx 2.996.$$

The notation $\log_e 20$ is seldom used. The notation in more common use is ln 20, where ln is an abbreviation for "natural logarithm." Thus, ln 20 = 2.996. ●

In general, to find ln x for any positive number x, use the change of base theorem to write

$$\ln x = \frac{\log x}{\log e}$$

$$\ln x = \frac{\log x}{.4343}$$

or $\ln x = 2.3026 \cdot \log x$ Since $1/.4343 \approx 2.3026$.

EXAMPLE 3   ln 897 = 2.3026 · log 897
               = 2.3026(2.9528)
          ln 897 = 6.799   ●

EXAMPLE 4   ln .0389 = 2.3026 · log .0389
                = 2.3026(.5899 − 2)
                = 2.3026(−1.4101)

Here we add the positive mantissa and the negative characteristic algebraically to get a single number.

          ln .0389 = −3.247   ●

9.5 EXERCISES

Write each of the following logarithms as a decimal to four significant digits. See Examples 1–4.

1. $\log_8 20$ 2. $\log_7 53$ 3. $\log_{12} 2$
4. $\log_5 17$ 5. $\log_8 27$ 6. $\log_{15} 36$
7. ln 28   8. ln 57   9. ln 386
10. ln 971   11. ln 28,000,000   12. ln 37,500,000
13. ln 15,700,000   14. ln 79,800,000   15. ln .0871
16. ln .00423   17. ln .00154   18. ln .00982
19. ln .0000568   20. ln .0479

The number of species in a sample is given by

$$S(n) = a \ln\left(1 + \frac{n}{a}\right),$$

where n is the number of individuals in the sample and a is a constant which indicates the diversity of species in the community. If $a = .36$, find $S(n)$ for the following values of n.

21. 100   **22.** 200   **23.** 150   **24.** 10

25. Find n if $S(n) = 9$ and $a = .36$.

Suppose the number of rabbits in a colony increases according to the relationship

$$y = y_0 e^{.4t},$$

where t represents time in months and y_0 is the initial population of rabbits.

26. Find the number of rabbits present at time $t = 4$ if $y_0 = 100$.

27. How long will it take for the number of rabbits to triple?

A city in Ohio finds its residents moving into the countryside. Its population is declining according to the relationship

$$P = P_0 e^{-.04t},$$

where t is time measured in years and P_0 is the population at time $t = 0$.

28. If $P_0 = 1,000,000$, find the population at time $t = 1$.

29. If $P_0 = 1,000,000$, estimate the time it will take for the population to be reduced to 750,000.

30. How long will it take for the population to be cut in half?

It can be shown that P dollars compounded continuously (every instant) at an annual rate of interest i would amount to

$$A = Pe^{ni}$$

at the end of n years. How much would $20,000 compounded continuously at 8% amount to for the following number of years?

31. 1 year

32. 5 years

33. Find the number of years it will take for $1000, compounded continuously at 7%, to double.

The amount of pollution in the air fluctuates with the seasons. It is lower after heavy spring rains and higher after periods of little rain. In addition to this seasonal fluctuation, the long-term trend is upward. An idealized graph of this situation is shown in the figure. Trigonometric functions can be used to describe the fluctuating part of the pollution levels. Powers of the number e can be used to show the long-term growth. In fact, the pollution level, P, in a certain area might be given by

$$P = 7(1 - \cos 2\pi t)(t + 10) + 100e^{.2t},$$

where t is time in years, with $t = 0$ representing January 1, 1981. Thus, July 1, 1981 *would be represented by t = .5, while October* 1, 1982, *would be represented by t =* 1.75. *Find the pollution levels on each of the following dates.*

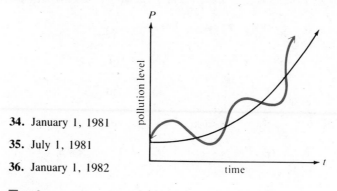

34. January 1, 1981

35. July 1, 1981

36. January 1, 1982

Chapter 9 Test

Simplify each of the following.

1. $\dfrac{3^4 \cdot 3^5}{3^6}$

2. $\dfrac{(5^8)^2 \cdot 5^9}{5^7 \cdot 5^6}$

Graph each of the following.

3. $y = 2^x$

4. $y = (1/3)^x$

Write each of the following in exponential notation.

5. $\log_2 32 = 5$

6. $\log 2 = .3010$

Write the following as logarithms.

7. $3^4 = 81$

8. $(2/3)^{-2} = 9/4$

9. $(.01)^{-2} = 10,000$

Find each of the following logarithms. Interpolate as necessary or use a calculator.

10. $\log .894$ **11.** $\log 2590$ **12.** $\log 76,980$ **13.** $\log .004761$

Find the value of the variable in each of the following. Interpolate as necessary or use a calculator.

14. $\log N = 3.5944$ **15.** $\log N = 8.9450 - 10$ **16.** $\log N = 1.4507$

Evaluate each of the following. Write answers with three significant digits.

17. $(97.4)^2$

18. $\sqrt[3]{52,700}$

19. $\dfrac{89.7}{(71.8)^{1.2}}$

Solve each of the following equations. If answer is not exact, write it to three significant digits.

20. $8^x = 128$ **21.** $7^x = 21$ **22.** $\log(x - 2) + \log(x - 11) = 1$

Find each of the following logarithms to three significant digits.

23. $\log_7 46.9$

24. $\ln 528$

Appendix

The Greek Alphabet

A	α	alpha	N	ν	nu
B	β	beta	Ξ	ξ	xi
Γ	γ	gamma	O	o	omicron
Δ	δ	delta	Π	π	pi
E	ϵ	epsilon	P	ρ	rho
Z	ζ	zeta	Σ	σ	sigma
H	η	eta	T	τ	tau
Θ	θ	theta	Υ	υ	upsilon
I	ι	iota	Φ	φ	phi
K	κ	kappa	X	χ	chi
Λ	λ	lambda	Ψ	ψ	psi
M	μ	mu	Ω	ω	omega

Values of Trigonometric Functions for Special Angles

Angle θ Degrees	Angle θ Radians	$\sin \theta$	$\cos \theta$	$\tan \theta$	$\cot \theta$	$\sec \theta$	$\csc \theta$
$0°$	0	0	1	0	undefined	1	undefined
$30°$	$\pi/6$	$1/2$	$\sqrt{3}/2$	$\sqrt{3}/3$	$\sqrt{3}$	$2\sqrt{3}/3$	2
$45°$	$\pi/4$	$\sqrt{2}/2$	$\sqrt{2}/2$	1	1	$\sqrt{2}$	$\sqrt{2}$
$60°$	$\pi/3$	$\sqrt{3}/2$	$1/2$	$\sqrt{3}$	$\sqrt{3}/3$	2	$2\sqrt{3}/3$
$90°$	$\pi/2$	1	0	undefined	0	undefined	1
$120°$	$2\pi/3$	$\sqrt{3}/2$	$-1/2$	$-\sqrt{3}$	$-\sqrt{3}/3$	-2	$2\sqrt{3}/3$
$135°$	$3\pi/4$	$\sqrt{2}/2$	$-\sqrt{2}/2$	-1	-1	$-\sqrt{2}$	$\sqrt{2}$
$150°$	$5\pi/6$	$1/2$	$-\sqrt{3}/2$	$-\sqrt{3}/3$	$-\sqrt{3}$	$-2\sqrt{3}/3$	2
$180°$	π	0	-1	0	undefined	-1	undefined
$210°$	$7\pi/6$	$-1/2$	$-\sqrt{3}/2$	$\sqrt{3}/3$	$\sqrt{3}$	$-2\sqrt{3}/3$	-2
$225°$	$5\pi/4$	$-\sqrt{2}/2$	$-\sqrt{2}/2$	1	1	$-\sqrt{2}$	$-\sqrt{2}$
$240°$	$4\pi/3$	$-\sqrt{3}/2$	$-1/2$	$\sqrt{3}$	$\sqrt{3}/3$	-2	$-2\sqrt{3}/3$
$270°$	$3\pi/2$	-1	0	undefined	0	undefined	-1
$300°$	$5\pi/3$	$-\sqrt{3}/2$	$1/2$	$-\sqrt{3}$	$-\sqrt{3}/3$	2	$-2\sqrt{3}/3$
$315°$	$7\pi/4$	$-\sqrt{2}/2$	$\sqrt{2}/2$	-1	-1	$\sqrt{2}$	$-\sqrt{2}$
$330°$	$11\pi/6$	$-1/2$	$\sqrt{3}/2$	$-\sqrt{3}/3$	$-\sqrt{3}$	$2\sqrt{3}/3$	-2
$360°$	2π	0	1	0	undefined	1	undefined

Fundamental Identities

$$\tan A = \frac{\sin A}{\cos A} \qquad \cot A = \frac{\cos A}{\sin A} \qquad \cot A = \frac{1}{\tan A} \qquad \csc A = \frac{1}{\sin A} \qquad \sec A = \frac{1}{\cos A} \qquad \sin^2 A + \cos^2 A = 1$$

$$\sin^2 A = 1 - \cos^2 A \qquad \cos^2 A = 1 - \sin^2 A \qquad \tan^2 A + 1 = \sec^2 A \qquad 1 + \cot^2 A = \csc^2 A \qquad \sin(-A) = -\sin A$$

$$\cos(-A) = \cos A \qquad \tan(-A) = -\tan A$$

Sum and Difference Identities

$$\cos(A - B) = \cos A \cos B + \sin A \sin B \qquad \cos(A + B) = \cos A \cos B - \sin A \sin B$$

$$\sin(A - B) = \sin A \cos B - \cos A \sin B \qquad \sin(A + B) = \sin A \cos B + \cos A \sin B$$

$$\tan(A - B) = \frac{\tan A - \tan B}{1 + \tan A \tan B} \qquad \tan(A + B) = \frac{\tan A + \tan B}{1 - \tan A \tan B}$$

Cofunction Identities

$$\sin\left(\frac{\pi}{2} - A\right) - \cos A \qquad \cos\left(\frac{\pi}{2} - A\right) = \sin A \qquad \tan\left(\frac{\pi}{2} - A\right) = \cot A$$

Multiple-Angle and Half-Angle Identities

$$\cos 2A = \cos^2 A - \sin^2 A \qquad \cos 2A = 1 - 2\sin^2 A \qquad \cos 2A = 2\cos^2 A - 1 \qquad \sin 2A = 2\sin A \cos A$$

$$\tan 2A = \frac{2\tan A}{1 - \tan^2 A} \qquad \cos\frac{A}{2} = \pm\sqrt{\frac{1 + \cos A}{2}} \qquad \sin\frac{A}{2} = \pm\sqrt{\frac{1 - \cos A}{2}} \qquad \tan\frac{A}{2} = \pm\sqrt{\frac{1 - \cos A}{1 + \cos A}}$$

Reduction Identity

$$a\sin A \pm b\cos A = \sqrt{a^2 + b^2}\,\sin(A + \alpha), \text{ where } \sin\alpha = b/\sqrt{a^2 + b^2} \text{ and } \cos\alpha = a/\sqrt{a^2 + b^2}$$

Sum and Product Identities

$$\sin x + \sin y = 2\sin\left(\frac{x + y}{2}\right)\cos\left(\frac{x - y}{2}\right)$$

$$\sin A \cos B = \frac{1}{2}[\sin(A + B) + \sin(A - B)]$$

$$\sin x - \sin y = 2\cos\left(\frac{x + y}{2}\right)\sin\left(\frac{x - y}{2}\right)$$

$$\cos A \sin B = \frac{1}{2}[\sin(A + B) - \sin(A - B)]$$

$$\cos x + \cos y = 2\cos\left(\frac{x + y}{2}\right)\cos\left(\frac{x - y}{2}\right)$$

$$\cos A \cos B = \frac{1}{2}[\cos(A + B) + \cos(A - B)]$$

$$\cos x - \cos y = -2\sin\left(\frac{x + y}{2}\right)\sin\left(\frac{x - y}{2}\right)$$

$$\sin A \sin B = \frac{1}{2}[\cos(A - B) - \cos(A + B)]$$

Table I   Squares and Square Roots

n	n^2	$\sqrt{n}$	$\sqrt{10n}$	n	n^2	$\sqrt{n}$	$\sqrt{10n}$
1	1	1.000	3.162	51	2601	7.141	22.583
2	4	1.414	4.472	52	2704	7.211	22.804
3	9	1.732	5.477	53	2809	7.280	23.022
4	16	2.000	6.325	54	2916	7.348	23.238
5	25	2.236	7.071	55	3025	7.416	23.452
6	36	2.449	7.746	56	3136	7.483	23.664
7	49	2.646	8.367	57	3249	7.550	23.875
8	64	2.828	8.944	58	3364	7.616	24.083
9	81	3.000	9.487	59	3481	7.681	24.290
10	100	3.162	10.000	60	3600	7.746	24.495
11	121	3.317	10.488	61	3721	7.810	24.698
12	144	3.464	10.954	62	3844	7.874	24.900
13	169	3.606	11.402	63	3969	7.937	25.100
14	196	3.742	11.832	64	4096	8.000	25.298
15	225	3.873	12.247	65	4225	8.062	25.495
16	256	4.000	12.649	66	4356	8.124	25.690
17	289	4.123	13.038	67	4489	8.185	25.884
18	324	4.243	13.416	68	4624	8.246	26.077
19	361	4.359	13.784	69	4761	8.307	26.268
20	400	4.472	14.142	70	4900	8.367	26.458
21	441	4.583	14.491	71	5041	8.426	26.646
22	484	4.690	14.832	72	5184	8.485	26.833
23	529	4.796	15.166	73	5329	8.544	27.019
24	576	4.899	15.492	74	5476	8.602	27.203
25	625	5.000	15.811	75	5625	8.660	27.386
26	676	5.099	16.125	76	5776	8.718	27.568
27	729	5.196	16.432	77	5929	8.775	27.749
28	784	5.292	16.733	78	6084	8.832	27.928
29	841	5.385	17.029	79	6241	8.888	28.107
30	900	5.477	17.321	80	6400	8.944	28.284
31	961	5.568	17.607	81	6561	9.000	28.460
32	1024	5.657	17.889	82	6724	9.055	28.636
33	1089	5.745	18.166	83	6889	9.110	28.810
34	1156	5.831	18.439	84	7056	9.165	28.983
35	1225	5.916	18.708	85	7225	9.220	29.155
36	1296	6.000	18.974	86	7396	9.274	29.326
37	1369	6.083	19.235	87	7569	9.327	29.496
38	1444	6.164	19.494	88	7744	9.381	29.665
39	1521	6.245	19.748	89	7921	9.434	29.833
40	1600	6.325	20.000	90	8100	9.487	30.000
41	1681	6.403	20.248	91	8281	9.539	30.166
42	1764	6.481	20.494	92	8464	9.592	30.332
43	1849	6.557	20.736	93	8649	9.644	30.496
44	1936	6.633	20.976	94	8836	9.695	30.659
45	2025	6.708	21.213	95	9025	9.747	30.822
46	2116	6.782	21.448	96	9216	9.798	30.984
47	2209	6.856	21.679	97	9409	9.849	31.145
48	2304	6.928	21.909	98	9604	9.899	31.305
49	2401	7.000	22.136	99	9801	9.950	31.464
50	2500	7.071	22.361	100	10000	10.000	31.623

Table II Trigonometric Functions in Degrees and Radians*

Angle θ									
Degrees	**Radians**	sin θ	csc θ	tan θ	cot θ	sec θ	cos θ		
0° 00′	.0000	.0000	No value	.0000	No value	1.000	1.0000	1.5708	90° 00′
10	029	029	343.8	029	343.8	000	000	679	50
20	058	058	171.9	058	171.9	000	000	650	40
30	.0087	.0087	114.6	.0087	114.6	1.000	1.0000	1.5621	30
40	116	116	85.95	116	85.94	000	.9999	592	20
50	145	145	68.76	145	68.75	000	999	563	10
1° 00′	.0175	.0175	57.30	.0175	57.29	1.000	.9998	1.5533	89° 00′
10	204	204	49.11	204	49.10	000	998	504	50
20	233	233	42.98	233	42.96	000	997	475	40
30	.0262	.0262	38.20	.0262	38.19	1.000	.9997	1.5446	30
40	291	291	34.38	291	34.37	000	996	417	20
50	320	320	31.26	320	31.24	001	995	388	10
2° 00′	.0349	.0349	28.65	.0349	28.64	1.001	.9994	1.5359	88° 00′
10	378	378	26.45	378	26.43	001	993	330	50
20	407	407	24.56	407	24.54	001	992	301	40
30	.0436	.0436	22.93	.0437	22.90	1.001	.9990	1.5272	30
40	465	465	21.49	466	21.47	001	989	243	20
50	495	494	20.23	495	20.21	001	988	213	10
3° 00′	.0524	.0523	19.11	.0524	19.08	1.001	.9986	1.5184	87° 00′
10	553	552	18.10	553	18.07	002	985	155	50
20	582	581	17.20	582	17.17	002	983	126	40
30	.0611	.0610	16.38	.0612	16.35	1.002	.9981	1.5097	30
40	640	640	15.64	641	15.60	002	980	068	20
50	669	669	14.96	670	14.92	002	978	039	10
4° 00′	.0698	.0698	14.34	.0699	14.30	1.002	.9976	1.5010	86° 00′
10	727	727	13.76	729	13.73	003	974	981	50
20	756	756	13.23	758	13.20	003	971	952	40
30	.0785	.0785	12.75	.0787	12.71	1.003	.9969	1.4923	30
40	814	814	12.29	816	12.25	003	967	893	20
50	844	843	11.87	846	11.83	004	964	864	10
5° 00′	.0873	.0872	11.47	.0875	11.43	1.004	.9962	1.4835	85° 00′
10	902	901	11.10	904	11.06	004	959	806	50
20	931	929	10.76	934	10.71	004	957	777	40
30	.0960	.0958	10.43	.0963	10.39	1.005	.9954	1.4748	30
40	989	987	10.13	992	10.08	005	951	719	20
50	.1018	.1016	9.839	.1022	9.788	005	948	690	10
6° 00′	.1047	.1045	9.567	.1051	9.514	1.006	.9945	1.4661	84° 00′
		cos θ	sec θ	cot θ	tan θ	csc θ	sin θ	**Radians**	**Degrees**
								Angle θ	

* Table I, "Four Place Values of Trigonometric Functions Angle θ in Degrees and Radians," from *Plane Trigonometry,* 3rd ed., Nathan O. Niles. Reprinted by permission of John Wiley & Sons, Inc. Copyright © 1959, 1968, 1976 by John Wiley & Sons, Inc.

Table II (continued)

Angle θ		sin θ	csc θ	tan θ	cot θ	sec θ	cos θ		
Degrees	**Radians**								
6° 00′	.1047	.1045	9.567	.1051	9.514	1.006	.9945	1.4661	84° 00′
10	076	074	9.309	080	9.255	006	942	632	50
20	105	103	9.065	110	9.010	006	939	603	40
30	.1134	.1132	8.834	.1139	8.777	1.006	.9936	1.4573	30
40	164	161	8.614	169	8.556	007	932	544	20
50	193	190	8.405	198	8.345	007	929	515	10
7° 00′	.1222	.1219	8.206	.1228	8.144	1.008	.9925	1.4486	83° 00′
10	251	248	8.016	257	7.953	008	922	457	50
20	280	276	7.834	287	7.770	008	918	428	40
30	.1309	.1305	7.661	.1317	7.596	1.009	.9914	1.4399	30
40	338	334	7.496	346	7.429	009	911	370	20
50	367	363	7.337	376	7.269	009	907	341	10
8° 00′	.1396	.1392	7.185	.1405	7.115	1.010	.9903	1.4312	82° 00′
10	425	421	7.040	435	6.968	010	899	283	50
20	454	449	6.900	465	6.827	011	894	254	40
30	.1484	.1478	6.765	.1495	6.691	1.011	.9890	1.4224	30
40	513	507	6.636	524	6.561	012	886	195	20
50	542	536	6.512	554	6.435	012	881	166	10
9° 00′	.1571	.1564	6.392	.1584	6.314	1.012	.9877	1.4137	81° 00′
10	600	593	277	614	197	013	872	108	50
20	629	622	166	644	084	013	868	079	40
30	.1658	.1650	6.059	.1673	5.976	1.014	.9863	1.4050	30
40	687	679	5.955	703	871	014	858	1.4021	20
50	716	708	855	733	769	015	853	992	10
10° 00′	.1745	.1736	5.759	.1763	5.671	1.015	.9848	1.3963	80° 00′
10	774	765	665	793	576	016	843	934	50
20	804	794	575	823	485	016	838	904	40
30	.1833	.1822	5.487	.1853	5.396	1.017	.9833	1.3875	30
40	862	851	403	883	309	018	827	846	20
50	891	880	320	914	226	018	822	817	10
11° 00′	.1920	.1908	5.241	.1944	5.145	1.019	.9816	1.3788	79° 00′
10	949	937	164	974	066	019	811	759	50
20	978	965	089	.2004	4.989	020	805	730	40
30	.2007	.1994	5.016	.2035	4.915	1.020	.9799	1.3701	30
40	036	.2022	4.945	065	843	021	793	672	20
50	065	051	876	095	773	022	787	643	10
12° 00′	.2094	.2079	4.810	.2126	4.705	1.022	.9781	1.3614	78° 00′
10	123	108	745	156	638	023	775	584	50
20	153	136	682	186	574	024	769	555	40
30	.2182	.2164	4.620	.2217	4.511	1.024	.9763	1.3526	30
40	211	193	560	247	449	025	757	497	20
50	240	221	502	278	390	026	750	468	10
13° 00	.2269	.2250	4.445	.2309	4.331	1.026	.9744	1.3439	77° 00′
		cos θ	sec θ	cot θ	tan θ	csc θ	sin θ	**Radians**	**Degrees**
								Angle θ	

Table II   (continued)

Angle θ		sin θ	csc θ	tan θ	cot θ	sec θ	cos θ		
Degrees	Radians	sin θ	csc θ	tan θ	cot θ	sec θ	cos θ		
13° 00′	.2269	.2250	4.445	.2309	4.331	1.026	.9744	1.3439	77° 00′
10	298	278	390	339	275	027	737	410	50
20	327	306	336	370	219	028	730	381	40
30	.2356	.2334	4.284	.2401	4.165	1.028	.9724	1.3352	30
40	385	363	232	432	113	029	717	323	20
50	414	391	182	462	061	030	710	294	10
14° 00′	.2443	.2419	4.134	.2493	4.011	1.031	.9703	1.3265	76° 00′
10	473	447	086	524	3.962	031	696	235	50
20	502	476	039	555	914	032	689	206	40
30	.2531	.2504	3.994	.2586	3.867	1.033	.9681	1.3177	30
40	560	532	950	617	821	034	674	148	20
50	589	560	906	648	776	034	667	119	10
15° 00′	.2618	.2588	3.864	.2679	3.732	1.035	.9659	1.3090	75° 00′
10	647	616	822	711	689	036	652	061	50
20	676	644	782	742	647	037	644	032	40
30	.2705	.2672	3.742	.2773	3.606	1.038	.9636	1.3003	30
40	734	700	703	805	566	039	628	974	20
50	763	728	665	836	526	039	621	945	10
16° 00′	.2793	.2756	3.628	.2867	3.487	1.040	.9613	1.2915	74° 00′
10	822	784	592	899	450	041	605	886	50
20	851	812	556	931	412	042	596	857	40
30	.2880	.2840	3.521	.2962	3.376	1.043	.9588	1.2828	30
40	909	868	487	994	340	044	580	799	20
50	938	896	453	.3026	305	045	572	770	10
17° 00′	.2967	.2924	3.420	.3057	3.271	1.046	.9563	1.2741	73° 00′
10	996	952	388	089	237	047	555	712	50
20	.3025	979	357	121	204	048	546	683	40
30	.3054	.3007	3.326	.3153	3.172	1.048	.9537	1.2654	30
40	083	035	295	185	140	049	528	625	20
50	113	062	265	217	108	050	520	595	10
18° 00′	.3142	.3090	3.236	.3249	3.078	1.051	.9511	1.2566	72° 00′
10	171	118	207	281	047	052	502	537	50
20	200	145	179	314	018	053	492	508	40
30	.3229	.3173	3.152	.3346	2.989	1.054	.9483	1.2479	30
40	258	201	124	378	960	056	474	450	20
50	287	228	098	411	932	057	465	421	10
19° 00′	.3316	.3256	3.072	.3443	2.904	1.058	.9455	1.2392	71° 00′
10	345	283	046	476	877	059	446	363	50
20	374	311	021	508	850	060	436	334	40
30	.3403	.3338	2.996	.3541	2.824	1.061	.9426	1.2305	30
40	432	365	971	574	798	062	417	275	20
50	462	393	947	607	773	063	407	246	10
20° 00′	.3491	.3420	2.924	.3640	2.747	1.064	.9397	1.2217	70° 00′
		cos θ	sec θ	cot θ	tan θ	csc θ	sin θ	Radians	Degrees
									Angle θ

Table II   (continued)

Angle θ									
Degrees	Radians	sin θ	csc θ	tan θ	cot θ	sec θ	cos θ		
20° 00′	.3491	.3420	2.924	.3640	2.747	1.064	.9397	1.2217	70° 00′
10	520	448	901	673	723	065	387	188	50
20	549	475	878	706	699	066	377	159	40
30	.3578	.3502	2.855	.3739	2.675	1.068	.9367	1.2130	30
40	607	529	833	772	651	069	356	101	20
50	636	557	812	805	628	070	346	072	10
21° 00′	.3665	.3584	2.790	.3839	2.605	1.071	.9336	1.2043	69° 00′
10	694	611	769	872	583	072	325	1.2014	50
20	723	638	749	906	560	074	315	985	40
30	.3752	.3665	2.729	.3939	2.539	1.075	.9304	1.1956	30
40	782	692	709	973	517	076	293	926	20
50	811	719	689	.4006	496	077	283	897	10
22° 00′	.3840	.3746	2.669	.4040	2.475	1.079	.9272	1.1868	68° 00′
10	869	773	650	074	455	080	261	839	50
20	898	800	632	108	434	081	250	810	40
30	.3927	.3827	2.613	.4142	2.414	1.082	.9239	1.1781	30
40	956	854	595	176	394	084	228	752	20
50	985	881	577	210	375	085	216	723	10
23° 00′	.4014	.3907	2.559	.4245	2.356	1.086	.9205	1.1694	67° 00′
10	043	934	542	279	337	088	194	665	50
20	072	961	525	314	318	089	182	636	40
30	.4102	.3987	2.508	.4348	2.300	1.090	.9171	1.1606	30
40	131	.4014	491	383	282	092	159	577	20
50	160	041	475	417	264	093	147	548	10
24° 00′	.4189	.4067	2.459	.4452	2.246	1.095	.9135	1.1519	66° 00′
10	218	094	443	487	229	096	124	490	50
20	247	120	427	522	211	097	112	461	40
30	.4276	.4147	2.411	.4557	2.194	1.099	.9100	1.1432	30
40	305	173	396	592	177	100	088	403	20
50	334	200	381	628	161	102	075	374	10
25° 00′	.4363	.4226	2.366	.4663	2.145	1.103	.9063	1.1345	65° 00′
10	392	253	352	699	128	105	051	316	50
20	422	279	337	734	112	106	038	286	40
30	.4451	.4305	2.323	.4770	2.097	1.108	.9026	1.1257	30
40	480	331	309	806	081	109	013	228	20
50	509	358	295	841	066	111	001	199	10
26° 00′	.4538	.4384	2.281	.4877	2.050	1.113	.8988	1.1170	64° 00′
10	567	410	268	913	035	114	975	141	50
20	596	436	254	950	020	116	962	112	40
30	.4625	.4462	2.241	.4986	2.006	1.117	.8949	1.1083	30
40	654	488	228	.5022	1.991	119	936	054	20
50	683	514	215	059	977	121	923	1.1025	10
27° 00′	.4712	.4540	2.203	.5095	1.963	1.122	.8910	1.0996	63° 00′
		cos θ	sec θ	cot θ	tan θ	csc θ	sin θ	Radians	Degrees
								Angle θ	

Table II   (continued)

Angle θ Degrees	Radians	sin θ	csc θ	tan θ	cot θ	sec θ	cos θ		
27° 00′	.4712	.4540	2.203	.5095	1.963	1.122	.8910	1.0996	63° 00′
10	741	566	190	132	949	124	897	966	50
20	771	592	178	169	935	126	884	937	40
30	.4800	.4617	2.166	.5206	1.921	1.127	.8870	1.0908	30
40	829	643	154	243	907	129	857	879	20
50	858	669	142	280	894	131	843	850	10
28° 00′	.4887	.4695	2.130	.5317	1.881	1.133	.8829	1.0821	62° 00′
10	916	720	118	354	868	134	816	792	50
20	945	746	107	392	855	136	802	763	40
30	.4974	.4772	2.096	.5430	1.842	1.138	.8788	1.0734	30
40	.5003	797	085	467	829	140	774	705	20
50	032	823	074	505	816	142	760	676	10
29° 00′	.5061	.4848	2.063	.5543	1.804	1.143	.8746	1.0647	61° 00′
10	091	874	052	581	792	145	732	617	50
20	120	899	041	619	780	147	718	588	40
30	.5149	.4924	2.031	.5658	1.767	1.149	.8704	1.0559	30
40	178	950	020	696	756	151	689	530	20
50	207	975	010	735	744	153	675	501	10
30° 00′	.5236	.5000	2.000	.5774	1.732	1.155	.8660	1.0472	60° 00′
10	265	025	1.990	812	720	157	646	443	50
20	294	050	980	851	709	159	631	414	40
30	.5323	.5075	1.970	.5890	1.698	1.161	.8616	1.0385	30
40	352	100	961	930	686	163	601	356	20
50	381	125	951	969	675	165	587	327	10
31° 00′	.5411	.5150	1.942	.6009	1.664	1.167	.8572	1.0297	59° 00′
10	440	175	932	048	653	169	557	268	50
20	469	200	923	088	643	171	542	239	40
30	.5498	.5225	1.914	.6128	1.632	1.173	.8526	1.0210	30
40	527	250	905	168	621	175	511	181	20
50	556	275	896	208	611	177	496	152	10
32° 00′	.5585	.5299	1.887	.6249	1.600	1.179	.8480	1.0123	58° 00′
10	614	324	878	289	590	181	465	094	50
20	643	348	870	330	580	184	450	065	40
30	.5672	.5373	1.861	.6371	1.570	1.186	.8434	1.0036	30
40	701	398	853	412	560	188	418	1.0007	20
50	730	422	844	453	550	190	403	977	10
33° 00′	.5760	.5446	1.836	.6494	1.540	1.192	.8387	.9948	57° 00′
10	789	471	828	536	530	195	371	919	50
20	818	495	820	577	520	197	355	890	40
30	.5847	.5519	1.812	.6619	1.511	1.199	.8339	.9861	30
40	876	544	804	661	501	202	323	832	20
50	905	568	796	703	1.492	204	307	803	10
34° 00′	.5934	.5592	1.788	.6745	1.483	1.206	.8290	.9774	56° 00′
		cos θ	sec θ	cot θ	tan θ	csc θ	sin θ	Radians	Degrees
								Angle θ	

Table II (continued)

Angle θ									
Degrees	**Radians**	**sin θ**	**csc θ**	**tan θ**	**cot θ**	**sec θ**	**cos θ**		
34° 00'	.5934	.5592	1.788	.6745	1.483	1.206	.8290	.9774	**56° 00'**
10	963	616	781	787	473	209	274	745	50
20	992	640	773	830	464	211	258	716	40
30	.6021	.5664	1.766	.6873	1.455	1.213	.8241	.9687	30
40	050	688	758	916	446	216	225	657	20
50	080	712	751	959	437	218	208	628	10
35° 00'	.6109	.5736	1.743	.7002	1.428	1.221	.8192	.9599	**55° 00'**
10	138	760	736	046	419	223	175	570	50
20	167	783	729	089	411	226	158	541	40
30	.6196	.5807	1.722	.7133	1.402	1.228	.8141	.9512	30
40	225	831	715	177	393	231	124	483	20
50	254	854	708	221	385	233	107	454	10
36° 00'	.6283	.5878	1.701	.7265	1.376	1.236	.8090	.9425	**54° 00'**
10	312	901	695	310	368	239	073	396	50
20	341	925	688	355	360	241	056	367	40
30	.6370	.5948	1.681	.7400	1.351	1.244	.8039	.9338	30
40	400	972	675	445	343	247	021	308	20
50	429	995	668	490	335	249	004	279	10
37° 00'	.6458	.6018	1.662	.7536	1.327	1.252	.7986	.9250	**53° 00'**
10	487	041	655	581	319	255	969	221	50
20	516	065	649	627	311	258	951	192	40
30	.6545	.6088	1.643	.7673	1.303	1.260	.7934	.9163	30
40	574	111	636	720	295	263	916	134	20
50	603	134	630	766	288	266	898	105	10
38° 00'	.6632	.6157	1.624	.7813	1.280	1.269	.7880	.9076	**52° 00'**
10	661	180	618	860	272	272	862	047	50
20	690	202	612	907	265	275	844	.9018	40
30	.6720	.6225	1.606	.7954	1.257	1.278	.7826	.8988	30
40	749	248	601	.8002	250	281	808	959	20
50	778	271	595	050	242	284	790	930	10
39° 00'	.6807	.6293	1.589	.8098	1.235	1.287	.7771	.8901	**51° 00'**
10	836	316	583	146	228	290	753	872	50
20	865	338	578	195	220	293	735	843	40
30	.6894	.6361	1.572	.8243	1.213	1.296	.7716	.8814	30
40	923	383	567	292	206	299	698	785	20
50	952	406	561	342	199	302	679	756	10
40° 00'	.6981	.6428	1.556	.8391	1.192	1.305	.7660	.8727	**50° 00'**
10	.7010	450	550	441	185	309	642	698	50
20	039	472	545	491	178	312	623	668	40
30	.7069	.6494	1.540	.8541	1.171	1.315	.7604	.8639	30
40	098	517	535	591	164	318	585	610	20
50	127	539	529	642	157	322	566	581	10
41° 00'	.7156	.6561	1.524	.8693	1.150	1.325	.7547	.8552	**49° 00'**
		cos θ	**sec θ**	**cot θ**	**tan θ**	**csc θ**	**sin θ**	**Radians**	**Degrees**
									Angle θ

Table II   (continued)

Angle θ									
Degrees	Radians	sin θ	csc θ	tan θ	cot θ	sec θ	cos θ		
41° 00′	.7156	.6561	1.524	.8693	1.150	1.325	.7547	.8552	49° 00′
10	185	583	519	744	144	328	528	523	50
20	214	604	514	796	137	332	509	494	40
30	.7243	.6626	1.509	.8847	1.130	1.335	.7490	.8465	30
40	272	648	504	899	124	339	470	436	20
50	301	670	499	952	117	342	451	407	10
42° 00′	.7330	.6691	1.494	.9004	1.111	1.346	.7431	.8378	48° 00′
10	359	713	490	057	104	349	412	348	50
20	389	734	485	110	098	353	392	319	40
30	.7418	.6756	1.480	.9163	1.091	1.356	.7373	.8290	30
40	447	777	476	217	085	360	353	261	20
50	476	799	471	271	079	364	333	232	10
43° 00′	.7505	.6820	1.466	.9325	1.072	1.367	.7314	.8203	47° 00′
10	534	841	462	380	066	371	294	174	50
20	563	862	457	435	060	375	274	145	40
30	.7592	.6884	1.453	.9490	1.054	1.379	.7254	.8116	30
40	621	905	448	545	048	382	234	087	20
50	650	926	444	601	042	386	214	058	10
44° 00′	.7679	.6947	1.440	.9657	1.036	1.390	.7193	.8029	46° 00′
10	709	967	435	713	030	394	173	.7999	50
20	738	988	431	770	024	398	153	970	40
30	.7767	.7009	1.427	.9827	1.018	1.402	.7133	.7941	30
40	796	030	423	884	012	406	112	912	20
50	825	050	418	942	006	410	092	883	10
45° 00′	.7854	.7071	1.414	1.000	1.000	1.414	.7071	.7854	45° 00′
		cos θ	sec θ	cot θ	tan θ	csc θ	sin θ	Radians	Degrees
								Angle θ	

284

Table III   Trigonometric Functions of Decimal Degrees*

θ deg	deg	min	sin θ	csc θ	tan θ	cot θ	sec θ	cos θ			
0.0	0	0	0.0000	No value	0.0000	No value	1.0000	1.0000	90	0	90.0
0.1	0	6	0.0017	572.96	0.0017	572.96	1.0000	1.0000	89	54	89.9
0.2	0	12	0.0035	286.48	0.0035	286.48	1.0000	1.0000	89	48	89.8
0.3	0	18	0.0052	190.99	0.0052	190.98	1.0000	1.0000	89	42	89.7
0.4	0	24	0.0070	143.24	0.0070	143.24	1.0000	1.0000	89	36	89.6
0.5	0	30	0.0087	114.59	0.0087	114.59	1.0000	1.0000	89	30	89.5
0.6	0	36	0.0105	95.495	0.0105	95.490	1.0001	0.9999	89	24	89.4
0.7	0	42	0.0122	81.853	0.0122	81.847	1.0001	0.9999	89	18	89.3
0.8	0	48	0.0140	71.622	0.0140	71.615	1.0001	0.9999	89	12	89.2
0.9	0	54	0.0157	63.665	0.0157	63.657	1.0001	0.9999	89	6	89.1
1.0	1	0	0.0175	57.299	0.0175	57.290	1.0002	0.9998	89	0	89.0
1.1	1	6	0.0192	52.090	0.0192	52.081	1.0002	0.9998	88	54	88.9
1.2	1	12	0.0209	47.750	0.0209	47.740	1.0002	0.9998	88	48	88.8
1.3	1	18	0.0227	44.077	0.0227	44.066	1.0003	0.9997	88	42	88.7
1.4	1	24	0.0244	40.930	0.0244	40.917	1.0003	0.9997	88	36	88.6
1.5	1	30	0.0262	38.202	0.0262	38.188	1.0003	0.9997	88	30	88.5
1.6	1	36	0.0279	35.815	0.0279	35.801	1.0004	0.9996	88	24	88.4
1.7	1	42	0.0297	33.708	0.0297	33.694	1.0004	0.9996	88	18	88.3
1.8	1	48	0.0314	31.836	0.0314	31.821	1.0005	0.9995	88	12	88.2
1.9	1	54	0.0332	30.161	0.0332	30.145	1.0005	0.9995	88	6	88.1
2.0	2	0	0.0349	28.654	0.0349	28.636	1.0006	0.9994	88	0	88.0
2.1	2	6	0.0366	27.290	0.0367	27.271	1.0007	0.9993	87	54	87.9
2.2	2	12	0.0384	26.050	0.0384	26.031	1.0007	0.9993	87	48	87.8
2.3	2	18	0.0401	24.918	0.0402	24.898	1.0008	0.9992	87	42	87.7
2.4	2	24	0.0419	23.880	0.0419	23.859	1.0009	0.9991	87	36	87.6
2.5	2	30	0.0436	22.926	0.0437	22.904	1.0010	0.9990	87	30	87.5
2.6	2	36	0.0454	22.044	0.0454	22.022	1.0010	0.9990	87	24	87.4
2.7	2	42	0.0471	21.229	0.0472	21.205	1.0011	0.9989	87	18	87.3
2.8	2	48	0.0488	20.471	0.0489	20.446	1.0012	0.9988	87	12	87.2
2.9	2	54	0.0506	19.766	0.0507	19.740	1.0013	0.9987	87	6	87.1
3.0	3	0	0.0523	19.107	0.0524	19.081	1.0014	0.9986	87	0	87.0
3.1	3	6	0.0541	18.492	0.0542	18.464	1.0015	0.9985	86	54	86.9
3.2	3	12	0.0558	17.914	0.0559	17.886	1.0016	0.9984	86	48	86.8
3.3	3	18	0.0576	17.372	0.0577	17.343	1.0017	0.9983	86	42	86.7
3.4	3	24	0.0593	16.862	0.0594	16.832	1.0018	0.9982	86	36	86.6
3.5	3	30	0.0610	16.380	0.0612	16.350	1.0019	0.9981	86	30	86.5
3.6	3	36	0.0628	15.926	0.0629	15.895	1.0020	0.9980	86	24	86.4
3.7	3	42	0.0645	15.496	0.0647	15.464	1.0021	0.9979	86	18	86.3
3.8	3	48	0.0663	15.089	0.0664	15.056	1.0022	0.9978	86	12	86.2
3.9	3	54	0.0680	14.703	0.0682	14.669	1.0023	0.9977	86	6	86.1
4.0	4	0	0.0698	14.336	0.0699	14.301	1.0024	0.9976	86	0	86.0
4.1	4	6	0.0715	13.987	0.0717	13.951	1.0026	0.9974	85	54	85.9
4.2	4	12	0.0732	13.654	0.0734	13.617	1.0027	0.9973	85	48	85.8
4.3	4	18	0.0750	13.337	0.0752	13.300	1.0028	0.9972	85	42	85.7
4.4	4	24	0.0767	13.035	0.0769	12.996	1.0030	0.9971	85	36	85.6
4.5	4	30	0.0785	12.746	0.0787	12.706	1.0031	0.9969	85	30	85.5
4.6	4	36	0.0802	12.469	0.0805	12.429	1.0032	0.9968	85	24	85.4
4.7	4	42	0.0819	12.204	0.0822	12.163	1.0034	0.9966	85	18	85.3
4.8	4	48	0.0837	11.951	0.0840	11.909	1.0035	0.9965	85	12	85.2
4.9	4	54	0.0854	11.707	0.0857	11.665	1.0037	0.9963	85	6	85.1
			cos θ	sec θ	cot θ	tan θ	csc θ	sin θ	deg	min	θ deg

Table III   (continued)

θ deg	deg	min	$\sin \theta$	$\csc \theta$	$\tan \theta$	$\cot \theta$	$\sec \theta$	$\cos \theta$			
5.0	5	0	0.0872	11.474	0.0875	11.430	1.0038	0.9962	85	0	85.0
5.1	5	6	0.0889	11.249	0.0892	11.205	1.0040	0.9960	84	54	84.9
5.2	5	12	0.0906	11.034	0.0910	10.988	1.0041	0.9959	84	48	84.8
5.3	5	18	0.0924	10.826	0.0928	10.780	1.0043	0.9957	84	42	84.7
5.4	5	24	0.0941	10.626	0.0945	10.579	1.0045	0.9956	84	36	84.6
5.5	5	30	0.0958	10.433	0.0963	10.385	1.0046	0.9954	84	30	84.5
5.6	5	36	0.0976	10.248	0.0981	10.199	1.0048	0.9952	84	24	84.4
5.7	5	42	0.0993	10.069	0.0998	10.019	1.0050	0.9951	84	18	84.3
5.8	5	48	0.1011	9.8955	0.1016	9.8448	1.0051	0.9949	84	12	84.2
5.9	5	54	0.1028	9.7283	0.1033	9.6768	1.0053	0.9947	84	6	84.1
6.0	6	0	0.1045	9.5668	0.1051	9.5144	1.0055	0.9945	84	0	84.0
6.1	6	6	0.1063	9.4105	0.1069	9.3573	1.0057	0.9943	83	54	83.9
6.2	6	12	0.1080	9.2593	0.1086	9.2052	1.0059	0.9942	83	48	83.8
6.3	6	18	0.1097	9.1129	0.1104	9.0579	1.0061	0.9940	83	42	83.7
6.4	6	24	0.1115	8.9711	0.1122	8.9152	1.0063	0.9938	83	36	83.6
6.5	6	30	0.1132	8.8337	0.1139	8.7769	1.0065	0.9936	83	30	83.5
6.6	6	36	0.1149	8.7004	0.1157	8.6428	1.0067	0.9934	83	24	83.4
6.7	6	42	0.1167	8.5711	0.1175	8.5126	1.0069	0.9932	83	18	83.3
6.8	6	48	0.1184	8.4457	0.1192	8.3863	1.0071	0.9930	83	12	83.2
6.9	6	54	0.1201	8.3238	0.1210	8.2636	1.0073	0.9928	83	6	83.1
7.0	7	0	0.1219	8.2055	0.1228	8.1444	1.0075	0.9925	83	0	83.0
7.1	7	6	0.1236	8.0905	0.1246	8.0285	1.0077	0.9923	82	54	82.9
7.2	7	12	0.1253	7.9787	0.1263	7.9158	1.0079	0.9921	82	48	82.8
7.3	7	18	0.1271	7.8700	0.1281	7.8062	1.0082	0.9919	82	42	82.7
7.4	7	24	0.1288	7.7642	0.1299	7.6996	1.0084	0.9917	82	36	82.6
7.5	7	30	0.1305	7.6613	0.1317	7.5958	1.0086	0.9914	82	30	82.5
7.6	7	36	0.1323	7.5611	0.1334	7.4947	1.0089	0.9912	82	24	82.4
7.7	7	42	0.1340	7.4635	0.1352	7.3962	1.0091	0.9910	82	18	82.3
7.8	7	48	0.1357	7.3684	0.1370	7.3002	1.0093	0.9907	82	12	82.2
7.9	7	54	0.1374	7.2757	0.1388	7.2066	1.0096	0.9905	82	6	82.1
8.0	8	0	0.1392	7.1853	0.1405	7.1154	1.0098	0.9903	82	0	82.0
8.1	8	6	0.1409	7.0972	0.1423	7.0264	1.0101	0.9900	81	54	81.9
8.2	8	12	0.1426	7.0112	0.1441	6.9395	1.0103	0.9898	81	48	81.8
8.3	8	18	0.1444	6.9273	0.1459	6.8548	1.0106	0.9895	81	42	81.7
8.4	8	24	0.1461	6.8454	0.1477	6.7720	1.0108	0.9893	81	36	81.6
8.5	8	30	0.1478	6.7655	0.1495	6.6912	1.0111	0.9890	81	30	81.5
8.6	8	36	0.1495	6.6874	0.1512	6.6122	1.0114	0.9888	81	24	81.4
8.7	8	42	0.1513	6.6111	0.1530	6.5350	1.0116	0.9885	81	18	81.3
8.8	8	48	0.1530	6.5366	0.1548	6.4596	1.0119	0.9882	81	12	81.2
8.9	8	54	0.1547	6.4637	0.1566	6.3859	1.0122	0.9880	81	6	81.1
9.0	9	0	0.1564	6.3925	0.1584	6.3138	1.0125	0.9877	81	0	81.0
9.1	9	6	0.1582	6.3228	0.1602	6.2432	1.0127	0.9874	80	54	80.9
9.2	9	12	0.1599	6.2547	0.1620	6.1742	1.0130	0.9871	80	48	80.8
9.3	9	18	0.1616	6.1880	0.1638	6.1066	1.0133	0.9869	80	42	80.7
9.4	9	24	0.1633	6.1227	0.1655	6.0405	1.0136	0.9866	80	36	80.6
9.5	9	30	0.1650	6.0589	0.1673	5.9758	1.0139	0.9863	80	30	80.5
9.6	9	36	0.1668	5.9963	0.1691	5.9124	1.0142	0.9860	80	24	80.4
9.7	9	42	0.1685	5.9351	0.1709	5.8502	1.0145	0.9857	80	18	80.3
9.8	9	48	0.1702	5.8751	0.1727	5.7894	1.0148	0.9854	80	12	80.2
9.9	9	54	0.1719	5.8164	0.1745	5.7297	1.0151	0.9851	80	6	80.1
			$\cos \theta$	$\sec \theta$	$\cot \theta$		$\csc \theta$	$\sin \theta$	deg	min	θ deg

286

Table III   (continued)

θ deg	deg min		sin θ	csc θ	tan θ	cot θ	sec θ	cos θ			
10.0	10	0	0.1736	5.7588	0.1763	5.6713	1.0154	0.9848	80	0	80.0
10.1	10	6	0.1754	5.7023	0.1781	5.6140	1.0157	0.9845	79	54	79.9
10.2	10	12	0.1771	5.6470	0.1799	5.5578	1.0161	0.9842	79	48	79.8
10.3	10	18	0.1788	5.5928	0.1817	5.5027	1.0164	0.9839	79	42	79.7
10.4	10	24	0.1805	5.5396	0.1835	5.4486	1.0167	0.9836	79	36	79.6
10.5	10	30	0.1822	5.4874	0.1853	5.3955	1.0170	0.9833	79	30	79.5
10.6	10	36	0.1840	5.4362	0.1871	5.3435	1.0174	0.9829	79	24	79.4
10.7	10	42	0.1857	5.3860	0.1890	5.2924	1.0177	0.9826	79	18	79.3
10.8	10	48	0.1874	5.3367	0.1908	5.2422	1.0180	0.9823	79	12	79.2
10.9	10	54	0.1891	5.2883	0.1926	5.1929	1.0184	0.9820	79	6	79.1
11.0	11	0	0.1908	5.2408	0.1944	5.1446	1.0187	0.9816	79	0	79.0
11.1	11	6	0.1925	5.1942	0.1962	5.0970	1.0191	0.9813	78	54	78.9
11.2	11	12	0.1942	5.1484	0.1980	5.0504	1.0194	9.9810	78	48	78.8
11.3	11	18	0.1959	5.1034	0.1998	5.0045	1.0198	0.9806	78	42	78.7
11.4	11	24	0.1977	5.0593	0.2016	4.9595	1.0201	0.9803	78	36	78.6
11.5	11	30	0.1994	5.0159	0.2035	4.9152	1.0205	0.9799	78	30	78.5
11.6	11	36	0.2011	4.9732	0.2053	4.8716	1.0209	0.9796	78	24	78.4
11.7	11	42	0.2028	4.9313	0.2071	4.8288	1.0212	0.9792	78	18	78.3
11.8	11	48	0.2045	4.8901	0.2089	4.7867	1.0216	0.9789	78	12	78.2
11.9	11	54	0.2062	4.8496	0.2107	4.7453	1.0220	0.9785	78	6	78.1
12.0	12	0	0.2079	4.8097	0.2126	4.7046	1.0223	0.9781	78	0	78.0
12.1	12	6	0.2096	4.7706	0.2144	4.6646	1.0227	0.9778	77	54	77.9
12.2	12	12	0.2113	4.7321	0.2162	4.6252	1.0231	0.9774	77	48	77.8
12.3	12	18	0.2130	4.6942	0.2180	4.5864	1.0235	0.9770	77	42	77.7
12.4	12	24	0.2147	4.6569	0.2199	4.5483	1.0239	0.9767	77	36	77.6
12.5	12	30	0.2164	4.6202	0.2217	4.5107	1.0243	0.9763	77	30	77.5
12.6	12	36	0.2181	4.5841	0.2235	4.4737	1.0247	0.9759	77	24	77.4
12.7	12	42	0.2198	4.5486	0.2254	4.4374	1.0251	0.9755	77	18	77.3
12.8	12	48	0.2215	4.5137	0.2272	4.4015	1.0255	0.9751	77	12	77.2
12.9	12	54	0.2232	4.4793	0.2290	4.3662	1.0259	0.9748	77	6	77.1
13.0	13	0	0.2250	4.4454	0.2309	4.3315	1.0263	0.9744	77	0	77.0
13.1	13	6	0.2267	4.4121	0.2327	4.2972	1.0267	0.9740	76	54	76.9
13.2	13	12	0.2284	4.3792	0.2345	4.2635	1.0271	0.9736	76	48	76.8
13.3	13	18	0.2300	4.3469	0.2364	4.2303	1.0276	0.9732	76	42	76.7
13.4	13	24	0.2317	4.3150	0.2382	4.1976	1.0280	0.9728	76	36	76.6
13.5	13	30	0.2334	4.2837	0.2401	4.1653	1.0284	0.9724	76	30	76.5
13.6	13	36	0.2351	4.2528	0.2419	4.1335	1.0288	0.9720	76	24	76.4
13.7	13	42	0.2368	4.2223	0.2438	4.1022	1.0293	0.9715	76	18	76.3
13.8	13	48	0.2385	4.1923	0.2456	4.0713	1.0297	0.9711	76	12	76.2
13.9	13	54	0.2402	4.1627	0.2475	4.0408	1.0302	0.9707	76	6	76.1
14.0	14	0	0.2419	4.1336	0.2493	4.0108	1.0306	0.9703	76	0	76.0
14.1	14	6	0.2436	4.1048	0.2512	3.9812	1.0311	0.9699	75	54	75.9
14.2	14	12	0.2453	4.0765	0.2530	3.9520	1.0315	0.9694	75	48	75.8
14.3	14	18	0.2470	4.0486	0.2549	3.9232	1.0320	0.9690	75	42	75.7
14.4	14	24	0.2487	4.0211	0.2568	3.8947	1.0324	0.9686	75	36	75.6
14.5	14	30	0.2504	3.9939	0.2586	3.8667	1.0329	0.9681	75	30	75.5
14.6	14	36	0.2521	3.9672	0.2605	3.8391	1.0334	0.9677	75	24	75.4
14.7	14	42	0.2538	3.9408	0.2623	3.8118	1.0338	0.9673	75	18	75.3
14.8	14	48	0.2554	3.9147	0.2642	3.7849	1.0343	0.9668	75	12	75.2
14.9	14	54	0.2571	3.8890	0.2661	3.7583	1.0348	0.9664	75	6	75.1
			cos θ	sec θ	cot θ	tan θ	csc θ	sin θ	deg min		θ deg

Table III (continued)

θ deg	deg	min	sin θ	csc θ	tan θ	cot θ	sec θ	cos θ			
15.0	15	0	0.2588	3.8637	0.2679	3.7321	1.0353	0.9659	75	0	75.0
15.1	15	6	0.2605	3.8387	0.2698	3.7062	1.0358	0.9655	74	54	74.9
15.2	15	12	0.2622	3.8140	0.2717	3.6806	1.0363	0.9650	74	48	74.8
15.3	15	18	0.2639	3.7897	0.2736	3.6554	1.0367	0.9646	74	42	74.7
15.4	15	24	0.2656	3.7657	0.2754	3.6305	1.0372	0.9641	74	36	74.6
15.5	15	30	0.2672	3.7420	0.2773	3.6059	1.0377	0.9636	74	30	74.5
15.6	15	36	0.2689	3.7186	0.2792	3.5816	1.0382	0.9632	74	24	74.4
15.7	15	42	0.2706	3.6955	0.2811	3.5576	1.0388	0.9627	74	18	74.3
15.8	15	48	0.2723	3.6727	0.2830	3.5339	1.0393	0.9622	74	12	74.2
15.9	15	54	0.2740	3.6502	0.2849	3.5105	1.0398	0.9617	74	6	74.1
16.0	16	0	0.2756	3.6280	0.2867	3.4874	1.0403	0.9613	74	0	74.0
16.1	16	6	0.2773	3.6060	0.2886	3.4646	1.0408	0.9608	73	54	73.9
16.2	16	12	0.2790	3.5843	0.2905	3.4420	1.0413	0.9603	73	48	73.8
16.3	16	18	0.2807	3.5629	0.2924	3.4197	1.0419	0.9598	73	42	73.7
16.4	16	24	0.2823	3.5418	0.2943	3.3977	1.0424	0.9593	73	36	73.6
16.5	16	30	0.2840	3.5209	0.2962	3.3759	1.0429	0.9588	73	30	73.5
16.6	16	36	0.2857	3.5003	0.2981	3.3544	1.0435	0.9583	73	24	74.4
16.7	16	42	0.2874	3.4800	0.3000	3.3332	1.0440	0.9578	73	18	73.3
16.8	16	48	0.2890	3.4598	0.3019	3.3122	1.0446	0.9573	73	12	73.2
16.9	16	54	0.2907	3.4399	0.3038	3.2914	1.0451	0.9568	73	6	73.1
17.0	17	0	0.2924	3.4203	0.3057	3.2709	1.0457	0.9563	73	0	73.0
17.1	17	6	0.2940	3.4009	0.3076	3.2506	1.0463	0.9558	72	54	72.9
17.2	17	12	0.2957	3.3817	0.3096	3.2305	1.0468	0.9553	72	48	72.8
17.3	17	18	0.2974	3.3628	0.3115	3.2106	1.0474	0.9548	72	42	72.7
17.4	17	24	0.2990	3.3440	0.3134	3.1910	1.0480	0.9542	72	36	72.6
17.5	17	30	0.3007	3.3255	0.3153	3.1716	1.0485	0.9537	72	30	72.5
17.6	17	36	0.3024	3.3072	0.3172	3.1524	1.0491	0.9532	72	24	72.4
17.7	17	42	0.3040	3.2891	0.3191	3.1334	1.0497	0.9527	72	18	72.3
17.8	17	48	0.3057	3.2712	0.3211	3.1146	1.0503	0.9521	72	12	72.2
17.9	17	54	0.3074	3.2536	0.3230	3.0961	1.0509	0.9516	72	6	72.1
18.0	18	0	0.3090	3.2361	0.3249	3.0777	1.0515	0.9511	72	0	72.0
18.1	18	6	0.3107	3.2188	0.3268	3.0595	1.0521	0.9505	71	54	71.9
18.2	18	12	0.3123	3.2017	0.3288	3.0415	1.0527	0.9500	71	48	71.8
18.3	18	18	0.3140	3.1848	0.3307	3.0237	1.0533	0.9494	71	42	71.7
18.4	18	24	0.3156	3.1681	0.3327	3.0061	1.0539	0.9489	71	36	71.6
18.5	18	30	0.3173	3.1515	0.3346	2.9887	1.0545	0.9483	71	30	71.5
18.6	18	36	0.3190	3.1352	0.3365	2.9714	1.0551	0.9478	71	24	71.4
18.7	18	42	0.3206	3.1190	0.3385	2.9544	1.0557	0.9472	71	18	71.3
18.8	18	48	0.3223	3.1030	0.3404	2.9375	1.0564	0.9466	71	12	71.2
18.9	18	54	0.3239	3.0872	0.3424	2.9208	1.0570	0.9461	71	6	71.1
19.0	19	0	0.3256	2.0716	0.3443	2.9042	1.0576	0.9455	71	0	71.0
19.1	19	6	0.3272	3.0561	0.3463	2.8878	1.0583	0.9449	70	54	70.9
19.2	19	12	0.3289	3.0407	0.3482	2.8716	1.0589	0.9444	70	48	70.8
19.3	19	18	0.3305	3.0256	0.3502	2.8556	1.0595	0.9438	70	42	70.7
19.4	19	24	0.3322	3.0106	0.3522	2.8397	1.0602	0.9432	70	36	70.6
19.5	19	30	0.3338	2.9957	0.3541	2.8239	1.0608	0.9426	70	30	70.5
19.6	19	36	0.3355	2.9811	0.3561	2.8083	1.0615	0.9421	70	24	70.4
19.7	19	42	0.3371	2.9665	0.3581	2.7929	1.0622	0.9415	70	18	70.3
19.8	19	48	0.3387	2.9521	0.3600	2.7776	1.0628	0.9409	70	12	70.2
19.9	19	54	0.3404	2.9379	0.3620	2.7625	1.0635	0.9403	70	6	70.1
			cos θ	sec θ	cot θ	tan θ	csc θ	sin θ	deg	min	θ deg

Table III   (continued)

θ deg	deg	min	$\sin \theta$	$\csc \theta$	$\tan \theta$	$\cot \theta$	$\sec \theta$	$\cos \theta$			
20.0	20	0	0.3420	2.9238	0.3640	2.7475	1.0642	0.9397	70	0	70.0
20.1	20	6	0.3437	2.9099	0.3659	2.7326	1.0649	0.9391	69	54	69.9
20.2	20	12	0.3453	2.8960	0.3679	2.7179	1.0655	0.9385	69	48	69.8
20.3	20	18	0.3469	2.8824	0.3699	2.7034	1.0662	0.9379	69	42	69.7
20.4	20	24	0.3486	2.8688	0.3719	2.6889	1.0669	0.9373	69	36	69.6
20.5	20	30	0.3502	2.8555	0.3739	2.6746	1.0676	0.9367	69	30	69.5
20.6	20	36	0.3518	2.8422	0.3759	2.6605	1.0683	0.9361	69	24	69.4
20.7	20	42	0.3535	2.8291	0.3779	2.6464	1.0690	0.9354	69	18	69.3
20.8	20	48	0.3551	2.8161	0.3799	2.6325	1.0697	0.9348	69	12	69.2
20.9	20	54	0.3567	2.8032	0.3819	2.6187	1.0704	0.9342	69	6	69.1
21.0	21	0	0.3584	2.7904	0.3839	2.6051	1.0711	0.9336	69	0	69.0
21.1	21	6	0.3600	2.7778	0.3859	2.5916	1.0719	0.9330	68	54	68.9
21.2	21	12	0.3616	2.7653	0.3879	2.5782	1.0726	0.9323	68	48	68.8
21.3	21	18	0.3633	2.7529	0.3899	2.5649	1.0733	0.9317	68	42	68.7
21.4	21	24	0.3649	2.7407	0.3919	2.5517	1.0740	0.9311	68	36	68.6
21.5	21	30	0.3665	2.7285	0.3939	2.5386	1.0748	0.9304	68	30	68.5
21.6	21	36	0.3681	2.7165	0.3959	2.5257	1.0755	0.9298	68	24	68.4
21.7	21	42	0.3697	2.7046	0.3979	2.5129	1.0763	0.9291	68	18	68.3
21.8	21	48	0.3714	2.6927	0.4000	2.5002	1.0770	0.9285	68	12	68.2
21.9	21	54	0.3730	2.6811	0.4020	2.4876	1.0778	0.9278	68	6	68.1
22.0	22	0	0.3746	2.6695	0.4040	2.4751	1.0785	0.9272	68	0	68.0
22.1	22	6	0.3762	2.6580	0.4061	2.4627	1.0793	0.9265	67	54	67.9
22.2	22	12	0.3778	2.6466	0.4081	2.4504	1.0801	0.9259	67	48	67.8
22.3	22	18	0.3795	2.6354	0.4101	2.4383	1.0808	0.9252	67	42	67.7
22.4	22	24	0.3811	2.6242	0.4122	2.4262	1.0816	0.9245	67	36	67.6
22.5	22	30	0.3827	2.6131	0.4142	2.4142	1.0824	0.9239	67	30	67.5
22.6	22	36	0.3843	2.6022	0.4163	2.4023	1.0832	0.9232	67	24	67.4
22.7	22	42	0.3859	2.5913	0.4183	2.3906	1.0840	0.9225	67	18	67.3
22.8	22	48	0.3875	2.5805	0.4204	2.3789	1.0848	0.9219	67	12	67.2
22.9	22	54	0.3891	2.5699	0.4224	2.3673	1.0856	0.9212	67	6	67.1
23.0	23	0	0.3907	2.5593	0.4245	2.3559	1.0864	0.9205	67	0	67.0
23.1	23	6	0.3923	2.5488	0.4265	2.3445	1.0872	0.9198	66	54	66.9
23.3	23	12	0.3939	2.5384	0.4286	2.3332	1.0880	0.9191	66	48	66.8
23.3	23	18	0.3955	2.5282	0.4307	2.3220	1.0888	0.9184	66	42	66.7
23.4	23	24	0.3971	2.5180	0.4327	2.3109	1.0896	0.9178	66	36	66.6
23.5	23	30	0.3987	2.5078	0.4348	2.2998	1.0904	0.9171	66	30	66.5
23.6	23	36	0.4003	2.4978	0.4369	2.2889	1.0913	0.9164	66	24	66.4
23.7	23	42	0.4019	2.4879	0.4390	2.2781	1.0921	0.9157	66	18	66.3
23.8	23	48	0.4035	2.4780	0.4411	2.2673	1.0929	0.9150	66	12	66.2
23.9	23	54	0.4051	2.4683	0.4431	2.2566	1.0938	0.9143	66	6	66.1
24.0	24	0	0.4067	2.4586	0.4452	2.2460	1.0946	0.9135	66	0	66.0
24.1	24	6	0.4083	2.4490	0.4473	2.2355	1.0955	0.9128	65	54	65.9
24.2	24	12	0.4099	2.4395	0.4494	2.2251	1.0963	0.9121	65	48	65.8
24.3	24	18	0.4115	2.4301	0.4515	2.2148	1.0972	0.9114	65	42	65.7
24.4	24	24	0.4131	2.4207	0.4536	2.2045	1.0981	0.9107	65	36	65.6
24.5	24	30	0.4147	2.4114	0.4557	2.1943	1.0989	0.9100	65	30	65.5
24.6	24	36	0.4163	2.4022	0.4578	2.1842	1.0998	0.9092	65	24	65.4
24.7	24	42	0.4179	2.3931	0.4599	2.1742	1.1007	0.9085	65	18	65.3
24.8	24	48	0.4195	2.3841	0.4621	2.1642	1.1016	0.9078	65	12	65.2
24.9	24	54	0.4210	2.3751	0.4642	2.1543	1.1025	0.9070	65	6	65.1
			$\cos \theta$	$\sec \theta$	$\cot \theta$	$\tan \theta$	$\csc \theta$	$\sin \theta$	deg	min	θ deg

Table III   (continued)

θ deg	deg	min	sin θ	csc θ	tan θ	cot θ	sec θ	cos θ			
25.0	25	0	0.4226	2.3662	0.4663	2.1445	1.1034	0.9063	65	0	65.0
25.1	25	6	0.4242	2.3574	0.4684	2.1348	1.1043	0.9056	64	54	64.9
25.2	25	12	0.4258	2.3486	0.4706	2.1251	1.1052	0.9048	64	48	64.8
25.3	25	18	0.4274	2.3400	0.4727	2.1155	1.1061	0.9041	64	42	64.7
25.4	25	24	0.4289	2.3314	0.4748	2.1060	1.1070	0.9033	64	36	64.6
25.5	25	30	0.4305	2.3228	0.4770	2.0965	1.1079	0.9026	64	30	64.5
25.6	25	36	0.4321	2.3144	0.4791	2.0872	1.1089	0.9018	64	24	64.4
25.7	25	42	0.4337	2.3060	0.4813	2.0778	1.1098	0.9011	64	18	64.3
25.8	25	48	0.4352	2.2976	0.4834	2.0686	1.1107	0.9003	64	12	64.2
25.9	25	54	0.4368	2.2894	0.4856	2.0594	1.1117	0.8996	64	6	64.1
26.0	26	0	0.4384	2.2812	0.4877	2.0503	1.1126	0.8988	64	0	64.0
26.1	26	6	0.4399	2.2730	0.4899	2.0413	1.1136	0.8980	63	54	63.9
26.2	26	12	0.4415	2.2650	0.4921	2.0323	1.1145	0.8973	63	48	63.8
26.3	26	18	0.4431	2.2570	0.4942	2.0233	1.1155	0.8965	63	42	63.7
26.4	26	24	0.4446	2.2490	0.4964	2.0145	1.1164	0.8957	63	36	63.6
26.5	26	30	0.4462	2.2412	0.4986	2.0057	1.1174	0.8949	63	30	63.5
26.6	26	36	0.4478	2.2333	0.5008	1.9970	1.1184	0.8942	63	24	63.4
26.7	26	42	0.4493	2.2256	0.5029	1.9883	1.1194	0.8934	63	18	63.3
26.8	26	48	0.4509	2.2179	0.5051	1.9797	1.1203	0.8926	63	12	63.2
26.9	26	54	0.4524	2.2103	0.5073	1.9711	1.1213	0.8918	63	6	63.1
27.0	27	0	0.4540	2.2027	0.5095	1.9626	1.1223	0.8910	63	0	63.0
27.1	27	6	0.4555	2.1952	0.5117	1.9542	1.1233	0.8902	62	54	62.9
27.2	27	12	0.4571	2.1877	0.5139	1.9458	1.1243	0.8894	62	48	62.8
27.3	27	18	0.4586	2.1803	0.5161	1.9375	1.1253	0.8886	62	42	62.7
27.4	27	24	0.4602	2.1730	0.5184	1.9292	1.1264	0.8878	62	36	62.6
27.5	27	30	0.4617	2.1657	0.5206	1.9210	1.1274	0.8870	62	30	62.5
27.6	27	36	0.4633	2.1584	0.5228	1.9128	1.1284	0.8862	62	24	62.4
27.7	27	42	0.4648	2.1513	0.5250	1.9047	1.1294	0.8854	62	18	62.3
27.8	27	48	0.4664	2.1441	0.5272	1.8967	1.1305	0.8846	62	12	62.2
27.9	27	54	0.4679	2.1371	0.5295	1.8887	1.1315	0.8838	62	6	62.1
28.0	28	0	0.4695	2.1301	0.5317	1.8807	1.1326	0.8829	62	0	62.0
28.1	28	6	0.4710	2.1231	0.5339	1.8728	1.1336	0.8821	61	54	61.9
28.2	28	12	0.4726	2.1162	0.5362	1.8650	1.1347	0.8813	61	48	61.8
28.3	28	18	0.4741	2.1093	0.5384	1.8572	1.1357	0.8805	61	42	61.7
28.4	28	24	0.4756	2.1025	0.5407	1.8495	1.1368	0.8796	61	36	61.6
28.5	28	30	0.4772	2.0957	0.5430	1.8418	1.1379	0.8788	61	30	61.5
28.6	28	36	0.4787	2.0890	0.5452	1.8341	1.1390	0.8780	61	24	61.4
28.7	28	42	0.4802	2.0824	0.5475	1.8265	1.1401	0.8771	61	18	61.3
28.8	28	48	0.4818	2.0758	0.5498	1.8190	1.1412	0.8763	61	12	61.2
28.9	28	54	0.4833	2.0692	0.5520	1.8115	1.1423	0.8755	61	6	61.1
29.0	29	0	0.4848	2.0627	0.5543	1.8040	1.1434	0.8746	61	0	61.0
29.1	29	6	0.4863	2.0562	0.5566	1.7966	1.1445	0.8738	60	54	60.9
29.2	29	12	0.4879	2.0598	0.5589	1.7893	1.1456	0.8729	60	48	60.8
29.3	29	18	0.4894	2.0434	0.5612	1.7820	1.1467	0.8721	60	42	60.7
29.4	29	24	0.4909	2.0371	0.5635	1.7747	1.1478	0.8712	60	36	60.6
29.5	29	30	0.4924	2.0308	0.5658	1.7675	1.1490	0.8704	60	30	60.5
29.6	29	36	0.4939	2.0245	0.5681	1.7603	1.1501	0.8695	60	24	60.4
29.7	29	42	0.4955	2.0183	0.5704	1.7532	1.1512	0.8686	60	18	60.3
29.8	29	48	0.4970	2.0122	0.5727	1.7461	1.1524	0.8678	60	12	60.2
29.9	29	54	0.4985	2.0061	0.5750	1.7391	1.1535	0.8669	60	6	60.1
			cos θ	sec θ	cot θ	tan θ	csc θ	sin θ	deg	min	θ deg

Table III   (continued)

θ deg	deg	min	$\sin\theta$	$\csc\theta$	$\tan\theta$	$\cot\theta$	$\sec\theta$	$\cos\theta$			
30.0	30	0	0.5000	2.0000	0.5774	1.7321	1.1547	0.8660	60	0	60.0
30.1	30	6	0.5015	1.9940	0.5797	1.7251	1.1559	0.8652	59	54	59.9
30.2	30	12	0.5030	1.9880	0.5820	1.7182	1.1570	0.8643	59	48	59.8
30.3	30	18	0.5045	1.9821	0.5844	1.7113	1.1582	0.8634	59	42	59.7
30.4	30	24	0.5060	1.9762	0.5867	1.7045	1.1594	0.8625	59	36	59.6
30.5	30	30	0.5075	1.9703	0.5890	1.6977	1.1606	0.8616	59	30	59.5
30.6	30	36	0.5090	1.9645	0.5914	1.6909	1.1618	0.8607	59	24	59.4
30.7	30	42	0.5105	1.9587	0.5938	1.6842	1.1630	0.8599	59	18	59.3
30.8	30	48	0.5120	1.9530	0.5961	1.6775	1.1642	0.8590	59	12	59.2
30.9	30	54	0.5135	1.9473	0.5985	1.6709	1.1654	0.8581	59	6	59.1
31.0	31	0	0.5150	1.9416	0.6009	1.6643	1.1666	0.8572	59	0	59.0
31.1	31	6	0.5165	1.9360	0.6032	1.6577	1.1679	0.8563	58	54	58.9
31.2	31	12	0.5180	1.9304	0.6056	1.6512	1.1691	0.8554	58	48	58.8
31.3	31	18	0.5195	1.9249	0.6080	1.6447	1.1703	0.8545	58	42	58.7
31.4	31	24	0.5210	1.9194	0.6104	1.6383	1.1716	0.8536	58	36	58.6
31.5	31	30	0.5225	1.9139	0.6128	1.6319	1.1728	0.8526	58	30	58.5
31.6	31	36	0.5240	1.9084	0.6152	1.6255	1.1741	0.8517	58	24	58.4
31.7	31	42	0.5255	1.9031	0.6176	1.6191	1.1753	0.8508	58	18	58.3
31.8	31	48	0.5270	1.8977	0.6200	1.6128	1.1766	0.8499	58	12	58.2
31.9	31	54	0.5284	1.8924	0.6224	1.6066	1.1779	0.8490	58	6	58.1
32.0	32	0	0.5299	1.8871	0.6249	1.6003	1.1792	0.8480	58	0	58.0
32.1	32	6	0.5314	1.8818	0.6273	1.5941	1.1805	0.8471	57	54	57.9
32.2	32	12	0.5329	1.8766	0.6297	1.5880	1.1818	0.8462	57	48	57.8
32.3	32	18	0.5344	1.8714	0.6322	1.5818	1.1831	0.8453	57	42	57.7
32.4	32	24	0.5358	1.8663	0.6346	1.5757	1.1844	0.8443	57	36	57.6
32.5	32	30	0.5373	1.8612	0.6371	1.5697	1.1857	0.8434	57	30	57.5
32.6	32	36	0.5388	1.8561	0.6395	1.5637	1.1870	0.8425	57	24	57.4
32.7	32	42	0.5402	1.8510	0.6420	1.5577	1.1883	0.8415	57	18	57.3
32.8	32	48	0.5417	1.8460	0.6445	1.5517	1.1897	0.8406	57	12	57.2
32.9	32	54	0.5432	1.8410	0.6469	1.5458	1.1910	0.8396	57	6	57.1
33.0	33	0	0.5446	1.8361	0.6494	1.5399	1.1924	0.8387	57	0	57.0
33.1	33	6	0.5461	1.8312	0.6519	1.5340	1.1937	0.8377	56	54	56.9
33.2	33	12	0.5476	1.8263	0.6544	1.5282	1.1951	0.8368	56	48	56.8
33.3	33	18	0.5490	1.8214	0.6569	1.5224	1.1964	0.8358	56	42	56.7
33.4	33	24	0.5505	1.8166	0.6594	1.5166	1.1978	0.8348	56	36	56.6
33.5	33	30	0.5519	1.8118	0.6619	1.5108	1.1992	0.8339	56	30	56.5
33.6	33	36	0.5534	1.8070	0.6644	1.5051	1.2006	0.8329	56	24	56.4
33.7	33	42	0.5548	1.8023	0.6669	1.4994	1.2020	0.8320	56	18	56.3
33.8	33	48	0.5563	1.7976	0.6694	1.4938	1.2034	0.8310	56	12	56.2
33.9	33	54	0.5577	1.7929	0.6720	1.4882	1.2048	0.8300	56	6	56.1
34.0	34	0	0.5592	1.7883	0.6745	1.4826	1.2062	0.8290	56	0	56.0
34.1	34	6	0.5606	1.7837	0.6771	1.4770	1.2076	0.8281	55	54	55.9
34.2	34	12	0.5621	1.7791	0.6796	1.4715	1.2091	0.8271	55	48	55.8
34.3	34	18	0.5635	1.7745	0.6822	1.4659	1.2105	0.8261	55	42	55.7
34.4	34	24	0.5650	1.7700	0.6847	1.4605	1.2120	0.8251	55	36	55.6
34.5	34	30	0.5664	1.7655	0.6873	1.4550	1.2134	0.8241	55	30	55.5
34.6	34	36	0.5678	1.7610	0.6899	1.4496	1.2149	0.8231	55	24	55.4
34.7	34	42	0.5693	1.7566	0.6924	1.4442	1.2163	0.8221	55	18	55.3
34.8	34	48	0.5707	1.7522	0.6950	1.4388	1.2178	0.8211	55	12	55.2
34.9	34	54	0.5721	1.7478	0.6976	1.4335	1.2193	0.8202	55	6	55.1
			$\cos\theta$	$\sec\theta$	$\cot\theta$	$\tan\theta$	$\csc\theta$	$\sin\theta$	deg	min	θ deg

Table III   (continued)

θ deg	deg	min	sin θ	csc θ	tan θ	cot θ	sec θ	cos θ			
35.0	35	0	0.5736	1.7434	0.7002	1.4281	1.2208	0.8192	55	0	55.0
35.1	35	6	0.5750	1.7391	0.7028	1.4229	1.2223	0.8181	54	54	54.9
35.2	35	12	0.5764	1.7348	0.7054	1.4176	1.2238	0.8171	54	48	54.8
35.3	35	18	0.5779	1.7305	0.7080	1.4124	1.2253	0.8161	54	42	54.7
35.4	35	24	0.5793	1.7263	0.7107	1.4071	1.2268	0.8151	54	36	54.6
35.5	35	30	0.5807	1.7221	0.7133	1.4019	1.2283	0.8141	54	30	54.5
35.6	35	36	0.5821	1.7179	0.7159	1.3968	1.2299	0.8131	54	24	54.4
35.7	35	42	0.5835	1.7137	0.7186	1.3916	1.2314	0.8121	54	18	54.3
35.8	35	48	0.5850	1.7095	0.7212	1.3865	1.2329	0.8111	54	12	54.2
35.9	35	54	0.5864	1.7054	0.7239	1.3814	1.2345	0.8100	54	6	54.1
36.0	36	0	0.5878	1.7013	0.7265	1.3764	1.2361	0.8090	54	0	54.0
36.1	36	6	0.5892	1.6972	0.7292	1.3713	1.2376	0.8080	53	54	53.9
36.2	36	12	0.5906	1.6932	0.7319	1.3663	1.2392	0.8070	53	48	53.8
36.3	36	18	0.5920	1.6892	0.7346	1.3613	1.2408	0.8059	53	42	53.7
36.4	36	24	0.5934	1.6852	0.7373	1.3564	1.2424	0.8049	53	36	53.6
36.5	36	30	0.5948	1.6812	0.7400	1.3514	1.2440	0.8039	53	30	53.5
36.6	36	36	0.5962	1.6772	0.7427	1.3465	1.2456	0.8028	53	24	53.4
36.7	36	42	0.5976	1.6733	0.7454	1.3416	1.2472	0.8018	53	18	53.3
36.8	36	48	0.5990	1.6694	0.7481	1.3367	1.2489	0.8007	53	12	53.2
36.9	36	54	0.6004	1.6655	0.7508	1.3319	1.2505	0.7997	53	6	53.1
37.0	37	0	0.6018	1.6616	0.7536	1.3270	1.2521	0.7986	53	0	53.0
37.1	37	6	0.6032	1.6578	0.7563	1.3222	1.2538	0.7976	52	54	52.9
37.2	37	12	0.6046	1.6540	0.7590	1.3175	1.2554	0.7965	52	48	52.8
37.3	37	18	0.6060	1.6502	0.7618	1.3127	1.2571	0.7955	52	42	52.7
37.4	37	24	0.6074	1.6464	0.7646	1.3079	1.2588	0.7944	52	36	52.6
37.5	37	30	0.6088	1.6427	0.7673	1.3032	1.2605	0.7934	52	30	52.5
37.6	37	36	0.6101	1.6390	0.7701	1.2985	1.2622	0.7923	52	24	52.4
37.7	37	42	0.6115	1.6353	0.7729	1.2938	1.2639	0.7912	52	18	52.3
37.8	37	48	0.6129	1.6316	0.7757	1.2892	1.2656	0.7902	52	12	52.2
37.9	37	54	0.6143	1.6279	0.7785	1.2846	1.2673	0.7891	52	6	52.1
38.0	38	0	0.6157	1.6243	0.7813	1.2799	1.2690	0.7880	52	0	52.0
38.1	38	6	0.6170	1.6207	0.7841	1.2753	1.2708	0.7869	51	54	51.9
38.2	38	12	0.6184	1.6171	0.7869	1.2708	1.2725	0.7859	51	48	51.8
38.3	38	18	0.6198	1.6135	0.7898	1.2662	1.2742	0.7848	51	42	51.7
38.4	38	24	0.6211	1.6099	0.7926	1.2617	1.2760	0.7837	51	36	51.6
38.5	38	30	0.6225	1.6064	0.7954	1.2572	1.2778	0.7826	51	30	51.5
38.6	38	36	0.6239	1.6029	0.7983	1.2527	1.2796	0.7815	51	24	51.4
38.7	38	42	0.6252	1.5994	0.8012	1.2482	1.2813	0.7804	51	18	51.3
38.8	38	48	0.6266	1.5959	0.8040	1.2437	1.2831	0.7793	51	12	51.2
38.9	38	54	0.6280	1.5925	0.8069	1.2393	1.2849	0.7782	51	6	51.1
39.0	39	0	0.6293	1.5890	0.8098	1.2349	1.2868	0.7771	51	0	51.0
39.1	39	6	0.6307	1.5856	0.8127	1.2305	1.2886	0.7760	50	54	50.9
39.2	39	12	0.6320	1.5822	0.8156	1.2261	1.2904	0.7749	50	48	50.8
39.3	39	18	0.6334	1.5788	0.8185	1.2218	1.2923	0.7738	50	42	50.7
39.4	39	24	0.6347	1.5755	0.8214	1.2174	1.2941	0.7727	50	36	50.6
39.5	39	30	0.6361	1.5721	0.8243	1.2131	1.2960	0.7716	50	30	50.5
39.6	39	36	0.6374	1.5688	0.8273	1.2088	1.2978	0.7705	50	24	50.4
39.7	39	42	0.6388	1.5655	0.8302	1.2045	1.2997	0.7694	50	18	50.3
39.8	39	48	0.6401	1.5622	0.8332	1.2002	1.3016	0.7683	50	12	50.2
39.9	39	54	0.6414	1.5590	0.8361	1.1960	1.3035	0.7672	50	6	50.1
			cos θ	sec θ	cot θ	tan θ	csc θ	sin θ	deg	min	θ deg

Table III   (continued)

θ deg	deg min		sin θ	csc θ	tan θ	cot θ	sec θ	cos θ			
40.0	40	0	0.6428	1.5557	0.8391	1.1918	1.3054	0.7660	50	0	50.0
40.1	40	6	0.6441	1.5525	0.8421	1.1875	1.3073	0.7649	49	54	49.9
40.2	40	12	0.6455	1.5493	0.8451	1.1833	1.3092	0.7638	49	48	49.8
40.3	40	18	0.6468	1.5461	0.8481	1.1792	1.3112	0.7627	49	42	49.7
40.4	40	24	0.6481	1.5429	0.8511	1.1750	1.3131	0.7615	49	36	49.6
40.5	40	30	0.6494	1.5398	0.8541	1.1708	1.3151	0.7604	49	30	49.5
40.6	40	36	0.6508	1.5366	0.8571	1.1667	1.3171	0.7593	49	24	49.4
40.7	40	42	0.6521	1.5335	0.8601	1.1626	1.3190	0.7581	49	18	49.3
40.8	40	48	0.6534	1.5304	0.8632	1.1585	1.3210	0.7570	49	12	49.2
40.9	40	54	0.6547	1.5273	0.8662	1.1544	1.3230	0.7559	49	6	49.1
41.0	41	0	0.6561	1.5243	0.8693	1.1504	1.3250	0.7547	49	0	49.0
41.1	41	6	0.6574	1.5212	0.8724	1.1463	1.3270	0.7536	48	54	48.9
41.2	41	12	0.6587	1.5182	0.8754	1.1423	1.3291	0.7524	48	48	48.8
41.3	41	18	0.6600	1.5151	0.8785	1.1383	1.3311	0.7513	48	42	48.7
41.4	41	24	0.6613	1.5121	0.8816	1.1343	1.3331	0.7501	48	36	48.6
41.5	41	30	0.6626	1.5092	0.8847	1.1303	1.3352	0.7490	48	30	48.5
41.6	41	36	0.6639	1.5062	0.8878	1.1263	1.3373	0.7478	48	24	48.4
41.7	41	42	0.6652	1.5032	0.8910	1.1224	1.3393	0.7466	48	18	48.3
41.8	41	48	0.6665	1.5003	0.8941	1.1184	1.3414	0.7455	48	12	48.2
41.9	41	54	0.6678	1.4974	0.8972	1.1145	1.3435	0.7443	48	6	48.1
42.0	42	0	0.6691	1.4945	0.9004	1.1106	1.3456	0.7431	48	0	48.0
42.1	42	6	0.6704	1.4916	0.9036	1.1067	1.3478	0.7420	47	54	47.9
42.2	42	12	0.6717	1.4887	0.9067	1.1028	1.3499	0.7408	47	48	47.8
42.3	42	18	0.6730	1.4859	0.9099	1.0990	1.3520	0.7396	47	42	47.7
42.4	42	24	0.6743	1.4830	0.9131	1.0951	1.3542	0.7385	47	36	47.6
42.5	42	30	0.6756	1.4802	0.9163	1.0913	1.3563	0.7373	47	30	47.5
42.6	42	36	0.6769	1.4774	0.9195	1.0875	1.3585	0.7361	47	24	47.4
42.7	42	42	0.6782	1.4746	0.9228	1.0837	1.3607	0.7349	47	18	47.3
42.8	42	48	0.6794	1.4718	0.9260	1.0799	1.3629	0.7337	47	12	47.2
42.9	42	54	0.6807	1.4690	0.9293	1.0761	1.3651	0.7325	47	6	47.1
43.0	43	0	0.6820	1.4663	0.9325	1.0724	1.3673	0.7314	47	0	47.0
43.1	43	6	0.6833	1.4635	0.9358	1.0686	1.3696	0.7302	46	54	46.9
43.2	43	12	0.6845	1.4608	0.9391	1.0649	1.3718	0.7290	46	48	46.8
43.3	43	18	0.6858	1.4581	0.9424	1.0612	1.3741	0.7278	46	42	46.7
43.4	43	24	0.6871	1.4554	0.9457	1.0575	1.3763	0.7266	46	36	46.6
43.5	43	30	0.6884	1.4527	0.9490	1.0538	1.3786	0.7254	46	30	46.5
43.6	43	36	0.6896	1.4501	0.9523	1.0501	1.3809	0.7242	46	24	46.4
43.7	43	42	0.6909	1.4474	0.9556	1.0464	1.3832	0.7230	46	18	46.3
43.8	43	48	0.6921	1.4448	0.9590	1.0428	1.3855	0.7218	46	12	46.2
43.9	43	54	0.6934	1.4422	0.9623	1.0392	1.3878	0.7206	46	6	46.1
44.0	44	0	0.6947	1.4396	0.9657	1.0355	1.3902	0.7193	46	0	46.0
44.1	44	6	0.6959	1.4370	0.9691	1.0319	1.3925	0.7181	45	54	45.9
44.2	44	12	0.6972	1.4344	0.9725	1.0283	1.3949	0.7169	45	48	45.8
44.3	44	18	0.6984	1.4318	0.9759	1.0247	1.3972	0.7157	45	42	45.7
44.4	44	24	0.6997	1.4293	0.9793	1.0212	1.3996	0.7145	45	36	45.6
44.5	44	30	0.7009	1.4267	0.9827	1.0176	1.4020	0.7133	45	30	45.5
44.6	44	36	0.7022	1.4242	0.9861	1.0141	1.4044	0.7120	45	24	45.4
44.7	44	42	0.7034	1.4217	0.9896	1.0105	1.4069	0.7108	45	18	45.3
44.8	44	48	0.7046	1.4192	0.9930	1.0070	1.4093	0.7096	45	12	45.2
44.9	44	54	0.7059	1.4167	0.9965	1.0035	1.4118	0.7083	45	6	45.1
45.0	45	0	0.7071	1.4142	1.0000	1.0000	1.4142	0.7071	45	0	45.0
			cos θ	sec θ	cot θ	tan θ	csc θ	sin θ	deg	min	θ deg

Table IV   Common Logarithms

n	0	1	2	3	4	5	6	7	8	9
1.0	.0000	.0043	.0086	.0128	.0170	.0212	.0253	.0294	.0334	.0374
1.1	.0414	.0453	.0492	.0531	.0569	.0607	.0645	.0682	.0719	.0755
1.2	.0792	.0828	.0864	.0899	.0934	.0969	.1004	.1038	.1072	.1106
1.3	.1139	.1173	.1206	.1239	.1271	.1303	.1335	.1367	.1399	.1430
1.4	.1461	.1492	.1523	.1553	.1584	.1614	.1644	.1673	.1703	.1732
1.5	.1761	.1790	.1818	.1847	.1875	.1903	.1931	.1959	.1987	.2014
1.6	.2041	.2068	.2095	.2122	.2148	.2175	.2201	.2227	.2253	.2279
1.7	.2304	.2330	.2355	.2380	.2405	.2430	.2455	.2480	.2504	.2529
1.8	.2553	.2577	.2601	.2625	.2648	.2672	.2695	.2718	.2742	.2765
1.9	.2788	.2810	.2833	.2856	.2878	.2900	.2923	.2945	.2967	.2989
2.0	.3010	.3032	.3054	.3075	.3096	.3118	.3139	.3160	.3181	.3201
2.1	.3222	.3243	.3263	.3284	.3304	.3324	.3345	.3365	.3385	.3404
2.2	.3424	.3444	.3464	.3483	.3502	.3522	.3541	.3560	.3579	.3598
2.3	.3617	.3636	.3655	.3674	.3692	.3711	.3729	.3747	.3766	.3784
2.4	.3802	.3820	.3838	.3856	.3874	.3892	.3909	.3927	.3945	.3962
2.5	.3979	.3997	.4014	.4031	.4048	.4065	.4082	.4099	.4116	.4133
2.6	.4150	.4166	.4183	.4200	.4216	.4232	.4249	.4265	.4281	.4298
2.7	.4314	.4330	.4346	.4362	.4378	.4393	.4409	.4425	.4440	.4456
2.8	.4472	.4487	.4502	.4518	.4533	.4548	.4564	.4579	.4594	.4609
2.9	.4624	.4639	.4654	.4669	.4683	.4698	.4713	.4728	.4742	.4757
3.0	.4771	.4786	.4800	.4814	.4829	.4843	.4857	.4871	.4886	.4900
3.1	.4914	.4928	.4942	.4955	.4969	.4983	.4997	.5011	.5024	.5038
3.2	.5051	.5065	.5079	.5092	.5105	.5119	.5132	.5145	.5159	.5172
3.3	.5185	.5198	.5211	.5224	.5237	.5250	.5263	.5276	.5289	.5302
3.4	.5315	.5328	.5340	.5353	.5366	.5378	.5391	.5403	.5416	.5428
3.5	.5441	.5453	.5465	.5478	.5490	.5502	.5514	.5527	.5539	.5551
3.6	.5563	.5575	.5587	.5599	.5611	.5623	.5635	.5647	.5658	.5670
3.7	.5682	.5694	.5705	.5717	.5729	.5740	.5752	.5763	.5775	.5786
3.8	.5798	.5809	.5821	.5832	.5843	.5855	.5866	.5877	.5888	.5899
3.9	.5911	.5922	.5933	.5944	.5955	.5966	.5977	.5988	.5999	.6010
4.0	.6021	.6031	.6042	.6053	.6064	.6075	.6085	.6096	.6107	.6117
4.1	.6128	.6138	.6149	.6160	.6170	.6180	.6191	.6201	.6212	.6222
4.2	.6232	.6243	.6253	.6263	.6274	.6284	.6294	.6304	.6314	.6325
4.3	.6335	.6345	.6355	.6365	.6375	.6385	.6395	.6405	.6415	.6425
4.4	.6435	.6444	.6454	.6464	.6474	.6484	.6493	.6503	.6513	.6522
4.5	.6532	.6542	.6551	.6561	.6571	.6580	.6590	.6599	.6609	.6618
4.6	.6628	.6637	.6646	.6656	.6665	.6675	.6684	.6693	.6702	.6712
4.7	.6721	.6730	.6739	.6749	.6758	.6767	.6776	.6785	.6794	.6803
4.8	.6812	.6821	.6830	.6839	.6848	.6857	.6866	.6875	.6884	.6893
4.9	.6902	.6911	.6920	.6928	.6937	.6946	.6955	.6964	.6972	.6981
5.0	.6990	.6998	.7007	.7016	.7024	.7033	.7042	.7050	.7059	.7067
5.1	.7076	.7084	.7093	.7101	.7110	.7118	.7126	.7135	.7143	.7152
5.2	.7160	.7168	.7177	.7185	.7193	.7202	.7210	.7218	.7226	.7235
5.3	.7243	.7251	.7259	.7267	.7275	.7284	.7292	.7300	.7308	.7316
5.4	.7324	.7332	.7340	.7348	.7356	.7364	.7372	.7380	.7388	.7396
n	0	1	2	3	4	5	6	7	8	9

Table IV (continued)

n	0	1	2	3	4	5	6	7	8	9
5.5	.7404	.7412	.7419	.7427	.7435	.7443	.7451	.7459	.7466	.7474
5.6	.7482	.7490	.7497	.7505	.7513	.7520	.7528	.7536	.7543	.7551
5.7	.7559	.7566	.7574	.7582	.7589	.7597	.7604	.7612	.7619	.7627
5.8	.7634	.7642	.7649	.7657	.7664	.7672	.7679	.7686	.7694	.7701
5.9	.7709	.7716	.7723	.7731	.7738	.7745	.7752	.7760	.7767	.7774
6.0	.7782	.7789	.7796	.7803	.7810	.7818	.7825	.7832	.7839	.7846
6.1	.7853	.7860	.7868	.7875	.7882	.7889	.7896	.7903	.7910	.7917
6.2	.7924	.7931	.7938	.7945	.7952	.7959	.7966	.7973	.7980	.7987
6.3	.7993	.8000	.8007	.8014	.8021	.8028	.8035	.8041	.8048	.8055
6.4	.8062	.8069	.8075	.8082	.8089	.8096	.8102	.8109	.8116	.8122
6.5	.8129	.8136	.8142	.8149	.8156	.8162	.8169	.8176	.8182	.8189
6.6	.8195	.8202	.8209	.8215	.8222	.8228	.8235	.8241	.8248	.8254
6.7	.8261	.8267	.8274	.8280	.8287	.8293	.8299	.8306	.8312	.8319
6.8	.8325	.8331	.8338	.8344	.8351	.8357	.8363	.8370	.8376	.8382
6.9	.8388	.8395	.8401	.8407	.8414	.8420	.8426	.8432	.8439	.8445
7.0	.8451	.8457	.8463	.8470	.8476	.8482	.8488	.8494	.8500	.8506
7.1	.8513	.8519	.8525	.8531	.8537	.8543	.8549	.8555	.8561	.8567
7.2	.8573	.8579	.8585	.8591	.8597	.8603	.8609	.8615	.8621	.8627
7.3	.8633	.8639	.8645	.8651	.8657	.8663	.8669	.8675	.8681	.8686
7.4	.8692	.8698	.8704	.8710	.8716	.8722	.8727	.8733	.8739	.8745
7.5	.8751	.8756	.8762	.8768	.8774	.8779	.8785	.8791	.8797	.8802
7.6	.8808	.8814	.8820	.8825	.8831	.8837	.8842	.8848	.8854	.8859
7.7	.8865	.8871	.8876	.8882	.8887	.8893	.8899	.8904	.8910	.8915
7.8	.8921	.8927	.8932	.8938	.8943	.8949	.8954	.8960	.8965	.8971
7.9	.8976	.8982	.8987	.8993	.8998	.9004	.9009	.9015	.9020	.9025
8.0	.9031	.9036	.9042	.9047	.9053	.9058	.9063	.9069	.9074	.9079
8.1	.9085	.9090	.9096	.9101	.9106	.9112	.9117	.9122	.9128	.9133
8.2	.9138	.9143	.9149	.9154	.9159	.9165	.9170	.9175	.9180	.9186
8.3	.9191	.9196	.9201	.9206	.9212	.9217	.9222	.9227	.9232	.9238
8.4	.9243	.9248	.9253	.9258	.9263	.9269	.9274	.9279	.9284	.9289
8.5	.9294	.9299	.9304	.9309	.9315	.9320	.9325	.9330	.9335	.9340
8.6	.9345	.9350	.9355	.9360	.9365	.9370	.9375	.9380	.9385	.9390
8.7	.9395	.9400	.9405	.9410	.9415	.9420	.9425	.9430	.9435	.9440
8.8	.9445	.9450	.9455	.9460	.9465	.9469	.9474	.9479	.9484	.9489
8.9	.9494	.9499	.9504	.9509	.9513	.9518	.9523	.9528	.9533	.9538
9.0	.9542	.9547	.9552	.9557	.9562	.9566	.9571	.9576	.9581	.9586
9.1	.9590	.9595	.9600	.9605	.9609	.9614	.9619	.9624	.9628	.9633
9.2	.9638	.9643	.9647	.9652	.9657	.9661	.9666	.9671	.9675	.9680
9.3	.9685	.9689	.9694	.9699	.9703	.9708	.9713	.9717	.9722	.9727
9.4	.9731	.9736	.9741	.9745	.9750	.9754	.9759	.9763	.9768	.9773
9.5	.9777	.9782	.9786	.9791	.9795	.9800	.9805	.9809	.9814	.9818
9.6	.9823	.9827	.9832	.9836	.9841	.9845	.9850	.9854	.9859	.9863
9.7	.9868	.9872	.9877	.9881	.9886	.9890	.9894	.9899	.9903	.9908
9.8	.9912	.9917	.9921	.9926	.9930	.9934	.9939	.9943	.9948	.9952
9.9	.9956	.9961	.9965	.9969	.9974	.9978	.9983	.9987	.9991	.9996
n	0	1	2	3	4	5	6	7	8	9

Answers to Selected Exercises

Exercises on Calculators

1. 4.5 to 5.5   **3.** 9.55 to 9.65   **5.** 8.945 to 8.955   **7.** 19.65 to 19.75   **9.** 253.7405 to 253.7415
11. 28,999.5 to 29,000.5   **13.** 3   **15.** 4   **17.** 4   **19.** 2   **21.** 5   **23.** 769,770
25. 12.5, 13   **27.** 9.00, 9.0   **29.** 7.13, 7.1   **31.** 11.6, 12   **33.** 76.42   **35.** 8.1
37. 28,300,000 (or 2.83×10^7)   **39.** 0.0057489   **41.** 0.0970   **43.** 0.0557   **45.** 8.6423
47. 9400 (or 9.4×10^3)   **49.** 0.0808   **51.** -108.1 **53.** $-28,000$ (or -1.8×10^4)   **55.** 2200 (or 2.2×10^3)

Chapter 1

Section 1.1 (page 7)

1. 8   **3.** -5 **5.** -15 **7.** -13 **9.** 10   **11.** -5.39579 **13.** II   **15.** III   **17.** None
19. None   **21.** II   **23.** IV   **25.** $x > 0, y > 0$ **27.** $x < 0, y < 0$ **29.** Positive   **31.** Negative
33. Positive   **35.** Positive   **37.** Negative   **39.** $\sqrt{18} = 3\sqrt{2}$ **41.** $\sqrt{50} = 5\sqrt{2}$ **43.** $\sqrt{34}$
45. $\sqrt{29}$ **47.** 4   **49.** 4   **51.** 8.1480   **53.** 6   **55.** 0   **57.** 7.994   **59.** $-2a^2 + 4a + 6$
61. $-2a^2 + 8$ **63.** $(-2, 11); (-1, 8); (0, 5); (1, 2); (2, -1); (3, -4)$
65. $(-2, -8); (-1, -3); (0, 0); (1, 1); (2, 0); (3, -3)$ **63.**
67. Domain: all reals; range: all reals; function
69. Domain: all reals; range: $y \geq 4$; function
71. Domain: all reals; range: $y \leq 4$; function
73. Domain: $x \geq 0$; range: all reals; not a function
75. Domain: $x \geq -4$; range: $y \geq 0$; function
77. Domain: all reals; range: $y \geq 1$; function
79. $x \neq 0$ **81.** $x \neq 7/3, x \neq -1/2$

65.

Section 1.2 (page 15)

1. 320°   **3.** 235°   **5.** 90°   **7.** 179°
9. 130°   **11.** 94.5937°   Answers other than the ones we
give are possible in Exercises 13–27.   **13.** 435°; $-285°$, quadrant I   **15.** 482°; $-238°$, quadrant II
17. 594°; $-126°$, quadrant III   **19.** 660°; $-60°$, quadrant IV   **21.** 78°; $-282°$, quadrant I   **23.** 152°; $-208°$,
quadrant II   **25.** 308°; $-412°$, quadrant IV   **27.** 201°; $-519°$, quadrant III   Your answers may differ a
little from ours in Exercises 29–41.   **29.** 45°   **31.** 225° or $-135°$ **33.** 53°   **35.** 158°   **37.** 171°
39. 30°   **41.** 330° or $-30°$ **43.** 1800°   **45.** 31° 25′ 47″   **47.** 89° 54′ 01″   **49.** 374.316°

Section 1.3 (page 20)

In Exercises 1–11 we give, in order, sine, cosine, and tangent. Your answers may differ a little from ours.
1. .26; .97; .27   **3.** .42; .91; .47   **5.** .57; .82; .70   **7.** .71; .71; 1.00   **9.** .82; .57; 1.43
11. .94; .34; 2.75   **13.** -3 **15.** -3 **17.** 5   **19.** 1   **21.** -1 **23.** 3   **25.** 1
In Exercises 27–49 we give, in order, sine, cosine, tangent, cotangent, secant, and cosecant.   **27.** 4/5; $-3/5$;
$-4/3$; $-3/4$; $-5/3$; 5/4   **29.** $-12/13$; 5/13; $-12/5$; $-5/12$; 13/5; $-13/12$ **31.** 4/5; 3/5; 4/3; 3/4; 5/3; 5/4
33. 24/25; $-7/25$; $-24/7$; $-7/24$; $-25/7$; 25/24   **35.** 1; 0; undefined; 0; undefined; 1   **37.** 0; 1; 0;
undefined; 1; undefined   **39.** $\sqrt{3}/2$; 1/2; $\sqrt{3}$; $\sqrt{3}/3$; 2; $2\sqrt{3}/3$ **41.** $-1/2$; $\sqrt{3}/2$; $-\sqrt{3}/3$; $-\sqrt{3}$;
$2\sqrt{3}/3$; -2 **43.** $-\sqrt{2}/2$; $\sqrt{2}/2$; -1; -1; $\sqrt{2}$; $-\sqrt{2}$ **45.** $-2/3$; $\sqrt{5}/3$; $-2\sqrt{5}/5$; $-\sqrt{5}/2$; $3\sqrt{5}/5$;
$-3/2$ **47.** $\sqrt{3}/4$; $-\sqrt{13}/4$; $-\sqrt{39}/13$; $-\sqrt{39}/3$; $-4\sqrt{13}/13$; $4\sqrt{3}/3$ **49.** $-\sqrt{10}/5$; $\sqrt{15}/5$; $-\sqrt{6}/3$;
$-\sqrt{6}/2$; $\sqrt{15}/3$; $-\sqrt{10}/2$ **51.** $-.34727$; .93777; $-.37031$; -2.7004; 1.0664; -2.8796 **53.** $-.5638$; $-.8259$;
.6826; 1.465; -1.211; -1.774 **55.** $-.633$; .774; $-.818$; 1.22; 1.29; -1.58

Section 1.4 (page 25)

1. 1/3 **3.** $\sqrt{5}/5$ **5.** .700692 **7.** 1/2 **9.** $\sqrt{3}$ **11.** -100 **13.** II **15.** III **17.** IV
19. II or IV **21.** I or II **23.** I or III In Exercises 25–35, we give, in order, sine and cosecant, cosine
and secant, tangent and cotangent. **25.** +; +; + **27.** −; −; + **29.** −; +; − **31.** +; +; +
33. −; +; − **35.** −; −; + **37.** Impossible **39.** Possible **41.** Impossible **43.** Possible
45. Possible **47.** Impossible **49.** Possible **51.** Impossible **53.** Impossible In Exercises 55–71,
we give, in order, sine, cosine, tangent, cotangent, secant, and cosecant. **55.** $-4/5$; $-3/5$; $4/3$; $3/4$; $-5/3$; $-5/4$
57. $7/25$; $-24/25$; $-7/24$; $-24/7$; $-25/24$; $25/7$ **59.** $1/2$; $-\sqrt{3}/2$; $-\sqrt{3}/3$; $-\sqrt{3}$; $-2\sqrt{3}/3$; 2
61. $-\sqrt{5}/5$; $2\sqrt{5}/5$; $-1/2$; -2; $\sqrt{5}/2$; $-\sqrt{5}$ **63.** $-5/6$; $\sqrt{11}/6$; $-5\sqrt{11}/11$; $-\sqrt{11}/5$; $6\sqrt{11}/11$; $-6/5$
65. $8\sqrt{73}/73$; $3\sqrt{73}/73$; $8/3$; $3/8$; $\sqrt{73}/3$; $\sqrt{73}/8$ **67.** $3\sqrt{13}/13$; $2\sqrt{13}/13$; $3/2$; $2/3$; $\sqrt{13}/2$; $\sqrt{13}/3$
69. .164215; $-.986425$; $-.166475$; -6.00691; -1.01376; 6.08958 **71.** $-.540362$; $-.841433$; .642193;
1.55716; -1.18845; -1.85061 **73.** a; $\sqrt{1-a^2}$; $a\sqrt{1-a^2}/(1-a^2)$; $\sqrt{1-a^2}/a$;
$\sqrt{1-a^2}/(1-a^2)$; $1/a$

Chapter 1 Test (page 27)

1. 4 **2.** 3 **3.** 5 **4.** $4\sqrt{5}$ **5.** 2 **6.** -8 **7.** $-a^2+3a+2$ **8.** 309° **9.** 186°
10. 72° In Exercises 11–15 we give, in order, sine, cosine, and tangent. **11.** $-\sqrt{2}/2$; $-\sqrt{2}/2$; 1
12. $-\sqrt{3}/2$; $1/2$; $-\sqrt{3}$ **13.** 0; -1; 0 **14.** 0; 1; 0 **15.** $15/17$; $-8/17$; $-15/8$ **16.** Possible
17. Impossible **18.** Possible **19.** $\cos\theta = -\sqrt{22}/5$; $\tan\theta = -\sqrt{66}/22$; $\cot\theta = -\sqrt{66}/3$; $\sec\theta = -5\sqrt{22}/22$;
$\csc\theta = 5\sqrt{3}/3$ **20.** $\sin\gamma = -\sqrt{39}/8$; $\tan\gamma = \sqrt{39}/5$; $\sec\gamma = -8/5$; $\csc\gamma = -8\sqrt{39}/39$;
$\cot\gamma = 5\sqrt{39}/39$

Chapter 2

Section 2.1 (page 32)

In Exercises 1–5, we give, in order, sine, cosine, tangent, cotangent, secant, and cosecant. **1.** $3/5$; $4/5$; $3/4$; $4/3$;
$5/4$; $5/3$ **3.** $21/29$; $20/29$; $21/20$; $20/21$; $29/20$; $29/21$ **5.** n/p; m/p; n/m; m/n; p/m; p/n
7. .759260; .650787; 1.16668; .857133; 1.53660; 1.31707 **9.** .87166; .49011; 1.7785; .56228; 2.0404; 1.1472
11. $\cot 40°$ **13.** $\sec 43°$ **15.** $\sin 37° 11'$ **17.** $\cot 64° 17'$ **19.** $\cos(90° - \gamma)$ **21.** $\csc(90° - 2A)$
23. $\sin(70° - \alpha)$ **25.** 30° **27.** 20° **29.** 12° **31.** 8° **33.** 70° **35.** True **37.** True
39. False **41.** True **43.** True

Section 2.2 (page 37)

In Exercises 1–11, we give, in order, sine, cosine, tangent, cotangent, secant, and cosecant. **1.** $\sqrt{3}/2$; $-1/2$; $-\sqrt{3}$;
$-\sqrt{3}/3$; -2; $2\sqrt{3}/3$ **3.** $1/2$; $-\sqrt{3}/2$; $-\sqrt{3}/3$; $-\sqrt{3}$; $-2\sqrt{3}/3$; 2 **5.** $-\sqrt{3}/2$; $-1/2$; $\sqrt{3}$;
$\sqrt{3}/3$; -2; $-2\sqrt{3}/3$ **7.** $-1/2$; $\sqrt{3}/2$; $-\sqrt{3}/3$; $-\sqrt{3}$; $2\sqrt{3}/3$; -2 **9.** $\sqrt{3}/2$; $1/2$; $\sqrt{3}$; $\sqrt{3}/3$; 2; $2\sqrt{3}/3$
11. $1/2$; $-\sqrt{3}/2$; $-\sqrt{3}/3$; $-\sqrt{3}$; $-2\sqrt{3}/3$; 2 **13.** $\sqrt{3}/3$; $\sqrt{3}$ **15.** $\sqrt{3}/2$; $\sqrt{3}/3$; $2\sqrt{3}/3$
17. -1; -1 **19.** $-\sqrt{3}/2$; $-2\sqrt{3}/3$ **21.** 1 **23.** $23/4$ **25.** $1/2 + \sqrt{3}$ **27.** $-29/12$
29. $-\sqrt{3}/3$ **31.** False **33.** True **35.** False **37.** True **39.** True **41.** 30°; 150°
43. 60°; 240° **45.** 120°; 240° **47.** 240°; 300° **49.** 135°; 315° **51.** 90°; 270° **53.** 0°; 180°

Section 2.3 (page 47)

1. 65° **3.** 255° **5.** 123° **7.** 98° 20′ **9.** 18° 30′ **11.** 228° 50′ **13.** 68.9°
15. 110° **17.** 161° 50′ **19.** 137.9° **21.** 82° **23.** 32° **25.** 75° **27.** 29° **29.** 2°
31. 65° 20′ **33.** 35.7° **35.** 69° 50′ **37.** 34° 30′ **39.** 39.1° **41.** .6248 **43.** 1.137
45. .8526 **47.** .3096 **49.** $-.7954$ **51.** .0105 **53.** $-.4120$ **55.** $-.3228$ **57.** $-.9965$
59. 1.142 **61.** -3.179 **63.** $-.3211$ **65.** 58° **67.** 30° 30′ **69.** 46° 10′ **71.** 81° 10′
73. 49.25° **75.** 114.21667° **77.** 32.6875° **79.** 128.70778° **81.** .86288 **83.** -6.04837
85. .27256 **87.** $-.72307$ **89.** 2×10^8 m/sec

Section 2.4 (page 53)

1. 4.5 to 5.5 pounds **3.** 9.55 to 9.65 tons **5.** 8.945 to 8.955 m **7.** 19.65 to 19.75 liters
9. 253.7405 to 253.7415 m **11.** 28,999.5 to 29,000.5 ft **13.** 3 **15.** 4 **17.** 4 **19.** 2

21. 5   **23.** 769; 770   **25.** 12.5; 13   **27.** 9.00; 9.0   **29.** 7.12; 7.1   **31.** 11.6; 12   **33.** .5704
35. 1.162   **37.** 2.171   **39.** .9052   **41.** .9686   **43.** .3404   **45.** .1951   **47.** 1.478
49. 1.562   **51.** .8121   **53.** 35° 44′   **55.** 25° 53′   **57.** 21° 48′   **59.** 23° 08′
61. 73° 27′   **63.** False   **65.** True   **67.** False   **69.** False   **71.** False

Section 2.5 (page 57)
1. $B = 53° 40′$; $a = 571$ m; $b = 777$ m   **3.** $M = 38.8°$; $n = 154$ m; $p = 198$ m   **5.** $A = 47.9108°$;
$c = 84.816$ cm; $a = 62.942$ cm   **7.** $A = 50°$; $a = 23$ ft; $c = 30$ ft   **9.** $A = 58°$; $b = 24$ m; $c = 45$ m
11. $B = 61°$; $a = 17$ in; $b = 31$ in   **13.** $A = 58°$; $a = 83$ m; $b = 52$m
15. $A = 27°$; $b = 4.5$ m; $c = 5.1$ m   **17.** $A = 47°$; $B = 43°$; $c = 109$ ft   **19.** $A = 68°$;
$B = 22°$; $c = 79$ m   **21.** $A = 70°$; $B = 20°$; $c = 4.0$ in   **23.** $B = 60° 30′$; $b = 1490$ cm; $c = 1710$ cm
25. $B = 57° 10′$; $a = 40.6$ m; $c = 74.9$ m   **27.** $B = 53° 40′$; $a = 57.1$ m; $b = 77.6$ m   **29.** $A = 71° 20′$;
$a = .282$ m; $b = .0954$ m   **31.** $B = 57° 07′$; $b = 107.9$ m; $c = 128.4$ m   **33.** $B = 60° 17′$; $a = 4.556$ cm;
$c = 9.191$ cm   **35.** $A = 71° 36′$; $B = 18° 24′$; $a = 7.413$ m   **37.** $A = 47.568°$, $b = 143.97$ m, $c = 213.38$ m
39. 28 in

Section 2.6 (page 61)
1. 33°   **3.** 13 m   **5.** 45 m   **7.** 29,000 ft   **9.** 8800 ft   **11.** 1300 ft   **13.** 120 mi   **15.** 38°
17. 350 m/min   **19.** 19.46 ft   **21.** 45.7 m   **23.** 7.49 mi   **25.** 183 m   **27. (a)** 34° **(b)** 10 cm
29. 1200 ft   **31.** 142 m

Chapter 2 Test (page 66)
In Exercises 1–4 we give, in order, sine, cosine, tangent, cotangent, secant, and cosecant.   **1.** 60/61; 11/61; 60/11;
11/60; 61/11; 61/60   **2.** $\sqrt{3}/2$; $-1/2$; $-\sqrt{3}$; $-\sqrt{3}/3$; -2; $2\sqrt{3}/3$ **3.** $-\sqrt{2}/2$; $-\sqrt{2}/2$; 1; 1; $-\sqrt{2}$; $-\sqrt{2}$
4. $-\sqrt{3}/2$; $1/2$; $-\sqrt{3}$; $-\sqrt{3}/3$; 2; $-2\sqrt{3}/3$ **5.** 10°   **6.** 10°   **7.** 1   **8.** $3 - 2\sqrt{3}/3$ **9.** $-5/3$
10. False   **11.** True   **12.** True   **13.** False   **14.** .9537   **15.** -1.356 **16.** $-.7159$
17. .7361   **18.** 1.558   **19.** 1.021   **20.** 37° 40′   **21.** 71.9°   **22.** 39° 30′   **23.** 55° 40′
24. 41° 40′   **25.** 12° 44′   **26.** 5   **27.** 3   **28.** 976   **29.** .000143   **30.** $B = 47°$; $b = 82$ m;
$c = 110$ m   **31.** $A = 10° 40′$; $a = 166$ cm; $b = 881$ cm   **32.** 82.6 ft   **33.** 1200 m

Chapter 3

Section 3.1 (page 72)
1. $\pi/3$ **3.** $\pi/2$ **5.** $5\pi/6$ **7.** $7\pi/6$ **9.** $5\pi/3$ **11.** $5\pi/2$ **13.** $\pi/9$ **15.** $7\pi/9$ **17.** .681
19. .742   **21.** 2.43   **23.** 1.12   **25.** 60°   **27.** 315°   **29.** 330°   **31.** $-30°$ **33.** 288°
35. 132°   **37.** 63°   **39.** 66°   **41.** 114.5916°; 114° 35′   **43.** 99.6947°; 99° 42′   **45.** 5.2254°;
5° 14′   **47.** .9847 radians   **49.** .8324 radians   **51.** $-.5185$ radians   **53.** $\sqrt{3}/2$ **55.** 1
57. $2\sqrt{3}/3$ **59.** 1   **61.** $-\sqrt{3}$ **63.** 1/2   **65.** -1 **67.** $-\sqrt{3}/2$ **69.** 1   **71.** 0
73. $-\sqrt{3}$ **75.** 1/2   **77.** We begin the answers with the blank next to 30°, and then proceed counterclockwise
from there: $\pi/6$; 45°; $\pi/3$; $\pi/2$; 120°; 135°; $5\pi/6$; π; $7\pi/6$; $5\pi/4$; 240°; 300°; $7\pi/4$; $11\pi/6$ **79. (a)** $5\pi/4$ **(b)** $3\pi/4$
81. $\pi/2$ **83.** π **85.** $2\pi/3$

Section 3.2 (page 78)
1. 25.1 in   **3.** 25.8 cm   **5.** 318 m   **7.** 5.05 m   **9.** 53.429 m   **11.** 1600 km   **13.** 1200 km
15. 3500 km   **17.** 5900 km   **19.** 7300 km   **21.** 21 m   **23.** .20 km   **25.** 2100 mi
27. 850 ft   **29.** 42 m^2 **31.** 1120 m^2 **33.** 1300 cm^2 **35.** 114 cm^2 **37.** 359 m^2
39. 760.34 m^2 **41.** 11.25° or 11° 15′; $\pi/16$ **43.** 15 ft   **47.** 282.488 cm^2 **49.** 164.964 mm^2

Section 3.3 (page 84)
1. .4877   **3.** .5317   **5.** .7314   **7.** .8004   **9.** .9981   **11.** 1.017   **13.** .9636   **15.** .4245
17. 1.213   **19.** $-.4436$ **21.** $-.7547$ **23.** $-.9967$ **25.** -3.867 **27.** $-.3090$ **29.** .3173
31. 2.282   **33.** -14.33 **35.** .6720   **37.** 1.2799   **39.** 1.2043   **41.** 1.4138   **43.** .5403
45. .3093   **47.** .9320   **49.** .2675   **51.** .9093   **53.** 58°   **55.** 84°   **57.** 66°   **61.** IV
63. II   **65.** 19°   **67.** 53°   **69.** 48°

Section 3.4 (page 88)
1. $5\pi/4$ radians   **3.** $\pi/25$ radians/sec   **5.** 9 min   **7.** 10.768 radians   **9.** $72\pi/5$ cm/sec

11. 6 radians/sec   **13.** 9.29755 cm/sec   **15.** 18π cm   **17.** 12 sec   **19.** $3\pi/32$ radians/sec
21. 24.8647 cm   **23.** $\pi/6$ radians/hr   **25.** $\pi/30$ radians/sec   **27.** $7\pi/30$ cm/min   **29.** 168π m/min
31. 1500π m/min   **33.** About 29 sec   **35.** (a) 2π radians/day; $\pi/12$ radians/hr   (b) 0
(c) $12{,}800\pi$ km/day or 533π km/hr   (d) 9050π km/day or 377π km/hr   **37.** 4.289 m

Chapter 3   Test   (page 91)
1. $\pi/4$ **2.** $2\pi/3$ **3.** $4\pi/9$ **4.** $35\pi/36$ **5.** $40\pi/9$ **6.** 225°   **7.** 162°   **8.** 168°
9. −216°   **10.** −110°   **11.** $\sqrt{3}$ **12.** $-1/2$ **13.** $-1/2$ **14.** $-\sqrt{3}$ **15.** $-\sqrt{3}$
16. 35.8 cm   **17.** 273 m^2 **18.** 41 yd   **19.** .8660   **20.** 2.798   **21.** .9703   **22.** −11.43
23. 1.675   **24.** −.9920   **25.** −.5048   **26.** .3898   **27.** 15/32 sec   **28.** $\pi/30$ radians/sec
29. $4\pi/75$ radians/sec   **30.** 1260π m/sec or 3960 m/sec

Chapter 4

Section 4.1   (page 99)

1.

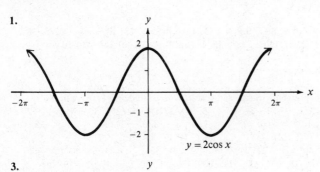

$y = 2\cos x$

3.

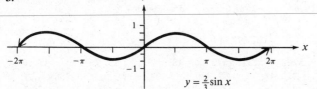

$y = \frac{2}{3}\sin x$

5.

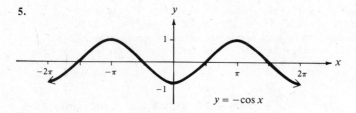

$y = -\cos x$

7.

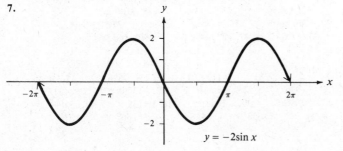

$y = -2\sin x$

9.

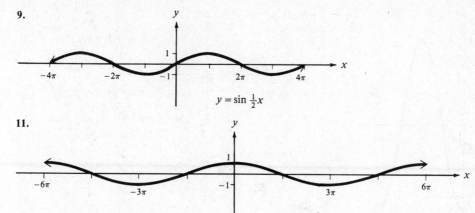

$$y = \sin \tfrac{1}{2}x$$

11.

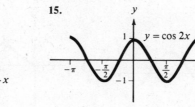

$$y = \cos \tfrac{1}{3}x$$

13.

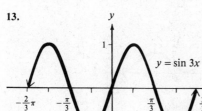

$$y = \sin 3x$$

15.

$$y = \cos 2x$$

17.

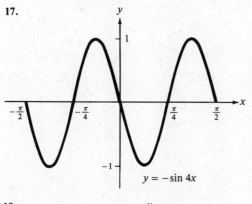

$$y = -\sin 4x$$

19.

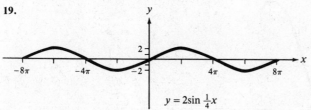

$$y = 2\sin \tfrac{1}{4}x$$

21.

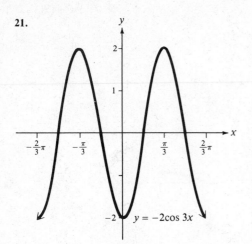

$y = -2\cos 3x$

23.

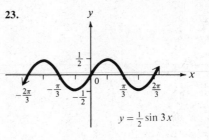

$y = \frac{1}{2}\sin 3x$

25.

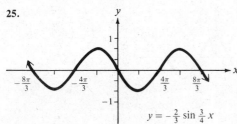

$y = -\frac{2}{3}\sin \frac{3}{4}x$

27.

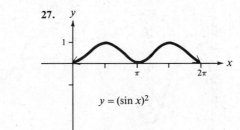

$y = (\sin x)^2$

29.

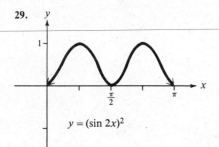

$y = (\sin 2x)^2$

31. 20   **33. (a)** 5; 1/60 **(b)** 60   **(c)** 5; 1.545; −4.045; −4.045; 1.545

(d)

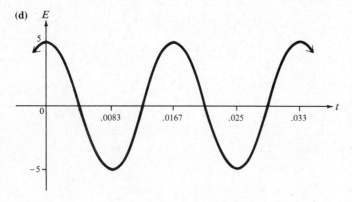

Section 4.2   (page 107)

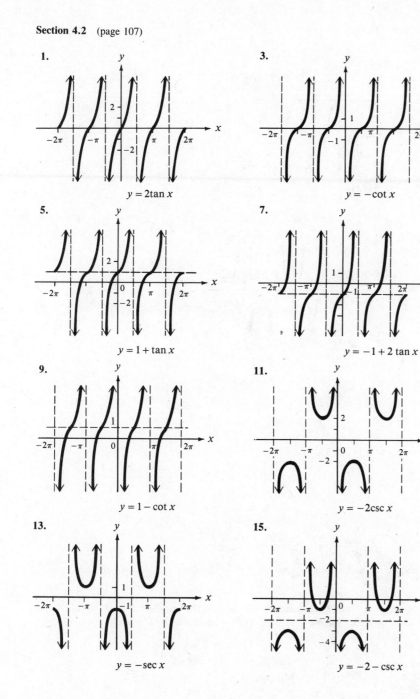

1.

$y = 2\tan x$

3.

$y = -\cot x$

5.

$y = 1 + \tan x$

7.

$y = -1 + 2\tan x$

9.

$y = 1 - \cot x$

11.

$y = -2\csc x$

13.

$y = -\sec x$

15.

$y = -2 - \csc x$

17. $\pi/2$

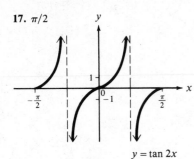

$$y = \tan 2x$$

19. $\pi/3$

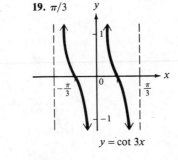

$$y = \cot 3x$$

21. $\pi/2$

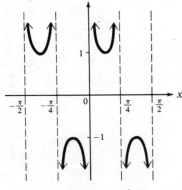

$$y = \csc 4x$$

23. 4π

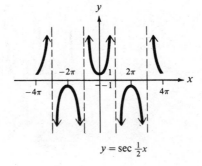

$$y = \sec \tfrac{1}{2}x$$

25. 4π

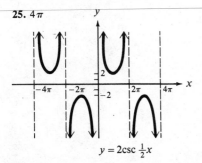

$$y = 2\csc \tfrac{1}{2}x$$

27. 0   **29.** -12.3 m   **31.** It leads to tan $\pi/2$, which does not exist.   **33.** 4 m   **35.** 63.7 m

Section 4.3   (page 112)

1. 2; 2π; none; none   **3.** 4; 4π; none; none   **5.** Not applicable; $\pi/2$; none; $\pi/2$ to the right   **7.** Not applicable; $\pi/3$; none; $\pi/12$ to the left   **9.** 1; $2\pi/3$; up 2; $\pi/15$ to the right   **11.** Not applicable; $\pi/4$; down 2; $\pi/4$ to the left

13.

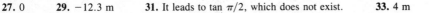

$$y = \cos\left(x - \tfrac{\pi}{2}\right)$$

15.

$$y = \sin\left(x - \tfrac{\pi}{4}\right)$$

17.

$$y = 2\cos\left(x - \tfrac{\pi}{3}\right)$$

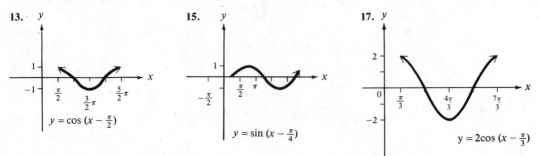

19.

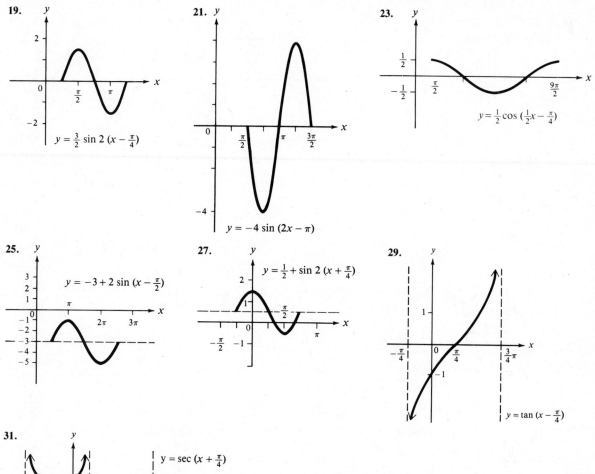

$y = \frac{3}{2} \sin 2 (x - \frac{\pi}{4})$

21.

$y = -4 \sin (2x - \pi)$

23.

$y = \frac{1}{2} \cos (\frac{1}{2}x - \frac{\pi}{4})$

25.

$y = -3 + 2 \sin (x - \frac{\pi}{2})$

27.

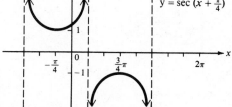

$y = \frac{1}{2} + \sin 2 (x + \frac{\pi}{4})$

29.

$y = \tan (x - \frac{\pi}{4})$

31.

$y = \sec (x + \frac{\pi}{4})$

Section 4.4   (page 114)

1.

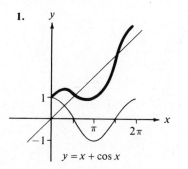

$y = x + \cos x$

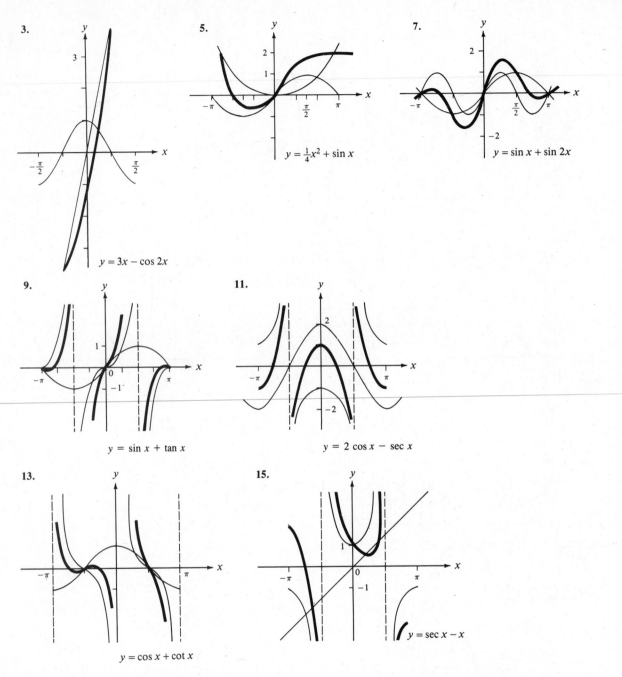

3.

$y = 3x - \cos 2x$

5.

$y = \frac{1}{4}x^2 + \sin x$

7.

$y = \sin x + \sin 2x$

9.

$y = \sin x + \tan x$

11.

$y = 2 \cos x - \sec x$

13.

$y = \cos x + \cot x$

15.

$y = \sec x - x$

17.

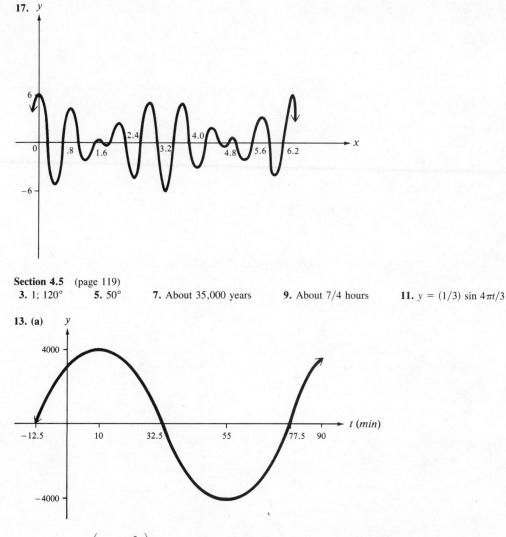

Section 4.5   (page 119)

3. 1; 120°   **5.** 50°   **7.** About 35,000 years   **9.** About 7/4 hours   **11.** $y = (1/3) \sin 4\pi t/3$

13. (a)

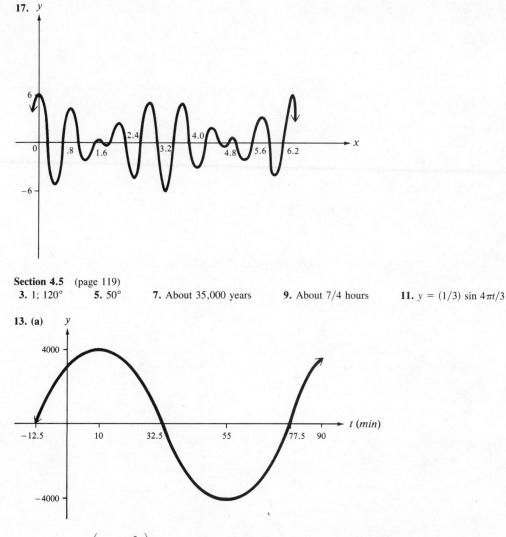

(b) $y = 4000 \sin \left(\dfrac{\pi}{45} t + \dfrac{5\pi}{18} \right)$ **(c) (i)** 2000 km north **(ii)** 2237 km south **(iii)** 1236 km south   **(d)** 3064 km north

Chapter 4   Test   (page 122)

In Exercises 1–6 we give, in order, the amplitude, period, and phase shift.   **1.** 2; 2π; none   **2.** None; $\pi/3$; none
3. 3; 2π; $\pi/2$ to the left   **4.** None; π; $\pi/8$ to the right   **5.** None; $2\pi/3$; $\pi/9$ to the right   **6.** None; 2π;
$3\pi/2$ to the left

7.

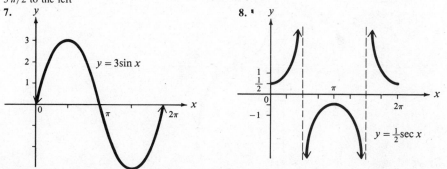

8.

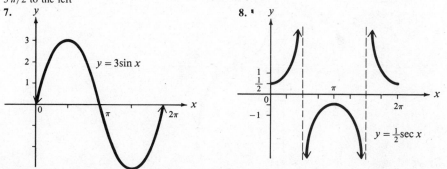

9.

$y = -\tan x$

10.

$y = -2\cos x$

11.

$y = \cot x + 2$

12.

$y = \csc x - 1$

13.

$y = \sin 2x$

14.

$y = \tan 3x$

15.

$y = 3\cos 2x$

16.

$y = \frac{1}{2}\cot 3x$

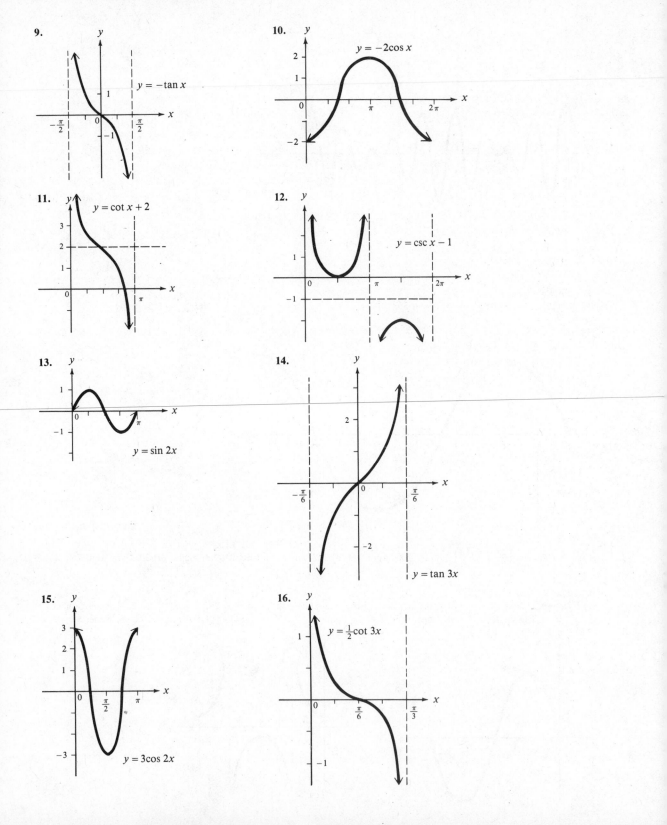

17.

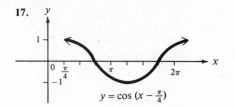

$$y = \cos\left(x - \frac{\pi}{4}\right)$$

18.

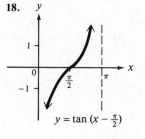

$$y = \tan\left(x - \frac{\pi}{2}\right)$$

19.

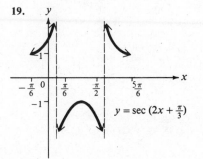

$$y = \sec\left(2x + \frac{\pi}{3}\right)$$

20.

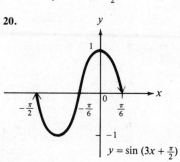

$$y = \sin\left(3x + \frac{\pi}{2}\right)$$

21.

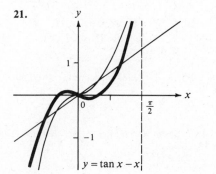

$$y = \tan x - x$$

22.

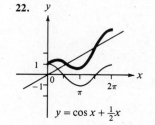

$$y = \cos x + \frac{1}{2}x$$

23.

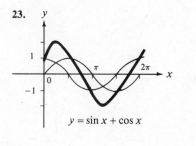

$$y = \sin x + \cos x$$

24.

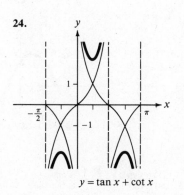

$$y = \tan x + \cot x$$

Chapter 5

Section 5.1 (page 129)

1. $\sqrt{7}/4$ **3.** $-2\sqrt{5}/5$ **5.** $\sqrt{21}/2$ **7.** $\cos\theta = -\sqrt{5}/3$; $\tan\theta = -2\sqrt{5}/5$; $\cot\theta = -\sqrt{5}/2$; $\sec\theta = -3\sqrt{5}/5$; $\csc\theta = 3/2$ **9.** $\sin\theta = -\sqrt{17}/17$; $\cos\theta = 4\sqrt{17}/17$; $\cot\theta = -4$; $\sec\theta = \sqrt{17}/4$; $\csc\theta = -\sqrt{17}$ **11.** $\sin\theta = 2\sqrt{2}/3$; $\cos\theta = -1/3$; $\tan\theta = -2\sqrt{2}$; $\cot\theta = -\sqrt{2}/4$; $\csc\theta = 3\sqrt{2}/4$

13. $\sin \theta = 3/5$; $\cos \theta = 4/5$; $\tan \theta = 3/4$; $\sec \theta = 5/4$; $\csc \theta = 5/3$ **15.** $\sin \theta = -\sqrt{7}/4$; $\cos \theta = 3/4$;
$\tan \theta = -\sqrt{7}/3$; $\cot \theta = -3\sqrt{7}/7$; $\csc \theta = -4\sqrt{7}/7$ **17.** (b)   **19.** (e)   **21.** (a)   **23.** (a)
25. (d)   **27.** 1   **29.** $-\sin \alpha$ **31.** 0   **33.** $(1 + \sin \theta)/\cos \theta$ **35.** 1   **37.** -1
39. $\sin^2 \theta/\cos^4 \theta$ **41.** 1   **43.** $(\cos^2 \alpha + 1)/(\sin^2 \alpha \cos^2 \alpha)$ **45.** $(\sin^2 s - \cos^2 s)/\sin^4 s$
47. $\cos x = \pm \sqrt{1 - \sin^2 x}$; $\tan x = \pm\sin x\sqrt{1 - \sin^2 x}/(1 - \sin^2 x)$; $\cot x = \pm \sqrt{1 - \sin^2 x}/\sin x$;
$\sec x = \pm \sqrt{1 - \sin^2 x}/(1 - \sin^2 x)$; $\csc x = 1/\sin x$ **49.** $\tan x = \pm \sqrt{\csc^2 x - 1}/(\csc^2 x - 1)$
51. $\cot s = \pm \sqrt{\sec^2 s - 1}/(\sec^2 s - 1)$ **53.** $\sin \theta = \sqrt{2x + 1}/(x + 1)$

Section 5.2 (page 133)
1. $1/(\sin \theta \cos \theta)$ **3.** $1 + \cos s$ **5.** 1   **7.** 1   **9.** $2 + 2 \sin t$ **11.** $(\sin \gamma + 1)(\sin \gamma - 1)$
13. $4 \sin x$ **15.** $(2 \sin x + 1)(\sin x + 1)$ **17.** $(4 \sec x - 1)(\sec x + 1)$ **19.** $(\cos^2 x + 1)^2$
21. $\sin \theta$ **23.** 1   **25.** $\tan^2 \beta$ **27.** $\tan^2 x$ **29.** $\sec^2 x$ **71.** Identity
73. Not an identity   **75.** Not an identity   **77.** Not an identity

Section 5.3 (page 140)
1. $\cot 3°$ **3.** $\sin 5\pi/12$ **5.** $\sec 104° 24'$ **7.** $\cos (-\pi/8)$ **9.** $\csc (-56° 42')$ **11.** $\tan$
13. $\cos$ **15.** $\csc$ **17.** True   **19.** False   **21.** True   **23.** $15°$ **25.** $140/3°$ **27.** $20°$
29. $(\sqrt{6} - \sqrt{2})/4$ **31.** $(\sqrt{2} - \sqrt{6})/4$ **33.** $(\sqrt{2} - \sqrt{6})/4$ **35.** 0   **37.** $\sqrt{2}/2$
39. $(\sqrt{2} \cos \theta)/2 + (\sqrt{2} \sin \theta)/2$ **41.** $(\sqrt{3} \cos \theta)/2 + (\sin \theta)/2$ **43.** $(\sqrt{2} \cos x)/2 - (\sqrt{2} \sin x)/2$
45. $(4 - 6\sqrt{6})/25$; $(4 + 6\sqrt{6})/25$ **47.** $16/65$; $-56/65$ **49.** $-77/85$; $-13/85$ **51.** $63/65$; $33/65$
53. $(\sqrt{105} - 4)/15$; $(\sqrt{105} + 4)/15$ **65.** $-.77917$ **67.** $.98209$

Section 5.4 (page 145)
1. $(\sqrt{6} - \sqrt{2})/4$ **3.** $2 - \sqrt{3}$ **5.** $(-\sqrt{6} - \sqrt{2})/4$ **7.** $(\sqrt{6} + \sqrt{2})/4$ **9.** $\sqrt{2}/2$ **11.** -1
13. 0   **15.** $\sqrt{2}/2$ **17.** $\sqrt{2}(\sin \theta + \cos \theta)/2$ **19.** $(\sqrt{3} \tan \theta + 1)/(\sqrt{3} - \tan \theta)$ **21.** $\sin \theta$
23. $\tan \theta$ **25.** $-\sin \theta$ **27.** $63/65$; $33/65$; $63/16$; $33/56$ **29.** $(4\sqrt{2} + \sqrt{5})/9$;
$(4\sqrt{2} - \sqrt{5})/9$; $(-8\sqrt{5} - 5\sqrt{2})/(20 - 2\sqrt{10})$; $(-8\sqrt{5} + 5\sqrt{2})/(20 + 2\sqrt{10})$
31. $77/85$; $13/85$; $-77/36$; $13/84$ **33.** $-33/65$; $-63/65$; $33/56$; $63/16$ **35.** 1; $-161/289$; undefined; $-161/240$
49. $.357072$ **51.** $.382273$ **53.** -2.09121

Section 5.5 (page 149)
1. $\sqrt{2} \sin (x + 135°)$ **3.** $13 \sin (\theta + 293°)$ **5.** $17 \sin (x + 152°)$ **7.** $25 \sin (\theta + 254°)$
9. $5 \sin (x + 53°)$ **11.** $-\sin \theta + \sqrt{3} \cos \theta$ **13.** $\sin \theta - \cos \theta$ **15.** $\cos \theta$
17. $2 \sin (x + 30°)$ **19.** $\sqrt{2} \sin (x + 135°)$

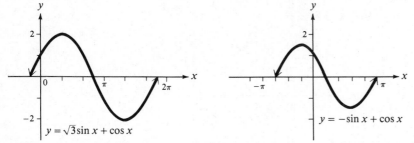

Section 5.6 (page 152)
1. $2\pi/5$ **3.** $\cos 2x$ **5.** $160°$; $160°$ **7.** $4k$; $\tan^2 4k$ **9.** $\cos^2$; $\sin^2$ **11.** $\cos \theta = 2\sqrt{5}/5$;
$\sin \theta = \sqrt{5}/5$; $\tan \theta = 1/2$; $\sec \theta = \sqrt{5}/2$; $\csc \theta = \sqrt{5}$; $\cot \theta = 2$ **13.** $\cos x = -\sqrt{42}/12$; $\sin x = \sqrt{102}/12$;
$\tan x = -\sqrt{119}/7$; $\sec x = -2\sqrt{42}/7$; $\csc x = 2\sqrt{102}/17$; $\cot x = -\sqrt{119}/17$ **15.** $\cos 2\theta = 17/25$; $\sin 2\theta = $
$-4\sqrt{21}/25$; $\tan 2\theta = -4\sqrt{21}/17$; $\sec 2\theta = 25/17$; $\csc 2\theta = -25\sqrt{21}/84$; $\cot 2\theta = -17\sqrt{21}/84$

17. $\tan 2x = -4/3$; $\sec 2x = -5/3$; $\cos 2x = -3/5$; $\cot 2x = -3/4$; $\sin 2x = 4/5$; $\csc 2x = 5/4$
19. $4\tan^2 x/(1 - 2\tan^2 x + \tan^4 x)$ **21.** $\cos 3x = 4\cos^3 x - 3\cos x$
23. $\cos 4x = 8\cos^4 x - 8\cos^2 x + 1$ **43.** $-.843580$ **45.** -1.57091

Section 5.7 (page 155)
1. $9°$ **3.** $194°$ **5.** $\tan 170°$ **7.** $-$ **9.** $+$ **11.** $\sin 22\,1/2° = (\sqrt{2 - \sqrt{2}})/2$;
$\cos 22\,1/2° = (\sqrt{2 + \sqrt{2}})/2$; $\tan 22\,1/2° = \sqrt{3 - 2\sqrt{2}}$ or $\sqrt{2} - 1$ **13.** $\sin 195° = -(\sqrt{2 - \sqrt{3}})/2$;
$\cos 195° = -(\sqrt{2 + \sqrt{3}})/2$; $\tan 195° = \sqrt{7 - 4\sqrt{3}}$ or $2 - \sqrt{3}$ **15.** $\sin(-\pi/8) = -(\sqrt{2 - \sqrt{2}})/2$;
$\cos(-\pi/8) = (\sqrt{2 + \sqrt{2}})/2$; $\tan(-\pi/8) = -\sqrt{3 - 2\sqrt{2}}$ or $1 - \sqrt{2}$ **17.** $\sin 5\pi/2 = 1$;
$\cos 5\pi/2 = 0$; $\tan 5\pi/2$ does not exist   **19.** $\sin\theta = \sqrt{5}/5$ **21.** $\cos x = -\sqrt{42}/12$ **37.** $84°$ **39.** $60°$
41. 3.9 **43.** $.892230$ **45.** -1.97579 **47.** $\sqrt{2}/(2 + \sqrt{2})$ or $\sqrt{2} - 1$

Section 5.8 (page 160)
1. $(1/2)(\sin 70° - \sin 20°)$ **3.** $(3/2)(\cos 8x + \cos 2x)$ **5.** $(1/2)[\cos 2\theta - \cos(-4\theta)] =$
$(1/2)(\cos 2\theta - \cos 4\theta)$ **7.** $-4[\cos 9y + \cos(-y)] = -4(\cos 9y + \cos y)$ **9.** $2\cos 45° \sin 15°$
11. $2\cos 95° \cos(-53°) = 2\cos 95° \cos 53°$ **13.** $2\cos(15\beta/2) \sin(9\beta/2)$ **15.** $-6\cos(7x/2)\sin(-3x/2) =$
$6\cos(7x/2)\sin(3x/2)$

Chapter 5 Test   (page 161)

1. $\sin x = -4/5$; $\tan x = -4/3$; $\sec x = 5/3$; $\csc x = -5/4$; $\cot x = -3/4$ **2.** $\sec x = -\sqrt{41}/4$;
$\cos x = -4\sqrt{41}/41$; $\cot x = -4/5$; $\sin x = 5\sqrt{41}/41$; $\csc x = \sqrt{41}/5$ **3.** $\sin(x + y) = (4 + 3\sqrt{15})/20$;
$\cos(x - y) = (4\sqrt{15} + 3)/20$ **4.** $\tan\theta = \sqrt{3}$ **5.** $\sin x = (\sqrt{2 - \sqrt{2}})/2$; $\cos x = (\sqrt{2 + \sqrt{2}})/2$;
$\tan x = \sqrt{3 - 2\sqrt{2}}$ or $\sqrt{2} - 1$ **6.** (b)   **7.** (j)   **8.** (a)   **9.** (i)   **10.** (c)   **11.** (h)
12. (d)   **13.** (g)   **14.** (b)   **15.** (a)   **16.** (c)   **17.** (f)   **18.** (h)   **19.** (e)   **20.** (d)
21. 1 **22.** $\cos^2\theta/\sin\theta$ **23.** $1/\cos^2\theta$ or $\sec^2\theta$ **24.** $(1 + \cos\theta)/\sin\theta$
25. $1/(\sin^2\theta \cos^2\theta)$ **26.** $-\cos\theta/\sin\theta$

Chapter 6

Section 6.1   (page 166)
1. Yes   **3.** No   **5.** Yes   **7.** No   **9.** Yes

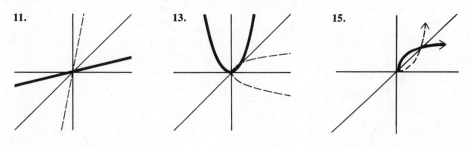

17.

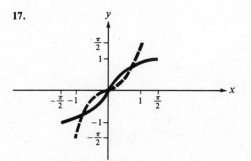

19.

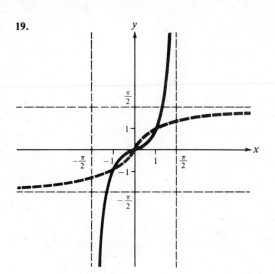

21. $y = x/2$ **23.** $y = (2x + 1)/3$
25. Not one-to-one   **27.** $y = (x + 1)^3$
29. Yes   **31.** No   **33.** Yes

Section 6.2 (page 172)
1. $-\pi/3$ **3.** $\pi/4$ **5.** $-\pi/2$ **7.** $\pi/3$ **9.** $5\pi/4$ **11.** $5\pi/6$ **13.** $-7° 40'$
15. $113° 30'$ **17.** $31° 00'$ **19.** .8378 from table; .8379 from calculator   **21.** 2.3155 radians
23. 1.1897 from table; 1.1898 from calculator   **25.** $\sqrt{5}/2$ **27.** $\sqrt{5}/5$ **29.** $-\sqrt{21}/2$ **31.** $\sqrt{34}/3$
33. 120/169   **35.** $-7/25$ **37.** 63/65   **39.** .957826   **41.** .123430   **43.** $\sqrt{1 - x^2}$
45. $(\sqrt{x^2 + 1})/x$ **47.** $\pm(\sqrt{1 - x^2})/x$ **49.** Real numbers, $0 < y < \pi$

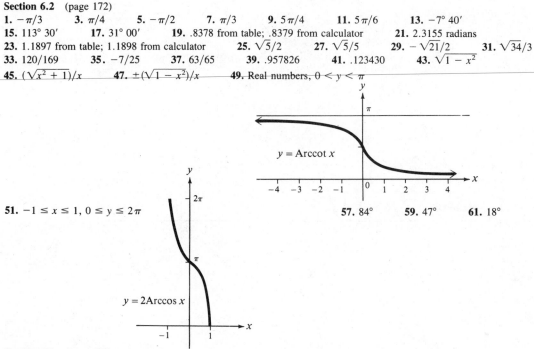

$y = \text{Arccot } x$

$y = 2\text{Arccos } x$

51. $-1 \le x \le 1, 0 \le y \le 2\pi$

57. $84°$ **59.** $47°$ **61.** $18°$

Section 6.3 (page 178)
1. $3\pi/4, 7\pi/4$ **3.** $\pi/6, 5\pi/6$ **5.** $\pi/4, 3\pi/4, 5\pi/4, 7\pi/4$ **7.** $\pi/6, 7\pi/6, 4\pi/3, 5\pi/3$
9. $\pi/3, 5\pi/3, \pi/6, 11\pi/6$ **11.** π **13.** $3\pi/2, 7\pi/6, 11\pi/6$ **15.** $\pi/4, 3\pi/4, 5\pi/4, 7\pi/4$
17. $71° 30', 251° 30', 63° 30', 243° 30'$ **19.** $45°, 135°, 225°, 315°$ **21.** $0°, 180°$ **23.** $90°, 270°, 60°,$
$120°, 240°, 300°$ **25.** $90°, 270°$ **27.** $33° 30', 326° 30'$ **29.** $0°, 90°, 180°, 270°$ **31.** $30°,$
$150°, 210°, 330°$ **33.** $0°, 90°$ **35.** $53° 40', 126° 20', 188° 00', 352° 00'$ **37.** $149° 40', 329° 40',$
$106° 20', 286° 20'$ **39.** No solution   **41.** $57° 40', 159° 10'$ **43.** 1/4 second   **45.** 2 seconds

Section 6.4 (page 181)
1. $0, \pi/2, \pi, 3\pi/2$ **3.** $\pi/4, 3\pi/4, 5\pi/4, 7\pi/4$ **5.** $\pi/12, 7\pi/12, 13\pi/12, 19\pi/12$ **7.** $3\pi/8, 5\pi/8, 11\pi/8,$ $13\pi/8$ **9.** $\pi/2, 3\pi/2$ **11.** $0, \pi/2, \pi, 3\pi/2$ **13.** $\pi/8, 3\pi/8, 5\pi/8, 7\pi/8, 9\pi/8, 11\pi/8, 13\pi/8, 15\pi/8$
15. $\pi/2$ **17.** $\pi/3, 5\pi/3, \pi$ **19.** $30°, 60°, 210°, 240°$ **21.** $0°$ **23.** $120°, 240°$ **25.** $270°,$
$30°, 150°$ **27.** $0°, 180°, 30°, 150°$ **29.** $60°, 300°$ **31.** $11° \, 50', 78° \, 10', 191° \, 50', 258° \, 10'$
33. $90°, 270°, 30°, 150°, 210°, 330°$ **35.** $\pi/12, \pi/2, 5\pi/12, 3\pi/2, 13\pi/12, 17\pi/12$ **37.** $0, \pi/4, 3\pi/4,$
$\pi, 5\pi/4, 7\pi/4$ **39.** $\pi/6, \pi/2, 3\pi/2, 5\pi/6$ **41. (a)** 1000 km, 100 km **(b)** 39 min., 61 min., 139 min.
(c) About 60 **43.** .001 **45.** .004

Section 6.5 (page 186)
1. $x = \arcsin y/4$ **3.** $x = (1/2) \arctan 2y$ **5.** $x = (1/2) \text{arccot } y/5$ **7.** $x = 4 \arccos y/6$
9. $x = (1/5) \arccos (-y/2)$ **11.** $x = (\arcsin y) - 2$ **13.** $x = \arccos(y + 3)$ **15.** $x =$
$\arcsin[(y + 4)/2]$ **17.** $2\sqrt{2}$ **19.** $\pi - 3$ **21.** $3/5$ **23.** $4/5$ **25.** 0 **27.** $1/2$
29. $-1/2$ **31.** 0 **33.** $t = (50/\pi)[\arccos(d - 550/450]$ **35. (a)** $t = [1/(2\pi f)][\arcsin e/E_{\max}]$
(b) .0007 **37. (a)** $x = \text{Sin } u, -\pi/2 \le u \le \pi/2$ **(b)**
(c) $\tan u = x/\sqrt{1 - x^2}$ **(d)** $u = \text{Arctan } (x/\sqrt{1 - x^2})$

Chapter 6 Test (page 188)
1. $y = (6 - 3x)/2$ **2.** $y = (30 + 7x)/5$ **3.** Not one-to-one **4.** $y = \sqrt[3]{x} - 5$ **5.** $\pi/4$ **6.** $\pi/4$
7. $2\pi/3$ **8.** $5\pi/6$ **9.** .5061 from table; .5062 from calculator **10.** 1.8850 from table; 1.8849
from calculator **11.** $-3/4$ **12.** $12/13$ **13.** $(\sqrt{10} + 2\sqrt{2})/6$ **14.** $(\sqrt{15} - 2)/6$ **15.** $60°, 300°$
16. $135°, 315°$ **17.** $270°$ **18.** $0°, 45°, 180°, 225°$ **19.** $90°, 270°, 45°, 225°$ **20.** $15°, 75°,$
$195°, 255°$ **21.** $x = \arccos[(3y - 1)/2]$ **22.** $x = (\arctan 2y) - 3$ **23.** 1 **24.** $\sqrt{3}/2$

Chapter 7

Section 7.1 (page 193)
1. $B = 62°, C = 90°, a = 8.17$ ft, $b = 15.4$ ft **3.** $A = 17°, C = 90°, a = 39.1$ in, $c = 134$ in **5.** $B = 41° \, 40',$
$C = 90°, a = 88.7$ mi, $c = 119$ mi **7.** $c = 85.9$ yd, $A = 62° \, 50', B = 27° \, 10', C = 90°$ **9.** $b = 42.3$ cm,
$A = 24° \, 10', B = 65° \, 50', C = 90°$ **11.** $B = 36° \, 36', C = 90°, a = 310.8$ ft, $b = 230.8$ ft **13.** $A = 50° \, 51',$
$C = 90°, a = .4832$ m, $b = .3934$ m **15.** 26.6 m **17.** $52° \, 30'$ **19.** 11.1 feet **21.** $35° \, 50'$
23. 40,600 ft **25.** 1590 ft **27.** 446 ft **29.** 114 ft **31.** 5.18 m **33.** 156 mi **35.** $54° \, 40'$
37. 1.91661×10^{13} mi

Section 7.2 (page 200)
1. $C = 83°, a = 11$ m, $b = 10$ m **3.** $C = 80° \, 40', a = 79.5$ mm, $c = 108$ mm **5.** $B = 37° \, 20', a = 38.4$ ft,
$b = 51.1$ ft **7.** $C = 57.36°, b = 11.13$ ft, $c = 11.55$ ft **9.** $B = 18° \, 30', a = 239$ yd, $c = 230$ yd
11. $A = 56° \, 00', c = 361$ ft, $a = 308$ ft **13.** $B = 109° \, 57', a = 27.01$ m, $c = 21.36$ m **15.** $A = 34° \, 43',$
$a = 3326$ ft, $c = 5704$ ft **17.** $C = 97° \, 34', b = 283.2$ m, $c = 415.2$ m **19.** 118 m **21.** 1.93 mi
23. 927 ft **25.** $111°$ **27.** 41.0 ft^2 **29.** 356 cm^2 **31.** 722.9 in^2 **33.** 1071 cm^2 **35.** 100

Section 7.3 (page 207)
1.
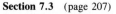
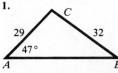
one possible triangle

3.
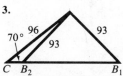
two possible triangles

5.
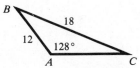
one possible triangle

7. $A_1 = 43°\,40'$, $C_1 = 106°\,40'$, $A_2 = 136°\,20'$, $C_2 = 14°\,00'$ **9.** $B = 26°\,30'$, $A = 112°\,10'$ **11.** No such triangle
13. $B = 27.19°$, $C = 10.68°$ **15.** $A = 43°\,50'$, $B = 6°\,52'$ **17.** $B = 20°\,40'$, $C = 116°\,50'$, $c = 20.6$ ft
19. No such triangle   **21.** $B_1 = 49°\,20'$, $C_1 = 92°\,00'$, $c_1 = 15.5$ km, $B_2 = 130°\,40'$, $C_2 = 10°\,40'$,
$c_2 = 2.88$ km   **23.** $A_1 = 52°\,10'$, $C_1 = 95°\,00'$, $c_1 = 9520$ cm, $A_2 = 127°\,50'$, $C_2 = 19°\,20'$, $c_2 = 3160$ cm
25. $B = 37.8°$, $C = 45.4°$, $c = 4.17$ ft   **27.** $A_1 = 53°\,14'$, $C_1 = 87°\,05'$, $c_1 = 37.16$ m, $A_2 = 126°\,46'$,
$C_2 = 13°\,33'$, $c_2 = 8.718$ m   **29.** Does not exist

Section 7.4 (page 212)
1. $a = 4.38$ in, $B = 80°\,10'$, $C = 60°\,00'$ **3.** $c = 6.47$ m, $A = 53°\,00'$, $B = 81°\,20'$ **5.** $a = 156$ cm,
$B = 64°\,50'$, $C = 34°\,30'$ **7.** $b = 9.529$ in, $A = 64.6°$, $C = 40.6°$ **9.** $a = 15.7$ m, $B = 21°\,30'$, $C = 45°\,40'$
11. $c = 139.0$ m, $A = 49°\,20'$, $B = 105°\,51'$ **13.** $A = 29°\,00'$, $B = 46°\,30'$, $C = 104°\,30'$ **15.** $A = 81°\,50'$,
$B = 37°\,20'$, $C = 60°\,50'$ **17.** $A = 42°\,00'$, $B = 35°\,50'$, $C = 102°\,10'$ **19.** $A = 47°\,40'$, $B = 44°\,50'$,
$C = 87°\,20'$ **21.** $A = 47°\,43'$, $B = 72°\,13'$, $C = 60°\,04'$ **23.** $A = 28°\,10'$, $B = 21°\,56'$, $C = 129°\,54'$
25. 257 m   **27.** 281 km   **29.** $14°\,30'$ **31.** 18 ft   **33.** 25.24983 mi   **35.** 140 in^2
37. 12,600 cm^2 **39.** 3650 ft^2 **41.** 1921 ft^2 **43.** 33 cans

Section 7.5 (page 218)
1. m and p, n and r **3.** m and p equal $2t$; or t is one-half m or p; also $m = 1p$ and $n = 1r$, $m = p = -q$; $r = -s$

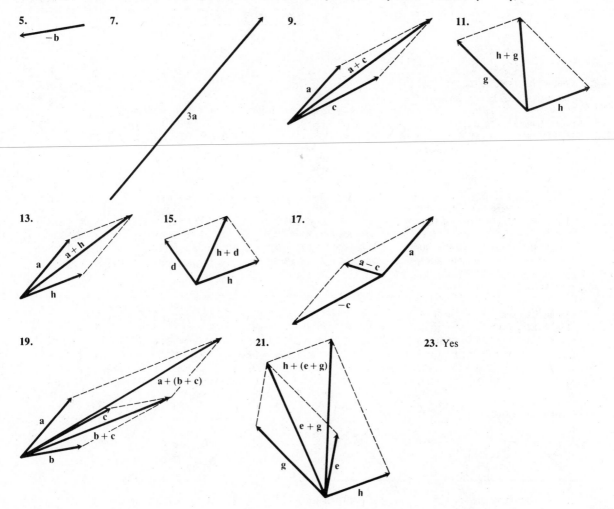

23. Yes

25.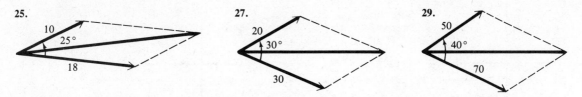

27.

29.

31. 14, 14   **33.** 14.2, 24.8   **35.** 13.7, 7.11   **37.** 123,155   **39.** 22.3, 65.4   **41.** 560
43. 27.2 lb   **45.** 88.2 lb   **47. (a) i)** 507,713 lbs; 88,163 lbs   **ii)** 532,089 lbs; 181,985 lbs   **iii)** 577,350 lbs;
388,675 lbs   **iv)** 500,000 lbs; 0 lbs   **(d)** 34° 33′

Section 7.6   (page 224)
  1. 94° 00′   **3.** 17   **5.** 18°   **7.** Magnitude 2.86, equilibrant makes an angle of 124.6° with the 4.72 lb force
9. Weight 64.8 lb, tension 61.9 lb   **11.** 190, 283 pounds respectively   **13.** 173°   **15.** 39.2
17. 237°, 470 mph   **19.** 358° 00′, 169 mph   **21.** 232 mph, 167°   **23. (a)** 280° and 36°   **(b)** Impossible
25. (a) 86 kph   **(b)** 89 kph

Chapter 7   Test   (page 227)
  1. $B = 42° 40′$, $c = 58.4$ cm   **2.** $A = 55° 20′$, $a = 14,200$ yd   **3.** $B = 74° 31′$ **4.** 63.7 m
5. $B = 25° 00′$ **6.** $B = 41° 40′$ **7.** $A = 19° 52′$ **8.** $B_1 = 74.6°$, $C_1 = 43.7°$, $c_1 = 61.9$ m,
$B_2 = 105.4°$, $C_2 = 12.9°$, $c_2 = 20.0$ m   **9.** .234 km^2 **10.** 153,600 m^2 **11.** 1300 ft
12. 13 m   **13.** 113 km   **14.** About 2.5 cans—better buy 3

15.

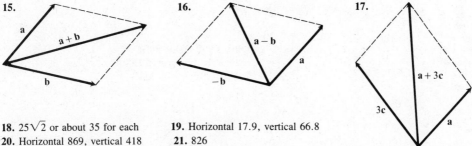

16.

17.

18. $25\sqrt{2}$ or about 35 for each   **19.** Horizontal 17.9, vertical 66.8
20. Horizontal 869, vertical 418   **21.** 826
22. 3° 50′   **23.** 105 lb   **24.** 7° 20′ at 8.3 mph

Chapter 8

Section 8.1   (page 232)
  1. $3i$ **3.** $8i$ **5.** $2i/3$ **7.** $3i\sqrt{2}$ **9.** $5i\sqrt{6}$ **11.** $3i\sqrt{3}$ **13.** $4i\sqrt{5}$ **15.** -1
17. 1   **19.** i **21.** $7 - i$ **23.** $3 - 6i$ **25.** $2 + i$ **27.** $8 - i$ **29.** $-14 + 2i$
31. $31 - 5i$ **33.** $3 + 4i$ **35.** 5   **37.** $25i$ **39.** $24 - 7i$ **41.** i **43.** $7/25 - 24i/25$
45. $13/20 - i/20$ **47.** $32/37 - 7i/37$ **49.** $-1 - 2i$ **51.** 4, 2   **53.** 2, -3 **55.** 1/2, 15
57. 14, 8   **59.** 10, -2 **61.** $E = 30 + 60i$ **63.** $Z = 233/37 + 119i/37$

Section 8.2   (page 236)

1.

3.

5.

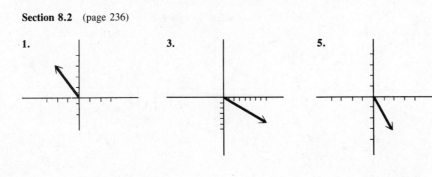

7.

9.

11. $1 + i$ **13.** $-2 + 2i$ **15.** $-2 + 4i$ **17.** $2 + 4i$ **19.** $7 + 9i$ **21.** $(2\sqrt{2}, 315°)$
23. $(3, 90°)$ **25.** $(5, 0°)$ **27.** $(2, 30°)$ **29.** $(2, 60°)$ **31.** $\sqrt{2} + i\sqrt{2}$ **33.** $-\sqrt{2}/2 + i\sqrt{2}/2$
35. $3i$ **37.** $-2 - 2i\sqrt{3}$ **39.** $\sqrt{3}/2 - i/2$ **41.** $\sqrt{2} + i\sqrt{2}$ **43.** $10i$ **45.** $-2 - 2i\sqrt{3}$
47. $\sqrt{3}/2 + i/2$ **49.** $5/2 - 5i\sqrt{3}/2$ **51.** $3\sqrt{2}(\cos 315° + i \sin 315°)$ **53.** $6(\cos 240° + i \sin 240°)$
55. $2(\cos 330° + i \sin 330°)$ **57.** $5\sqrt{2}(\cos 225° + i \sin 225°)$ **59.** $(\sqrt{13}, 56° 20')$, $\sqrt{13}(\cos 56° 20' + i \sin 56° 20')$
61. $-1.0179 - 2.8221i$; $(3, 250° 10')$ **63.** $-1.8794 + .6840i$; $2(\cos 160° + i \sin 160°)$
65. (a) Earth: $107 + 54.5i$, Sun: $-39.4 + 30.8i$, Moon: $-9.08 - 17.8i$ **(b)** $58.5 + 67.5i$ or $(89.3, 49°)$

Section 8.3   (page 241)
1. $6i$ **3.** 4 **5.** $12\sqrt{3} + 12i$ **7.** $-15\sqrt{2}/2 + 15i\sqrt{2}/2$ **9.** $-3i$ **11.** -8 **13.** 1
15. $27/2 - 27i\sqrt{3}/2$ **17.** $-16\sqrt{3} + 16i$ **19.** $-128 + 128i\sqrt{3}$ **21.** $128 + 128i$ **23.** $3\sqrt{3}/2 + 3i/2$
25. $-1 - i\sqrt{3}$ **27.** $-1/6 - i\sqrt{3}/6$ **29.** $2\sqrt{3} - 2i$ **31.** $-1/2 - i/2$ **33.** $\sqrt{3} + i$
35. $2.39 + 15.0i$ **37.** $.378 + 3.52i$ **39.** $5520 + 9550i$

Section 8.4   (page 245)
1. $(\cos 120° + i \sin 120°)$,
   $(\cos 240° + i \sin 240°)$,
   $(\cos 0° + i \sin 0°)$

3. $2(\cos 90° + i \sin 90°)$,
   $2(\cos 210° + i \sin 210°)$,
   $2(\cos 330° + i \sin 330°)$

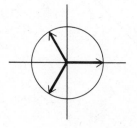

5. $4(\cos 60° + i \sin 60°)$,
   $4(\cos 180° + i \sin 180°)$,
   $4(\cos 300° + i \sin 300°)$

7. $\sqrt[3]{2}(\cos 20° + i \sin 20°)$,
   $\sqrt[3]{2}(\cos 140° + i \sin 140°)$,
   $\sqrt[3]{2}(\cos 260° + i \sin 260°)$

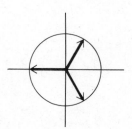

9. $\sqrt[3]{4}(\cos 50° + i \sin 50°)$, $\sqrt[3]{4}(\cos 170° + i \sin 170°)$, $\sqrt[3]{4}(\cos 290° + i \sin 290°)$

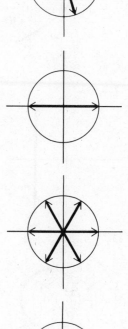

11. $(\cos 0° + i \sin 0°)$, $(\cos 180° + i \sin 180°)$

13. $(\cos 0° + i \sin 0°)$, $(\cos 60° + i \sin 60°)$, $(\cos 120° + i \sin 120°)$,
$(\cos 180° + i \sin 180°)$, $(\cos 240° + i \sin 240°)$, $(\cos 300° + i \sin 300°)$

15. $(\cos 45° + i \sin 45°)$, $(\cos 225° + i \sin 225°)$

17. $(\cos 0° + i \sin 0°)$, $(\cos 120° + i \sin 120°)$, $(\cos 240° + i \sin 240°)$ **19.** $(\cos 90° + i \sin 90°)$,
$(\cos 210° + i \sin 210°)$, $(\cos 330° + i \sin 330°)$ **21.** $2(\cos 0° + i \sin 0°)$, $2(\cos 120° + i \sin 120°)$,
$2(\cos 240° + i \sin 240°)$ **23.** $(\cos 45° + i \sin 45°)$, $(\cos 135° + i \sin 135°)$, $(\cos 225° + .i \sin 225°)$,
$(\cos 315° + i \sin 315°)$ **25.** $(\cos 22\,1/2° + i \sin 22\,1/2°)$, $(\cos 112\,1/2° + i \sin 112\,1/2°)$,
$(\cos 202\,1/2° + i \sin 202\,1/2°)$, $(\cos 292\,1/2° + i \sin 292\,1/2°)$ **27.** $2(\cos 20° + i \sin 20°)$, $2(\cos 140° + i \sin 140°)$,
$2(\cos 260° + i \sin 260°)$ **29.** $1.3606 + 1.2637i$; $-1.7747 + .5464i$; $.4141 - 1.8102i$
31. $1.6309 - 2.5259i$, $-1.6309 + 2.5259i$

Section 8.5   (page 250)

1. $x^2 + y^2 - 2y = 0$ or $x^2 + (y - 1)^2 = 1$

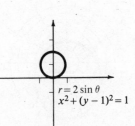

$r = 2 \sin \theta$
$x^2 + (y - 1)^2 = 1$

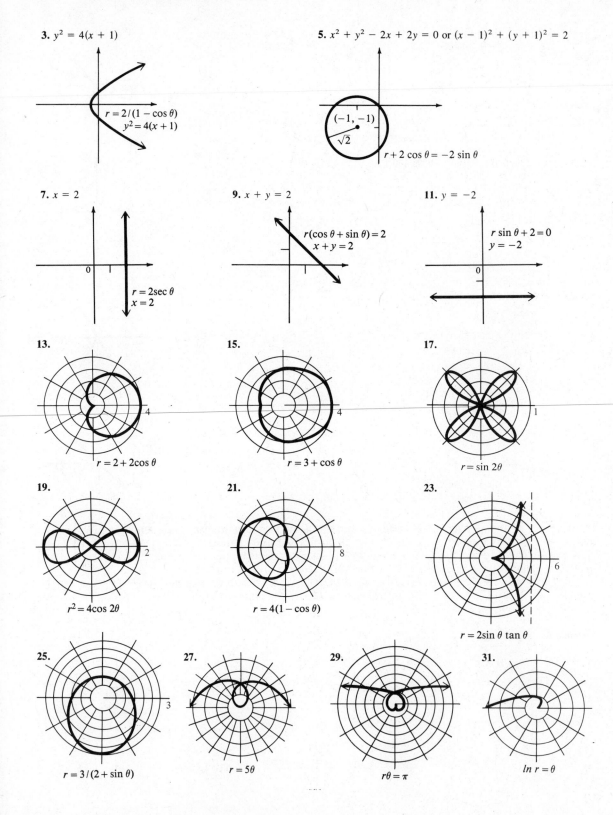

3. $y^2 = 4(x + 1)$

$r = 2/(1 - \cos \theta)$
$y^2 = 4(x + 1)$

5. $x^2 + y^2 - 2x + 2y = 0$ or $(x - 1)^2 + (y + 1)^2 = 2$

$(-1, -1)$
$\sqrt{2}$
$r + 2 \cos \theta = -2 \sin \theta$

7. $x = 2$

$r = 2\sec \theta$
$x = 2$

9. $x + y = 2$

$r(\cos \theta + \sin \theta) = 2$
$x + y = 2$

11. $y = -2$

$r \sin \theta + 2 = 0$
$y = -2$

13. $r = 2 + 2\cos \theta$

15. $r = 3 + \cos \theta$

17. $r = \sin 2\theta$

19. $r^2 = 4\cos 2\theta$

21. $r = 4(1 - \cos \theta)$

23. $r = 2\sin \theta \tan \theta$

25. $r = 3/(2 + \sin \theta)$

27. $r = 5\theta$

29. $r\theta = \pi$

31. $\ln r = \theta$

Chapter 8 Test   (page 251)
1. $3i$ **2.** $2i\sqrt{3}$ **3.** $2i\sqrt{5}/5$ **4.** i **5.** $x = -7/3$, $y = -9/2$ **6.** $5 + 4i$

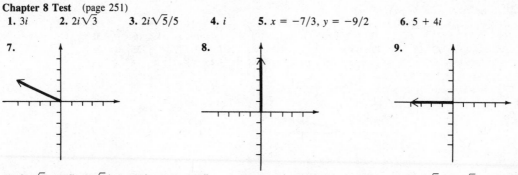

7.   **8.**   **9.**

10. $(2\sqrt{2}, 135°)$, $2\sqrt{2}(\cos 135° + i \sin 135°)$ **11.** $3i$, $3(\cos 90° + i \sin 90°)$ **12.** $\sqrt{2} - i\sqrt{2}$, $(2, 315°)$
13. $10 - 2i$ **14.** $-4 - i$ **15.** $7 - 24i$ **16.** 5 **17.** $-11 - 7i$ **18.** $-10 + 28i$ **19.** $1/5 - 3i/5$
20. $-3 - 3i\sqrt{3}$ **21.** $-8 - 8i\sqrt{3}$ **22.** -2 **23.** $-128 + 128i$ **24.** $\sqrt[6]{2}(\cos 105° + i \sin 105°)$,
$\sqrt[6]{2}(\cos 225° + i \sin 225°)$, $\sqrt[6]{2}(\cos 345° + i \sin 345°)$ **25.** $4x^2 + 3y^2 - 2y - 1 = 0$

26.

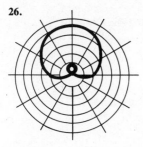

Chapter 9

Section 9.1   (page 256)
1. 3^{11} **3.** 7 **5.** 6^3 **7.** 8^{18} **9.** 2^8 **11.** $1/2^3$ **13.** 3 **15.** $1/9^2$ **17.** 5
19. 8 **21.** 3 **23.** $5/3$ **25.** -2 **27.** -2 **29.** -3 **31.** $1/4$

33.   **35.**   **37.**

$y = 3^x$ $y = (\tfrac{1}{3})^x$ $y = 2^{x+1}$

39.   **41.**

$y = 2^{-x}$ $y = 3^x - 3$

43. $1{,}000{,}000$ **45.** $4{,}000{,}000$ **47.** 289 g   **49.** \$1191.02   **51.** \$1196.68

Section 9.2 (page 260)

1. $\log_3 243 = 5$ **3.** $\log_{10} 10000 = 4$ **5.** $\log_6 1/36 = -2$ **7.** $\log_{2/3} 9/4 = -2$ **9.** $4^2 = 16$
11. $10^3 = 1000$ **13.** $7^1 = 7$ **15.** $(3/4)^2 = 9/16$ **17.** $4^{-2} = 1/16$ **19.** 16   **21.** 3
23. 3   **25.** 9/4   **27.** 16   **29.** 5/4   **31.** $\log_6 45$ **33.** $\log_5 12/7$ **35.** $\log_2 28/5$
37. $\log_3 16$ **39.** $\log_8 \sqrt{7}$ **41.** $\log_2 81/25$ **43.** 1.1461   **45.** 1.4471   **47.** 2.4080
49. 3.1242   **51.** 0.3471   **53.**

$y = \log_4 x$

Section 9.3 (page 265)

1. 0.4456   **3.** 4.9926   **5.** 5.8745   **7.** .7716 − 3   **9.** 722   **11.** 2330   **13.** .114
15. .00571   **17.** .6899   **19.** 4.5797   **21.** −1.5357 or 8.4643 − 10   **23.** 2.743   **25.** 2635
27. .005082   **29.** .0000187   **31.** 9.58   **33.** 70.8   **35.** .0104   **37.** .0000219 or 2.19×10^{-5}
39. 96,810   **41.** .1749   **43.** 1.969   **45.** 3.2   **47.** 1.8   **49.** 2.0×10^{-3} **51.** 1.6×10^{-5}
53. 1.1509 db

Section 9.4 (page 268)

1. 3   **3.** 1/5   **5.** 3/2   **7.** 4/3   **9.** 8   **11.** 3   **13.** .477   **15.** −.824   **17.** 1.29
19. 1.26   **21.** 1.78   **23.** −1.43   **25.** 2.99   **27.** 16   **29.** 5   **31.** $\sqrt[3]{10}$ or 2.15
33. 1/100 or .01   **35.** About 15 seconds   **37.** 46 days

Section 9.5 (page 271)

1. 1.441   **3.** .2789   **5.** 1.585   **7.** 3.332   **9.** 5.956   **11.** 17.15   **13.** 16.57   **15.** −2.441
17. −6.476   **19.** −9.776   **21.** 2   **23.** 2   **25.** 2.59×10^{10} **27.** About 3 months
29. About 7 years   **31.** $21,665.74   **33.** About 9.9 years   **35.** 258   **37.** 296

Chapter 9 Test (page 273)

1. 3^3 **2.** 5^{12} **3.**   **4.**

$y = 2^x$

$y = (\frac{1}{3})^x$

5. $2^5 = 32$ **6.** $10^{.3010} = 2$ **7.** $\log_3 81 = 4$ **8.** $\log_{2/3} 9/4 = -2$ **9.** $\log_{.01} 10,000 = -2$
10. 9.9513 − 10 or .9513 − 1   **11.** 3.4133   **12.** 4.8864   **13.** 7.6777 − 10 or .6777 − 3   **14.** 3930
15. .0881   **16.** 28.23   **17.** 9490   **18.** 37.5   **19.** .531   **20.** 7/3   **21.** 1.56   **22.** 12
23. 1.98   **24.** 6.27

Index